EDUCATION IN THE DEVELOPING WORLD:
CONFLICT AND CRISIS

Education in the developing world

Conflict and Crisis

Sarah Graham-Brown

On behalf of World University Service (WUS) UK
and WUS Germany

LONGMAN
London and New York

Longman Group UK Limited,
Longman House, Burnt Mill, Harlow,
Essex CM20 2JE, England
and Associated Companies throughout the world.

Published in the United States of America
by Longman Publishing, New York

First published 1991

British Library Cataloguing in Publication Data
Graham-Brown, Sarah
  Education in the developing world: conflict and crisis
  1. Education
  I. Title   II. World University Service
  370

  ISBN 0–582–06431–7

Library of Congress Cataloging in Publication Data
Available from Publisher

Set in Times

Produced by Longman Group (FE) Limited
Printed in Hong Kong

CONTENTS

LIST OF PLATES MAPS FIGURES AND TABLES

Plates

16   A school in the 'homeland' of Bophuthatswana. Per
capita expenditure on education in the 'homelands' is
even lower than for blacks in the rest of South Africa,
while the demand for education is rising rapidly
17   Some groups of refugees have succeeded in organising
their own education programmes. These refugees, who
have returned to El Salvador from camps in Honduras
are running their own school. The Salvadorean teachers
union ANDES has been instrumental in promoting
literacy programmes in refugee camps in Honduras, as
well as supporting returning refugees
18   A child teaches her mother to read and write in
Bluefields, on the Atlantic coast of Nicaragua
19   Villagers organized their own open-air literacy class in
this FMLN-controlled area of Morazan province, El
Salvador

Maps

Figures

Tables

PREFACE

Education world-wide faces a deepening crisis, related to the wider economic problems faced by the countries of the South, but exacerbated by political repression and conflict. It is against this background that World University Service (WUS) has been working in support of education for development.

WUS is an international, non-governmental organization focusing on education. It is made up of a network of national committees and partners in sixty countries which involve academics and students in international programmes. WUS has consultative status with several United Nations agencies. Since its foundation in 1920 under the name European Student Relief, the organization has moved beyond its European focus to become world-wide. Its initial concern to assist individual students and academics has evolved into a policy linking the resources of the education sector to the education and development needs of the community as a whole. WUS has five priority programme areas: education and training for refugees, returning exiles and victims of discrimination; human rights; women; community development; and academic co-operation.

WUS(UK) runs scholarship programmes for refugees from Southern Africa, Central America and the Horn of Africa, and for workers from non-governmental organizations in the South. It also supports educational projects in Southern Africa, the Horn of Africa, Latin America and the Israeli-Occupied Territories. WUS(UK) provides an education advice service for refugees and asylum-seekers in the UK, and runs public information campaigns on education for development, refugee and women's education issues.

WUS(UK) embarked upon a detailed examination of the deepening world education crisis in 1989, joined by WUS(Germany) and with financial support from the European Commission, the Ford Foundation and the Government of Norway. But this was not to be merely an academic exercise: our purpose is change. We need to understand the nature and causes of the crisis in order that, with the involvement of our constituencies and the public, we can work for improvements in international educational and development policies and practices. For this reason we have sought to base the book in real-life experiences, gathered first-hand by WUS and its partner organizations in Africa and Latin America. Given the scale of this project and our limited resources, it has not been possible to cover the whole world in detail. Reflecting our wish to ground the research in our own experience, we have focused on certain key regions in which WUS works: Southern Africa, Central America and the Horn of Africa. These regions include a variety of countries facing different economic and political challenges. They are also regions characterized by war and civil conflict – realities that cannot be excluded from the examination of education and development.

The book concludes with a series of recommendations to the international community, which could, if it chose, give real support to people's aspirations and initiatives and could begin to tackle the root causes of the education crisis. Whilst inefficiency and injustice in the South cannot be ignored, the deepest roots of the crisis lie with the international community, and especially with the industrialized countries of the North.

There is no doubt that radical changes are necessary if we are to arrest and reverse the crisis and build the skills and confidence which are necessary for development. Sensitive and appropriate aid must be stepped up at least to United Nations target levels, and specific targets should be established for the proportion of aid to education. Debts must be written off, exchanged and re-scheduled. There must be a new initiative to define and make sacrosanct a charter of educational rights. These are just some of the recommendations described in more detail at the end of this book. They are ambitious, but progress *is* possible and all of us have a part to play.

Nineteen-ninety was International Literacy Year and also saw the holding of a World Conference on Education for All. There have also been dramatic changes in Eastern Europe and in Southern Africa. These events all offer opportunities for positive change, though it will be of critical importance to ensure that aid to Eastern Europe is not at the expense of the South, and that support for education is not at the expense of equally important initiatives in the fields of health or the environment. Awareness of the education crisis is growing and the international community has been forced to pay attention to it, but existing initiatives are inadequate. Fundamental changes will come about only through the expression of wide public concern and action. This book is not an end in itself – it is the beginning of a process of awareness-building and campaigning to bring the necessary changes in thinking and in policy internationally.

There is no reason why the education crisis should not be the focus for a level of world-wide awareness and action similar to that now mobilized around environmental issues. Skills, learning, knowledge and understanding are as critical to human survival as a sustainable environment. The causes of the educational and environmental crises also have much in common: no progress can be made in either arena unless we can find means to change our global agenda from one dominated by the pursuit of personal or national self-interest to one which emphasizes equity, democracy, the quality of life, basic needs and sustainability.

We all have an interest in resolving the education crisis; we all have a contribution to make. We can inform ourselves and others; we can write to our elected representatives; we can ask our banks to write off Third World debt (in respect of which they have probably already made provision for non-payment); we can support the work of Third World practitioners and organizations through solidarity and human rights organizations and through development agencies. I hope that when you have read this book you will feel moved to action – your help is needed and valued.

If you wish to learn more, and to find ways to work in support of education for development and in support of the book's recommendations, I hope you will contact WUS. There is probably a committee in your country whose address can be found through any of those listed below.

WUS (UK)	WUS Germany	WUS International
20 Compton Terrace	Goebenstr. 35	5 Chemin des Iris
London NI 2UN	6200 Wiesbaden	1216 Geneva
UK	Germany	Switzerland

Jane Freeland
Chair, Executive Committee, WUS(UK)

ACKNOWLEDGEMENTS

World University Service (UK) commissioned me to write this book as part of a wider initiative to raise awareness of the education crisis in the South.

I consulted many people in many countries. It is impossible to thank them all individually but their contributions – of ideas, research material and contacts – are greatly appreciated.

Colleagues at WUS (UK) have shared their expertise on particular regions and on areas of education and education policy. My special thanks go to the two WUS editors, Elana Dallas and Philip Marfleet, for their skill and patience. WUS Executive Committee members Jane Freeland and Pauline Dodgson were generous with their knowledge of and contacts in Central America and Zimbabwe respectively.

Members of the editorial committee set up to support the project have provided valuable comments, advice and contacts. My particular thanks go to Dr David Stephens of the University of Sussex and Dr Trevor Coombe of the Institute of Education, London University, for help with work on Mozambique and Zambia, and to Dr Teame Mehbratu of Bristol University for allowing me to share in a discussion at the School of Education with graduate students from a number of African countries.

Jane Freeland, Dr Kenneth King of Edinburgh University, Dr Teame Mehbratu and Dr Trevor Coombe all provided helpful comments and criticisms on the manuscript. Others who were kind enough to read and comment on the draft were Dr Deniz Kandiyoti, Dr Maxine Molyneux and Kitty Warnock.

Much research for the book was carried out by our partners in the case-study regions, without whose contributions the work could not have been completed. They often worked in difficult conditions but still managed to produce material in good time. In Costa Rica I would like to thank Mario Lungo Uclés and Ethel Romero of CSUCA, and América Rodriguez; in South Africa, Yogesh Narsing of the University of Witwatersrand and other researchers associated with the National Education Crisis Committee; in Zimbabwe, Sithembiso Nyoni and Sibangele Jamela of the Organisation of Rural Associations for Progress (ORAP); and in Sudan, Dr Medani Ahmed of the Institute for African and Asian Studies in the University of Khartoum.

Members of other WUS groups also provided me with invaluable help and hospitality. In particular I would like to mention Kambiz Ghawami and Petra Loch of WUS Germany; Cesar Quinteros, WUS Regional Co-ordinator for Central America, and the staff of WUS El Salvador in Mexico City; Silvia Villagra and Annabella Caldera of WUS Nicaragua; and members of WUS Sweden. Many others gave help which made my brief country visits so profitable, especially Anna Keane, who acted as guide and interpreter in Nicaragua, and Deborah Eade of Oxfam, Mexico, who helped me to obtain publications in Spanish. John Campbell and Collete Tilley in Johannesburg, and Dr Vinayagum Chinapah at the University of Stockholm, kindly allowed me to use their office space and helped in arranging interviews.

In a number of countries I was granted interviews by education and development specialists in international organizations, aid agencies and universities, often at short notice. In particular I would like to thank those whom I interviewed at Unesco and the International Institute for Educational Planning in Paris; Deutsche Gesellschaft für Technische Zusammenarbeit (GTZ) and the Federal Ministry for Economic Co-operation in Germany; the Swedish International Development Authority (SIDA) and the University of Stockholm in Sweden; the European Commission in Brussels; the World Bank in Washington; Unicef in New York; the International Labour Organization and the World Council of Churches in Geneva; the United Nations Human Rights Commission (UNHCR) in Costa Rica; the University of Zimbabwe; and the Universities of Witwatersrand, Natal, the Western Cape and Cape Town in South Africa. Publications and interviews by individuals who are directly quoted are cited in the footnotes.

A number of non-governmental organizations in Europe gave me interviews and information and responded to a questionnaire. My thanks for their co-operation.

Several writers and academics have generously allowed me to use unpublished interviews and research. Thanks go especially to David Archer and Patrick Costello for their material on Guatemalan refugees in Mexico; to Jane Freeland for her interview with Johnny Hodgson from Nicaragua; to John Gultig of the University of Natal in Pietermaritzburg and Research on Education in South Africa (RESA, University of Essex) for permission to quote his forthcoming article on schooling and political violence in Natal; and to Judith Marshall for use of her conference paper on structural adjustment programmes in Mozambique.

- WUS (UK) and WUS (Germany) acknowledge the financial support of the Commission of the European Communities, the Ford Foundation, the Norwegian Agency for Development Co-operation (NORAD) and Ausschuß für Entwicklungsbezogene Bildung und Publizistik (ABP), which has made this research project possible.

The Publishers are grateful to the following for permission to reproduce copyright material;

ANDES for translated extracts from *Alfabetizar bajo la guerra: la educacion popular en El Salvador* by E. Toledo Hermosillo (pub EDIMAR/ANDES, 1990); International Labour Office for an extract from p78 from *Stabilisation, adjustment and poverty. A collection of papers presented at an informal ILO expert group meeting*, International Employment Policies Working Paper No 1, Geneva 1986, copyright 1986, International Labour Organization, Geneva); Jenny Matthews © Plates 1, 5, 6, 7, 10, 11, 12, 14, 17, 18 & 19; International Defence Aid Fund for Southern Africa © Plates 2, 8, 13, 15 & 16; Jeremy Hartley © Plates 3 & 9; Don Edkins © Plate 4; Professor Gail P. Kelly of the University at Buffalo, State University of New York (Footnote 18 of Chapter 5); Claude Tibi of the Institut International de Planification de l'Education, Paris (Footnotes 16 & 20 of Chapter 4); Rolph van der Hoeven of Unicef (Footnote 8 in Chapter 3 and Footnote 1 in Chapter 4); International Monetary Fund (IMF) for Figure 2.2a; Organization for Economic Co-operation & Development (OECD) for Table 19.1, UCA Editores, Universidad Centroamericana Jose Simeon Canas for the article 'La Familia en la sociedad salvadorena' by S. Montes in *Estudios Centroamericanos* No 4, 1986.

The Publishers have been unable to trace the following and would appreciate any information that would enable us to do so;

Mujer y educación en tres areas rurales del Peru by R Vargas Vega (pub CELAE/Ministry of Public Education, 1989); *Formación de Educadores Populares: Cuarto experiencias latinoamericanas* (pub Consejo de Educación de Adultos de América Latina, 1989); Figure 10.2, Tables 10.1 and 13.1 (Department of Education & Training, South Africa).

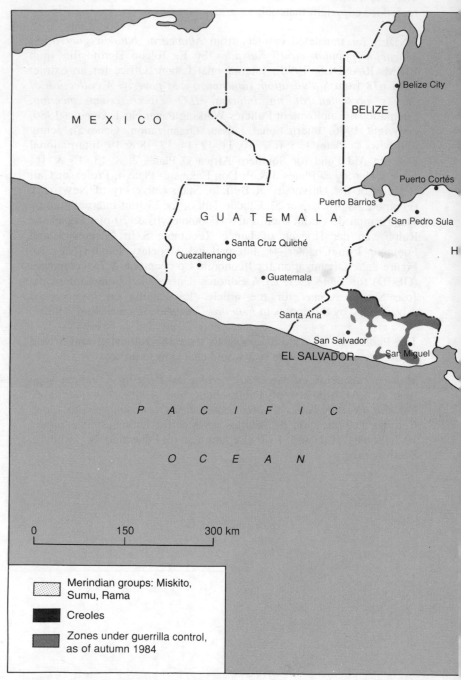

*Map 1   **Central America***

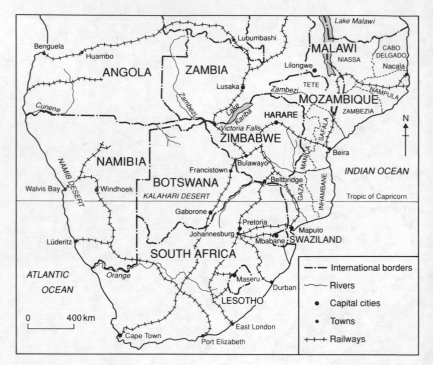

*Map 2   **Southern Africa***

Map 3 **Zimbabwe**

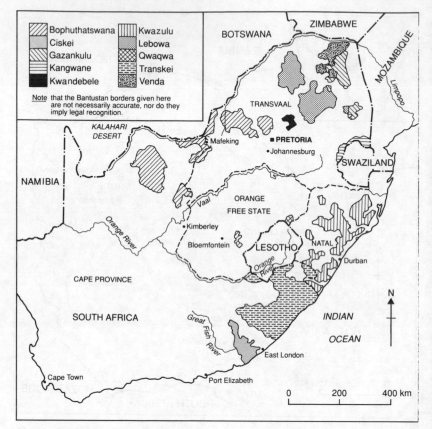

Map 4   South Africa, including Bantustans

CHAPTER 1

Introduction

Education for all?

'I would have liked the children to study a lot so that they wouldn't have to live a life as hard as ours, but the economic situation makes it impossible; they have to go out to work.' A Colombian peasant mother expresses her hopes for her children and her belief in education as a way to a better life.[1]

In many of the villages, refugee camps and shanty towns of Africa, Latin America and Asia, children are not at school. Significant numbers have to work to survive, as farm labourers, as street vendors, as prostitutes. For many, there is no school to go to. According to World Bank and Unesco estimates, there are over 150 million children world-wide between the ages of six and eleven who are not at school. Over 90 per cent of these children live in the poorest countries, and 60 per cent of them are girls.

In many countries of the South the debt crisis of the 1980s exacerbated these problems and ended an era of unprecedented growth for education. Countries severely affected by the economic crisis, often compounded by military and political conflict, have seen the numbers of children enrolling in school fall, and a marked increase in drop-out rates among children who do start school. Many of them find themselves sitting on the floor with fifty or sixty others, with no books, in front of a harassed teacher who has to do another job in order to make ends meet. Few make it to secondary school. Parents, particularly mothers bringing up families on their own, are meanwhile struggling to survive.

For many people in the South, the opportunity to give children an education has represented a new dawn which gave them hope for the future. Their own lives might not change, but for their children, schooling would open new vistas. In 1948 the United Nations proclaimed that education is a basic human right. In countries where colonial domination or indigenous repressive regimes had deprived people of educational opportunities, access to education was seen as part of a process of liberation. For governments, particularly in newly independent states, the promise of 'education for all' was both an act of faith in the future of the country and an important way of increasing their political legitimacy in the eyes of their people.

Between 1950 and 1970, the numbers of those enrolled in schools rose dramatically on a global level, and literacy levels rose, though not as rapidly as had been hoped. Rural communities, and especially rural women, still missed out on educational opportunities. None the less, the hope was that access to education would deliver many benefits: for the nation, a skilled workforce to contribute to economic development, national unity and social cohesion, and in some countries, popular participation in politics. For the individual, it promised an escape from poverty, greater social prestige and mobility, and the prospect of a good job, preferably in town. In practice these hopes were often unfulfilled, particularly among the least privileged social groups, but they remained powerful aspirations.

In the 1980s, the growth in education has slowed down, and in some cases, is even being reversed. Enrolments are not keeping up with population growth, and educational expenditure is static or falling. This has been most evident in Africa, in a number of countries in Latin America and in parts of Asia. Among the consequences has been a decline in access to education for the poorest groups and a marked deterioration in the quality of education at all levels. In the poorest developing countries, both governments and the majority of their peoples have watched the goal of 'education for all' fade into the distant future. Furthermore, the falling quality of education and the lack of job prospects mean that education is no longer automatically associated with wealth, status or security.

A researcher in India, talking to villagers, found that they regarded their children's education as a lottery. You do not really expect to win, but you take a ticket just in case you, or in this case your child, draws a lucky number. The hope has not disappeared, but for many people, experience has taught scepticism.

What went wrong? Clearly, there is no one simple answer to cover all societies. But there are some common themes and experiences. The first is the continuing inequalities in economic and political relationships between the industrialized North and most states of the South. Whatever the policies of governments in the South, they are subject to external economic pressures to which education, along with other types of social provision, is very vulnerable. Economic crises are not solely of their own making, but are brought about by trends in the global economic system, and by the policies of governments in the industrialized North. In the worst instances, these new difficulties have combined with political conflicts to bring national development efforts to a virtual standstill. Education has not escaped these pressures.

The second common theme is the inequalities and divisions within each society: between social classes and ethnic or religious groups. Finally, there are the inequalities in status and access to resources between men and women. These divisions influence who receives education and for how long, and what is learnt. Education plays a complex part in either changing or reproducing these divisions. Some of the earlier hopes that the provision of education would automatically transform society were undoubtedly naive, or wishful thinking.

Certainly, there is some hard thinking to be done about the goals and purposes of education. But the changes in the economic climate over the last ten to fifteen years have reduced many countries to a state of permanent crisis management, where simply keeping the system afloat represents an achievement. In such a climate education can hardly be expected to prosper or demonstrate its full potential in social and economic development.

Economic recession has encouraged a tendency on the part of academics, governments and international organizations to measure everything in terms of cost and returns to investment. In this view, education becomes a commodity. A residual belief may remain in a humanistic interpretation of the goals of education – as a human right, as part of the social provision the state should provide, or as part of the development of a 'whole' person. But the main emphasis is on 'human capital' and on returns to education measured in strictly economic terms. This narrow cost-benefit approach is used to assess both the process and the product of education. It forms the basis of many reform strategies being proposed for the education systems of developing countries.

This approach to education is not reserved only for the debtor countries but has also become common currency in the United Kingdom, in some European nations and in the United States. However, as far as debtor nations are concerned, it seems to be part of a wider tendency to take the international economic status quo as the point of departure. Countries near bankruptcy are told that their education systems must match their resources, or lack of them. No one would argue for grandiose and unnecessarily expensive schemes for poor countries, a trap into which some have fallen before. The questions remain: why are they so poor, and is there any good reason, apart from the highly unequal world order, why they should be condemned to remain so?

Out of these crises have also emerged some new approaches to educational provision. Old certainties have been called into question, in education no less than in other aspects of social policy. It is difficult now to see education as the panacea for all social and economic ills which some envisaged in the 1950s and 1960s. As one young Zambian put it: 'We need to destroy the myth of education as the miraculous solution – that's the type of thing which leads to the problems we have now.' But having abandoned the 'miracle' concept, a more sophisticated analysis is required which locates education within the economic and social structure of society, rather than treating it as a largely independent variable. Only in this way can the limitations and potential strengths of particular educational strategies be assessed.

In response to these problems, individuals and communities have taken their own initiatives to help the poorest families, first to eat and survive, and then to keep their children at school. Organized groups of women, trade unionists, Christian communities, liberation movements and many others have tried to create their own kinds of education, community support and development initiatives. But although there is much that communities and their organizations can do, their efforts alone cannot solve the wider economic and political problems on the international and national level.

Focus

The book focuses on the impact of economic and political pressures on the provision of basic education: that is, the provision of schooling at primary and secondary level and of out-of-school education to people of all ages. It does not aim to give a detailed economic analysis of the crisis, but rather to draw out some of its specific implications for education.

The effects of the crisis have been most severe among marginal communities; that is, those who have least access to political power, economic influence and social benefits. The groups which are marginal vary from society to society, but we examine a variety of situations in which marginality restricts people's right to an education.

The book is divided into five sections. Part One looks at the debt crisis and how it has affected both government education policies and communities' access to education. The main themes addressed in Part One are elaborated through a series of country case studies in the next three sections. Part Two studies the variety of government responses to debt, structural adjustment and political crisis, and the effects this has had on their educational policies and goals. Part Three explores, with the help of more detailed case studies, how families, teachers and pupils in poor and marginal communities have dealt with educational problems and what their attitudes to education are. Part Four examines how both governments and non-governmental organizations, resistance movements and community-based groups have responded to demands for literacy and alternative forms of education. Finally, Part Five looks to the future, examining the economic options, the role of the international community and its response to the debt crisis. This is related to the need to develop more equitable and democratic approaches to education.

Among the key issues addressed are:

- The need for increased awareness in the North of the economic and political conditions in which education has to function in the South.
- The open and hidden costs of these crises to education and their particular impact on economically and socially marginal groups, especially women.

- The widespread tendency to adopt a purely technocratic approach to educational planning and development, in apparent isolation from other crucial aspects of economic and political reality.
- The development of educational initiatives which do not assume that the poor have to be passive victims of economic and political crisis. These may involve governments, liberation movements, non-governmental organizations, churches, trade unions and associations of women or peasants.
- The responsibility of Northern industrialized countries in the debt crises and political conflicts of the South, and how they should contribute to their resolution.
- How and why Northern economic, political and humanitarian institutions intervene in these areas, what impact they have on education and what changes or modifications can and should be made to their role.

The book will not deal with technical and vocational education in a formal classroom setting, nor with higher and further education. This is not because these are any less important, but they are large areas, and the problems they encounter are distinct from those of basic education.

Universities and colleges depend for the effectiveness of their work on having students coming to them well prepared from the school system. In many countries students come out of the school system not only ill-prepared for university on an academic level, but also robbed of the ability to think for themselves and assess critically what they are taught. A school system which is able to teach students not only knowledge and skills, but teach them to think independently, is crucial. Higher education institutions can be an important reservoir, not only for the development of skills, including the training of teachers, but also for ideas and debate on all aspects of education and social policy. The economic crisis has hit higher education in many developing countries so hard that 'low morale and the flight of talent in many centres of higher education' has reduced 'this critical capacity'.[2]

Other critical areas of education which are only touched on for lack of space are pre-school education, and education for people with disabilities. These are areas which are beginning to be taken more seriously in a number of countries and are vital to any policy which advocates education for all.

Case studies

World University Service (WUS) and other agencies working in this field have become more and more aware of the complex interaction of political and economic factors in the provision of education. The work of WUS, both on displaced and under-privileged groups and on human rights and higher education, has alerted it to the importance of these factors. This book is an attempt to explore some of these interactions and their effects, and to suggest priorities for future work. This can create dialogue, not only among Northern agencies, but also with practitioners in the South.

The focus of the book reflects the particular concerns of WUS, concentrating on the main regions in which WUS(UK) works; WUS (Germany) also works in Asia. The case studies centre on countries in three regions: Central America (El Salvador, Nicaragua, Guatemala, Honduras and Costa Rica); Southern Africa (Zambia, Zimbabwe, Mozambique, South Africa and Namibia); and to a lesser extent, on the Horn of Africa (Sudan). The emphasis on the least privileged groups, particularly women and refugees, also reflects the work of groups which WUS supports in these regions.

As far as the debt crisis is concerned, these countries represent a spectrum of indebtedness, according to World Bank criteria.

Severely indebted low income	Severely indebted middle income	Moderately indebted middle income
Mozambique	Costa Rica	Guatemala
Sudan	Honduras	Zimbabwe
Zambia	Nicaragua	

El Salvador falls just outside the last category (moderately indebted, middle income) and South Africa, though not included in debtor categories, does have a substantial foreign debt.[3]

The studies reflect a wide range of political and educational strategies: from efforts at popular mobilization for mass education in Nicaragua and Mozambique to policies of racial exclusion in South Africa. The educational status of the population varies from the very high levels of illiteracy in Mozambique and Sudan to the very low levels in Costa Rica.

It may be said that most of these countries are not 'representative' in that they do not reflect 'normal' economic and political conditions, but these 'abnormal' conditions, including war and civil conflict, can be found in many parts of the globe. Living through such conflicts, displacement and disruption constitutes the daily experience of millions of people. In Asia, there are parallels in the Laos/Vietnam/Kampuchea region, in Sri Lanka, Afghanistan and the Philippines; in the Middle East in Lebanon, the Israeli-occupied West Bank and Gaza Strip, Iran and Iraq; in the Horn of Africa; and in Latin American states such as Colombia and Peru. On the other hand, several countries included here – Costa Rica, Zambia and to a lesser extent Zimbabwe – are not directly affected at the moment by internal or international conflict.

Certainly, these case studies do not reflect conditions in the richer countries of the South, the more prosperous states of South-east Asia or the oil-rich states of the Middle East. Nor do they necessarily mirror the situation in the large and populous developing states – Brazil, Mexico, Argentina, India or Nigeria. Yet they reflect aspects of those realities, and the dilemmas faced by policy-makers. The experience of teachers, students and communities are not dissimilar to those faced in other debt- and conflict-blighted countries.

Data

Most of the data for Part One come from secondary sources. It is noticeable that much of the writing on the impact of the debt crisis and solutions to it comes from Northern academic institutions, bilateral and multilateral agencies concerned with aid and from Northern non-governmental organizations. Some work by analysts from the South is produced under the auspices of the United Nations agencies or the World Bank. This in itself is a commentary on the unequal power relations and capacity to influence policy debate which exists between North and South and the 'relative invisibility' of education research from the South.

However, visits to the case-study regions and collaboration with local academics and organizations revealed more material. Though by no means so widely distributed, it presents different perspectives on these issues. To mention only a few institutions under whose auspices valuable research has been produced: there are regional organizations in Central America, such as Confederación Universitaria Centro-americana (CSUCA), Instituto Mexicano para el Desarrollo Comunitario (IMDEC – which works on popular education), and the UN Economic Commission for Latin America and the Caribbean (CEPAL); and several Central American universities, especially the University of El Salvador, the Universities of Central America in El Salvador and Nicaragua, Universidad Autonomía de Nicaragua (UNAN), and the University of Costa Rica. The teachers' union ANDES in El Salvador has begun to publish accounts of its members' teaching experiences during the conflicts of the 1980s; while in Mexico there has been a proliferation of research institutes 'in exile' focusing on various countries in Central America.

In Southern Africa, the University of Zambia has produced several major research documents on basic education, and the University of Zimbabwe is now doing a survey of the impact of economic adjustment measures on social policy. In South Africa, units in several universities have been carrying out important research on basic education and literacy: in particular, the University of Witwatersrand, the University of Natal, the University of the Western Cape and the University of Cape Town. In addition, a variety of independent organizations have produced analyses of literacy and education issues. In Namibia, much of the documentation has been done through church organizations, the United Nations Institute for Namibia, and the Namibian Extension Unit in co-operation with the International Extension College and solidarity groups abroad. In Sudan, the University of Khartoum – and its research institutes – though severely circumscribed by political difficulties and extreme shortage of funds, have continued to do some research.

For the case studies, both at the national and community levels, a variety of sources were used, but the basic research was done on behalf of WUS by local partners: in Central America by CSUCA; in Zimbabwe by a local non-governmental organization, the Organization of Rural Associations for Progress (ORAP); in South Africa by researchers associated with the National Education Crisis Committee (NECC) working in education in various communities; and in Sudan by the Department for African and Asian Studies at the University of Khartoum.

Each of the research partners provided us with as much statistical and factual data as possible, but the main aim of the research was to gain some impression of how people viewed the education system and their experiences of it, as teachers, students or parents in poor or marginal communities. The techniques used by the researchers varied, but usually included structured interviews with individuals or groups, with relatively small numbers of people.

Limitations on the scope of the research were imposed by political and security problems in several of these countries. In South Africa, the study conducted for WUS was limited by the state of emergency which, in mid-1989, was still in full force. For example, in northern Transvaal the researcher wrote: 'Small-scale interview surveys conducted in Northern and North-eastern Transvaal were hampered by the security situation in mid-1989, especially in the "homeland" of Venda, and limited the areas in which data could be collected.' Another survey, kindly contributed by the Education Policy Unit at the University of Witwatersrand, stressed the problems of reaching teachers and students for interviews and the difficulty of getting information on issues relating to police and security force activity in schools.

CSUCA's researcher encountered difficulties in obtaining data and on occasion in conducting interviews, especially in El Salvador because of security force surveillance. In Sudan, the research work was carried out after the 1989 coup, which made the conduct of any kind of field study extremely difficult and curtailed the scope of the project. The severe economic crisis which prevails in Khartoum and lack of basic materials, down to paper and typewriters, also hampered the work. Our thanks for the efforts and persistence of all our research partners and also to all those who participated, as groups or individuals, in interviews, both with the author and with our research partners. In some cases the names of interviewees were not provided or have been withheld to protect them.

Material from the case studies has been used throughout the book without individual references. Likewise, interviews conducted by the author in the case-study countries are not footnoted. We do not claim that these studies provide a comprehensive or definitive picture, but they represent a cross-section of ideas and perceptions, particularly from marginal communities whose voices are rarely heard in debates about education.

Notes

1. Vélez (1988), p.11 (translated from Spanish).
2. King (1988), p.15.
3. World Bank, *World Debt Tables 1989–90*, p.51.

PART ONE

Education and International Inequalities

Education in the South has been seriously affected by the international debt crisis and the efforts made to remedy it through stabilization and structural adjustment programmes. Internal political conflicts have also caused severe disruption in many countries. Those who have suffered most as a result of these problems have generally been the poorest and most marginal communities.

CHAPTER 2

The indebted South

In July 1989, the financial pages of major newspapers reported that negotiations on the International Coffee Agreement had broken down and the agreement which had controlled coffee market dealing had been suspended. Within hours of the suspension the average value of a pound of 'green' coffee had dropped from about US$1.20 to 65 cents. For citizens of Europe and the USA, this news, if noticed at all, might cause complaints about the continued high price of coffee on supermarket shelves. But in Colombia, the world's second biggest coffee producer it was reported that, 'Some 800,000 families are dependent on coffee for their livelihood, of whom 90 per cent farm less than eleven acres. If the coffee price is high they have schools. If it falls they starve.' In some twenty indebted countries of the South, government revenues and the incomes of hundreds of thousands of workers depend on how much coffee is exported and at what price.[1]

It may seem a long way from a village school in Latin America or Africa to the centres of economic power in London or New York, but in fact a web of connections, some concealed, others quite direct, joins them. Despite the achievement of political independence, the vast majority of countries in the South have remained locked into positions in the international economic order which impose constraints on national decision-making of a quite different magnitude from those which affect most countries in the North. In the 1980s these inequalities in power and influence have been brought into sharper focus by a global recession and a widespread debt crisis among developing countries.

A recent study covering 107 developing countries, of which forty-one were categorized as 'least developed countries', found the following disturbing trends since 1980:

- Gross Domestic Product (GDP) per capita has fallen in 54 per cent of the least developed countries and 64 per cent of the other developing countries.
- Public expenditure per capita has fallen in 58 per cent of the least developed countries and in 67 per cent of the other developing countries.
- Private consumption per capita has decreased in 81 per cent of the least developed countries and in 64 per cent of other developing countries.

- Debt service (the amount of money paid in interest and other charges on loans) has increased to claim a greater share of export earnings in 87 per cent of the least developed countries and in 84 per cent of the other developing countries.[2]

For a number of states in Latin America, and for some in Africa, difficulties in repaying international loans had already started in the 1970s, with the 1973 oil price rises bringing the first major shock to more fragile economies. In sub-Saharan Africa, GDP per capita had grown at over 3 per cent a year between 1965 and 1973 but had stagnated between 1973 and 1980. Between 1980 and 1988 it fell by about 25 per cent.

A handful of countries have, by various routes, achieved substantial industrialization, a fairly diversified economic base and relatively high income levels. However, the majority of nations of the South still rely heavily on primary commodity production. The constraints which affect policy-making in South Korea or Taiwan are worlds away from those which bear down on Ghana, Malawi, or countries with large populations, such as Egypt or India. Equally, the oil-rich states of the Gulf with their small populations present a very different picture from other oil producers, such as Nigeria or Mexico. These differences within the so-called 'Third World' have been sharpened by the global recession of the 1980s.

This book focuses not on the small group of countries which have been in a relatively strong position to weather this recession, but on those countries and regions which have remained largely dependent on primary commodity production, and therefore have been most vulnerable to its effects. It is generally agreed that the worst hit regions are sub-Saharan Africa and Latin America, though countries with serious debt problems can be found in other regions – for example, the Philippines and Sri Lanka; Morocco and Egypt.

Getting into debt

Among the primary commodity producers, the impact of the global recession has varied in intensity, depending on the previous state of the economy and a nexus of other political and social factors. Generally speaking, the key economic problems have been:

- An overall decline in terms of trade for primary products, both agricultural and mineral, combined with dramatic price fluctuations (see Figure 2.1) and, particularly in Africa, stagnating export volumes. In many cases, drought and environmental deterioration have compounded this problem. The International Monetary Fund (IMF) calculates an index for the purchasing power of a basket of primary commodities, excluding gold and oil. It stood at 100 in 1957, rose back to that level in the early

1970s, and fell by 1985 to 66. Even for oil producers, the effects of price fluctuations are substantial. For example, for Mexico it is estimated that a one-dollar variation in the price of a barrel of oil means a shift of almost US$500 million in annual export earnings.[3]

• A growing trend towards protectionism in Europe and the United States. For some agricultural products Northern farmers are heavily subsidized, leading to over-production, which increases the pressure to exclude similar products from the developing world.

• Changing patterns of demand in industrialized countries, with declining demand for some types of minerals and other industrial inputs.

• The heavy dependence of many developing countries on imports of both capital and consumer goods, for which prices have generally been rising. In addition, the price of vital oil imports peaked in 1973, in the early 1980s and again in 1990.

• The resulting balance of payments difficulties led many countries to increase external borrowing rapidly to bridge the gap.

• Rising real rates of interest, combined with falling export revenues, have made it much harder to pay the loans back. Increased interest payments raise the level of debt service. For Mexico, every 1 per cent rise in annual interest rates means a US$700 million rise in debt payments.[4]

Most of these problems originate in economic trends and policy decisions taken by Northern industrialized countries, or in economic and financial institutions dominated by them, not by the primary commodity producers of the South. The only major exception to this pattern has been the case of the Organization of Petroleum Exporting Countries (OPEC).

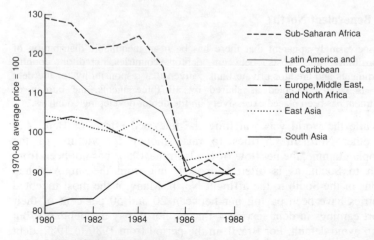

Figure 2.1 **Developing countries: terms of trade**
Source: World Bank, World Development Report 1990 p.14.

In sub-Saharan Africa, most external debts are owed to governments or multilateral agencies. For states with more complex or diversified economies, with oil resources, or a measure of industrialization, severe indebtedness may be the result of other processes. In the 1970s, very large-scale and expensive development projects were in vogue, encouraged by international agencies and Northern banks seeking investment opportunities. Consequently several countries in Latin America and Africa – for example, Brazil, Argentina, Mexico, Nigeria and Sudan – embarked on very ambitious economic and infrastructural projects. In the case of oil producers such as Mexico and Nigeria, this economic boom was mainly fuelled by high oil prices after 1973, but Northern commercial banks were also queuing up to provide them with credit. However, with the downturn in the international economy from the late 1970s, these countries' exports could no longer keep up with loan repayments and they fell deeply into debt.

Once the debtor nation is no longer able to keep up payments, except by further borrowing on disadvantageous terms (that is, short-term, high-interest credits), it is the creditor nations and institutions in the North which inevitably call the shots.

• The less the debtor country is able to pay, the worse its credit rating becomes, making it more difficult to borrow either from government and multilateral agencies or from commercial banks.

• The debt crisis finally leads to default, or recourse to the IMF, which negotiates rescheduling agreements on condition that certain economic 'stabilization' measures are taken. If these are rejected, other international loans are unlikely to be forthcoming.

The Benevolent North?

It is increasingly apparent that there has been an inequitable distribution of responsibility and costs between debtor countries, creditor country governments and creditor private banks: given that responsibility for the debt crisis is widely accepted as shared by all three agents, the burden of adjustment has been placed excessively on the debtor developing countries.[5]

While the world was watching the televised efforts of Band Aid and other Northern charities to raise money for victims of the Ethiopian famine, the net flow of funds in the 1980s has not been from North to South, as is often supposed, but from the impoverished nations of the South to the affluent North. Many of the most indebted countries have been paying out between 20 and 50 per cent of their export earnings in debt service – that is, not to pay the debts off, but just to avoid default. For Brazil, in the period from 1980 to 1982, debt service reached 62 per cent of export revenues.[6]

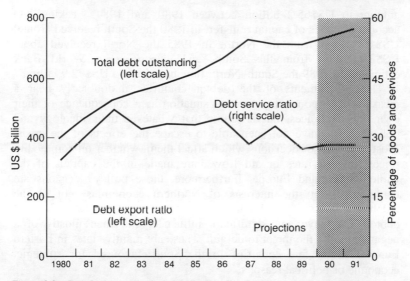

*Figure 2.2a **Developing countries: debt outstanding and ratios of debt service to exports: countries with debt-servicing difficulties***
Note: The debt service ratio is the ratio of debt service to exports, including workers' remittances.
Source: IMF, *World Economic Outlook,* May 1990, Chart 22.

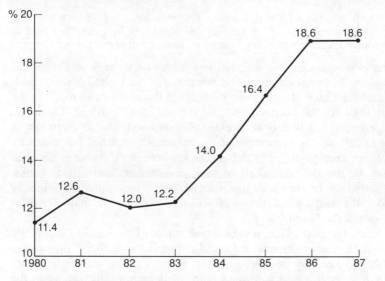

*Figure 2.2b **Ratio of debt service to exports for low-income Africa***
Source: World Bank, *World Debt Tables, 1988-89*

In addition, there has been large-scale capital flight from countries in deep economic trouble, as companies and wealthy individuals move their money out. In Latin America, capital flight from seven countries, including Argentina, Brazil, Mexico and Venezuela, was estimated to amount to US$65.2 billion between 1980 and 1984.[7] Taking into account all types of capital transfer, in 1980 the South received around US$40 billion from the North. In 1985 the North received about US$31 billion from the South, and, according to World Bank estimates, in 1989 the South–North flow had risen to US$42.9 billion.

The governments of the debtor countries undoubtedly bear a measure of responsibility for this situation as a consequence of their own policy choices, but it seems that whatever their ideology and policies, they have not been able to escape the effects of the crisis. Most of the major decisions which affect them, whether on commodity prices, interest rates or aid flows, are made in the capitals of the United States and Europe. Furthermore, those policy decisions are made largely in the interests of Northern economies, not of the indebted nations of the South. Only the largest and most influential debtors can have any significant influence, and then mostly of a negative kind – the threat to default. These are mainly states in Eastern Europe, and a few countries in the South favoured for strategic, economic or political reasons.

Harsh Medicine: The Effects of Stabilization and Structural Adjustment Programmes

The vast majority of the developing countries have been affected by the adjustment process. . . . Stabilization and adjustment have therefore become a predominant feature of policy-making in the first half of the 1980s.[8]

The consequences of indebtedness have been very different for countries of the South than, for example, for the United States, which is running a huge deficit. Debt itself is not the problem so much as the inability of the economies to finance the burden. Economic 'adjustment' has largely been externally imposed, and its main aim is not to develop the economies of the countries concerned but to ensure that they keep paying their debts. The key role in this process has been taken by the IMF on behalf of both governments and private banks. Negotiations on rescheduling official debts are undertaken mostly under the auspices of the 'Paris Club', a group of major creditor nations of the North.

Since the mid-1970s, a substantial number of countries, especially in Africa, Latin America and the Caribbean, have found themselves unable to keep up debt repayments. In the ensuing economic crises they have been faced with the choice of defaulting, or turning to the IMF. On average, every year from 1980 to 1985, there were forty-seven countries with IMF programmes. A number more have carried out adjustment programmes either on their own or with World Bank adjustment loans and credits.

What do 'stabilization' and 'structural adjustment' mean?

The IMF's solution to debt problems has been a more or less standard package of short-term 'stabilization' measures which aim to reduce demand and expenditure within the economy of the debtor country. They typically include:

● currency devaluation
● public expenditure cuts
● removal of state subsidies
● restraints on wages and public sector employment
● limits on credit expansion.

However, it became increasingly evident that the IMF's short-term support programmes were not resolving the economic problems of debtor countries. More emphasis was then placed on longer-term 'structural adjustment' loans.

These loans have mainly come from the World Bank, and are conditional on further and more comprehensive economic reforms, including devaluation of the currency, liberalization of price mechanisms and reform of financial structures. In order to receive such a loan, a country usually has to have complied with IMF 'stabilization' requirements. Structural adjustment loans are more flexible than IMF measures, but they usually require measures to 'streamline' the public sector and make it more efficient, while at the same time providing incentives to the private sector to take over some of the public sector's functions. In addition, there are often pressures to open the country to foreign investment and remove all forms of protection of local production, and impose wage restraint while developing greater export orientation, especially in agriculture.

Loan payments are conditional on adherence to these policies, and, with few exceptions, little account seems to be taken of the specific social and political conditions in the country concerned. A number of countries, including Zambia, Zimbabwe, Tanzania, Honduras and Costa Rica, have, at various times, pulled out of World Bank or IMF programmes, or had payments frozen because of political or economic objections to the measures proposed. However, the pressure to conform to the demands of these institutions is considerable. Not only are further loans from major international agencies usually contingent on compliance with these measures, but even debt rescheduling agreements with private- or public-sector creditors may depend upon it. Essentially, stabilization and adjustment policies are imposed by Northern financial institutions on behalf of Northern creditors, leaving the indebted nations of the South with little room to manoeuvre.

The World Bank tends to be more growth-oriented than the IMF, but in the 1980s has followed the IMF's guidelines more and more closely in its lending policies. One result is that concepts such as cost recovery, efficiency and adjustment have shifted the emphasis away from discussion of broader issues of development, particularly the concern to promote equity and social well-being rather than simply economic growth. This climate of opinion has also deflected any challenge to the structure of the international economy, and to its role in the creation of these economic difficulties in the South. For countries in so deep an economic crisis, some fairly drastic changes are necessary. But are these particular measures the most effective and are their human costs acceptable?

Notes

1.   Jonathan Curling, *Independent*, 10 March 1989.
2.   Lewin and Berstecher (1989), pp.59–60.
3.   Dziedzic (1989) p.34.
4.   Ibid.
5.   Griffith-Jones and Sunkel (1989), p.141.
6.   Heyneman (1989), Table 5.
7.   Ghai and Hewitt de Alcántara (1989), p.14.
8.   Cornia *et al.* (1987), vol. 1, p.49.

CHAPTER 3

The human costs

Debt may be born in the treasuries and central banks of the developed countries . . . fluctuations in commodity prices may seem to be the preoccupation of the commodity markets of the world's great financial centres, but they end up in the living rooms of the poor. *Frank Judd*, Oxfam[1]

'Structural adjustment' has entered the vocabulary of everyday life, not in London, Paris or New York, where it is the province of the specialists, but in streets and homes in debtor countries around the world. The debt crisis and adjustment measures have not only affected governments, banks and economic institutions, but have also quite dramatically eroded the living standards of ordinary people, especially in Africa and Latin America. Some countries have now experienced a decade or more of economic crisis. The remedies applied by the IMF and the World Bank have exacerbated the poverty and deprivation of substantial sections of their populations and are threatening the fabric of social and educational services.

It is not always easy to distinguish between the effects of the ailment – debt – and the attempted cure – stabilization and structural adjustment. The latter, however, have had certain definable effects, superimposed on already difficult economic conditions:

- Reduced spending on public services causes a decline in the quality or quantity of services. Health, education, housing, transport and water supplies suffer. Often state subsidies for basic consumer goods on which the poor particularly depend are cut. How the cuts are imposed on particular sectors depends on government choices and political and economic priorities.
- Cutbacks in public sector employment often affect the urban middle classes as well as poorer groups. They have the most dramatic impact in countries where the public sector provides a large proportion of jobs in the formal sector, particularly for those with post-primary education.
- Sharp rises in prices of basic commodities as a result of currency devaluation or cuts in subsidies, when combined with wage curbs, have meant an acute fall in living standards.
- Continued economic stagnation and low levels of investment in many debtor countries mean that new opportunities for employment are limited. With high unemployment the norm in many countries, people rely on the so-called 'informal' sector; that

is, various kinds of self-employment. This can range from selling matches or food in the streets to running a small manufacturing or service business. Although some informal workers earn a lot, for the great majority earnings are low and erratic. With a stagnating economy, there are often too many people competing for limited markets.

One indicator of the sharp drop in living standards is the decline in real GDP per capita (that is, taking account of the erosion of its value by inflation) in both Latin America and sub-Saharan Africa.

The Inter-American Development Bank describes how the figures on GDP per capita in Latin America understate the problem:

The deterioration of GDP per capita comes at a time when fiscal spending is being cut back and alternative employment programmes and safety nets are inadequate. It is therefore likely that data for GDP per capita understate the worsening situation of the lower income population.[2]

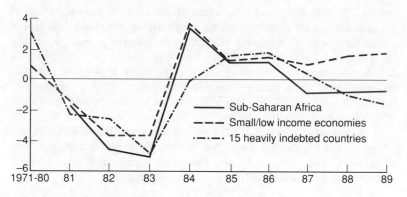

*Figure 3.1 **Real per capita GDP: annual changes in percentages***
Source: Derived from IMF World Economic Outlook, October 1989

Squeezing the poor

The effect of economic crisis on general living standards is now fairly widely known. What is less clear is the specific impact on different sections of society. In many cases, these economic shocks have hit societies which are already socially polarized with very wide gaps between the top 10 or 20 per cent and the population at large. As a consequence, falls in living standards have very different results on different groups. The affluent may have more to lose, but they have greater economic margins before they experience any real deprivation.

The urban middle class has felt the squeeze, especially in Latin America and the Philippines, as have the large number of public-sector employees in many African states. However, other sections of the affluent classes, particularly those with strong international financial connections and bank accounts in the United States or Europe, have actually profited from the crisis, and have been sheltered from the effects of domestic inflation and currency devaluation.

For those who are already living on the margins of survival, cuts of any kind in living standards can prove disastrous. The numbers of people who are living in absolute poverty – that is, unable to meet basic needs for food, shelter and clothing – has been increasing. In Central America, for example, up to 40 to 50 per cent of the population is now considered to be living in absolute poverty.

Even among the poorest sections of society, the economic stress has not been spread evenly. People in urban and rural areas have been affected in different ways. For the urban poor, the main problems have been the removal of subsidies on basic goods, especially food, and price rises. Where the urban population depends on imported food, devaluation of the currency, making imports more expensive, also contributes to rising prices. Even for a country like Zambia which produces much of its own staple food, maize, devaluation brought inflationary pressures on maize prices through the imported fertilizers, fuel and machine parts used to produce it.

Declining wages evidently hit the poor urban population hardest. In some cases, the declines are sharpest for low earners: in Chile, for example, real wages fell 16 per cent between 1981 and 1984, but in 1981–82 alone, real income for the poorest 40 per cent of wage earners fell 10 per cent. In Brazil, in 1986–87 there was a 38 per cent drop in urban wages.[3] In Africa, even in a relatively affluent country such as Kenya, these trends have brought a marked increase in urban inequality.

For the poorest families, this means longer hours of work to provide for basic needs and more family members contributing to income. Worst off are households headed by women, because in most countries women's earning power is less than men's. Women's wages in the formal sector are generally lower, while women are usually to be found in the least lucrative 'informal' jobs, taking in washing or sewing, selling food and doing domestic work.

One of the stated goals of IMF and World Bank programmes for indebted countries has been to even out the economic disparities between what were perceived as more privileged urban areas and marginalized rural areas. However, over the past ten to fifteen years, drought and rural poverty in Africa have driven increasing numbers of rural people into the towns to seek work. In many Latin American countries where large numbers of rural people have little or no land, this rural–urban flow has been going on for decades. Now the people who live in squatter and shanty towns on the fringes of most major cities have themselves become highly vulnerable, and the economic crisis has increased their difficulties.

It is certainly true that rural areas have generally suffered most from governmental neglect. Agriculture has been, for the most part, a low priority, or has been left in the hands of a land-owning elite. In remote rural areas government services such as health and education have been very thin on the ground.

The reforms advocated by the multilateral agencies have focused on raising agricultural producer prices and switching to export crops. Although in some instances the new price policies have brought quite widespread benefits, these depend very much on whether rural people have access to sufficient land to make a living as cultivators. So far the evidence seems to suggest that most of the benefits of these policies have gone to larger-scale commercial farmers, not to peasant smallholders. For example, in Kenya, these measures have mostly benefited large farmers who make up less than 20 per cent of the farming community. Small producers have few resources to fall back on if experiments with new crops fail. Some have sometimes switched to more profitable crops away from food production, only to be caught in a trap of indebtedness when problems arise with production and marketing.

Small farmers at risk

In Costa Rica, as part of the policy of promoting non-traditional export crops (known as *agricultura de cambio*), the Ministry of Agriculture encouraged small farmers to increase cocoa production. Although non-traditional exports seem to have had some success in Costa Rica, early production difficulties hit small farmers who had few reserves of capital. Production levels were lower than expected, apparently because of the poor quality of the seed authorized by the Ministry. As a result of poor harvests, these small producers found themselves deep in debt to the bank which had given loans for cocoa production. The farmers marched on the capital, San José, bearing placards saying, 'This is the funeral of *agricultura de cambio*, born in San José, died in the countryside.'

Efforts to boost production, and therefore incomes, in the countryside also have to take account of rising prices of imported fertilizers and fuel, and the state of the country's rural infrastructure. Rural transport systems are often weak. Shortages of fuel and spare parts cause serious problems in access to markets. Material for sacks or packaging may not be available when needed, causing another bottleneck.

In sub-Saharan Africa, 60 per cent of all agricultural work is done by women, but they rarely have a legal claim to land and are frequently ignored in schemes giving rural credit or advice to farmers. Many of these women, as the poorest subsistence farmers, have not seen the benefits of new measures geared to commercial farming. Furthermore, people in drought-affected areas of Africa have barely been able to grow enough food for their needs, let alone a surplus to sell. In these circumstances, increased producer prices do not help them much, but they are vulnerable to consumer price rises if they have to buy in food.

Rural people who work for wages on other people's land are even more vulnerable to consumer price rises. A survey of rural wage workers in Brazil showed that before the recession the average diet included rice, beans, manioc and corn, plus some kind of animal protein. This was replaced by a diet of rice and beans only. The only items consumed by all families surveyed were rice, sugar and salt. The last two were consumed in larger quantities than are healthy, because they give a temporary sensation of fullness.[4]

After a decade of adjustment, it seems that whatever the intentions of the policy-makers, both rural and urban inequality has been on the increase in the majority of debtor countries. Certainly this trend cannot be blamed entirely on adjustment programmes themselves. Many other factors have also played their part: natural and man-made disasters, further declines in terms of trade, and political and military conflict. However, the macro-economic focus of stabilization and adjustment programmes has meant that the poor, or rather the reasons why people are poor, seem to have been 'invisible to the designers'.[5]

Staying afloat

The people who have been hardest hit by the economic crisis have often responded with considerable ingenuity to the problem of keeping themselves and their families afloat. An important means by which families cope is through mutual support networks of neighbours, friends and kin. Sometimes these are quite informal – women giving one another food when one family is particularly short. Various kinds of mutual aid to help with bills and fees have been established, as have neighbourhood savings societies. In many African countries, where the links between extended family members are still strong, it may be possible to retreat to the village if living conditions become too difficult in town. In towns where there is some spare land, people start to grow their own produce to keep food costs down. In Ghana, where the economy has been in crisis for many years, people began to abandon money altogether and returned to a barter economy.

In some countries, crisis has extended these forms of organization. One example is the development of 'popular economic organizations' in the poor districts of the Chilean capital, Santiago. These organizations have a variety of origins. Some are based on a particular neighbourhood, others on association with a workplace, a religious community or shared political beliefs. They cover a wide range of social needs, including access to cheaper food and basic supplies. Production groups provide goods and services for sale at below market prices; organizations provide support for the many unemployed, while others deal with the problems surrounding provision of housing, water and electricity; yet others address health, education and entertainment needs.[6]

Without support from formal and informal organizations of these kinds some families would not survive, and certainly would not be able to keep children at school. This is especially true in countries where family ties have been eroded by economic change. Green comments:

Traditional security systems have been eroded – probably a trend well-established in the 1960–79 period but much more nakedly evident since. Kinship and locality or origin groups are less able to support poor members/relatives – especially in urban and natural (or other) disaster stricken rural areas. This is not simply a result of shifts towards less extended families and urban residence, relevant as these are. With economic contraction fewer and fewer group members have resources (especially of cash or food) to spare – all boats are sinking lower.[7]

Safety nets – are they enough?

Although people have taken their own initiatives to provide safety nets within their communities, the scale of the problem requires wider solutions. In the early 1980s, the prevailing wisdom in international agencies was that the debt crisis could be resolved in a relatively short time, mainly by applying sharp shock treatment to the economies of debtor countries. As years passed and indebtedness remained at very high levels or continued to rise, it became evident that the problem was a longer-term one. Furthermore, when basic indicators of social well-being began to send out danger signals, the 'human costs' of adjustment began to appear on international agendas.

The argument that the human costs of debt and adjustment have fallen disproportionately on the poor has been made most forcibly by the United Nations Children's Fund (Unicef), through its monitoring of child survival, health and nutrition. Unicef found that after a few years of economic crisis, negative signs began to appear in indicators of infant and child mortality, morbidity (that is, sickness), nutritional levels, school attendance and retention. Further research suggested that children from the poorest layers of society were worst affected.

Subsequently, other major agencies including the World Bank have acknowledged the existence of these human costs, though both the IMF and the World Bank had long sustained the argument that the adverse effects of adjustment would mainly fall on the more affluent sectors of society in the urban areas.

While concern may be growing over the plight of poor and marginal groups, the practical response to the problem on an international level has so far been limited. The World Bank, the United Nations Development Programme (UNDP) and the African

Development Bank have initiated a project to assist governments to set up household surveys which would register some of the problems which adjustment programmes cause for the poorest groups. However, this project was only in its early stages in 1990.

Giving with one hand, taking with the other

Pamscad stands for 'Programme of actions to mitigate the social costs of adjustment' and involves the World Bank, the British government's Overseas Development Administration (ODA), the World Food Programme and a number of UN agencies, including Unicef, UNDP and the World Health Organization (WHO).

By 1985, two years after Ghana's Economic Recovery Programme (ERP) was launched, the negative social effects of this macro-economic adjustment strategy were becoming clear. However, it was not until 1988 that Pamscad was launched. The total cost was put at US$84 million over two years, including a foreign exchange component of $38 million and $11 million in food aid. The projects proposed have:

● a strong 'poverty' focus (that is, they are highly targeted);
● high economic and social rates of return and evidence of cost-effectiveness;
● modest institutional requirements to ensure speedy implementation;
● avoidance of 'any distortions' to the wider goals of the ERP;
● 'high visibility to enhance confidence in adjustment'.[8]

The projects fall under a number of headings, including community initiatives to restore socio-economic infrastructure, including schools; employment-generating projects; support for redundant civil servants; basic needs and educational support projects, including assistance with paper and printing of textbooks and exercise books; and food stocks to go into a revolving fund for the bulk purchase of food for secondary boarding schools. Target groups are rural households with low productivity, low income or under-employed urban households and redundant workers. Women have also been identified as a vulnerable group in need of support, but it remains to be seen whether the programme will come to grips with the specific problems which women have experienced as a result of the crisis.

Although the programme may help to repair some of the damage to social services caused by the economic crisis and subsequent adjustment policies, the underlying economic uncertainties remain. Prices for cocoa, Ghana's main export crop, rose in 1990 and may have stabilized after the extension of an international pricing agreement. However, during the first year of the Pamscad programme, in 1988, Ghana lost US$120 million from the fall in cocoa prices.

The World Bank has initiated some programmes in Africa – in Ghana, the Ivory Coast, the Gambia, Guinea, Mauritania and Senegal – which aim to mitigate the effects of adjustment on the poor. The largest and furthest advanced of these is the Pamscad programme in Ghana, a country whose economy has been in crisis since the beginning of the 1970s.

Unicef, along with some non-governmental organizations, has advocated policies to sustain child survival and support the health and income of their mothers. Examples of such projects viewed as particularly successful were in Botswana, Zimbabwe and Chile. These targeted programmes consisted largely of nutritional support for children and primary health-care measures, particularly immunization. However, these successes have mostly been in countries where the overall economic conditions have been less severe. It is also unclear whether such targeting strategies can succeed if recessionary conditions and cuts persist over a long period. They may allow people in marginal groups to survive, but they do not alter fundamental social inequalities or the lack of economic growth and development.

Recently, Unicef has shifted the emphasis of its campaign away from compensatory programmes towards a medium-term strategy which involves building consideration of 'human factors' into adjustment policies. This would alter priorities in setting economic targets, and would involve much longer time-scales, with the goal of development and not merely economic growth. It is also suggested that growth should be accompanied by a more equitable distribution of wealth, though no attempt is made to confront the political implications of such a statement for governments. In addition, the Commonwealth Secretariat has recently produced a report which argues strongly for much more account to be taken of gender issues when considering the social effects of the crisis. The impact of economic and social crisis on the lives of poor women is clearly distinct from that of men, because their roles in both production and reproduction are different. However, little concrete action has yet resulted from these proposals, and they will have to be pressed with great vigour to convince the international community of their central importance for the future. (For further discussion on strategies to resolve the debt crisis, see Part Five.)

Invisible communities

If the 'human costs' of adjustment are to be assessed, and in future avoided, one important factor is the availability of reliable data on a range of social and economic issues. There is still a great shortage of evidence which can fill the gap between the level of individual anecdote and macro-economic trends. Richard Jolly of Unicef has recently suggested that if the people planning adjustment policies are to take more account of social factors, they should collect and publish social indicators in the same way that they publish fiscal and economic data.[9] The Commonwealth Secretariat report, *Engendering Adjustment for the 1990s,* has also emphasized the need for gendered statistics.

The main problems with statistical data in general are, first, that they are not necessarily reliable or comprehensive, and second, that they are frequently selective. Furthermore, social statistics are difficult to gather and have often been considered unimportant. Consequently, efforts to identify particular social groups which have suffered from the effects of debt and adjustment are often frustrated, since they are frequently made invisible by the available statistics. This can happen in a number of ways.

In some countries, the information is simply never collected. This may be deliberate policy, or because that particular statistic is not considered relevant. This applies particularly to gender breakdowns of statistics. For example, gender-disaggregated statistics on school enrolment and retention rates are difficult to find for many developing countries, and gender breakdowns of teaching staff are also rare.

Definitions of employment and unemployment are notoriously problematic. In many of the countries studied, those employed in the formal sector of the economy are more or less an elite. For this group there are some indications from wage and price statistics as to whether their standard of living is going up or down. But for the large numbers of people who work in the informal sector, for many women working in agriculture, and those who actually do not have any work, the impact of economic change is very difficult to measure.

In many African countries, women comprise the majority of small farmers, but official employment statistics do not reflect this fact, since women are considered family workers and therefore not 'employed'. The household, as a unit for analysis, is often ignored. When household surveys are carried out, questions are rarely asked as to who controls property, which is an important basis of gender and generational power relations within the family and affects the way decisions are made, for example, on children's education.

In Zimbabwe, efforts have been made to include gender breakdowns in statistics, particularly in education. However, a recent conference in Harare noted that efforts to address issues of women in development, especially the changing situation in the rural sector where the majority of women live, were being hampered by lack of data. It was suggested that this lack of data was linked to attitudes towards women in development: 'It was believed that benefits to men of all development programmes would always filter down to the women folk. Consequently, the various agencies of change developed information systems in which women were invisible.'[10]

However, the lack of statistics may also be the result of a shortage of funds to support a proper statistical department. In many countries severely affected by economic crisis, the quality of data collection has declined. War and internal conflict may further inhibit collection of data. For example, in Angola and Mozambique much data is now not available after the early 1980s and what there is can be little more than guesswork. In El Salvador, the census planned for the beginning of the 1980s was never carried out because of the war, so that the latest census data available is from 1971 – twenty years out of date.

Particular linguistic and ethnic groups may also have been excluded or ignored in official data. In Guatemala, the last census was carried out in 1982, at the height of the counter-insurgency campaign. This inevitably raises questions about the quality of the data, particularly on the indigenous Indian communities, many of which at the time were being destroyed or dispersed by the Guatemalan army.

In South Africa, racial segregation has resulted in the multiplication of separate government departments, and therefore of differently compiled statistical data. Take the case of education. More than fifteen departments cover the education of whites, coloureds, Indians, blacks who live in white areas, blacks who live in 'homelands', and blacks who live in 'independent homelands'. One of the outcomes of this bizarre situation is that compilation of country-wide statistics proves very difficult. The statistics not only come from different sources, but they are also based on different assumptions, so that the various sets of data are not strictly comparable. As a result there are no reliable national figures for enrolments and drop-outs, and no clear idea of how many people are illiterate. At a political level, it also allows the South African government to shirk responsibility for the state of education in the 'homelands' by designating them as separate entities.

Furthermore, in some countries, there is deliberate 'cooking' of data for political reasons: under-estimates, over-estimates, suppression of data. Sometimes this is for internal political consumption, sometimes for the benefit of international agencies. Sometimes figures are made to appear better than they are, in order to show the progress being made. Sometimes figures are made to look worse, in order to stress the urgent need for aid and to qualify for the status of 'Less Developed Country'.

Aside from deliberate omissions and distortions, national averages hide great discrepancies, typically between metropolitan areas and remote rural areas, or between prosperous and poor regions of the country. Generally speaking, the more polarized the society, the more misleading national averages will be. For example, per capita GNP in El Salvador in 1987 was US$860 – ranking it as a middle/lower middle-income country. However, according to official figures from the Ministry of Planning in 1985, 50.6 per cent of the population received only 5.5 per cent of national income, while the wealthiest 10 per cent of the population received 63.1 per cent of total income.

In education, a high rate of enrolment at primary school or high rates of literacy may be encouraging, but this also needs to be disaggregated by region and gender. For example, in Costa Rica, considered educationally the most successful country in Central America, the 1984 census showed only 6.9 per cent of the total population over ten years old to be illiterate. But when this aggregate was broken down by region, the proportion of illiterates varied from about 20 per cent in Los Chiles, one of the poorest districts, to 2 per cent in the capital, San José.

Apart from these general problems, there are groups of people who are particularly likely to be left out of the statistics altogether. People who do not have legal or documented status often exist in this kind of statistical twilight – squatters whose position has not been legalized, street children working below the legal age, undocumented refugees and illegal migrants.

Aside from the weaknesses and omissions in the statistics, a particular difficulty in assessing the impact of economic crisis is the time lag between an economic shock and the social consequences reflected in statistical indicators of health and education. The trends in school enrolments can only be judged over a period of years, though some health indicators like malnutrition and increases in morbidity or mortality may appear more rapidly. Even then, macro-statistics may show falling enrolments, rising drop-out rates and repetition of grades, and increasing numbers of street children, but unless they can be disaggregated by region, community and gender, no clear picture can be achieved of the precise impact of economic crisis.

Political conflict and economic recession

In a large number of countries, the global recession and domestic economic problems have been accompanied by varying levels of military conflict or internal political unrest. In the Philippines and Sri Lanka, in most of the states of Southern Africa and Central America, in Peru and Colombia, political instability and conflict have meant that governments allocate large proportions of their budget to defence and internal security, to keep the regime in power and to defend the country against external military threats. In economic recessions, when overall budgets cannot be increased, the demand for military expenditure further limits what can be spent on education, health and other services. The exceptions are regions of high strategic importance which receive large aid packages: for example, Honduras and El Salvador from the United States, while Ethiopia, Cuba and Nicaragua have in the past received assistance from the Soviet Union and Eastern European countries. However, most of this type of aid is spent on the military.

Conflict disrupts already weak economies and undermines prosperous ones. Vietnam is still suffering the effects of thirty years of war. Angola, though potentially a rich country, has its economy in ruins as a result of civil war and war with South Africa. Sudan's already weakened economy has disintegrated under pressures of civil war and a flood of refugees from neighbouring states. Countries in Africa and Central America which have not been party to the conflicts have none the less suffered from the strain of accommodating many thousands of refugees. Certainly for a large number of countries peace and the resolution of political conflicts are prerequisites for any kind of renewed economic growth, not to mention social equity.

Recession, and adjustment policies themselves, have raised political tensions and in already repressive societies tend to increase the severity of repression. Food riots, whether in Brazil, Argentina, Zambia or Morocco, express the anger of people who feel they have been pushed too far, and also resentment that many of the wealthy have not born the brunt of debt and of the harsh medicine prescribed to cure it. In Brazil, Panama, Haiti and Peru, this anger has contributed to the fall of governments. Indeed, concern in international circles for the plight of the poor has not been unmixed with anxiety about the political stability of favoured regimes and with fear of the rise of radical forces on the waves of discontent thus created.

Notes

1. Frank Judd, Oxfam, at UN–NGO Workshop, Oxford, Sept. 1987, p.3.
2. Inter-American Development Bank (1988), p.21.
3. Canak and Levi in Weeks (ed.) (1989), pp.143f.
4. Unicef (1989), *Invisible Adjustment*, p.91.
5. Colclough and Green (1988), p.3.
6. Cornia *et al.* (1988), vol. 2, p.83.
7. Green in ILO (1986), p.78.
8. Jolly and van der Hoeven (1989).
9. Hewitt and Wells (1989), pp.51f.
10. Hedman (1989).

CHAPTER 4

The state and the school system – where is adjustment leading?

Deteriorating health and education conditions are not only depriving many families [of] a decent living, but also . . . affect the deployment of their capabilities in the future. Many developing countries are not only 'eating into their stock of physical capital' as a result of low investment levels, but are also 'eating into their stock of human capital'. This is perhaps one of the most serious effects and will be felt for many years to come.[1]

R. Van der Hoeven, Unicef

Moves towards universal education

What had been achieved by the end of the 1970s? The global statistics on education since the 1950s show several major trends: first, a rapid increase in overall school enrolments, numbers of schools and numbers of teachers; second, a relatively large proportion of national budgets spent on education; and third, how small these amounts were in absolute terms when compared to educational spending by nations of the North.

For many countries, the first boom in enrolments was in the primary sector, as children entered the school system for the first time. Subsequently the 'bulge' in enrolments moved to secondary and finally to the tertiary level. Although the proportional growth of secondary and tertiary education was striking, the number of enrolments represented only a fraction of those who entered the school system in primary year one. Many dropped out before and during secondary school, or repeated the same grade once or more.

On the whole, even the poorest countries of the South have spent quite large proportions of their budgets on education. In fact, some have spent proportionately more than their counterparts in the North, but the actual sums of money are minuscule in comparison. For example, in 1985, the United Kingdom spent US$22.5 billion on education, while the Philippines, with roughly the same population size, spent US$402.4 million. Guatemala, with a population the size of Sweden's, spent only one-fiftieth of the sum allocated to education in Sweden. With over 60 per cent of the world's students, the South has only 11.6 per cent of the world's total educational budget.

The result is that the poorest countries spend only tiny amounts per student. This has not only the obvious effect on the books, materials and laboratories available to each student, but it also means that if cuts or savings have to be made, the effects are much more drastic. Thus governments in low-income countries which aim to provide free and universal education face serious problems of financing, whatever their motives and priorities. This is aggravated by medium to high levels of population growth, experienced especially in many African and Middle Eastern states over the past two decades.

Table 4.1a   Enrolment ratios in primary school

Country	1975	1980	Latest year*	(female enrolment)
Sub-Saharan Africa				
Botswana	72	92	112	(115)
Kenya	104	115	96	(93)
Malawi	56	60	66	(59)
Mozambique	111	99	68	(59)
Sudan	47	50	49	(n.a.)
Tanzania	53	93	66	(66)
Zambia	97	90	97	(92)
Zimbabwe	70	85	128	(126)
Latin America				
Brazil	88	99	103	(n.a.)
Chile	112	109	102	(101)
Costa Rica	107	105	98	(97)
El Salvador	74	75	79	(81)
Guatemala	63	71	76	(70)
Honduras	88	93	106	(108)
Mexico	105	115	118	(116)
Nicaragua	82	99	99	(104)
Asia				
Bangladesh	73	62	70	(64)
Philippines	107	113	106	(107)
Sri Lanka	77	103	104	(102)

* Between 1986 and 1988

Notes: These are official statistics from reporting countries mentioned in the text and show enrolments of all age groups in first level schooling as a ratio of the primary school age group. This varies in length (4–7 years) and starting age. But for the most part children should be reaching the end of the first cycle by the age of 11–13. However, these gross enrolment ratios include children who do not fall into this age group. This is evidently the case where the figure is over 100 but is also true for those countries with lower gross enrolment ratios.

The most these figures can do is suggest what the trends in enrolments may be. They also do not necessarily imply that every child counted completes the cycle – many drop out before this.

Source: Unesco Yearbook 1989, Table 3.2

Although the impacts of debt and adjustment on poor and marginal groups are now increasingly widely discussed, until recently the effects on education have not been much scrutinized. In a crisis people

Table 4.1b   **Growth of enrolments 1960–80**[a]

Region	Level of education	Number enrolled (000's)			Percentage increase 1960–80
		1960	1970	1980[b]	
Developed countries	Primary	124,077	137,711	125,454	1
	Secondary	46,429	70,519	80,574	72
	Higher	9,599	21,105	29,719	214
	Total	180,105	229,335	235,747	31
Africa	Primary	19,312	33,372	61,284	218
	Secondary	1,885	5,353	13,798	636
	Higher	185	479	1,366	709
	Total	21,382	39,204	76,448	259
Latin America	Primary	27,601	47,062	64,549	134
	Secondary	3,039	7,428	17,655	493
	Higher	573	1,640	5,156	831
	Total	31,212	56,229	87,361	182
South Asia	Primary	73,595	121,296	168,854	128
	Secondary	16,196	37,439	61,561	298
	Higher	1,818	4,821	9,819	411
	Total	91,602	163,556	236,234	163

[a]Does not include the People's Republic of China, the Democratic People's Republic of Korea, and Namibia.
[b]Adjusted for country differences in the length and official age span of elementary schooling.

Source: UNESCO, *Trends and Projections of Enrolment, 1960–2000 (as assessed in 1982)* (Paris: UNESCO, Division of Statistics on Education, Office of Statistics, March 1983), pp. 60–2. Cited in Coombs (1985), p.99

tend to focus on life-threatening problems – for example, hunger and disease – whereas education seems a less urgent priority. According to Claudio de Moracastro of the ILO.

It's a conflict between the important and the urgent. On the political side, we find that from a limited point of view there are two powerful constituencies – the accountants who want the debts paid back, and on the other hand the political clout of death and starvation. The predicament of education is that it fits into neither category – between death and debt there is no room for education, no political space.[2]

However, from a longer-term perspective, ignoring or shelving educational development can have serious consequences for future economic and social development.

   Like the wider impact of debt and adjustment, effects on education can be assessed from two points of view: first, the effect on the availability of education, its quality and scope; and second, on people's ability to take advantage of it. It is not just a question of what education the state or other agencies can provide, but also of who is in a position to take it up. For example, most urban middle-class families, even those which have been quite severely affected by the crisis, are unlikely to consider not educating at least their male children to the end of the primary, and probably into the secondary, cycle of school. On the other hand, whatever the aspirations of people in some of the more vulnerable social groups, schooling for all their children cannot be their priority. Thus economic crisis both affects the system directly, by influencing the amount and quality of resources (financial and human) which are invested in it, and indirectly, by the pressures it puts on the finances of the poorest groups.

The culture of cuts

In most developing countries, the state can claim most of the credit for the expansion of education systems. Until the 1980s, the state was generally regarded as the main provider for a national education system. Equipment, teachers and curricula would come from the government, even if communities were building the schools. This was, first, because of the wish to create a more or less coherent national system of education; second, for ideological and political reasons, many governments have wished to take credit for increasing access to education. The third reason was that, in poor countries, there is rarely sufficient private capital to invest in a national education system, rather than in individual private schools tailored to the needs of the elite. Although there is quite a strong tradition of private schooling in Latin America and substantial numbers of missionary schools in Africa, for the most part they make up a relatively small proportion of total provision, and play a more important part in the secondary than in the primary cycle.

By the end of the 1970s, expenditure on education in real terms was in many cases already levelling off, or declining, especially where levels of inflation were high. Between 1970 and 1979, out of a group of twenty-eight developing countries, only six had increased educational spending as a proportion of total expenditure, while in eleven countries spending had declined and a further eleven had remained static.[3]

During the 1980s, many governments in Africa and some in Latin America entered what has been described as a 'culture of cuts', in which planning was reduced essentially to crisis management. The tendency for government departments to live hand to mouth is reinforced in countries where there are substantial annual fluctuations in national income. Lewin comments:

It is characteristic of educational expenditure in many developing countries that it has fluctuated widely from year to year, without necessarily following a long-term trend. This is . . . especially prominent in African countries, many

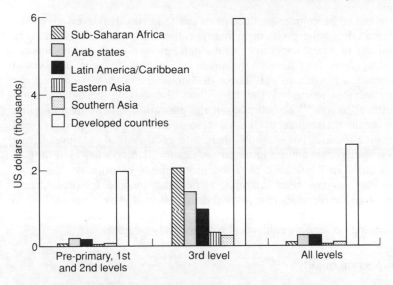

Figure 4.1 **Public current expenditure on education per pupil (1987)**
Source: Unesco (1990) *Basic Education and Literacy: World Statistical Indicators,*
Figure 10.

of which have been amongst those affected most by recession, violent price
fluctuation, and unstable exchange rates.[4]

Some governments have chosen, whether out of ideological conviction
or political calculation, to maintain the proportion of expenditure
going to education, while cutting other social sectors. This strategy is
commonly employed in sub-Saharan Africa. Zambia, for example,
chose to make a cut in health expenditure while sustaining educational
expenditure as a proportion of its total budget. Other countries – for
example, in most of Latin America – have sustained expenditure on
health, with education more vulnerable to cuts. In some 'adjusting'
countries, cuts have been very severe: in the Philippines, education
spending per capita in 1984 was 30 per cent below the 1979 level,
with a consequent decline in primary school enrolment rates between
1980 and 1987 (see Table 4.1a). In Jamaica, per capita expenditure on
education for children under 15 was cut by 40 per cent.

However, when real levels of expenditure are falling overall, the
absolute sums available in education budgets may be declining even
when education's share of the total has not fallen. There is a further
problem in that populations are growing by 2 to 3 per cent or more a
year. Budgets therefore need to rise annually to keep up with rising
levels of demand, leaving aside the need for expenditure to keep up
with inflation.

Waste and inefficient use of resources, sometimes on a large scale,
undoubtedly exist in most education systems. Therefore, some savings
and even cuts can be made which might improve the system and not

turn out to be counter-productive in the long run. However, given the magnitude of the problem in many countries, such savings are very unlikely to be sufficient to close the gap between needs and resources.

Decisions then have to be made as to how to keep the system running, and what to cut. These decisions are taken not only on the technocratic merits of the case, but also giving consideration to political factors. When all parts of the education system are struggling to obtain their share of limited resources, the power struggles can become intense. For example, there is a good deal of pressure at least to maintain expenditure in tertiary education. Universities tend to have more political influence than the protagonists of primary education, but they too have been struggling to maintain income. In some African countries, universities have closed down because they cannot afford to remain in operation. Cuts in higher education may lead to increased spending on sending students abroad to study overseas.

Impact on quality

In the early 1980s, 20 per cent of schools in the Ed Duneim district in Sudan had no water, and 57 per cent had no latrines. In the Kilosa district of Tanzania, 42 per cent of schools were without water and 10 per cent without latrines.[5] In Nigeria, many schools in the north have no roofs, or collapsed walls. In some parts of the south, children can be seen carrying their own desks to school each day.[6]

Primary education in both Latin America and sub-Saharan Africa has suffered a severe squeeze. Since in many indebted countries primary level education already has the lowest levels of expenditure per pupil, reductions in funding have had some drastic consequences, especially for the least privileged regions and sectors. Textbooks, exercise books, blackboards, chalk, desks, chairs, pencils: all the ordinary objects which we identify with a classroom are often scarce or non-existent.

In sub-Saharan Africa, budgets for materials and equipment have in some cases declined to zero, with the government no longer taking any responsibility for their provision. Between 1975 and 1985 the proportion of educational expenditure on teaching materials was almost halved in Africa – from 7.6 per cent to 4.2 per cent. In Latin America and the Caribbean it fell even more sharply, from 4.4 to 1.8 per cent.[7] Expenditures per primary student on teaching materials in the 1980s were less than US$1 in Ghana, Bangladesh, Botswana and Chile, among a number of others. The comparable figure for the United Kingdom was US$34 and for Denmark US$161.3.[8]

Maintenance of buildings and school property has also been badly hit. Leaking roofs, lack of light, and even lack of water are not uncommon problems, certainly in Africa and Central America. Of course, cuts and shortages in other sectors of the economy also affect education, whether it is power cuts, water shortages or lack of transport and fuel to bring materials to schools, especially in remote rural areas. Sometimes there are shortages of raw materials caused by production and transport bottlenecks or lack of foreign exchange: for example, paper for books, or cement and other building materials for repairs or new classrooms.

In budgetary terms, all these are classified as recurrent costs. In the category of investment spending for the future of the system, there has also been a sharp downward curve. In some countries that is because most of the educational infrastructure was built in earlier decades. For the most part, whatever the state of the infrastructure, new developments are out of the question unless external funding can be found. These limitations also apply to the vital areas of teacher training, curriculum research and development of educational materials.

At primary school level, teachers' salaries make up the largest proportion of any education budget, and are politically the most sensitive item. Although in many countries teachers are among the strongest and most organized groups of employees, this has not necessarily allowed them to maintain, let alone improve, their salary levels. Susan George cited the following story of a primary school teacher in Bolivia, on strike for a living wage:

Under pressure from the IMF, the government has frozen salaries. Depending on the category, a teacher earns between (US$10 and $40 monthly at the May 1986 rate). . . . The minimum family food basket as calculated by the (Central Trade Union Organisation) costs (US$160). We knew we'd never get that from the government, so we asked for (US$60). Well, the government won't even negotiate. They just said that any teacher who wasn't in the classroom Monday was fired and his job would be considered vacant. I don't think enough will go back to stop the movement. Teachers all have to do another job anyway to survive. Some drive taxis or deal on the black market.

The real long-term problem is the quality of teaching. Nobody's motivated to teach with salaries like that, or to prepare the lessons. A lot of children are dropping out in the early grades now in order to work trampling the coca leaves (the first stage in cocaine processing). . . . The ones that do come to school are malnourished – their parents don't have enough money to feed them – and they arrive with empty stomachs so they can't concentrate or they fall asleep in class.[9]

This may seem an extreme case, but most of the main features – salaries slipping below subsistence, teachers taking several jobs and demoralization in the classroom – have become a feature of life in much of Central and Latin America and sub-Saharan Africa. A World Bank study of primary teachers' salaries in eighteen countries of sub-Saharan Africa found that real salaries had declined in all but two between 1980 and 1985. In eleven countries, including Kenya, Zambia, Zimbabwe and Senegal, the falls were 10 per cent or more.[10]

Teachers' pay has declined, not necessarily because of pay cuts but because the purchasing power of their salaries has fallen dramatically – along with those of other public sector workers. In some African countries, teachers are paid irregularly or have to wait months for their pay packets. In Cameroon, there have been times when teachers were waiting a year for their full pay. In Nigeria, after the dramatic fall in oil revenues in 1981, schools were closed down because there was no money to pay teachers for up to eighteen months at a time. Between 1983 and 1986, more than 80,000 teachers left the profession or were made redundant.[11]

Working conditions have inevitably deteriorated. The combination of large classes, sometimes working double shifts (many countries run two or three shifts a day in primary school), or taking second and even third jobs outside teaching is tiring enough. When the teacher is the sole learning resource in the classroom because there are no books and equipment, this imposes a further burden which most teachers are not properly trained to cope with. It takes a highly innovative and motivated teacher to create or have pupils create learning aids out of whatever materials are available. Far more often, teachers will fall back on conservative 'chalk and talk' practices – that is, if there is any chalk. For example, if there is only one textbook per class, the teacher will write a section of it on the blackboard (if there is one) and have the students copy or memorize it.

In Central and Latin America, multi-grade schools are very common in rural areas. In these schools, one teacher can be expected to teach several grades. For example, in Guatemala 54 per cent of schools only have one teacher. In Ecuador, the figure is 85 per cent in rural schools.[12] This situation is also common in Nicaragua and Colombia. Educationists have differing views as to the viability of this system for a small school, but certainly the teachers need training and equipment to do the job, training which they rarely receive. Rural teachers sometimes have to travel long distances to school, and isolation and lack of advice or professional support add to their frustrations. In rural areas, housing and other facilities for teachers are often rudimentary in the extreme and, along with all the other disincentives, make it very difficult to recruit and retain staff in rural schools.

The net result of all these problems has been to make teaching an undesirable profession in a number of countries, with a high level of drop-outs. Those who remain are frequently too busy earning money elsewhere to prepare lessons or take teaching seriously. Moonlighting among teachers is nothing new, but the scale of the problem now seems to be out of control.

Lack of teacher training and poor teacher training is another serious problem. Especially in sub-Saharan Africa and Central America there are large numbers of unqualified or poorly qualified teachers, especially since qualified teachers are leaving the profession. Teaching, whether at primary or secondary level, is not now widely regarded as an attractive prospect for a school graduate. Investments in teacher training are vital but have not always been prioritized, and now most governments do not have the funds to upgrade their teacher training, or to implement large-scale, in-service teacher training. Even projects based on distance learning do not come cheap.

Alternatives in teacher training

In Colombia, the *escuela nueva* programme is a long-term scheme to improve rural education. It was launched in 1976 and now covers about one-third of rural schools. The initiative grew out of earlier unsuccessful attempts to improve provision of rural schooling. The project has benefited from considerable external support – in the first phase, from USAID, and in the second phase from the World Bank, which will also support phase three, designed to extend the scheme to all rural schools. Its aim is to increase the availability and quality of schooling while keeping costs down and it places particular emphasis on teacher training and continuous in-service upgrading.

The World Bank outlines its main characteristics:

The strategies used to implement the program focus on curriculum, teacher training, administration and the school–community relationship. The curriculum content, which is readily adaptable to the circumstances of a particular community, is simple and sequential with an emphasis on problem-solving skills. Presented in the form of semi-programmed learning guides, the curriculum is organized to permit a flexible promotion system. To complement the curriculum materials and to meet the challenges of multi-grade teaching techniques, Escuela Nueva has developed a special classroom design based on resource corners, simple classroom furniture and a 100-book library.[13]

Teachers are expected to deal with multi-grade classes because of the difficulties and cost of providing schools with different teachers for each grade where there are scattered rural populations. However, they are given training and back-up to cope with the task. Teachers participate in active training workshops, rather than informative courses, both before the introduction of the programme and during the school year. The education authorities have brought in salary incentives for teachers completing the in-service training programme and introducing the new methods in their schools. This was partly to meet objections from teachers that in-service training was not being taken sufficiently into account when deciding promotions.

Although there is no clear evidence of marked differences in drop-outs between *escuelas nuevas* and traditional rural schools, studies from the World Bank suggest that student motivation and creativity were greater and teachers generally had a positive response to the new system.[14]

Clearly, these conditions damage the learning environment and the morale of teachers and students. They also affect the quality of education, already low in many places. However, measuring quality is difficult. The most technocratic approach is to measure pass rates from grade to grade, and examination results. On a global level, this is of limited value, because a variety of criteria are used for promotion from grade to grade, with some systems allowing automatic promotion through certain grades. As far as examinations are concerned, many education systems regularly move the goalposts by altering the standard of marking according to the quota of passes required.

None the less, some detailed studies using these criteria suggest that many children can hardly read after four years of primary school, and show particular weaknesses in science subjects and practical subjects, as many schools have no facilities for practical work.

The 'culture of cuts' also affects prospects for change and reform in the education system. For example, a number of countries have made efforts to revise school curricula, to make them more relevant or accessible to pupils. But these changes can have little effect on what goes on in the classroom if books and support materials are not available to teachers and pupils. Materials and equipment for practical work are crucial not only for academic science courses, but also for most types of vocational training in schools and colleges, introduced in a number of countries to increase the usefulness of what is learnt. Under these conditions the experience of education is not necessarily a pleasant one: lack of books, harassed teachers and poor physical environment are often combined with tired, unwell or malnourished pupils whose capacity to learn is likely to be much reduced and whose home situation – crowded, noisy, without proper light – does not help them to study. It says a great deal for the determination and resilience of many children that they do get something out of their education. It also reflects the dedication and skills of at least a section of the teaching force.

Shifting the burden

The crisis caused by the shortage of public funds for education in most developing countries has reopened the debate about who should pay for education. Before the drive for universally accessible education, which began in the 1950s, various forms of non-governmental resources played a larger part in educational provision. In both Latin America and sub-Saharan Africa there were a variety of private schools for those who could afford the fees. Schools of this kind, especially at secondary level, are still the option for the wealthier classes in both regions. Many such schools are run by religious orders or groups. In addition, missionaries have played an important role in providing low cost or free education, especially in rural areas.

This role was particularly important in Africa in colonial times, since for the most part the colonial state provided minimal resources for the education of colonized peoples. However, these 'private' forms of education were still quite limited in their coverage. Some missionary schools also subjected students to pressures to follow their religious beliefs. After political independence, church and missionary schools have continued to play a role, though a more limited one. However, in a few countries – for example, Cameroon – churches continued to play an important part in the education system, especially in the provision of primary schooling. Since local churches there have taken over schools previously funded by Northern church organizations, they too are often short of money, and the economic crisis has made it increasingly difficult to maintain schools.

Aside from the provision of schools by private or voluntary bodies, 'private' funding from communities and families is increasingly used to support publicly funded state education. In Africa particularly, some degree of community participation, particularly in building schools, has been commonplace. Over the past ten years, the range of charges on the community, and the size of those charges relative to income, has shown a marked increase. This has been the commonest way of coping with governments' inability to provide funds, not just for new buildings, but also for recurrent expenses. Only teachers' salaries remain for the most part in government hands.

Consequently, even within the state education sector an increasing financial burden falls on parents. Sometimes this takes the form of direct fees, sometimes it consists of payments into building funds or school activity funds. Parents are expected to pay for school uniforms (where these are compulsory), exercise books and writing materials, and sometimes textbooks when they are available. As a consequence, in India, for example, it is estimated that parents already pay a substantial proportion of the cost of state education. This is particularly the case at secondary school level where school fees and examination charges plus the costs of books and equipment are high.

Organizations such as the World Bank are actively encouraging the charging of user fees and 'cost recovery' mechanisms, to cut or level off government expenditure on education, and 'decentralize' its administration. However, a frequently voiced concern about this strategy is its effect on equity in educational provision. For middle-class parents with a child in an urban secondary school, these fees and charges may seem high, but will take up a relatively small proportion of the family income. For the child of a slum dweller, or a peasant with a large family, such charges make a more significant dent in income. At the same time, the quality of education the child receives will, in most cases, not compare with that available to the middle-class child.

Where such charges are already in operation, the economic crisis has made it even harder than before for the poorest sectors to afford these payments for several children. If 'cost recovery' is to be further intensified, the poorest people will only be able to keep their children in school by sacrificing other vital expenses or falling heavily into debt. Lewin and Berstecher comment:

Charging user fees is likely to have a disproportionate impact on poor families. These generally have more members of school age, have less disposable income and experience greater fluctuations from year to year in income than do rich families. . . . [Furthermore] family incomes have fallen in many sub-Saharan African countries at the very time when school fees have been introduced or raised. . . . School avoidance rates are highest amongst the lowest income groups in Sri Lanka; the major factor identified for this is the inability to provide the basic requirements of attendance – bus-fares, uniforms, writing materials, etc. Increased user fees, other things being equal, are likely to discourage regular enrolment amongst the poorest and, in many societies, affect adversely the enrolment of girls, where they are in competition for declining family income.[15]

Some of the strategies to collect funds can also sharpen inequalities between and within communities or schools. Some countries have allowed schools or groups of schools to set fees according to the wishes of parents. However, if the community consists of a range of income groups, richer members often bid up the fees because they want better facilities, to a level beyond the means of the poorest families. Meanwhile, schools serving largely poor communities are simply not able to raise much money and so have much poorer facilities. The differences in communities' abilities to fund education then result in substantial discrepancies between schools. One strategy used in Sri Lanka is to establish 'clusters' of schools which form a unit both to disburse state funds and to raise funds from the communities within their catchment area. Though there may be benefits in co-operation between such a cluster of schools, a potential danger is that larger and wealthier schools take the lion's share of funds raised from the communities, thus accentuating inequalities between schools within the cluster.

One study of schools of similar size using various combinations of private and public funds suggests that there are more disparities in resource allocation between institutions which receive funds from several sources, that is, including private parental contributions. Least disparities are found between those funded by central government. These disparities in funding are most acute for non-salary expenditures; that is, for materials, equipment and maintenance.[16]

Another alternative is to create schools which are wholly financed by communities. For more affluent areas, especially where parents are very committed to educating their children beyond the first level, this may produce flourishing schools. In less favourable circumstances, however, this can lead to an 'underclass' of poor schools. This problem has arisen in the well-established *harambee* community schools in Kenya. These are mainly secondary schools, though some primary schools are also built and funded by the community.

Although *harambee* schools have certainly increased the number of children who get to secondary school, when compared to the state-funded schools, their quality is generally judged to be low. Evidence from both Kenya and Tanzania also suggests that these self-help school projects can sometimes increase social and regional inequalities. In very poor communities, people may labour to build schools but then are unable to afford the direct and indirect costs of running them.

Only in exceptional circumstances, related mostly to political patronage can [*harambee*] schools claim to offer much more than an educational facade. As such, although the anticipated reward may make them appear to be worthwhile investments, they are actually a burden on communities.[17]

Although there are situations in which community-run schools have advantages, they are not a blanket prescription for relieving the education crisis. Their effects on educational quality and coverage depend not only on the intrinsic merits of the project itself, but also the socio-economic context in which it is introduced.

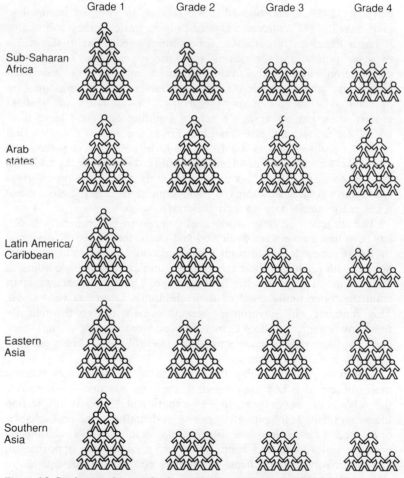

*Figure 4.2 **Staying at primary school: survival rates (initial year 1986)***
Source: Unesco (1990) *Basic Education and Literacy, Figure 4.*

'Reaching the unreachable'

Experience in several countries has suggested that community involvement in schools, or the creation of schools as part of community development projects, may increase rather than decrease pressures on the government to improve and expand its services.

In Bangladesh, less than half of primary school-age children enrol in state schools, and half the pupils quit school before completing third grade. The figures for girls, especially in rural areas, are even higher. Government expenditure on rural schools is very meagre, the quality of schooling is generally poor, and curricula are irrelevant.

The Bangladesh Rural Advancement Committee (BRAC) works in community development, primary health care and agriculture. Since 1985, it has been developing a system of 'non-formal' schools to cater for those children who do not get into the state system or drop out early. By 1989, it had opened 2,500 schools in villages, intended to give 'unreachable' children a chance to learn basic literacy and maths. It has a three-year programme for children aged eight to ten and a two-year programme for eleven- to fourteen-year-olds. Teachers are drawn from among the more educated members of the local community, trained by BRAC on short courses, with close monitoring of their subsequent classroom teaching. Communities or landless groups often put up a simple school building and then lease it to BRAC for a low rent, just enough to cover the cost of materials and repairs. Because teachers are from the local community, parents are more likely to become involved in running the schools. In addition, other aspects of BRAC's work, particularly the provision of rural credit, have somewhat improved living conditions, and therefore made it easier for parents to send their children to school.

The attraction of these schools, in contrast to government schools, has been that teachers are dedicated and interested; curricula, designed by BRAC, are relevant to rural life; the schools are close to students' homes, with relatively short school days, and are flexible according to the rhythms of economic life in the village. The cost to parents, apart from the 'opportunity cost' of their children's labour, is very small. This contrasts with government schools which, though theoretically free, now charge for books, materials and exams. BRAC has been particularly successful in attracting girls to enrol in its schools, and has generally low drop-out rates.

The main problem facing the organization as the schools become more successful is how they relate to the state education system. Are the schools 'to serve primarily as experimental models for testing ideas and methods for providing primary education to the unreachable' or to expand further into a country-wide system? BRAC's relationship with the government has been co-operative rather than oppositional, and it is involved in a scheme to improve community participation in state primary schools.

However, some of its younger group of students go on into state schools. This creates various dilemmas. How much should BRAC adapt its curriculum to fit with that of state schools? Many pupils in state schools only succeed because their parents pay for private tutoring; how then can the poorest students succeed when their parents cannot pay for tutors? Finally, many parents simply cannot afford the charges at state schools. BRAC cites the case of a very bright girl who graduated from one of their schools and transferred to fourth grade in a state school. However, she could not move on to the fifth grade because her parents could not afford the exam fee.

BRAC is supported by a number of external funders: Interpares (Canada), Swedish International Development Authority (SIDA), Norwegian Agency for Development Co-operation (NORAD), Britain's Overseas Development Administration (ODA) and Unesco. Obviously without this funding (about US$1.4 million between 1985 and 1989) its work could not continue. Though the sums are relatively small, a continuous and reliable flow of aid is needed to keep the schools going.

In terms of its relationship with the state education sector, it seems likely that BRAC's work will in the long-term actually put pressure on the government, both to take note of BRAC's innovative methods, and to devote more funds to the development of rural schooling.[18]

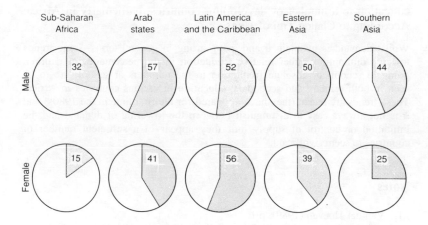

Figure 4.3 **Secondary school: adjusted gross enrolment ratios by sex (%), developing countries, 1987**
Source: Unesco (1990) *Basic Education and Literacy, Figure 5.*

Some people advocate expanding private fee-paying education in developing countries, but there is no realistic possibility that it could serve the needs of more than a small élite. To be commercially viable, the fees charged are beyond the reach of the average family, and with the exception of a few boarding schools, private schools are mostly located in urban centres and do not serve rural populations. A problem which has also been experienced both in sub-Saharan Africa and Central America has been the lack of control over the quality of schooling provided, which, despite high fees, often leaves much to be desired.

However, the economic crisis has served to emphasize further the gap between well-equipped, if not always well-run, private schools and ramshackle public-sector schools and community schools. Through this discrepancy the opportunity gap between rich and poor is further reinforced, even if some bright and determined students manage to cross the line, with the help of scholarships or though sacrifices made by their parents. It also undermines confidence in state education. In sub-Saharan Africa as Wright noted:

Those who desire good quality teaching, successful examination results, high standards of discipline and sound all round development are increasingly prepared to forsake their own public education systems and make inordinate sacrifices in pursuit of their desires. . . . Even where most parents cannot afford to send their children abroad or to private schools, they manifest a lack of confidence in the public education system by investing in private lessons with teaching syndicates, where they hope at least to have good quality teaching and successful examination results.[19]

Changes in patterns of educational funding have combined with other factors which limit access to education to reduce the take-up of education in a number of developing countries, particularly in Africa. According to Claude Tibi of Unesco:

Whilst demand is maintained and even strong in general terms, some trends towards diminution, either relative (reduction in the percentages of children going to school) or absolute (reduction in the numbers at school) are to be seen in both primary and secondary education in various countries in Africa. These trends are recent (they have appeared for the first time in the 1980s) and it is not always easy to distinguish between the lowering of demand and the limitation or control of supply, but they appear in a sufficient number of countries to seem significant.[20]

Notes

1. Van der Hoeven (1989), p.1.
2. Claudio de Moracastro, ILO, interview with the author, 1989.
3. Coombs (1985), p.144.
4. Lewin (1988), p.15.
5. Caillods and Postlethwaite (1988), p.8.
6. Hinchcliffe (1989), p.9.
7. Heyneman (1989), Table 17.
8. Lockheed and Verspoor (1990), Table 22.
9. George (1988), p.151.
10. Zymelman and DeStefano (1989), p.35.

11. 'Adjusting Education to Economic Crisis' *IDS Bulletin* 20, p.9.
12. Caillods and Postlethwaite (1988), p.7.
13. Lockheed and Verspoor (1990), p.110.
14. Ibid.; Colclough and Lewin (1990), Appendix, pp.46-9.
15. Lewin and Berstecher (1989), p.70.
16. Tibi (1988), p.109.
17. Bray and Lillis (1988), p.128.
18. Lovell and Fatema (1989).
19. Wright (1989), p.92.
20. Tibi (1989), pp.108–9.

CHAPTER 5

Marginal groups and education

Debt and structural adjustment affect various social groups in already polarized, inequitable and divided societies very differently. The problems of the least privileged sections of the population did not begin with the debt crisis but have been exacerbated by it. The crisis does not only affect the availability and quality of schooling. Broader factors need to be considered, particularly the interaction between school and society and government policies. The question is complicated by the fact that divisions are not simply between social classes, between the wealthy and the poor. Other forms of inequality, between different linguistic or ethnic groups, and between men and women, play an important part in making people 'marginal'.

Although education can play an important part in changing social attitudes and aspirations, it also socializes people into particular roles in society. A series of filters, both within the education system itself and in the wider economy and society, tend to reproduce existing social hierarchies. These filters are of different types and intensities, depending on the goals and character of particular governments and societies. The following are some of these forms of selection:

- those overtly defined by government policy: for example, exclusions based on race or language;
- those created by gaps in the education system (especially in rural areas);
- those caused by the inability of certain disadvantaged groups to enrol in or to remain at school because of language, gender or the poverty or isolation of the community;
- the way the formal education system selects through examinations – although it may be formally accessible to all, relatively few are expected to complete all its stages;
- the chances of a child completing school depend on his or her socio-economic circumstances, including the economic situation of the family, the educational background of the parents and the perceived relevance of education;
- different types of education in a particular society are given differing social and economic values: for example, private/public, academic/vocational, formal/non-formal;
- the value placed on different types of work and skills: for example, manual as opposed to white-collar work.

Education based on a formal system of schooling has created new demands and aspirations. People are led to believe that it will offer social mobility and a way of escaping from poverty. However, in many developing countries, there is a considerable tension between the ideal of education as a means of democratizing knowledge and creating a meritocratic society, and the limited opportunities offered by dependent economies. Educational provision is limited by lack of funds, so that the poorest and most marginal people are least likely to gain access to education. Poor quality education also limits the numbers who reach the higher grades. Thus effective education remains largely the preserve of the élite.

Furthermore, as Martin Carnoy argues, the model of education used in most developing countries, derived from systems created in Northern industrialized countries, widens the gap between the meritocratic aspirations created by education and its relevance to the majority of the population. 'Failing' in school is the rule rather than the exception. Carnoy argues that this can create a vicious circle in which education, rather than empowering people, reinforces a sense of powerlessness. '. . . .Failing in school, even in schools where very few succeed, helps to pacify those who might otherwise claim increased access to resources and political power, since such claims are officially restricted to those of proven merit.'[1]

Low-income families and educational choice

In a shanty area of Colombo, K. Leelawathie, aged 46, lives in a 'temporary structure' with her three children.

She works as a daily wage labourer on construction sites. Pay is Rs60 a day but there are long spells of unemployment during the rainy season or when work is slack. Family poverty has forced her 14-year-old son to take paid work as well. He works alongside her on the construction site, receiving the same wage. The work is gruelling, beginning at 7 a.m. and often ending at midnight; lunch and tea are provided on site.

Earlier, as a casual labourer, K. Leelawathie and her family had been able to survive as a result of assistance from her sisters and from state subsidies, which supplemented her own meagre income. But with a reduction in the rice and fuel subsidies and increasing inflation, her main concern has been to feed the children: 'We could not live for more than a few days on food and kerosene stamp cards. The prices of food and kerosene increased so much.' She then contracted tuberculosis and had a long period without paid work: the ensuing difficulties and poverty compelled her son to drop out of school in Grade 3 and her elder daughter in Grade 2. Her younger daughter (aged 9) longs to go to school. 'Where can I find the means?' she asks.[2]

This story is just one example of the ways in which poverty, illness and cuts in government expenditure can affect children's chances of education. They are also highlighted by the disparities in the percentages of children from different regions and social groups who go to school.

The difference in gross enrolment ratios at primary level (the ratio of children of whatever age enrolled in primary schools to the number in the primary school age range) between different regions in one country can be dramatic. In Kenya, in 1984, the highest regional enrolment ratio was 119, suggesting that almost all children were passing through the primary system whether or not they were of the appropriate age, while the lowest regional enrolment ratio was 22. In Malawi in 1987 the figures were 72 and 25 respectively, and for Brazil in 1982, 101 and 74. In Brazil, moreover, children in rural areas were three times more likely to drop out of primary school.[3]

There are also sharp differences according to social class. In Chile, a country which historically has had a well-developed education system, in 1979 first grade repetition among the poorest 40 per cent of the population was 53 per cent, compared to 8 per cent among the children of the wealthiest 40 per cent.

Clearly, cuts in educational budgets are one factor in this trend but not the only one. In Chile, for example, whereas there has been an overall cut in government budgets to education since the military coup in 1973, budgets for primary education increased in both absolute and relative terms up to the early 1980s. But during the same period enrolment and retention rates began to fall. This was particularly marked in the area of the capital city, Santiago. Here the reasons for the decline seem to have been connected with the government's economic policies, which led to a sharp fall in real incomes, employment and living standards, especially among the urban poor in the late 1970s and early 1980s.[4]

For the poorest families, there are push-and-pull factors in deciding on the educational future of a child. By sending children to school and keeping them there, the family may sacrifice their potential earning power. In Latin America, children as young as five and six work as street vendors, dodging in and out of the traffic jams to sell chewing gum, newspapers or bags of fruit.

Female-headed households tend to be poorer, and therefore there is more pressure for children to leave school and contribute to family income. If mothers with young children are forced to go out to work when there are no nurseries and no older relatives to look after the children, young girls may be kept at home to look after the youngest children and do domestic tasks which the mother cannot cope with.

A study by the Brazilian Ministry of Labour (1985) found that 30 per cent of poor families in cities and 12 per cent in rural areas were headed by women, and many other families had male heads who could not work because of disablement. One of the results of this was that substantial numbers of these families are largely, or even wholly, supported by the labour of their children. And among poor, female-headed households, one-fifth of the children who worked were under ten years old.[5]

Women are often obliged to act as 'shock-absorbers' for economic and social crisis. It is not merely the long hours of work involved, including time-consuming domestic chores without the help of labour-saving devices, but the fact that the various roles women have to play compete for a finite number of hours. As paid work takes up more and more time, there is less opportunity to care for or supervise children or give them support as they grow up. Where state services have been cut, community activities to substitute for these services take up more of women's (unpaid) time. In these circumstances, the health of families, and their education, both at school and in the home, evidently suffer.

These were among the conclusions of a study of the effects of economic crisis and adjustment on a low-income community in Ecuador. It found that about 15 per cent of women were 'burnt out' – no longer able to cope or to hold their families together. Perhaps more significantly, it found that 55 per cent were 'hanging on', just managing by using up future resources – for example, using children to make up shortages of paid or unpaid labour needs, and thus depriving them of schooling or the chance of making the best of their time at school.[6] In the most extreme cases, children are abandoned by mothers who simply cannot cope any more. The rise in the number of street children in major cities of the South is indicative of this crisis.

The large numbers of children who are not in the designated age group for their grade also points to delays in starting school. In poor communities, it is not uncommon for children to start school at nine or ten instead of six or seven. Erratic attendance and frequent repetition of grades may be explained by the need for school-age children to work at certain times. In rural areas it is a common practice to withdraw children from school for the harvest season, because all hands are needed to pick the crop. Children may be taken out of school for a time when the family is going through a bad patch and parents cannot afford to send them.

In rural areas, the distance, difficulty or expense of transport to school is also a deterrent factor. In some African countries, children walk many miles to school every day. Where they have to use public transport, economic crisis has frequently put up the cost. One report showed that in Egypt, where educational coverage in terms of numbers of schools is relatively good, 94 per cent of boys and 72 per cent of girls enrolled when there was a school within 1 kilometre. When the distance rose to 2 kilometres, enrolments fell to 90 per cent and 64 per cent respectively.[7] The frequent movements of families and individuals seeking work and greater prosperity also has its impact on children's schooling. The idea of education as an escape route from poverty has often been associated with physical mobility: for example, for poverty-stricken sugar-cane cutters in north-eastern Brazil, education is regarded as the way one's children can get out to the city. However, the economic scales are still heavily against education – it is estimated that there is a 50 per-cent drop-out rate at primary level.

Furthermore, since the economic crisis began in the early 1980s, conditions in the cities have become so bad that people are even returning to the region, which is likely to dampen former aspirations.[8]

In a number of countries, especially in Latin America, large numbers of *campesinos* (peasants) are landless labourers, often moving from area to area with their families in search of work. For example, since the early 1970s more and more rural Mexicans have not been able to make ends meet on the land and have become day labourers or migrant workers. Between 1981 and 1983, minimum agricultural wages fell more than 30 per cent. As a result, a study shows that

a new phenomenon has emerged. In the past, it was common for the day labourer to migrate, leaving his family in his parent's home or in his own small house. Today, because a single wage is inadequate as a 'family wage', wives also have to look for paid agricultural work. In other words, in order to achieve the same purchasing power as was given by the father's wage in 1975, in 1985 the father, the mother and one child have to find paid employment. The fact that families have to travel from one place to another, their lack of social relations with a stable community, and the precarious nature of domestic life, destroy the family's role as a social, affective, residential and educational unit.

Both constant movement and the need for children to work put paid to hopes for a stable schooling, or in some cases, any schooling at all.[9]

Poverty, whether rural or urban, also affects the performance and prospects of those children who do go to school. Malnutrition has a marked effect on their ability to learn and to concentrate. Early childhood malnutrition retards intellectual development, and malnourished mothers are likely to have children with serious deficiencies. Bad housing conditions are another adjunct of poverty which affects school performance. Whether in shanty towns, villages or refugee camps, overcrowding, noise, lack of light and hunger all make it difficult to study, on top of the demands which are placed on children outside school hours to help their families by working.

Finding a job

For those who manage to complete primary or secondary school, there is the question of what job prospects there are. If the labour market offers more and better-paid jobs for school graduates, clearly there is more incentive to make sacrifices in order to keep children at school. If school-leavers are virtually predestined to join the unemployment queue, or if the type of education offered is viewed as irrelevant to the economic and social needs of the community, the value of education comes into question.

Long before the economic crises of the 1980s, many countries confronted the problem that their school systems produced graduates for white-collar jobs, and to a limited extent for 'modern' industries, which provided only a small proportion of employment. One result was bureaucracies overloaded with school and university graduates, large numbers of educated unemployed and a growing paper chase after qualifications.

What became known as the 'diploma disease' has had a strong influence on what education means to people. It is seen not so much as a process but as an outcome – the graduation certificate. The kind of education offered in the majority of schools and examination systems in developing countries originates from colonial education systems, or has been strongly influenced by European models. One inheritance is a hierarchy of learning and skills: in the British-influenced systems particularly, an inferior status is accorded to manual skills and vocational training.

Another problem in many countries is that the rural sector has been generally neglected, so education in rural areas has had little relevance to people's lives. Since working in agriculture (as opposed to being a land-owner) is associated with inferior social status, 'improvement' has been associated with finding urban employment.

In urban areas, the majority of people do not work in white-collar or regular waged employment: however, the education system reflects and reinforces the fact that these kinds of work are the aspiration: others are under-valued. Furthermore, the decline in salaried employment in many countries of sub-Saharan Africa and Latin America in the 1980s has sharpened these dislocations between the education system, popular aspirations and the reality of the job market.

Where there are high levels of unemployment among school-leavers there may also be disillusionment with the rewards to be had from keeping children in school. If professionals earn relatively poorly after many years of training, as one Zambian student remarked, 'some youngsters find it better to do unskilled manual labour – like that they earn more than professionals. Graduates often can't get jobs, so education becomes meaningless'.[10]

However, people do make extraordinary efforts and sacrifices to keep their children at school if they believe that it will bring economic advancement and individual betterment. This view can be very persistent even in the face of discouragement. For example, in countries such as Zambia and Uganda, where there has been a long period of economic or political turmoil, the demand for education has remained buoyant.

Political struggle and education

The political and cultural atmosphere also affects attitudes to education. A government which actively encourages and prioritizes education, not only for the élite, and which stresses the importance of education for women, may legitimize education for those who previously thought it was not for them or their families. In the same way, a society which has historically valued the idea of education for all is likely to continue to do so, although conviction wears thin when the education system cannot cope with demand nor deliver access to land and employment.

On the other hand, government policies provoke scepticism about education if it is perceived as irrelevant to people's needs and of poor quality; if its benefits are seen to be reserved for those who are already privileged; if it is deliberately segregated along class or racial/ethnic lines; or, lastly, if the wider economy cannot offer some economic and social rewards to its graduates.

Education has often been a tool of repressive regimes and at the same time the vehicle for popular protest against them. Interference in the educational process through censorship of curricula, books and educational materials prevents 'sensitive' issues being addressed in the classroom. Staff and students are denied a voice in educational issues, particularly where they are organized in professional or student unions, which are often banned. The issues which mobilize students and teachers may be to do with the education system itself: bad conditions in schools, corrupt education authorities, poor teachers' pay and conditions, arrest and harassment of colleagues. They may address wider political, economic or social grievances. Round the world, from China and South Korea to Israel, South Africa and Eastern Europe, political protest has been initiated on university campuses and in secondary schools: the idea that these institutions are somehow insulated from wider conflicts cannot be sustained.

In some cases, the state takes punitive action against protesters, through bannings, breaking up demonstrations, imprisonment, exile, disappearances, executions. Students and teachers form a significant proportion of the cases taken up by Amnesty International, particularly in Latin America. A final resort is to close down schools and universities: the most comprehensive recent case has been the Israeli government's reaction to the Palestinian uprising or *intifada*. The education system in the Occupied Territories, from kindergartens to universities, has been shut down for many months at a time over a period of more than three years, effectively punishing the population by withdrawing opportunities for education.

Sometimes particular groups are excluded from power and influence through lack of access to the language of power and government, and through the suppression or neglect of particular indigenous languages and their cultures. In many parts of Latin America, Spanish speakers dominate a variety of indigenous Amerindian groups (*indígenas*). This creates a dilemma for those who receive education which can become the means by which they are distanced from their own culture. It also reinforces the isolation and oppression of those who remain outside the dominant culture. It can also lead to the devaluation not only of the indigenous culture and language but also of the ways of learning embedded in it.

The dilemma of choosing an official language for education faces countries with a multiplicity of indigenous languages. In many African countries, governments have opted for the language of the former colonial power in the interests of national unity and 'nation building'. Although this may avoid favouring any particular indigenous language group, it tends to reinforce further the legacy of educational values and attitudes from the metropole, while downgrading the importance of local languages and cultures. In other instances, for example, in South Africa, language has played a divisive political role. While enforcing the use of Afrikaans in schools for black South Africans for many years, the government has also, through the Bantustan, or 'homelands' policy, promoted the idea that black South Africans are divided by tribal and language barriers.

War, civil conflict and government repression have created millions of refugees and displaced persons world-wide. There are, of course, different categories of refugees. Those who have money and are well educated may suffer the traumas of persecution and exile but are usually better equipped to survive in other societies, and are more likely to find education for their children and jobs for themselves. A much greater shock is encountered by the many peasants and nomads who find themselves either in refugee camps or trying adapt to city life.

They are marginal in similar ways to illegal or semi-legal migrants: they have problems with access to work and services, including education, and they often face hostility and harsh treatment by the host authorities. In camps, people are more likely to have a minimum of services but may feel isolated and helpless. Many also bear the physical and psychological burden of traumatic events from which they fled. Much depends on the state of the economy in the host country: where debt and adjustment problems are severe, refugees may be less than welcome. Displaced people, adrift within their own country, are often in an even more vulnerable position, without access to protection and frequently losing out in terms of health, education and other services.

Gender difference

Added to the disparities of educational opportunity created by class and ethnic divisions is the effect of gender. Access to education for women has been regarded as a particularly important indicator of social progress. Education for women is seen as crucial to family planning and child health and the key to integrating more women into the workforce. In more radical terms, it has been regarded as instrumental in changing attitudes to gender relations.

Certainly, in many countries, the present generation of girls has educational opportunities their mothers and grandmothers would not have dreamed of, and governments extol this as an example of their achievements. The statistics show that there have been marked improvements in female enrolment in many countries. However, in the majority, enrolments continue to lag behind those of boys, especially at secondary level.

Exceptions

A number of countries hit by economic recession or war have seen reversals in the upward trend of primary school enrolment rates which were prevalent in the 1960s and 1970s. In some cases, these crises appear to have hit male enrolment more than female.

Women and girls, as well as men, may be involved in war and civil conflict, but it is mainly young men and boys who leave home and school to fight. For example, in El Salvador, female enrolment has at some periods overtaken that of males. In 1975, the gross enrolment ratio in the seven to fifteen age-group for males was seventy-six, rising only to seventy-seven by 1987. Female enrolment overtook that of males, rising from seventy-three to eighty-one. A similar pattern was seen among the sixteen- to eighteen-year-olds.[11]

In Nicaragua, although enrolments rose for both sexes between 1974 and 1987, female enrolment overtook male. In this case, the government took clear initiatives to promote education for girls after 1979. But both conscription into the army during the Contra war and poverty – the tendency for boys to start work young – were also part of the reason.

In a few countries where female enrolment actually exceeds that of males, especially at secondary level, this may reflect a relatively low economic and social value placed on formal education. This is much more likely to apply in poorer sectors rather than in the middle class, where education and status tend to be more closely linked. In South Africa and Namibia, young men frequently drop out of school to become migrant workers or take local manual employment. Here the added factor has been the lack of opportunities for educated blacks of either sex (see Chapter 13).

In Botswana and Lesotho, girls outnumber boys at the lower end of the educational spectrum, and even at secondary and university level the numbers of women are substantial, compared with most neighbouring countries. This is a historical trend due to the nature of the traditional cattle-herding economy, where boys were educated by their elders and 'modern' education was, therefore, not much prized. The attractions for young men of migrant labour in the mining industry at home and in South Africa have also discouraged them from staying on at school.

With the exception of some Latin American countries, this inequality of access remains prevalent, especially in Africa and in South Asia, a pattern suggested by the figures for Zimbabwe, Zambia, Malawi and Kenya. Furthermore, among those who are still illiterate, whether old or young, women still form the majority.

Within this gendered inequality of access lie other factors already referred to: class and ethnicity. An under-privileged child, male or female, stands far less chance of getting through the education system than a wealthy one. Girls from élite families have a much better chance of getting to the end of secondary school than boys from poor families. But a girl from a poor family stands less chance than all of them. Under economic pressure, a daughter's school career will almost always be curtailed rather than a son's.

Cultural factors can also inhibit girls' access to education. Women are considered the bearers of indigenous or 'traditional' culture, especially in communities where that identity is under threat. Sometimes they are therefore excluded from receiving an 'alien' education, an extension of a commonly held male view, especially in rural communities, that formal education is 'irrelevant' to women.

A study discussing the role of education in the lives of mainly indigenous peasant women in Peru shows how education can appear at the same time attractive and threatening:

For women, school is an opportunity for autonomy in the face of the vicious circle in which they are normally locked: [moving] from the paternal home to her new home (as a married woman) in which she will always be considered as labour, as reproducer [of the family] and in charge of domestic chores. In this sense, school becomes a socializing arena where the exchange of experiences between girls with similar backgrounds is a vital priority.

However, especially among the indigenous population . . . school is not necessarily perceived as an agent of socialization, insofar as it is perceived as embodying Western [culture] and as such could represent another of the institutions which destroys ethnic identity (Quechua/Aymara). The social and psychological cost of contact with the outside world is very high for indigenous people: their home and community become the only spaces where their identity does not cause shame, and traditions are kept alive. Thus we can say that women's lower levels of literacy and access to formal education are a means of defence against external, assimilating forces.[12]

Attitudes to female roles in the family and marriage also affect access to and achievement in school. A survey of women in Lomé, Togo, found that families were reluctant to keep girls at school on the grounds that it was a waste of money, since when they got married they moved out of their parents' household. In most areas where wives move to their husband's family home when they marry, this is undoubtedly a consideration.[13]

In many different cultures, there is fear of the 'dangers' facing young women outside the boundaries of their home and the control of the family. Control of girls' sexuality is often a major concern. As a

Colombian peasant put it, 'there are many dangers facing girls outside the home. You know, many more than for men'.[14]

The economic pressures of the past two decades are, in many communities, gradually eroding the family structures which legitimized these views. For example, while the informal education by mothers of their children may have been diminished by overwork and stress, it has not been replaced by other forms. In many cases, this has created ambivalent attitudes to education for women and girls.

In all but the most isolated communities, families are now faced with decisions about sending children to school at least for a brief period, but the issues relating to girls and sexual control are most acute when they reach the age of puberty. Even where marriage is not regarded as the first and immediate option, the fear of girls becoming pregnant has become one of the major disincentives to keeping girls at school into their teens. In sub-Saharan Africa, this issue is most explicitly and widely discussed, though it appears as a problem in Latin America too. It has led to a new kind of marginalization: young girls who have been at school and have become pregnant are routinely debarred from continuing their education.

Argentina in the 1980s has seen a marked increase in early pregnancies and adolescent mothers, due to changes in patterns of social behaviour and reactionary policies on contraception and sex education. A recent study noted:

The position of these women is particularly difficult: they are branded socially as having sinned, they have no independent income because the pregnancy interrupts their education and affects their possibilities of employment, and in general they have little chance of being accepted into and being protected by the networks of mutual aid based on kinship because of the increasing scarcity of resources in the lower classes as a whole. In these conditions it is not just the woman but also her children who will suffer the consequences of this situation for life.[15]

In Zimbabwe, this situation has revealed itself in the much-publicized problem of baby dumping. In opinion surveys and in most media coverage of the issue, it is evident that the prevailing tendency is to blame the problem on the increasing 'irresponsibility' of young women, rather than on broader social attitudes towards women and sexuality. According to Caroline Allison,

In countries as diverse as Ghana, Tanzania and Namibia, drop-out rates caused by schoolgirl pregnancies pose additional questions as to the underlying causes and possible solutions. Pregnancy influences not only the formal educational participation of girls who actually become pregnant – since the price of pregnancy is nearly always expulsion – but that of girls in general, since fear of pregnancy (and hence wasted investment – both labour and cash) is one of the major reasons for parents attaching higher preference to the education of sons than daughters.[16]

Women, schooling and employment

How much does schooling in fact change women's prospects in life, and their opportunities for employment? To what extent does education empower them, either in their relations with men or with the community at large? Clearly, there are no simple answers which cover all regions in the developing world. Women often speak of education as something which will empower them and give them confidence. In practice, very often girls' experience of school is that it reinforces ideas about 'appropriate' roles, whether in relation to employment or to the family and to men.

This reinforcement occurs in a number of ways: through the content of the curriculum and the approach and images presented in textbooks (where these exist). Equally important are the attitudes of teachers. All too often, they exacerbate the biases in teaching materials, favour the boys in class and discourage girls from taking certain subjects.

The links between length of schooling and employment prospects for women are not as clear-cut as the optimistic predictions of the 1960s and 1970s envisaged. The data suggest that the high hopes for education as the bearer of gender equality did not come to fruition. In some, though not all, parts of the South there are now more women in paid employment. There have been increases in professional employment, especially in Latin America and parts of the Middle East and Asia, though the largest numbers of women are concentrated in so-called 'traditional' women's professions such as teaching, nursing and welfare work.

However, the vast majority of employed women form a cheap labour force for national and multinational enterprises in agriculture and manufacturing. Many more work in the largely undocumented informal sector or as part of the family labour force in rural areas. In many countries, externally funded development projects have encouraged 'income generation' for women. This is usually treated as distinct from training men for 'jobs', even in the informal employment sector, so that women are still being cast in economically marginal roles.

In Latin America, more women have joined the wage labour force but, since the recession, larger numbers have also been appearing in the unemployment statistics. Even where women work in the same jobs as men, in the vast majority of cases (in many European countries as well as in the South) they do not receive the same wages, although many countries have passed equal pay legislation. Arguably, economic crises, rising prices and falling wages have further limited choice and bargaining power for the poorest groups of women who are obliged to work in order to survive.

Neither education nor legislation alone can change this situation, but only changes in the structures within which women work – whether they are paid or unpaid. Kelly comments:

Gender stereotypes in textbooks

One influence on women's self-image and self-esteem is the content of the textbooks used at school. For girls from poor families, these may be the only books they see while they are growing up. In Togo, a survey of secondary school textbooks showed that many presented women and girls as subordinates, either by excluding them or by making them passive victims of circumstance. In other instances they appeared to be actively dangerous, sometimes engaging in witchcraft. Careers for girls were generally shown as 'traditional' ones – childcare, nursing or midwifery, cottage industry and market trading. Among the few 'modern' careers, a recurring example was an air-stewardess – a 'glamorous' service job. Only men were portrayed in leadership roles, as senior teachers, in business or the police, although many girls would be aware from their own experience that there are women in Togo who have business and professional jobs. Another problem is that many of the textbooks were produced in France, and made assumptions about the nature of family life and women's roles which were irrelevant to the Togolese situation.

In Costa Rica, a survey of primary school textbooks showed similar problems. The survey covered books produced both by the Ministry of Education and by commercial publishers, which were used in schools in 1975 and 1985. In the commercially produced books, the bias against women, both in terms of male–female balance and of negative stereotypes, did not improve over the decade. Males appear as historical figures, involved in intellectual activity and agriculture; females in domestic work, childcare and sometimes as students. A story about women from one of these books stresses their limited horizons: a poor street vendor, dreaming about a better future, drops her basket of wares. The text asks, 'What should the woman have been doing instead of imagining future possibilities?'

Government textbooks showed some improvement in the portrayal of women, with the publication of a new series of textbooks in 1984 and 1985 with assistance from USAID. Females still appear much less often than males, but there have been some efforts to represent women in less stereotyped roles, while men are shown more often in domestic and childcare activities.[17]

Education was seen as a means of enabling women to work like men at a job for a wage and, unlike men, in the household bearing and rearing children. Reforms in education have not been accompanied by changes in women's roles in the household, the structure of occupations, workforce segregation, discrimination against women in employment and in remuneration. Education, in short, can only provide knowledge, skills and credentials, but the extent to which these translate into equality in society depends on whether the structures which keep women subservient to men are changed.[18]

Even governments and political movements which aim to reform or remould society on more equitable lines have rarely succeeded in confronting these structures, particularly as they exist within the family. While it is widely asserted that the family is one of the basic units of social life, it is equally common to hold that relationships within the family – especially male–female relationships – are 'private' affairs. Certainly, challenging male–female relationships in marriage, property relations and decision-making within the family have proved difficult. Even radical political leaderships have generally preferred to limit their interventions to actively encouraging women's participation in education and the workforce.

Notes

1   Carnoy and Samoff (1990), p.66.
2. From a case study prepared for the Commonwealth Secretariat by S. Jayaweera, Centre for Women's Research, Sri Lanka, in *Engendering Adjustment* (1989), p.25.
3. Lockheed and Verspoor (1990), p.102.
4. Cornia *et al.* (1988), vol.2, ch.3, *passim*.
5. Unicef (1987), *Invisible Adjustment*, p.86.
6. Moser (1989) in *Invisible Adjustment,* passim.
7. Lockheed and Verspoor (1990), p.102.
8. Information from Françoise Caillods, International Institute for Educational Planning.
9. Arizpe *et al* (1989) in *Invisible Adjustment*, p.258.
10. Student discussion group with author, Bristol University, 1989.
11. Figures from Unesco *Yearbook 1989*.
12. Vargas Vega *et al.* (1989), pp.38–9 (translated from Spanish).
13. Togo case study in Kate Young (ed.) (1988).
14. Vélez (1988), p.10 (translated from Spanish).
15. Unicef (1987), *Invisible Adjustment*, p.47.
16. Allison in Rose (ed.) (1985), p.117.
17. Togo: Beraimeh (1988); Costa Rica: M. Gonzalez-Suarez (1987), *Barriers to Female Achievement: Sex Stereotypes in Textbooks*, quoted in M. Lockheed *et al*, (1990), p.104.
18. G.P. Kelly (1990), p.139.

CHAPTER 6

Other ways of learning: the effects of the crisis on non-formal education

Most people associate education with schools, colleges and universities; that is, the 'formal sector'. In terms of state budgets, numbers of students and employees, this is certainly the predominant form of education today, even in the poorest societies. But there are many other types of learning, for all age groups. Dividing formal education from out-of-school or so-called non-formal education is artificial in many ways. But in some countries, this division reflects the gulf between government provision through the school system, on the one hand, and the needs and interests of marginal populations who are most alienated from that system, on the other.

In many respects, especially with regard to literacy, there is no simple way to separate the two. For many years, there was a commonly held belief that universal primary education would gradually lead to the eradication of illiteracy. If this were the case, a one-off literacy campaign aimed at illiterate adults would be sufficient to meet out-of-school need. In fact, educational coverage has not become universal in the developing world. Substantial numbers of young people never go to school or drop out of school before they have achieved functional literacy. So the number of illiterates continues to grow in absolute and, in some cases, in proportional terms. For example, in Kenya, a country with high, though now declining, enrolments at primary level, a recent survey of people enrolled in the literacy programme launched at the beginning of the 1980s showed that more than half the learners were below the age of thirty. Half of the total had also attended school for three to four years. Seventy per cent of those enrolled were women.[1]

Education for adults and for those of any age who have missed out on mainstream formal schooling is characteristically very diffuse. Its content varies greatly, as do its providers, which range from the state to various kinds of non-governmental organizations. It is also a sector in which Northern non-governmental organizations are now particularly interested and involved.

Non-formal education takes many forms. These include literacy and basic education for adults, 'catching-up' programmes for school drop-outs, pre-school education for young children, political and trade-union education and various kinds of educational work linked with development initiatives, including agricultural extension and training programmes, and health education. These also shade over into a broad variety of both state and privately sponsored vocational training programmes.

The purposes and goals of these forms of education are equally varied. As a result, it is extremely difficult to generalize about the effects of economic and political crisis on their evolution. None the less, some trends have become apparent during the 1980s. On the whole, long-term needs for out-of-school education have increased at the same time as material resources are diminishing.

With few exceptions, whatever the ideology of the government in power, adult basic education and literacy work supported by state budgets have suffered badly from the effects of economic cutbacks. For the most part, non-formal and out-of-school education has little political clout in government circles and therefore is easily cut back. Even governments strongly committed to literacy campaigns and continuing education, such as Mozambique and Nicaragua, have been forced to shelve or restrict programmes because of economic recession and the difficulties of sustaining programmes in war conditions. The other option has been to depend to an increased extent on external sources of funding.

Other important sectors of educational provision have been slow to develop in many countries, hampered by lack of resources. These include pre-school education for young children and support for both children and adults with disabilities. The absence of crèches and pre-school facilities can have a knock-on effect on access to education for older children, as school-age daughters are withdrawn from school to care for the younger children.

Economic difficulties and the need to work longer hours may also cut down the time available to adults to go to classes or community meetings. This is particularly evident among adult women, who are generally the main recipients of non-formal education. Lack of free time is also a problem for projects run by volunteer teachers. Poverty may deter individuals from investing even in the basic materials required for classes – paper, pencils and sometimes textbooks or workbooks. This chapter examines how these problems have affected literacy work and popular education initiatives.

Motives for literacy

Many of the difficulties arising in literacy work lie in assumptions about literacy itself. Whether it is regarded as a technical skill or a means of empowerment, literacy has now become a catchword in international development circles. It is often put forward as the key to the solution of a variety of other social and economic problems. However, the experiences of literacy work and literacy campaigns suggest that it is actually a very problematic concept – mainly because the value and significance of reading, writing and numeracy, as well as effective ways of teaching, seem to vary from society to society. Both the practice and the outcomes vary considerably. No single satisfactory formula for achievement has emerged. Effectiveness seems to depend on a variety of factors: the nature of the society, the political and economic environment – its structures of power (national, community and family) – and the relevance of the materials and techniques used to develop literacy. It is certainly not amenable to any simple formula of cost and efficiency.

Counting literates

Measuring the number of people who are illiterate requires deciding on who is literate. John Smyth of Unesco suggests that literacy figures are a 'rubber yardstick': literacy should be seen as a continuum, not something you have or you do not have. But this obviously makes meaningful statistical measurement very difficult. Unesco, for example, estimates that in 1990 there were 963 million illiterates in the world. While such statements may be important to draw attention to the magnitude of the problem, the figures themselves are certainly questionable. First, Unesco has to rely on government figures, which are not particularly reliable. Although Unesco has its own definition of literacy, this is not necessarily followed by all countries. The data given to international bodies are collected by a variety of means. Sometimes it is the result of some kind of literacy test, sometimes self-definition; it may be the result of sample surveys, or of a national census, not all of which produce comparable results. Furthermore, most national statistics count anyone who has been to school as literate, though this is certainly not true.

Distinctions also have to be made between absolute illiteracy and functional illiteracy. The Unesco definition distinguishes between 'literacy' and 'functional literacy'. A literate person 'can with understanding both read and write a short simple statement on his (/her) everyday life'. A functionally literate person must be able to 'engage in all those activities in which literacy is required for effective functioning of his (/her) group and community and also for enabling him (/her) to continue to use reading, writing and calculation for his (/her) own and the community's development'.[2]

It is also useful to distinguish alphabetic literacy from ability to 'read' visual and oral symbols, a skill often more highly developed in non-literate cultures.

The nature of literacy itself is still in dispute. Certainly what constitutes 'functional' literacy in one society may be dysfunctional in another because of language or cultural differences. For example, some argue that in Europe and the United States people will soon not be considered fully literate if they are unable to understand computer languages.

It is often assumed that everyone, given the chance, wishes to become literate. In fact, literacy – defined as reading, writing and numeracy – may not be a high priority at all times and in all communities. Those who live in isolated areas with little contact with literate communities may have highly developed non-literate skills and feel no real need to become literate. They may also speak languages which have not been fully written down. People who live in extreme poverty often regard food, housing, access to land and clean water, and health care for their children as much more urgent priorities than learning to read.

There are, therefore, dangers in presenting literacy as an escape from a state of ignorance, or the cure to a disease. In a largely oral culture, this approach may denigrate the skills, knowledge and ways of communicating of those who are not literate and encourage people to regard them as less important members of society. It may marginalize language groups and so encourage new forms of élitism and exclusivism. It may also reinforce a sense of failure in those who do not manage to become literate or remain so. If literacy is imposed in this way it is not necessarily liberating.

Knowledge and experience

La Asociación Jarhuajperakua works in a rural area of Mexico training rural popular teachers. It gives the following description of the communities (both indigenous and Spanish-speaking *campesinos*) with whom it works:

Communication is by the spoken word. The written language is almost never used and it could be said that it isn't necessary while the structures which marginalize [these communities] remain. Literacy is of little use. Mathematical forms of language depend on mental calculations and in general, requests to learn are for (adding, subtracting, multiplying and dividing) and for calculating percentages.

All the communities have their own knowledge based on experience: popular wisdom which is incorporated into informal educational processes. Informal education has a strong socializing power.

Formal education is structured through rural schools which are modelled on urban schools. There is a hierarchy of power which controls the children's education, though in formal and non-formal adult education, this [hierarchy] is not so apparent as it lacks a structured framework.[3]

Some groups and organizations promoting out-of-school education have begun to develop methods of work which take a broader view of what literacy means. They place greater emphasis on first developing people's abilities to express their needs and act on them. This is now regarded as part of the process of education, not separate from it. In this way, achieving functional literacy is only one part of the process. Whether the actual skills of reading and writing are the most important element will depend very much on the social and economic context. This approach contrasts sharply with the functional approach, which assumes that learning to read and write is an end in itself. Another aspect of this approach is to reinforce people's abilities to use language to express their needs and discuss problems. In Lesotho and in Jamaica, drama groups have played an important part in developing community participation, while in some Latin American countries, videos have been used to develop visual skills and analysis of familiar images. Cassettes and radio programmes are also used to help with languages which are not written.

Some development workers have found that health care and agriculture are the main preoccupations, especially for women, and that an interest in literacy may grow out of work in those areas, rather than preceding it. In Zimbabwe, though in general there is an interest in literacy, especially among rural women who have not had a chance to go to school, not all consider it a first priority. In some of the numerous income-generating projects which have been established, people expressed more interest in practical skills than in literacy *per se*.

Even in societies where literacy is held up as the norm, motives for participating in literacy work vary considerably. Participants in the Kenyan literacy programme had a variety of motivations for becoming literate, depending on their socio-economic situation. For example, there were differences between the motivations of two rural communities: in Kiirua, a recent settlement where farming is prosperous, learners saw literacy as a tool to improve their productive skills, and their immediate well-being. South Maragoli is a poorer, over-populated area where most of the men migrate to the towns to work. Here, the majority of women left behind wanted to be literate first and foremost in order to write letters to migrant family members and read their replies. They also needed literacy and numeracy skills to receive remittances and to run small farm businesses.

Where religious groups are strong and are involved in literacy work, reading may be strongly associated with piety. In a recent display of statements by the newly literate in Maputo, Mozambique, one woman said she was pleased to be literate because 'I like to be able to read the Bible.'

Self-respect and the ability to articulate demands are also important considerations. In communities which are well organized and where there are opportunities to participate in decision-making, interest in learning to read, write or count is generally high. For example, in Nicaragua and Mozambique, literacy was part of a political process, rather than a bid to obtain practical skills. However, a further incentive to become literate in highly organized communities is that participation in local groups or committees may require literacy. Women, particularly, are often excluded from participation in such groups because they are not literate.

In countries where a number of different languages are spoken, both literacy promoters and communities are faced with the choice of which language to learn in. The answer is not always obvious. It is usually easier to teach people to read and write in their mother tongue if they have no knowledge of another language, or an imperfect grasp of it. It is also the right of those learners to become literate first of all in their own language. However, if literacy is in a mother tongue which is not the language of power and the prevailing language in the society, it may serve to marginalize those learners and deny them a voice at national level. Sometimes those who are potential learners are very aware of this issue. For example, in Bolivia, the government has initiated literacy programmes in indigenous Indian languages, only to find that indigenous communities want to learn Spanish. However if there is resistance to the prevailing linguistic culture, people may insist on mother-tongue learning.

The state and literacy

During the 1980s, political conflicts as much as economic problems have sharpened awareness of the issues in non-formal education. Literacy is increasingly seen as a political issue by governments. High illiteracy figures are regarded as revealing failures in their education systems – hence the embarrassment of countries like the United Kingdom in admitting that it still has a problem with illiteracy. It has also become a political issue in the developing world, as the expectation of receiving an education and therefore becoming literate has grown.

Governments of all political persuasions have therefore made at least sporadic efforts to promote literacy among adults, sometimes with substantial funding from international organizations. However, literacy has slipped down the list of government priorities in many countries during the 1980s. In the 1970s there was a fairly widespread belief that literacy was a sound economic investment which would lead to increased productivity. In the recessionary climate of the 1980s, the short-term returns on literacy have been called into question, and generally speaking the long-term rewards of education have received less attention. Furthermore, with high levels of unemployment, there are usually sufficient literate candidates for the shrinking numbers of jobs requiring literacy.

The outcomes of government-sponsored literacy programmes and campaigns have been extremely mixed. Literacy work has taken two forms. Short campaigns involving mass mobilization have been one method. Literacy programmes involving ongoing work over a period years, either nationally or targeting selected communities or regions, have been the other. It is generally agreed that in societies undergoing major political change, revolutionary governments have been more able to mobilize and inspire people both to teach and to learn.

Nicaragua's short campaign of 1980 is perhaps the best example of this. Other, longer campaigns, in Mozambique, Ethiopia and Tanzania, were also launched by governments advocating social and political change. These had some success, though sustaining the enthusiasm of both learners and literacy workers over a longer period of time has often proved a problem. In countries where there is little popular identification with the regime, especially under authoritarian governments, efforts at literacy promotion may be regarded with suspicion or even contempt. It is in these circumstances that non-government literacy initiatives have become a focus of interest. Where such projects have made an impact, greater community involvement and organization may in turn generate challenges to the government – demands for democracy, land reform, and greater access to services such as education.

Literacy campaign in Ecuador

A mass literacy campaign which sought to build on the Nicaraguan experience took place in Ecuador in 1989. A campaign for greater community participation in education was explicitly linked to human rights issues. The literacy campaign was three months long and the literacy workers were mostly senior high-school pupils who taught as part of their compulsory curriculum. Learners were organized locally into 'popular literacy circles'.

As in Nicaragua, the goal was mutual learning between the students and the literacy learners – the exposure of youngsters to the lives and experiences of others being seen as a very valuable part of the work. However, the parallels with the Nicaraguan campaign did not include the level of popular mobilization and enthusiasm inspired in 1980, and the campaign was not accompanied by other kinds of social and educational change, as was the case in Nicaragua. The student teachers for the most part did not live in the communities where they taught, so there was not the same intensity of urban–rural contact that was achieved in the Nicaraguan case. While a great deal of effort was put into the preparation of teaching and learning materials, there appear to be few structures in place to follow up on the initial campaign. Ongoing literacy work is in the hands of a relatively small number of voluntary adult teachers who receive only a token payment.[4]

'Popular education'

The failure of formal education to create a literate population is not simply a question of shortages and lack of resources, important though these factors are. It reflects the alienation of substantial sectors of the population from the education system and its providers. As a report on literacy in Honduras remarked, formal education frequently increased political and economic marginalization, 'impeding access to the forms of expression of the "erudite culture". At the same time, it devalues the popular cultural heritage.' In other words, the problem is not merely economic impoverishment, but cultural and political impoverishment.

In regions of acute conflict, literacy has been increasingly associated with political struggles for liberation and national or ethnic identity. Where state and élite policies have deprived people of educational opportunities, or suppressed and distorted cultures through education, literacy can have a very powerful symbolic as well as practical value. For this reason, many liberation movements have run literacy programmes in exile or in liberated areas, from the South West African People's Organisation (SWAPO) in Namibia to the Frente Farabundo Marti para la Liberación Nacional (FMLN) in El Salvador.

These problems with formal education have led to the proliferation of education programmes run by community and religious organizations, trade unions, and women's and peasants' organizations. Such initiatives, particularly numerous in Latin America, are clearly distinct from those which simply involve the state or local government imposing an obligation on people to provide for their children's education, or to become literate, without at the same time introducing any element of democratic choice into the process of education.

The most influential practitioner and protagonist of what has come to be known as 'popular education' is the Brazilian educator Paulo Freire. His major contribution to the debate on literacy has been to challenge the view that literacy is simply a skill or technique to be acquired. He sees it rather as a means to empower people, to enable them to comprehend their political and economic position, confront their oppression and seek collectively to change it. Learning involves discussion and dialogue rather than the transfer of knowledge from teacher to learner, he maintains.

Variations on this 'pedagogy of liberation' have been influential in Latin America since the 1970s and have subsequently spread further afield. Recently, these ideas have begun to have some influence in Southern Africa. In some cases, such education is seen as compensating for the failures of state provision. In others, it is seen as part of a process of developing a new and different education system, changing both what is taught and how it is taught, and the relationships between teachers, learners and the wider community.

Broadly speaking, what has been defined as popular education can serve a variety of goals, among which are:

● to increase access to education for those who have been excluded from schooling;

- to challenge the goals of education as provided under the existing government and economic system;
- to establish alternative forms of education, particularly concentrating on its relevance to the experience and needs of dispossessed or marginalized groups;
- to mobilize people for political struggle through conscientization;
- to empower communities and individuals.

Although some remarkable results have been achieved, not least by Freire himself in Brazil and Guinea-Bissau, the methodological and practical problems of working in this way have been considerable. Particular problems have arisen in developing ways of breaking down authoritarian relations between teacher and learner. Rosa Maria Torres, who has had long experience of literacy campaigns in Latin America comments on the difficulty of dealing with this issue:

Dialogue occurs between equals but a power relation exists between educator and learner. If this is denied, the relation will remain because the resistance to change comes as much from learners as teachers. To construct dialogue, teachers must first understand why it is difficult to generate it.[5]

The small scale and lack of political weight of most popular education projects in relation to state-run education systems can be a strength if this leads to autonomy and freedom to change and experiment, but there are other, more negative aspects. The organizations involved frequently need to rely on funding from external sources. Even when funders are generally supportive of their goals, this kind of dependence can impose limitations. Second, the concept of education as a received package of knowledge affects people as well as governments, and there are often difficulties in persuading people that this is 'proper' education, especially if there is no certification.

Those who favour national, state-sponsored campaigns argue that such localized literacy programmes organized by non-governmental organizations do not reach a large enough number of people. The same is true of popular education initiatives which in most, though not all, instances reach only a relatively small number. But the more effective of these initiatives are designed to challenge the policies of the government, both on education and other economic and social issues, not just to provide 'alternative' education for a small community.

In recent years, the terminology associated with Freire's work has increasingly been appropriated by a wide range of educators and even governments. Their intentions are often very different from the goals of challenging governments and their policies. The language and, even to an extent, the methodology of 'popular education' has also been used to legitimize political and social control, whether by governments or by external funding agencies which now look with greater favour on projects couched in terms of 'empowerment'.

Barriers to learning: women and literacy

There are social and practical impediments to becoming literate, even when the desire to do so is strong. For the most part, rural dwellers, especially women, still have least access to literacy programmes. Women make up the majority of illiterates, especially among adults. But women frequently suffer from controls exerted by their husbands, fathers or male relatives, who prevent or discourage them from attending classes. In urban areas, the more determined sometimes go anyway, without permission, if the man works long hours away from home. But village life does not favour clandestine attendance at literacy classes. In some cases men object particularly to women attending mixed classes. But another problem arises if women are the majority of participants in non-formal educational courses, which are then perceived by men as 'just for women' and therefore unimportant.

Women frequently have little time or energy to spare to attend classes and study. Women's tasks increase in times of economic crisis, and literacy classes can simply become another time-consuming effort in an over-burdened day. Fatigue and irrelevant learning materials also explain why women who say they are eager to learn appear to be quickly discouraged and drop out. For example, in Tanzania rural women have been eager for information and enthusiastic about the national literacy programme. However, they have frequently been disappointed by the lack of materials of interest and relevance to them. In the late 1980s, the Women's Education Section of the Tanzanian Institute of Adult Education launched a series of books based on interviews with village women. In them, they talk about their daily problems and how they solved them, with accounts of projects they had started and photographs from the villages. The aim is to combine reading materials with useful information and ideas.[6]

Although many non-formal education projects now include a particular emphasis on skills training and literacy for women, the results have been mixed. For example, a recent study of a number of non-formal education projects for women in West Africa found major problems remained in reaching women effectively in rural areas. It examined projects in countries where illiteracy rates among women are generally very high – for example, Mali where 89 per cent of women are illiterate and Niger with 91 per cent. Some of the projects examined were run by local non-governmental organizations, some by government ministries, mostly with external funding or support. While the authors argue that literacy work should form an integral part of broader development work, such as income-generating projects, they warn that 'education cannot be treated as an after-thought, piggy-backed onto projects'. It needs to be built into the project from the outset.[7] Women's eagerness for literacy and skills is greater when other aspects of their lives are changing: for example, when, as small farmers, they have access to credit and agricultural advice.

The consequences for adult women of becoming literate are complex and little studied. Lalage Bown points out that most studies of the effects of education on women have focused on those who have passed through formal education, rather than those who have received education in adulthood. Measurement of the outcomes of literacy and adult education is also more difficult, and has to take into account subjective as well as objective criteria.

School-based studies generally suggest that education influences women's behaviour as mothers, with educated women having healthier children who are more likely to stay at school. On the question of family size the evidence is more mixed. It seems likely that becoming literate later in life will also affect women's attitudes to health and education in their families, especially if these issues have been addressed as part of the literacy process. However, Bown points out that there are other ways in which women's lives are affected outside the family. In the case of adult learning, much depends on the economic and social environment in which the learners live as to what benefits literacy is likely to bring.

Finally, the least measurable outcome of literacy may be self confidence, increased self valuation and an ability to participate more fully in life outside the home. It has been suggested that adult education is more likely to achieve these outcomes than formal schooling, in which, as noted earlier, women often internalize a variety of negative stereotypes.[8] Nonetheless, the achievement of greater confidence and willingness to participate in community affairs sometimes sets women new challenges, when men are threatened by their newly-found confidence and seek to prevent them from exercising it.

Learning strategies

There are several other aspects of literacy work which have proved to be crucial to effectiveness: training and motivation of literacy workers; the quality and relevance of materials; and the reinforcement of literacy.

Experiences of various literacy campaigns suggest that both the commitment and skills of literacy promoters are very important. Reliance on revolutionary fervour or personal commitment have not always proved sufficient, as was often assumed in early experiments with popular education. This has been one of the difficulties of the Freirean model, which tended to idealize the teacher's role as the agent of conscientization. Success was assumed to be essentially a matter of political will and individual dedication. However, the difficulties encountered in successive experiments have led practitioners to take more account of the need for some kind of initial training in methods of promoting dialogue and discussion and the use of materials. One of the criticisms of the Nicaraguan campaign was that the 'cascade' system of training meant that the training process was gradually diluted, so that the young *brigadistas* at several removes from the original set of trainers had few skills to bring to their work. Their commitment carried them over many of the problems in a short campaign. But when in difficulties they tended to fall back on somewhat authoritarian school teaching methods, the only model they had. Other projects in Latin America have suffered from the same problem. Rosa Maria Torres, who was one of the advisers to the Nicaraguan campaign, has recently helped in the Ecuadorian literacy campaign, which has placed much more emphasis on both training of promoters and back-up once they are in the field.

Learner participation in dialogue and discussion is not easy to achieve or sustain and does not necessarily happen spontaneously. Often too, the teachers are young and are not automatically accepted or appreciated. When they are, the relationship can be very fruitful, but in some instances they are not regarded as 'proper teachers', especially by older learners. The Asociación Jarhuajperakua points out that the communities with which they work in rural Mexico have a strong sense of hierarchy. If the rural educator they have trained is of low social status in the eyes of the community, this will make his or her task more difficult. In some societies, this would apply to women educators.

Relying on voluntary teachers with limited back-up and preparation can be a major drawback, particularly when levels of political commitment are lower. The West African study cited earlier suggests that high drop-out rates and learning problems stem at least in part from the use of poorly trained volunteer teachers. They tend to 'dabble' in literacy work, and have neither the motivation nor the skills to mobilize people. Motivations for participating in literacy work also vary. In Kenya, a sample of full-time, paid literacy teachers expressed satisfaction with their work, which gave them status in the community, though some were concerned with their lack of certification. Among voluntary teachers, mainly living in the community where they work, the main incentive seems to have been the hope that this would be a step towards a full-time job in teaching.[9]

There has been a good deal of innovation in the development of materials to support both literacy and post-literacy work. This is most evident in Latin America, where centres of popular education have generated new ideas and approaches. There is now much more emphasis on using materials which have direct relevance to people's daily lives, with less emphasis on political sloganizing for its own sake. Whereas in many cases both governments and non-governmental organizations are able to obtain external funding to produce literacy and post-literacy materials, shortage of funds has been one factor in seeking to generate literacy materials from within the community. But probably the more important factor has been the effort to create materials to which learners can relate. Hard experience has shown that while people may be impressed with well-produced materials, the key question is whether those who are learners can relate to the contents – both written and visual. The use of visual materials is increasingly regarded as an important part of the learning process, to generate dialogue and discussion, rather than simply to illustrate a text. Other issues emerge along the way – particularly the visual and textual representation of women. Awareness of this issue has been slow to emerge, and may be one of a number of factors which have discouraged women from persisting in literacy classes.

Once people achieve basic literacy, whatever its precise form, the process creates further demands for post-literacy education, whether to 'catch up' on missed formal education, or to develop organizational or practical skills. At this point, the demands become much more complex and potentially more expensive. This has proved to be one of the most difficult aspects of adult education, though experiences in many countries have shown that unless literacy skills can be used, whether through provision of an environment in which reading and writing are part of everyday experience, or through further education, those made literate will soon lapse into functional illiteracy.

In the future, there may be a large demand for a variety of educational initiatives beyond the formal school system, and this may continue even when primary school enrolments are at a high level. This could be one of the most challenging areas for both governments and non-governmental organizations. The nature and scope of demand will depend on the state of the economy and on popular attitudes towards education. One option is the provision by the government of some form of 'accelerated primary' education, as has been the case in Nicaragua. This gives new literates a chance to 'catch up' on formal schooling and qualifications, though teaching techniques need to be adapted to adult learners. Another option is skills-oriented courses. At present, courses of this kind tend to be most developed in urban areas, but they could be based in rural areas and focus on agricultural skills useful to small farmers, especially women.

Distance learning, a form of self-tuition through radio or television programmes, reinforced by written materials and study groups, has proved a useful strategy, especially in attempts to reach scattered rural populations. However, it has certain limitations. It seems to be most effective for learners who already have some experience of studying and are able to cope with working alone. It is therefore more suitable for upgrading skills than learning from scratch, or in situations where there are small groups of learners working together. Distance techniques are also of little use for teaching 'hands-on' skills. Various experiments with all these methods suggest that they cannot be achieved 'on the cheap'. Initially, they are expensive in terms of time and personnel, for training, groundwork and ensuring reliable communications with institutions or individual learners in more isolated areas.

There is another problem with promoting education outside the school system. Unless the school system is discredited for mainly political reasons, a lower valuation is put on non-formal education, especially for young people. This is something that post-literacy programmes have to deal with. In the current political and educational climate, this attitude is encouraged by those who argue that non-formal education is cheaper, because costs are usually borne by communities or voluntary organizations. Only where the value placed on these kinds of education is changed, where they are seen as offering new approaches which can influence formal education and initiate change, can they be effective in the long run. Governments and other organizations involved need to throw their weight behind legitimizing the status of non-formal education. Too often it is treated as an afterthought or a side-show, especially when the formal education system is in crisis.

Despite all the pitfalls and problems of literacy and post-literacy work, and the perennial shortages of funds and skills which face many groups and governments, some of the most interesting and innovative experiments in developing countries have been in out-of-school education. They have challenged some of the assumptions and methods which are still the norm in the formal sector. They have also raised questions about the nature of education and its content, the training of teachers, relations between teachers and learners, the development and use of materials, and the use of language and visual images.

Notes

1. Carron *et al.* (1989), pp.99ff.
2. Quoted in Lind (1988), p.11.
3. CEAAL (1989), p.27 (translated from Spanish).
4. Archer and Costello (1990), pp.78ff.
5. R.M. Torres quoted in Archer and Costello (1990), p.80.
6. Rafferty (1988), pp.130–2.
7. Unesco/Unicef (1988), *passim.*
8. Bown (1990) *passim.*
9. Carron *et al.*

PART TWO

The Debt Crisis, Politics and Educational Policy

International economic and political forces place severe constraints on individual governments' decision-making, particularly if that nation is economically under-developed. None the less, neither governments nor peoples are simply passive victims. Choices are still made, though external circumstances may limit the initial range of options and may also affect the outcome of the policy chosen. In this section, we examine how these forces affect governments' role in the provision of education.

Profile of the case-study regions: the international and regional context

All the countries of the South cannot be lumped together if the processes which affect education are to be understood. Historical experiences and cultural assumptions differ and there are great variations in wealth, population size and ideology. However, there are certain common themes. These include the legacies of previous regimes, whether colonial, semi-colonial or indigenous, and the strong influence of Western ideas and technologies on concepts of 'modernity' and 'progress' espoused by many political élites in the South. Education is often used as an ideological tool by regimes of very different political persuasions, and sometimes itself becomes a site of political conflict. Sharp inequalities between different classes and ethnic groups and between men and women are often exacerbated by debt and economic crisis. To assess the impact on education, we turn to some specific cases. The examples in the following sections draw primarily on case studies in Central America, Southern Africa and Sudan.

In recent decades, these three regions have been the focus of political, economic and military interventions by the great powers. In Southern Africa, the major regional power, South Africa, has also played a highly interventionist role in neighbouring countries. For the most part, with the exception of South Africa, these are relatively poor states, with economies that are still largely tied to the export of primary commodities and are particularly vulnerable to external economic pressures and fluctuations in the world economy. With the exception of Costa Rica, these countries have recent histories of domination by authoritarian or colonial regimes, and of insurgency and resistance or even outright civil war. While each nation has its own culture and history, in recent years each has been affected by events in the surrounding region.

South Africa stands in apparent contrast to the rest of the states considered here: a regional military superpower with a relatively strong and diversified economy, built on its mineral wealth and on the exploitation of the cheap labour of its black majority. None the less, its heavy dependence on exports of minerals, especially gold and diamonds (which make up about 80 per cent of export earnings), make it vulnerable to fluctuations in the world market, and to sanctions imposed by some members of the international community. In the 1980s, the economy was affected by recession and the government

Table 7.1   **Statistical profiles**

Country	Date	GNP per capita**	Infant mortality rate[1]	Population millions 1988*	% urban 1988*	% literate adults 1985*** m/f
Central America						
Costa Rica	1975	950	33.1			
	1980	1,950	20.1			
	1986	1,500	17.2	2.7	45	94/93
El Salvador	1975	430	88.0			
	1980	740	74.8			
	1986	820	63.8	5.0	44	75/69
Guatemala	1975	570	87.2			
	1980	1,120	74.8			
	1986	1,050	65.6	8.7	33	63/47
Honduras	1975	360	98.0			
	1980	640	87.2			
	1986	770	59.0	4.8	42	61/58
Nicaragua	1975	650	95.8			
	1980	690	82.8			
	1986	730	66.5	3.6	59	[74]+
Southern Africa						
Mozambique	1975	–	143.7			
	1982	190	132.8			
	1986	220	120.0	14.9	24	55/22
South Africa	1975	1,410	98.0			
	1980	2,160	87.8			
	1986	1,840	67.9	34.0	58	– –
Sudan	1975	250	133.8			
	1980	430	123.2			
	1986	300	112.0	23.8	21	33/14
Zambia	1975	550	96.4			
	1980	600	90.4			
	1986	270	92.5	7.6	54	84/67
Zimbabwe	1975	570	88.8			
	1980	710	82.4			
	1985	590	73.9	9.3	27	81/67

[1]Deaths per thousand live births under the age of 1
* Urban percentage and population from *World Development Report 1990, Tables 1 and 31.*
** In current US dollars
*** Literacy rates from *State of the World's Children 1989* Table 4.
+ Literacy rate for Nicaragua (1986) from Inter-American Development Bank, *Economic and Social Progress in Latin America* 1988, p.464.

Sources: derived from World Bank, *World Tables 1988–89*; *World Development Report, 1990*. Unicef, *State of the World's Children*, 1989 was forced to negotiate the rescheduling of its external debts. It has also resorted to austerity policies which have affected prices, employment and real wages. Despite the relative strength of the economy, apartheid ideology and economic policies have kept the majority of the population living in poverty, at a level more comparable to the countries of Central America than to that of the affluent South African whites. Overall illiteracy rates among the black population are still thought to stand above 50 per cent, and schooling is not accessible to many black children. The segregated education system is geared to keeping the majority of black people in subordination, while health and housing conditions are poor and, most importantly, black people have been deprived of political and human rights.

In the 'front-line' states bordering on South Africa, the apartheid regime and the organized resistance to it have had serious repercussions. South Africa has pursued a policy of violent destabilization in Mozambique, and, to a lesser extent, in Zimbabwe. It has invaded Angola on several occasions, and has launched punitive raids on alleged African National Congress (ANC) bases in a number of neighbouring countries. These actions have created large numbers of refugees and displaced people, who have been spread through most of the countries in the region. The costs of these conflicts, in terms of the damage to their economies and social welfare, as well as of lives lost, has been considerable. The states most severely affected have been Mozambique, Angola and Namibia, but even countries not centrally involved in the fighting – Zambia, Zimbabwe and the two states most immediately dependent on South Africa, Botswana and Lesotho – have felt its effects. Furthermore, most of the front-line states are dependent on transport routes through South Africa, which has imposed substantial increases in transit costs, tightening its hold on their economies and raising the cost of imports.

Losses associated directly and indirectly with regional conflict between 1980 and 1988 are estimated at US$16 to 17 billion. This figure covers losses to GDP in Malawi, Zimbabwe, Botswana, Zambia, Tanzania, Swaziland and Lesotho. It does not include the countries directly involved in the war: Angola, Mozambique and Namibia. Zambia's losses alone were put at US$4.75 to 5 billion and Zimbabwe's at US$7.5 to 8 billion.[1]

Central America, meanwhile, is regarded by the United States as its 'backyard', and successive US governments since the nineteenth century have intervened in its internal political struggles. Since the late 1970s, regional conflict has intensified, and so has the role of the United States, which provides large amounts of both military and civil aid to governments which it supports. The main sources of regional tension in the 1980s have been the civil war in El Salvador, where the United States has provided ever-increasing amounts of military aid to a succession of right-wing governments, and the role of the United

States and the US-backed Contras in undermining the Sandinista government in Nicaragua. From May 1985 this included a trade embargo and an economic blockade, mining Nicaraguan ports, large-scale support for the Contras and various undercover operations to disrupt the economy. By the end of the 1980s the Nicaraguan economy was on the verge of collapse. The Sandinistas lost the 1990 elections to UNO, a loose coalition of opposition groups of both right and left.

These conflicts have had repercussions throughout the region. For example, there are large refugee populations in the surrounding states, while Honduras has seen a greatly increased US presence and the growing militarization of its society. These conflicts, combined with the debt crisis, have also contributed to a sharp decline in intra-regional trade which had been built up through the Central American Common Market.

Sudan has, meanwhile, suffered a series of calamities during the 1980s: drought has caused severe economic problems, loss of life and massive movements of people, exacerbated by the rekindling of the civil war between the north and the south. It is surrounded by states with internal conflicts and has received successive waves of refugees. In the late 1970s, people streamed north from the civil war in Uganda. During the whole of the 1980s, refugees fled from the wars in Chad and in Ethiopia.

A particular problem in dealing with regions in turmoil is the difficulty of making even short-term predictions. This is not simply a problem which affects writers and journalists, but more importantly it plagues the lives of people in those regions, and those in government who try to plan for the future. In both Central America and Southern Africa today, and in the Horn of Africa, there are prospects for change, yet the future is filled with imponderables. These are necessarily reflected in this book, not least through the voices of people from the region: beyond a certain point second-guessing is not possible. Both the book, and the peoples, governments and liberation movements of the regions are forced to live with these uncertainties.

In order to examine in more detail the interaction between socio-political context, economic problems and educational policies pursued by governments, the case-study countries are grouped according to key problems and the variety of ways in which governments have attempted to deal with them. Each section emphasizes some of the themes dealt with in Part One: the impact of economic constraints on educational policy and practice; the role of political factors in access to education, its content and outcomes; the relationship between state and community in financing education; the effects of government policies on social inequalities.

In terms of educational provision and state policies, the case-study countries represent a wide spectrum, from variably successful attempts to universalize basic education (Zimbabwe, Mozambique, Zambia,

Nicaragua, Costa Rica); to widespread neglect of large sections of the population (El Salvador, Honduras, Sudan); to a history of active discrimination against particular sections of it (Guatemala, South Africa, Namibia). In most cases, education has been viewed as politically significant by both governments and oppositions, whether as a major force for change, or as a way of bolstering the existing regime.

Within each region, there are:

• Countries where educational difficulties over the last decade have been caused mainly by economic problems related to the burden of debt service and the effects of stabilization and adjustment policies designed to cope with them. The cases to be discussed here are Zambia, Zimbabwe and Costa Rica

• Countries where existing economic problems affecting education have been compounded by war and insurgency. The examples used here are Nicaragua, Mozambique and Sudan.

• States where internal political conflict has permeated the education system itself: South Africa and Namibia, El Salvador, Honduras and Guatemala.

Notes

1.   Unicef (1989), *Children on the Front Line*, p.37.

Planning under pressure: debt, adjustment and education policy in Zambia, Zimbabwe and Costa Rica

At a meeting in Harare of African finance officials in July 1989, it was argued that development is being held up by the tendency for government policy-makers to be involved in short-term crisis management for structural adjustment programmes, and responding to the demands of large numbers of foreign advisers. (*Radio Zimbabwe*, 6 July 1989)

A senior official in the Zambian Ministry of Planning was recently quoted as saying that development aid has to be spent more on sustaining than developing. There are no new secondary schools, no expansion in education and health facilities, only lost opportunities. 'How can we place a value, in any real terms, on the lack of growth and development when we are always running to catch up?' (Quoted in *Apartheid Terrorism*)[1]

Zambia, Zimbabwe and Costa Rica have invested heavily in education, which has played an important role in legitimizing political parties and governments. Their rhetoric has emphasized national unity and social cohesion, as well as the development of skills for the economy. However, their historical development as nations has differed considerably. Zambia and Zimbabwe have a somewhat similar background of colonial rule, while Costa Rica has just celebrated 100 years as an independent state. Since the late 1970s, all have experienced economic crises of varying severity in which international factors have played a significant part. Zambia and Costa Rica have experienced very serious debt crises. Costa Rica has partially recovered, though without solving its underlying economic problems. It has done so at the expense of sharp cuts in living standards and in expenditure on its long-established system of social services and free education. Zambia's economic problems, despite a number of stabilization and structural adjustment packages negotiated with the IMF and the World Bank, show little sign of diminishing.

Zimbabwe, now independent for a decade after a prolonged war of liberation against a white minority regime, has been primarily concerned to throw off its colonial legacy. Considerable strides have been made, especially in priority areas such as education, and its debt position is much less severe than either Zambia's or Costa Rica's. None the less, while it has managed to avoid the dramatic slashing of budgets, the government is operating in an economic straitjacket and development on all fronts is dogged by a stagnant economy with inadequate investment levels, lack of foreign exchange and high defence expenditure.

Zambia and Zimbabwe: reforming the colonial legacy

British colonial rule took different forms in Zimbabwe and Zambia. White settler governments in Zimbabwe had full internal self-government from 1923, while Zambia was ruled by a conventional colonial administration answerable to the Colonial Office in London. None the less, as far as education was concerned, the policies followed were not dissimilar. In both cases, educational provision for the black majority was largely left in the hands of missionaries. Towards the end of the colonial period, missionary schools increasingly received government grants, and some government schools for blacks were established in urban areas. Mass education for black people, particularly beyond primary school, was not encouraged. While white settlers and colonial civil servants were provided with both government schools and a number of fee-paying private schools, many of them regarded the expansion of educational provision for the black population as politically dangerous.

As a result, educational structures were weak at independence, with very limited coverage above primary level for the majority of the population. For example, in Zambia in 1964, the year of independence, only 961 African pupils were known to have passed the School Certificate, the secondary school leaving exam.[2] During seventy years of colonial rule, no university had been established. High illiteracy rates and a chronic lack of skilled manpower meant that the new government regarded educational provision as politically and economically important and popular demand for it at all levels was considerable.

In Zimbabwe, the political significance of education was even greater. Zambia achieved political independence without a prolonged conflict, but in Zimbabwe it took more than a decade of military and political struggle to overthrow white minority rule. At independence in 1980, the country was suffering from the limited coverage of the education system under the white minority regime. Schools and other infrastructure had been destroyed and society disrupted during the armed struggle. The white supremacist Rhodesian Front government (1962–79) had actually reduced the proportion of expenditure on black education from 8 per cent of GNP in 1965 to 2 per cent thereafter[3], largely handing financial responsibility over to African local councils which did not have the funds or capacity to run a school system. In 1980, the illiteracy rate was estimated to be 40 per cent of the population over the age of fifteen, with a further 15 per cent semi-literate. Only a small percentage of black children were able to remain at school beyond primary level.

During the liberation struggle, the two liberation movements, the Zimbabwe African Peoples' Union (ZAPU) and the Zimbabwe African National Union (ZANU), had set up some education programmes for fighters and for refugees. The ZANU government, which came to power in 1980, had two major educational goals: to expand access to education and to end the racist bias of the previous system. In 1981, Prime Minister Robert Mugabe made this comment on the goals of education:

In Zimbabwe today, education must fundamentally orient itself towards the revolutionary transformation now taking place in many spheres of our society. Education must, at all costs, eschew all tendencies or even appearances of a commitment to the maintenance and reproduction of the unjust social order and undemocratic value system to the overthrow of which we sacrificed so much in the struggle. It must be designed to constitute an essential component of those forces making for positive change in our country.[4]

In both countries, therefore, the priority given to education was reflected in high levels of expenditure. But over the years both internal difficulties and external economic and regional pressures have put these policies under strain. They have also revealed weaknesses within the current education systems. Zambia came to independence in 1964 with one major economic asset, on which the colonial economy had been based: copper. In the decade after independence, the relatively high price of copper allowed the government to finance a very substantial expansion of education and other social services. Zambia's first development plan set the ambitious goal of providing primary school places for all children by 1970. There was also an emphasis on getting all urban and 75 per cent of rural children through seven grades of primary school. This rapid expansion, combined with a large teacher training programme, was a mammoth task. Many communities contributed by building schools, often makeshift buildings with even more makeshift accommodation for teachers, if any at all.

The government began by taking on much of the financial responsibility for education, with the exception of some school building. The rapid expansion of enrolments, teacher numbers and the volume of materials and support services meant that budgets grew very rapidly. Until 1975, while copper prices were high, this burden was bearable. But as the price plunged, the government saw its sources of funding evaporating. In 1982 the price of copper was the lowest in real terms for forty years, falling even further by 1986. The overall index of terms of trade fell from 100 in 1970 to 24 in 1982.[5] The recent price recovery cannot make up for that much lost ground. Zambia became caught in a vicious circle because the mining industry is also heavily dependent on increasingly expensive imports, so that over time, output, investment and productivity fell. Moreover, Zambia's copper deposits are running down so that the industry is threatened with extinction early in the next century. With a very limited manufacturing base and agricultural production of foodstuffs insufficient to feed the country, Zambia became highly exposed to the vagaries of international markets.

The government has been criticized for not making enough effort during the period of high copper prices to diversify Zambia's economic base, and especially to encourage agricultural development. If this diversification had been achieved, it is argued, the worst effects of the fall in copper prices might have been avoided. Subsequent attempts to diversify the economy have foundered not only on corruption and inefficiency, though these have played a part, but because Zambia could not mobilize the funds for new investment, since the growing debt burden took a larger and larger share of the national cake. An added burden throughout this period has been the additional costs of routing the bulk of Zambian exports and imports through South Africa. Zambia has also suffered economically from destabilization and economic sabotage first by the white Rhodesian regime and then by South Africa, and from the knock-on effects of the wars in neighbouring Angola and Mozambique. M.J. Kelly has observed:

The current deteriorating standards of living and acute social problems that owe so much of their origin to the decline in the economy suggest that the inheritance at the time of Independence of a highly developed mining sector was a very mixed blessing: the lack of balance it occasioned in the economic base has resulted in serious economic and social disequilibrium with the locus of control resting as much with decisions made in the London Metal Market as with policies established in Lusaka.[6]

Zambia's balance of payments situation steadily worsened after 1975, and by 1978 the IMF was arranging the first of a series of standby facilities, and one extended fund facility (1981–83). The World Bank, in addition, lent large sums for the rehabilitation of the mining industry. These were accompanied by a succession of stabilization and adjustment measures. There were sharp cuts in government expenditure which, although they eased the deficit in the short term, also led to further slowing down of the economy as a whole. This impasse was made worse by continued falls in copper prices until the mid-1980s. Furthermore, these economic policies have put severe political pressure on an erratically authoritarian regime whose remaining credibility depends mainly on provision of services. This led to the decision to withdraw from IMF agreements in May 1987.

Zambia returned to the IMF fold in early 1990 on the basis of an agreed economic restructuring programme and debt rescheduling, which has also released new aid flows. However, the question of its approximately US$1 billion debt to the IMF and the World Bank remained to be resolved. An immediate outcome of the government's efforts to implement this programme and raise basic consumer prices was the outbreak of riots in June 1990 which further highlighted the government's unpopularity. Like most of its neighbours, including Zimbabwe and Mozambique, Zambia's economic plans were also jeopardized by sharp rises in oil prices at the beginning of the Gulf crisis in August 1990.

Zimbabwe, achieving independence in the 1980s, faced leaner economic times than had Zambia in the 1960s. However, it embarked on an even larger programme of educational expansion, with the result that education has consistently been one of the largest budget items. Zimbabwe's economy is not based on a single commodity like Zambia's and it did not experience the mass exodus of whites and 'scorched earth' policies of the Portuguese in Mozambique and Angola. After independence, the ZANU government opted for a policy of reconciliation rather than confrontation with its white settler population, and by association with its direct southern neighbour, South Africa.

Zimbabwe inherited severe social and economic inequalities, with a limited social infrastructure for the black community. None the less, its economy had in some ways benefited from the diversification and protection from external competition which resulted from international sanctions imposed after the unilateral declaration of independence by the white minority government in 1965. The Zimbabweans inherited a relatively strong economy compared with Zambia. Zimbabwe has both a more developed industrial base and a more extensive commercial farming sector. This sector continues to be dominated by a largely white farming community, with the addition of members of the new black élite. No large-scale land reform or redistribution has taken place, in part because of restrictions placed on the government by the pre-independence Lancaster House agreement. Now that period of restriction has ended, there is political pressure on the government to embark on a more comprehensive and equitable policy of land distribution.

Zimbabwe's rulers are not entirely masters in their own house. They have to take account not only of local white vested interests, but, more importantly, of foreign and multinational capital which controls a substantial proportion of its industries, though the government has been buying out some foreign, especially South African, firms. Over the years, the economic pressures have grown, partly as a result of government policies which committed it to high levels of spending, and partly because of external factors such as declining terms of trade and smaller than anticipated flows of aid after independence. Total aid in 1987 was US$295 million, compared with US$212 million in 1981. The 1987 figure amounted to US$32.6 per capita, compared, for example with Botswana's US$135.6 per capita. Zimbabwe's traditional agricultural and mining sectors still make up the major portion of exports and are vulnerable to price changes. Drought has caused further problems in the agricultural sector, both for domestic consumption and exports.

By 1983, Zimbabwe had approached the IMF and was presented with the standard package of reform measures, but by 1984 had reached a parting of the ways with the Fund. The government deviated from its prescriptions in several ways. For example, although they raised prices as the IMF wished, they insisted on minimum wage requirements. Despite the 1984 break with the IMF, economic stringency measures remained in force though they were gradually reduced in the following years. However, in 1990 the government launched a full-scale economic restructuring package for which it sought World Bank support. It included trade and financial liberalization, and the ending of price controls on all but a handful of basic goods and services. There have also been proposals for cuts in public spending.

Spending on education remained high in spite of the earlier crisis. Expenditure rose substantially from 13 per cent of total expenditure in 1978/79, to 24 per cent in the early and mid-1980s, with a slight decline in 1983/84 when financial difficulties were at their height, levelling off at 22 per cent in the late 1980s. The government has not, however, taken responsibility for all the expenses of education expansion, emphasizing from the outset the role of the community in financing education. In the decade from 1979 the number of primary schools almost doubled from 2,401 to 4,504, while pupil numbers increased by 178 per cent. At secondary level, where provision in the colonial period was extremely limited, the expansion has been even more spectacular, with the number of schools increasing from 177 to 1,502 and the number of pupils by 950 per cent. This has undoubtedly been a welcome and popular policy.

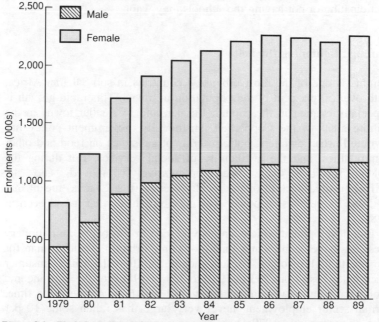

Figure 8.1 Zimbabwe: primary school enrolment
Source: Zimbabwe Ministry of Education and Culture, *Annual Reports* 1979–1989.

In order to finance expansion on this scale, the government has relied heavily on payments and other inputs from the community. Primary education was made free and compulsory in 1980, but all secondary schools are fee-paying. Furthermore, the government only directly controls and finances 5.8 per cent of primary schools and 12.8 per cent of secondary schools. For these schools, the government pays for maintenance, teachers' salaries and equipment. At secondary level, tuition fees are paid by families. At all levels, there is a general-purpose fee payable by families for extra-curricular and additional facilities. This is set on a sliding scale, depending on whether the school is primary or secondary, day or boarding.

The vast majority of schools are 'government-aided' and are run by district councils or missions. There are also a few 'élite' schools – mainly former white boarding schools. The government pays teachers' salaries in district council schools, and a grant to cover primary tuition costs. There are also grants available to cover about a quarter of the cost of putting up new school buildings.

It is estimated by Fay Chung, the Minister of Education and Culture, that parental input since independence into school capital expenditure is in the region of Z$50 million for primary schools (about Z$10 per family per year) and Z$126 million (Z$30 per pupil per year) at secondary level. Contributions to recurrent costs were about Z$420 million (about Z$100 per pupil per year).[7] This parental involvement is theoretically voluntary, but parents are presented with the option of participating or not having the schools they want.

Zambia: tightening the belt

Zambia is one of the most urbanized countries in sub-Saharan Africa, with over 50 per cent of the population in towns. This rapid growth is especially evident in the capital, Lusaka, and in smaller towns in the mining areas of the Copperbelt. Historically, government policy has favoured urban dwellers, both in terms of subsidies on food and other commodities, and the availability of social services. But during the 1980s, subsidies have been progressively removed, and the IMF-sponsored auction of the local currency (the kwacha) meant that by 1987 its purchasing power was only one-third what it had been in 1983.

In a development which can also be seen in Zimbabwe, inflationary pressures have been greater for low-income urban households than for those with high incomes. For low-income families, the urban consumer price index rose from 203 in 1980 to 733 in 1986; for the high-income group the figures were respectively 189 and 644. At the same time, formal sector employment, never very large, has fallen some 10 per cent since the mid-1970s because of economic stagnation, and the informal sector is now overcrowded and income therefore low. One outcome of this is that those on low incomes either reduce the amount they eat, or eat food of lower nutritional value, which particularly affects growing children. Among the most vulnerable households are those headed by women – at the last census in 1980 approximately one-third of rural households were female-headed, and less than one-fifth in town.

Inflation hits the urban poor

Jessy lives in a low income area of a town in Zambia. Her husband was recently laid off from his construction job and is now employed part-time as a night watchman. Jessy works in the home and grows vegetables, selling what she can and keeping the rest for the family. Her earnings are minute. They have two daughters in school and two much younger children. . . .

Since 1983, prices of food and clothing have risen markedly and her husband's income has failed to keep pace. His recent change of job meant a further drop in income . . .

One item that has become much more expensive recently is education. There have been increases in school charges, books and uniforms. Jessy and her husband feel it is a priority that their children go through school, but are already worried that they will not be able to afford to send the eldest to secondary school. They may send the middle children to Jessy's parents in an attempt to get the eldest through secondary school.[8]

Figures on poverty levels are not easy to come by. According to data from the Prices and Incomes Commission, the proportion of urban households living below the Poverty Datum Line rose from 35 per cent in 1985 to 55 per cent in 1987. One study summed up the overall situation as follows:

Altogether, the 1980s have seen reduced inequality in income distribution between urban and rural activities. While the urban groups have experienced substantial reductions in real income, their rural cousins have maintained and maybe improved their incomes. However, the income distribution within the rural sector seems to have deteriorated.[9]

Zambia is one of the countries in which the government has made an effort to sustain expenditure on education and its share in GDP has not actually fallen. None the less, considerable cuts have been made in real terms, with per capita expenditure in education falling 10 per cent between 1975 and 1985. Within these constraints the government has also chosen to put relatively high levels of finance into the secondary and tertiary sectors, and a relatively low percentage into primary education. Capital expenditure on primary education has declined dramatically in real terms – from 288 million kwacha in 1977 to 30 million kwacha in 1985. Recurrent budgets at primary and secondary

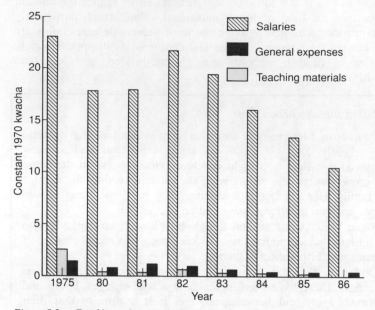

Figure 8.2a   Zambia: unit current spending, primary education
Source: Derived from Kelly (1988) *Financing Education in Zambia.*

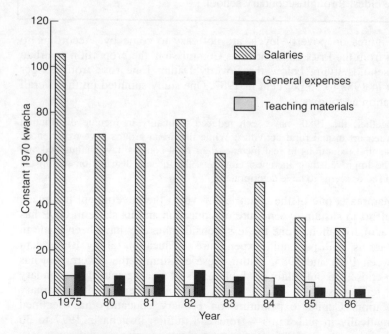

Figure 8.2b   Zambia: unit current spending, secondary schools
Source: Derived from Kelly (1988) *Financing Education in Zambia.*

levels have been particularly hard hit, while spending on universities has been sustained. This contradicts the rhetorical commitment of the government to give priority to primary education and reflects strong political pressure to retain higher levels of funding for tertiary education. The political clout of the primary education sector in the struggle for resources is clearly limited. Another problem is that the Ministry of Education itself cannot retain highly qualified and experienced staff because of low pay and poor conditions.

Teachers' salaries make up an increasingly large proportion of recurrent budgets, especially at primary level, with other expenditures pared down to almost nothing. In these circumstances, one can scarcely talk about planning, but rather a response to 'inescapable commitments'.[10] Teachers are unionized and a powerful enough group to prevent the decoupling of their salary levels from those of other public-sector employees, but none the less by 1985 they had seen the real value of their salaries fall to half their value a decade earlier. At the same time there are administrative distortions, such as poor distribution of teaching staff. In some schools, particularly in urban areas, there are teachers who are not teaching or are teaching very few hours, while in others teachers are coping with very large classes. There has also been a decline throughout the decade in spending on teacher training, though the recently initiated Self Help Action Programme in Education (SHAPE) project may increase the effectiveness of in service training.

This situation has not led to a decline in enrolments: except for a brief period at the beginning of the crisis, the demand for education has been sustained. Despite the difficulties, people still regard access to education for their children as a 'passport out of poverty'. In contrast to some other low-income countries in Africa, most children do eventually get to primary school and stay there for a few years. Parents continue to send children to school, even where physical conditions are very poor because of lack of maintenance. The question is whether they are likely to learn anything. The major difficulties are overcrowding, lack of books and materials, and low teacher morale.

There are substantial bottlenecks in the primary system – at first grade in urban schools (causing large numbers of children to start school late), and at fifth grade in rural schools. The major hurdle, however, is entry into secondary school. While gross primary enrolment ratios in 1986 were 102 for males and 92 for females, for secondary school the ratios were respectively 23 and 13. Furthermore, one way of saving money has been to allow larger classes, with severe overcrowding in some urban primary classrooms. More than 100 children have been reported in a class, though the national average was forty-one, for Lusaka fifty-one and for Kitwe fifty-four. The running of multiple sessions has been another means of saving which, though not always a problem, has led to truncated teaching sessions, late-coming and absenteeism on the part of teachers and pupils.

The SHAPE education reform project

The SHAPE project, launched in 1985, grew out of the educational reforms proposed in the late 1970s but never systematically carried through because of the economic crisis. These reforms had envisaged reorienting the ten-year basic education programme away from its highly academic content, towards more practical and vocational aspects. It also envisaged strengthening education with production, that is, treating the school as a productive and income-generating unit where students learn through practical application of their knowledge.

SHAPE, under the auspices of the Ministry of General Education, Youth and Sport and the Ministry of Higher Education, aims to strengthen teacher competence at local level by encouraging teachers, head teachers and local administrators to initiate their own productive work linked to teaching, and to evolve their own techniques and materials. SHAPE has also been introduced in pre-service training in teacher training colleges. It is still at an experimental stage and has not yet been implemented country-wide. It has evidently met with considerable enthusiasm, but there has been initial resistance from some staff and parents who still favour a more academic approach to teaching and learning. It has also suffered from insufficient links in the school between production and learning and from shortages of space in some schools to accommodate productive activities. There are signs in some schools that the most successful activities have been those which mainly involve boys, and that home economics and other subjects taken mainly by girls have fared less well. On the other hand, girls have not participated strongly in male-dominated subjects.

However, further research is needed to confirm these impressions. Finally, the liaison and back-up from the regional and national levels of the SHAPE administration are not strong enough, partly because the size of the country, and shortages of fuel and transport, hamper regular communication and visits to schools by school inspectors and SHAPE co-ordinators.

The acute shortages of public funds for basic education in Zambia over the past decade have led to an increasing reliance on external aid to finance educational initiatives. SHAPE is a prime example of this, with much of its funding coming from Scandinavian national aid agencies as well as the British Council. Observers have pointed to the potential contradictions of a self-help project which is heavily reliant for its continuation on external funding.[11]

Teacher absenteeism is also exacerbated by general shortages of goods and services: teachers, like other employees, can spend half their days chasing scarce consumer goods for their families, instead of being in the classroom. Many also have second or third jobs to make ends meet.

The government no longer provides funds for textbooks and materials in schools. Parents have to buy them – that is, if they are available. The supply problem is such that it is difficult to tell whether parents cannot afford to buy the books, or whether no copies are available. A research survey in 1986/87 in a random sample of schools country-wide showed that, whereas most teachers had the prescribed handbooks, pupils frequently had no textbooks. For example, 127 out of 196 schools did not have a single English textbook in grade one and 80 per cent had no maths books. At grade four (the level at which basic literacy is supposed to be achieved), in forty-one out of 189 schools, there was not a single English reader. Most head teachers questioned thought the position was worse than it had been five years earlier. This, combined with declining real salaries, has a severe effect on teacher morale. [12]

It is clear that people are still eager to send their children to school. They are also willing, within reason, to pay towards this schooling. In the survey already mentioned, more than half the parents questioned appeared willing to provide funds for school needs, materials and maintenance. Only 20 per cent, however, were willing to assume any responsibility for payment of teachers' salaries.

In the sphere of parental contributions, regional inequalities are marked: in 1985 in Lusaka annual parental expenditure per child was 206 kwacha a year, while in the poorest regions, for example Western, Luapula and North-western, the amounts were 67, 87 and 51 kwacha respectively. With government, central or regional, unable to make up the difference between parents' ability to pay and the needs of schools, sharp differences in quality of education are inevitable. [13]

Community demand for education is still strong, and puts further pressures on government resources. For example, communities are still building schools, but the government cannot afford to pay the salaries of teachers to staff these schools. Ministers and other politicians continue to tell the public that education will continue to grow, in order to retain political credibility – since education is considered an important issue – while at the same time telling administrators to cut budgets.

Of course, for the wealthiest strata there is always the option of sending their children to élite private schools, while other urban parents make sacrifices to send their children to the fee-paying schools which have sprung up since 1977 especially to meet the unfulfilled demand for secondary education. However, these are for the most part of very low quality and certainly cannot meet the needs of the poorest sectors. [14]

Zimbabwe: the pressures of growth

Generally speaking, Zimbabwe's economic situation is a good deal healthier than that of many other African countries. However, by no means all groups in the population have benefited equally from prosperity or from generous expenditure on social services. The Zimbabwean government has sustained its high level of educational spending in the face of a growing debt burden, the economic burden of the war in Mozambique and the cost of trade routes through South Africa.

There are indications, however, that the government is now trying to put the brakes on further expansion. Where parent-teacher associations are initiating new building projects, according to Minister of Education Fay Chung, the Ministry is no longer encouraging them. There have also been complaints from some members of parliament about the high levels of educational expenditure in comparison with other services. In 1990, during discussions about economic restructuring, the Minister of Finance, Economic Planning and Development, Bernard Chidzero, hinted that primary school fees might be re-introduced as part of cuts in public sector spending. None the less, demand for education is still high, at primary and secondary levels, and with an annual population growth rate of 3.5 per cent, shows no sign of slackening.

The very rapid expansion of the education system has left support systems running to catch up. The picture is very uneven. There are flourishing schools which reflect the growing affluence and improved living conditions of a portion of the population, but there are other schools which are little more than shells, with few materials and facilities. In these schools, double shifts, known as 'hot-seating', are the norm.

As far as the provision of books, materials, tools and other educational facilities are concerned, a good deal of the cost of provision falls on families. But some of the country's economic difficulties have direct and indirect effects on provision. While these problems are not on the scale found in Zambia, they are becoming more acute. There are major bottlenecks in the transport system, mainly because of foreign exchange problems. Shortages of fuel and vehicles affect delivery of materials and cause problems for supervisory staff visiting rural areas. A long-standing cement shortage often leaves buildings started by the community unfinished.

Creating a teaching force which is adequate to the rapidly growing system has been another problem. In Zimbabwe, black teachers' pay was increased at independence to the levels paid to white teachers. Certainly they are much better off compared with teachers in, for example, Malawi or Zambia. The problem now is that with expenditure levelling off, pay cannot rise further, especially as more teachers are employed. Spending can be limited by controlling the speed of promotions but this discourages those contemplating going into the profession.

The poorest schools, especially in rural areas, have great difficulties in attracting and retaining staff. There are many complaints about the poor quality of housing for teachers. Also, whereas teaching was one of the main professional careers open to black Zimbabweans in the colonial period, other more attractive options are now (at least theoretically) open to school and university graduates. R.J. Zvobgo highlights these points:

We seem to be failing in producing the kind of teacher who is committed to national service today. Like his [*sic*] colleagues in most developing countries, he is, to say the least, unprepared and unwilling to serve in rural areas and has to be forced to do so although he is fully aware that rural areas and people are most undeveloped and disadvantaged because of lack of human, material and financial resources. . . . There is also much more mobility from the teaching profession to other professions. . . . The teaching profession is, for most people, only a stepping stone to a more lucrative profession.[15]

Teaching is still an important option for less privileged groups: for example, for school graduates in rural areas where there are few opportunities for professional employment and for both urban and rural women, whose range of job opportunities is still far more limited than men's.

Despite relatively high levels of pay, there remains a shortage of trained teachers. A large percentage of the untrained teachers are in the non-government sector. In non-government schools (that is, mainly district council schools) in 1987, untrained teachers made up 50 per cent of the total at primary level and 45 per cent at secondary level; for government schools the figures were much lower – 7 and 19 per cent respectively. The government has resorted to a variety of expedients to deal with teacher shortages. University students taught in schools in the long vacations, and expatriate teachers were hired, especially in rural areas. In addition, some primary school teachers who held 'O' level certificates were upgraded to teach in secondary schools. The continuing shortage of science teachers led to an agreement with Cuba to train several hundred secondary science teachers. This is despite considerable efforts to create innovative ways of developing teacher training in the post-independence period.

There has been considerable discontent among teachers over pay and conditions. In June 1990 during a strike of non-graduate teachers over their pay award, the government brought emergency regulations into force. After end of the strike a number of striking teachers were not reinstated and many of these were said to have left the country to seek work in Botswana. An academic at the University of Zimbabwe in the department of Educational Administration, K.P. Dzvimbo, pointed to another, broader problem. He noted that teachers as a group were supposed to be agents of change, 'but the environment within which the teacher operates has not changed'. Teachers are not trained

New teacher training initiatives in Zimbabwe

The government's response to the problem of teacher shortages was to launch new kinds of teacher training programmes. The idea was to provide a large proportion of the teacher's training on the job. This saves on training facilities and teacher trainers and also helps fill the gaps in the ranks of the existing teaching force. The first of these, for primary teachers, was the Zintec programme (National Teacher Education Course) which started in 1981. The training lasted four years, and had only two terms of formal instruction in college – the first and the last. The rest of the time the students, who were paid a salary, were deployed to teach in schools throughout the country, with the back-up of distance learning materials and periodic supervisory visits from National Centre staff. On graduation they received a university-accredited certificate.

By the mid-1980s, the rapid growth of secondary education induced the government to introduce a modified version of the Zintec programme for non-university secondary school teacher training, based in teacher training colleges round the country. This programme involves two years (the first and last) at college, and two years' teaching in schools. The individual colleges bear the responsibility for preparing materials and supervising students. Undoubtedly, these schemes have allowed more teachers to be trained in a short period, without a very large expansion in the institutional teacher training facilities. However, although it is too soon to assess the overall pedagogical value and cost effectiveness of the secondary programme, some difficulties have emerged.

The first relates to the capacity of the teacher training colleges adequately to supervise their scattered students. Effective distance education depends on good communications and support for the learners. The distance education materials are prepared by each of the training colleges involved, and seem to have been much less effective than in the Zintec programme, with its central distance learning unit.

The main difficulty has been that teachers allocated to rural schools, especially local district council schools, found themselves virtually without back-up. Many of these schools exist on a shoe-string and lack a library, books and all kinds of teaching aids, especially for practical subjects. Many such schools are headed by 'teachers in charge' who only have primary teacher qualifications. The distance learning materials do not always reach the students when needed, and a survey indicated that they rarely received more than one visit a year from their supervisor because of the shortage of transport. Thus students living in poor accommodation, often isolated and without external support, become disillusioned with the experience of teaching, and put off the idea of teaching in a rural area where qualified teachers are needed most.[16]

as innovators and much of the content of teacher training colleges' curricula is not relevant to this approach. Once in the classroom the teacher is restricted by the core curriculum and general workload and lack of equipment.[17]

Social inequalities

Although Zimbabwe has had some success in redressing racial inequalities, there have been limits on how far social inequalities have been checked. Whereas the domination of the white population, now only about 1 per cent of the total, has faded, new class structures have been developing. Education has not been immune from this process, and some would argue that it has helped to create new social divisions.

The quality of schools still varies widely. For example, children going to former white schools in Harare, now known as 'Group A' schools, are likely to get a far better education and have much better facilities than children going to most of the schools, known as 'Group B' schools, in the 'high density suburbs' (formerly segregated black townships). Although children are bussed into the 'A' schools from poorer neighbourhoods, their location in the richer suburbs means that the majority of pupils are from either black or white middle-class families. There are even wider discrepancies between urban and rural schools. This was in part the outcome of a deliberate government policy to avoid losing professionals and industrialists. Government policy was not to reduce the privileges of those who enjoyed privileges, but rather to make them pay.

However, the slow development of the economy acts as a limiting factor on how far 'levelling up' takes place for those in less privileged positions. In terms of social equity, Fay Chung admits that the major disadvantage of this educational policy is

that of class differentiation, with wealthier parents paying substantially more than poorer parents, resulting in lavish provision on the one hand and very meagre provision on the other. Government has attempted to overcome severe discrepancies by establishing a Disadvantaged Schools Programme which seeks to provide capital development for communities which are extremely poor. This is, however, a small programme of only Z$5 million per annum.[18]

Apart from differences in educational opportunities, a combination of economic and social factors over the past few years has sharpened stratification within the black population. A new urban middle class has emerged, but at the other end of the social scale there are many people unemployed, especially young people, in the urban high density suburbs.

In the rural areas, lack of access to land, drought (which has not only destroyed crops but has meant that impoverished people have had to sell their livestock and have even been forced off the land by hardship), and rising prices have further marginalized poor rural dwellers. It is estimated that about 15 per cent of the population, mostly in the rural areas, earn less than Z$100 a year, and it is this group which is facing the most difficulties in keeping their children at school.

The modest resettlement programme in rural areas which aimed to improve the grossly inequitable distribution of land prevailing during the colonial period was less effective than had been hoped, and was cut back by the stabilization measures taken in 1982–84. The government has provided substantial help for the communal areas and resettlement schemes, in terms of agricultural extension services, greater access to credit and health care facilities. However, prolonged drought, and in Matebeleland armed conflict, have limited its effectiveness.

Many of the poorest households are headed by women farmers who do not have cattle, an important source of wealth. Many are dependent on remittances from migrant relatives. Inflationary pressures on the standard of living are now substantial. Those who work in the formal sector are partly protected by the continued existence of a minimum wage requirement, but for the majority of those in the informal sector or in peasant agriculture, there is no such security.

Regional differences in educational provision are substantial. In Matabeleland, the conflict between the government and dissidents between 1982 and 1987 effectively condemned the region to years of not only destruction and deaths, but also to general neglect. As Fay Chung remarked, Matabeleland, though not the poorest region of the country, is ten years behind in development terms.[19] Since the unity pact, which healed the rift between ZANU and ZAPU (with its political base predominantly in Matabeleland), development funds have been flowing in, but education and all other aspects of services and development have still to recover, especially in sparsely populated rural districts.

Another region which suffered badly both during the liberation struggle and in recent years is the North-eastern region in the Zambezi valley. Long isolated and under-developed, it still has very few secondary schools. These only cover the first two years, so that most secondary schoolchildren have to leave the region to complete their education. In recent years, killings and abductions by the South African-backed movement fighting the Mozambican government, Renamo, have increased the difficulties. Army protection is needed to keep schools open and teachers in place. Similar problems have occurred in the Eastern Highlands, although educational provision is generally better.

Children of employees on the large commercial farms – still mainly run by whites – suffer problems left from the colonial past. If distances to local rural district council schools are too great, they have to rely on whatever education is provided by the farmer. Though this problem is not as widespread or invidious as in South Africa, it still affects a significant number of children. Many of these farm workers originally migrated from Zambia or Mozambique, but some have been in Zimbabwe for a generation or more though they have no regularized status. Some of their children never get to school.

A 1988 Ministry of Health survey of immunization and maternity services examined education and other social services available on a sample of commercial farms. On 67 per cent of the farms there was no primary school, and only 5 per cent had adult literacy classes, of which only one-third were judged to be satisfactory. The authors warn that the data need to be treated with caution because it was not clear how many of the farms surveyed had substantial numbers of permanent workers for whom schools or adult education should be provided. But in general, they say that 'there are gross inadequacies in educational facilities. The quality of the existing facilities is also very questionable'.[20]

These differences are reflected in the ways in which community contributions to education have worked out. The formation of parent–teacher associations (PTAs) was instigated by the government. Though it is clear that some PTAs have become highly organized and participate actively in the life of their schools, there are considerable variations across the country.

On the whole the poorest communities have had most difficulties, where parents are illiterate or semi-literate and have little money or time to spare. Problems have also arisen where there are sharp social or political rifts in the community, and where a school catchment area includes a wide disparity of income levels. If more than half the parents are fairly well off and eager to expand facilities in their school, they can set levels for school charges which are beyond the means of the poorer parents (fee levels are set by the government). It has also been noted that influential local people use the provision of school facilities, extra classrooms, libraries, more teachers and lower teacher/pupil ratios as a way of enhancing their own status and prestige.

Drop-outs

Drop-outs from the school system are still substantial. At primary level, the drop-out rate rose to 30 per cent in the cohort which finished seven years of school in 1987 and then fell to 16.4 per cent for those finishing in 1989. A government study of primary school drop-outs listed the following reasons:

● lack of encouragement from illiterate parents;
● religious beliefs;
● drought or famine;
● financial problems;
● early marriages;
● broken families.

The vast majority of children do attend school for all or part of the primary school cycle. Some 24 per cent of children drop out at the transition from primary to secondary school, while at secondary level there has recently been a significant rise in the drop-out rate. This rate has risen significantly for the cohorts reaching Form Four from 1987 onwards (see Table 8.1). This seems to reflect primarily the increasing cost of school fees, combined with rises in the cost of living. The poor prospects for employment, and the well-known fact that many people fail 'O' levels, undoubtedly also play their part.[21]

A study of gender and enrolment patterns since 1980 reveals that, although there has been an enormous increase in the absolute numbers of both girls and boys attending school, at secondary level the drop-out rate for girls is not only high, but in proportional terms fewer girls reach fourth to sixth form ('O' and 'A' level grades) than was the case in the 1970s, when for the most part only privileged whites reached these levels.

Table 8.1   Zimbabwe: average drop-out rate from secondary education

Year	Form	Enrolment	Drop-out rate (%)
1980	1	24,569	10.4
1983	4	22,201	
1981	1	83,491	14.9
1984	4	71,014	
1982	1	97,752	8.4
1985	4	89,517	
1983	1	110,725	11.6
1986	4	97,820	
1984	1	138,904	18
1987	4	113,915	
1985	1	148,002	24
1988	4	112,965	
1986	1	166,168	26.5
1989	4	122,118	
Average			17.3

Source: Ministry of Education and Culture: *Annual Reports,* 1979–89

School-leavers – where to?

In the last few years, academics, the press and even government reports in Zimbabwe have noted a dramatic and frightening rise in school-leaver unemployment. In rural areas, employment opportunities are almost nil, while in the towns the numbers working in the informal sector have increased markedly. By 1986 there were estimated to be about half as many people in informal work as are employed in the formal sector. Employment in the formal sector has stagnated, and where opportunities are available, school-leavers often do not have the specific skills required. Another option is migration, whether to the urban areas where work is thought to be available – though this is often an illusion – or to South Africa and Botswana.

In formal sector employment, women still represent no more than 8 per cent of workers (up from 5 per cent in 1980). This is a legacy from the colonial period, when the majority of formal sector workers were male migrants from the rural areas. The majority of women remained in the 'tribal trustlands' as subsistence farmers, relying on remittances to supplement their meagre income from farming. In the industrial sector, for example, in textiles, there are still relatively few women on the shop-floor. They are employed mainly in clerical and administrative work. Large numbers of women still work in the non-formal sector and in agriculture, but this does not show up in statistics.

Slow growth in the economy and in employment opportunities is also putting pressure on the credibility of the examination system, which is still modelled on the old British 'O' and 'A' level system. After independence, a curriculum reform committee was established. Some significant advances have been made in removing the colonial view of history and society which virtually blotted out all history and culture, apart from that of Europe and European settlers in Africa. Innovations have been introduced to the science curriculum and the 'O' level syllabus has been made somewhat more relevant. The Zimbabwe Scientific Programme (ZIMSCI) project is designed to support teachers not trained in science and to provide a complete science package with low-cost kits for the first years of secondary school. The scheme is generally considered successful in making science more enjoyable and accessible for students, though the goal of independent practical work by students has for the most part not been achieved. The distribution of the special ZIMSCI materials has been a major headache.

The curriculum is still, for the most part, geared to a very academic style of learning. Both upper primary and secondary school are conducted in English, a second language. The examinations, tailored to be selective, make no concession to this, nor do they make allowance for the wide range of academic ability and preparedness among the candidates. Thus, especially among rural pupils, 'O' level failure rates are very high – up to 90 per cent. This represents a great deal of frustration, a sense of failure and a lot of parental income felt to be wasted. This is made worse by the fact that five 'O' levels are the necessary qualification for a wide range of white-collar jobs, and therefore are regarded as a talisman for success. But with the shortage of such jobs, the system is turning out too many school graduates not well qualified for any other kind of work.

The question often raised is whether this education system is relevant to Zimbabwe's needs. There is now a trend away from an exclusively academic curriculum towards teaching more practical subjects in schools. The first moves in this direction began soon after independence, with the 'Education with Production' programme. One major consideration in its introduction was an attempt to generate income from schools. The experiment seems to have worked to some extent in rural schools with farms attached. However, in most urban schools, such manual tasks as tending school gardens or technical work are generally regarded both by pupils and teachers as a form of punishment. A further unforeseen difficulty for schools doing any kind of agricultural work has been the widespread drought of the mid-1980s, which is still affecting some parts of the country.

In the latter part of the 1980s, the government has initiated a more wide-ranging change in the curriculum so that all secondary school pupils should do one or more 'practical' subjects. The main difficulty is the expense of proper equipment for practical teaching in all schools. Given that many rural schools do not even have properly equipped science laboratories, it is hard to see how they will be able to afford equipment for carpentry, metalwork and building. Teacher training colleges which are to train teachers in these subjects will also require funds for equipment.

Advocating the value of vocational skills in a society where social status and financial rewards are generally concentrated in white collar occupations is not easy. This is a problem in many countries, but in ex-colonial countries in this region prejudice against vocational skills is particularly strong because it formed part of the discriminatory policy of white regimes. These quite explicitly linked vocational education with the low status black people were expected to occupy in the social hierarchy. These reactions may fade over time, but at the moment they are still quite a strong influence in Zimbabwean society.

Costa Rica: eroded gains?

Costa Rica presents a contrast in many ways both to its neighbours in Central America and to the southern African countries discussed above. A small, mountainous country with a population of under three million people, it has long been free from colonial domination. Compared with the rest of Central America, it has not experienced severe political or military conflict since a brief and limited civil war in 1948. Costa Rica has established a reputation as a liberal democracy in which education plays an important part in giving its citizens access both to individual social mobility and to democratic rights.

These liberal ideas date back to the 1880s, but it was the thirty years from 1950 to 1980 that saw the greatest expansion of educational provision. State provision of education has been paramount, although private schools do exist. The right to education is embodied in the constitution, and the fundamental law of education states that it is to be free, obligatory and provided by the state to an adequate standard. This law also includes rights to education for adults. In all these respects, Costa Rica's history of educational provision is very different from that of its neighbours. It has the highest average literacy rate in the region and, another indicator of relative social health, the lowest infant mortality rate.

During the 1970s, educational expenditure was very high, taking up about 6 per cent of GDP, and up to 35 per cent of central government expenditure. The main explanation for this extraordinarily high proportion is that Costa Rica does not have an army, only a small civil guard, so that expenditure on defence has been unusually low. Costa Rica has recently begun to develop 'non-traditional' agricultural exports such as flowers, ornamental plants, spices and vegetables as well as cocoa. Despite the relative success of these new crops, it is still, like its neighbours, dependent for national income on the export of its 'traditional' primary commodities – coffee, sugar and bananas. Prices for these exports have plunged several times in the last fifteen years and have never remained stable from year to year. During the 1970s, Costa Rica also increased its investments, both in the social sector and in new economic initiatives. As a consequence of these two factors, by the end of the 1970s this small country had one of the highest levels of per capita debt in Latin America, rising from US$95.8 per person in 1970 to US$1,511 per head in 1985.[22]

The debt crisis

The economic crisis came to a head in mid-1981, when the government announced that it could no longer pay either principal or interest payments on its debts. This resulted in a series of rescheduling agreements with the IMF, and a structural adjustment loan. The initial effects of the crisis sent shock waves through the economy: the average annual rise in consumer prices reached over 80 per cent in 1982, and in 1983 real per capita income had fallen by 2.2 per cent from the previous year (in the 1970s it had been rising at about 5 per cent a year). The cost of servicing the debt rose from 16.8 per cent of export earnings in 1980 to 51.6 per cent in 1983.

The IMF demanded that Costa Rica put in place a range of stabilization measures to alter the exchange rate regime and to reduce the fiscal deficit, mainly by raising taxes, tariffs and prices, and removing some subsidies. The government of President Carazo resisted the IMF's demands. His successor, President Monge, whose government came to power in 1982, was more willing to co-operate, and rescheduling arrangements and a standby loan were agreed.

Though the economic situation has now somewhat improved, it has affected both government expenditure and living standards over the entire decade. Furthermore, the debt problem is far from resolved. The government of President Arias paid only a portion of the interest due on its commercial loans in 1986, arguing that the debt service burden was excessive and beyond the ability of the country to pay. Agreements were finally ratified in late 1989 with commercial banks for debt buy-backs, with the Paris Club (representing the main official creditors) to reschedule about one-third of its US$930 million debt, and with the World Bank for a structural adjustment loan. This will lessen the debt burden, but these arrangements remain conditional on IMF-dictated austerity measures including cuts in public spending and domestic credit.

The effects on public expenditure have not been as drastic as might have been expected. There seem to be two major reasons for this. The first is that the impact of the debt crisis has been considerably cushioned by injections of aid from the United States which rose from US$14 million in 1980 to over US$160 million in 1987. However, this aid comes with conditions. USAID, the main US donor, will not disburse payments if the country is in dispute with the IMF over the terms of its rescheduling or loan agreements. At the same time, in political terms, Costa Rica has been drawn much more closely into the US sphere of influence during the 1980s, moving away from the neutral stance it previously took, so that for a time it was one of the host countries for the US-backed Nicaraguan Contras.

The second consideration is the internal significance of maintaining public services, at least for those political parties committed to this type of welfare state. In the first years of 'stabilization', the government put in place various measures, including feeding programmes, to assist the most vulnerable groups in society. The Arias government did not reduce public expenditure, especially on social sectors and education, as much as the opposition proposed nor as much as the IMF advocated. Despite this resistance, however, there have been marked declines in the proportion of expenditure on both health and education. This contrasts with, for example, policy in Zambia, where the proportion of educational expenditure has been sustained, though at a much lower absolute level. The centre-right government of Rafael Angel Calderón, elected in February 1990, may continue to impose public spending cuts, encouraged by the IMF. It is likely to face stiff opposition from trade unions, including the teachers' union, if it does so.

The impact on education

The pressures of the debt crisis in Costa Rica since the beginning of the 1980s have led to cuts in social expenditure in both proportional and absolute terms. Levels of government expenditure on education dropped from over 30 per cent of national expenditure and 6 to 7 per cent of GNP in the mid-1970s to 22 per cent and 4 per cent respectively in 1985. Health spending fell from 5 to 7 per cent of GNP in the late 1970s to 2.6 per cent in 1985. These restrictions on funding over the decade have begun to put pressure on the relatively well-developed education system. They have accentuated the inequalities of provision, with rural areas in the remoter mountains feeling the most strain.

Table 8.2   Costa Rica: educational indicators through the period of the economic crisis, 1975–88*

	1979	1980	1982	1984	1986	1988
Education expenditure as a % of GDP	6.2	6.2	4.3	4.3	4.3	
Primary school enrolments (000)	354.0	348.7	342.5	350.7	380.4	409.6
Secondary school enrolments (000)	169.3	137.8	165.7	147.6	141.7	143.1

* Population growth rate, 2.7%
Source: CSUCA Research Project; Inter-American Development Bank (1988). *Economic and Social Progress in Latin America* Table IV–6.

In 1986, a Ministry of Public Education document highlighted the difficulties caused by lack of funds. It suggested that the system was not just marking time but actually losing ground in some areas:

Falling budget allocations are beginning to cause near paralysis in the activities of the Ministry of Education, both at central level and in the regional directorates and schools and colleges. In recent months, the physical condition of equipment and buildings has deteriorated alarmingly, due to lack of maintenance, and due also to the lack of basic expenditure on light, water, security guards, chalk, stationery, publications and books. . . . In both central and regional offices staff members who provide technical and administrative support to educational centres are semi-paralysed in their work by lack of transport, of travel allowances, petrol and educational materials.[23]

These pressures on budgets show no signs of letting up. In 1989, a government decree banned the creation of any new posts in public sector institutions and companies.

In 1979, the education system was reorganized into regional directorates, and those in the poorer regions are now finding difficulties in responding to local needs. Liliana Carvajál, of the regional directorate of education in San Carlos, described in 1989 how shortages affect the work of the directorate itself:

In this regional centre we have 15 schools and two colleges, but we have very limited supplies of paper and carbons for the year and there are no stencils. This limits the activities of the educational institutions in the region and makes it difficult for the administrative centres to do their job, which includes developing technical training projects and teacher training.

As a result, she adds, teachers have to pay towards their own training because the Ministry cannot provide materials and documents.

Schools in the poorest areas, already short of resources, are certainly feeling the pinch. Carvajál pointed out that in rural areas such as those around San Carlos there were schools without functioning water pumps or sanitary services. 'It's rather illogical', she points out, 'to have a school with no water.' In 1985, 45 per cent of primary level schools, mainly in rural areas, were run by a single teacher (teaching all grades). Combined with shortages of books and equipment and the poor state of maintenance of many schools, the situation for teachers, especially those posted to rural areas, can be discouraging. Teachers' salaries are relatively low compared with those for other professions requiring the same duration of training, so that there is no great incentive to become a teacher. A teacher from an urban school, discussing the reasons for a recent teachers' strike, said that not only were salaries low when the amount of time worked outside classroom hours was taken into account, but also teachers often had to pay for classroom materials out of their own pockets, if they wanted to have any. Despite a long tradition of education, there is still a lack of qualified teachers: in 1986 almost 400 teaching posts were not filled for lack of trained applicants.

A fifteen-day teachers' strike in September 1989, supported by other workers, reflected some of these economic and professional concerns, though the Costa Rican teachers' union is not considered militant. Apart from direct demands relating to pay and conditions for teachers, demands included: recognition of the professional status of teachers; establishment of a technical commission on the financial needs of the Ministry of Public Education; policies to defend the social welfare system; elimination of taxes on books and educational materials; and funding for student transport and school meals.

Although most Costa Ricans do try to send their children to school, the system still suffers from substantial drop-out and repetition rates. Nation-wide, the 1980s have seen downward trends in enrolments, and increases in drop-out and repetition rates. In the primary levels (two cycles of three years from age six to eleven), numbers enrolled showed a decline in the years after 1975 and did not return to the 1975 level until ten years later. Drop-out levels at this level improved after the early years of the 1980s but repetition rates have increased from about 6 per cent in 1975 to almost 11 per cent in 1985 and 1988. At secondary level, enrolments have declined steadily since the beginning of the 1980s, while drop-outs rose from a low of 9.5 per cent in 1976 to 16.3 per cent in 1987 and repetition from 5.3 per cent in 1975 to a high of 13.5 per cent in 1985. However, the pattern varies considerably according to region and social class. In rural areas the levels of drop-out, repetition and absenteeism are much higher. For example, in the San Carlos district, of the children who begin first grade, 95 per cent do not finish secondary school. Many children are taken from school after about five years because of economic or family problems.

In Costa Rica, the common pattern of rapidly declining female enrolment after the primary level is reversed. It is girls who tend to stay at school longer and in the secondary cycle outnumber boys (making up 52 per cent of total enrolment in 1985). The reason for this seems to be that the opportunity cost of keeping boys at school when they could go out to work is greater than for girls, especially for poor rural families. On the other hand, in urban areas there are now more opportunities for women with high school education to find jobs.

The economic crisis of the early 1980s played a part in this decline in take-up of education, and hit the poorest sectors of society hardest, sharpening social differentiation and the concentration of wealth. According to Villasuso,

In 1977, 25 per cent of all Costa Rican families were unable to meet their basic needs to some extent and 13 per cent lived in extreme poverty. The rural areas contained 34 per cent of poor families and 19 per cent of extremely poor families. No great change occurred in this situation until the outbreak of the crisis and the introduction of the adjustment policies. A comparison of 1970 and 1983 shows that the share of the poor sections of the population declined in favour of the higher income groups: this was mainly an urban phenomenon. Furthermore, according to a MIDEPLAN [state planning] study, 41.7 per cent of wage earners were poor (i.e. not able to meet basic needs to some extent) in 1980, and this proportion rose to 56.4 per cent in 1981 and 70.7 per cent in 1982, indicating the impoverishment of wage earners as a result of the crisis and the adjustment. The causes must be sought in the drop in real wages and employment, the higher public tariffs and the cutback in government assistance programmes.[24]

According to the same official report, the rural areas fared no better, with the proportion of families classified as poor rising from 58 per cent in 1980 to 82 per cent in 1982.

Although education is theoretically free in Costa Rica, parents still have to pay the increasingly high costs, relative to income, of school clothing, books, materials and transport costs. For a family with several school-age children, even the minimum as outlined by the Ministry of Public Education in 1986 (notebooks, pencils and crayons) would cost about 200 colones a child. According to Carvajál, for secondary school children the costs could go as high as 3,000 to 4,000 colones a month to provide materials, books and other necessities (equivalent to US$33 to 44).

Since the height of the crisis in the early 1980s, living standards have risen again but many of those living on the margins have not made up lost ground. As an inhabitant of Chacarita, a marginal *barrio* (district) in Puntarénas, put it:

The world has an image of this country as democratic, the Switzerland of Central America, and when the tourists come, they only go to the beautiful parts, but they don't go to other parts like Batan, Limón, Los Chiles, the peasant [communities] in the southern zone, where people live in difficult situations.

The crisis of resources in public education has also brought to a head questions about the relevance of the present curriculum, which has been criticized as too academic and élitist, and the rigidity of the education system generally. Tito Quiros, specialist in adult education at the University of Costa Rica, argues that the curriculum is adapted to the culture and needs of the middle class, which is the minority. 'It does not address the daily needs of the majority, or help them to have the resources to survive.' While the education system is deemed to be 'successful' by the outside world, there are limits on the possibilities for change and innovation.

Some efforts are now being made to confront these problems. The Ministry of Education has launched regional upgrading campaigns in four areas regarded as having the most serious problems: San Carlos, Limón, Los Santos and Santa Cruz. These projects include curriculum development, educational philosophy and goals, teacher upgrading and in-service training. They also endeavour to increase the participation of local organizations in educational planning.

However, as an official in San Carlos admitted, their work is constrained by shortage of resources. This has led to a departure from the generally accepted principle of state funding for educational projects. In the four areas in which this upgrading is taking place, foundations have been established to raise private funds for educational projects, though they are still in the early stages of development. This goes well beyond the past practice of small-scale fundraising through 'raffles or fairs'. 'The aim is that the foundation will go and talk with the people of this region who have big farms, or business people and explain to them special projects and ask for funds.' The official admitted that more prestigious types of education projects might seem more attractive than other, more mundane ones, but they have not yet had sufficient experience in 'selling' projects to be sure.

There are already numerous private schools, especially in San José, and private foundations funding education already exist – for example, the Omar Dengo foundation which funds computer resources in schools. But this latest initiative is to raise funds for specific projects, initiated from the state sector, and which before the crisis would automatically have been funded by the state. It is not yet clear whether this signals a more general change in the government's approach to the funding of education.

Notes

1. Johnson and Martin (1989), p.99.
2. Kelly (1987), p.20.
3. Riddell (1988), pp.25–27.
4. ZIMFEP (1986), 'Education in Zimbabwe'.
5. Kelly (1987), p 27; Clark and Keen (1988), p.6.
6. Kelly (1987), p.26.
7. Chung (1989), p.15.
8. Extract from a case study prepared for the Commonwealth Secretariat by Alison Evans, Institute of Development Studies, University of Sussex, quoted in *Engendering Adjustment* (1989), p.24.
9. Andersson and Kayizzi-Mugerwa (1989), p.12.
10. Kelly (1987), p.43.
11. Lubasi *et al.* (1989); Coombe (1988), pp.9–14.
12. Kelly (1987), p.73–76.
13. Silanda and Tuijnman (1989), *passim.*
14. Kaluba (1986), *passim.*
15. Zvobgo (1986), p.104.
16. Material in this section is derived mainly from Chivore (1986b).
17. 'Education in the new Zimbabwe' (1988).
18. Chung (1989), p.16.
19. Interview, Oxford, Sept. 1989.
20. Government of Zimbabwe, Ministry of Health (1988), p.26.
21. Government of Zimbabwe, Ministry of Education and Culture (1990).
22. Vargas (1987), p.125.
23. Ministerio de Educación Pública 'Situación actual de la educación y políticas educativas de corto plazo', San José, May 1986, quoted in Romero (1987), p.6 (translated from Spanish).
24. Villasuso (1987), p.110.

CHAPTER 9

Battling for survival: war, debt and education in Mozambique, Nicaragua and Sudan

In countries facing military attack and destabilization, as well as external economic pressures, education becomes a battle, both for governments and participants. Two such countries are Mozambique and Nicaragua, where revolutionary governments embarked on campaigns of social and economic transformation in which education played a key role. Sudan has suffered many years of intermittent internal strife between governments dominated by northerners and separatist movements in the south. It has also been severely affected by debt and regional conflicts. Like Mozambique and Nicaragua, it is struggling to survive, with its education system in chaos. However, in contrast, successive Sudanese governments have made little attempt to initiate radical social transformation.

Transforming society: education and revolution in Mozambique and Nicaragua

The histories of Nicaragua and Mozambique over the past two decades have similarities. Both the Sandinistas and Frelimo came to power after a liberation struggle against highly repressive regimes. As governments, both have faced hostility from a powerful neighbour. Both came to power with a goal of mobilizing the population for social and economic change, based on the idea that people's political and social consciousness could be changed, along with material conditions.

As part of this process, education was expected to play a crucial role in changing attitudes, not simply in creating national unity and skills to improve the national economy. In this they went beyond the goals set by Zambia or Zimbabwe. Education became part of an act of political will. In both cases, an early priority was a nation-wide literacy campaign to 'catch up' the lost years of education. Major changes were undertaken in basic school education, in terms of access, curricula and the running of schools. In both countries these and other social policies have been short-circuited by war and destabilization, and by the slide into a major debt crisis.

Yet there were also differences, not only in educational policies and responses to economic and military crisis, but also in the legacy with which they had to deal. Despite the repression practised by the

Somoza regime in Nicaragua, its legacy of under-development was not on the same scale as that left by some 400 years of Portuguese colonial rule in Mozambique. As far as education was concerned, for example, Frelimo's point of departure was an illiteracy rate of 93 per cent, compared with about 50 per cent in Nicaragua.

Mozambique

'After independence, we had to start everything new,' recalls one Mozambican education official. In 1975 there were only about forty university graduates in the country and the departure of the Portuguese settlers who had monopolized skilled and white-collar jobs left the economy in a state of collapse. Education and health, as well as land, were immediately nationalized. Frelimo already had some experience of developing schools in the liberated zones before independence, when education was intended to contribute to the liberation struggle, to change people's consciousness and attitudes and to promote production and combat.

Initially, the newly nationalized school system expanded very rapidly, with enrolments doubling in the course of a few years. There were efforts to democratize school management structures, encouraged by the establishment of communal villages and co-operatives. The first phases of a mass literacy campaign were launched. Both the need and the demand for basic education were evident. However, education policy has embodied a constant tension between the pursuit of more democratic forms of education, and a more technocratic approach which emphasized uniformity, discipline and the development of standardized skills to meet economic needs. This problem, also experienced to some extent in Nicaragua, has been particularly acute in Mozambique because of the high levels of illiteracy and shortages of skilled people at all levels, and the legacy of a highly authoritarian colonial school system.

By the beginning of the 1980s, there was a trend towards more centralization, and away from the sometimes rather anarchic experiments in local school democracy of the 1970s. In 1981, President Samora Machel stressed not democratic participation in school management but the responsibility of pupils to achieve good marks to justify the money and effort expended by the community.

With their work, with their daily effort . . . paying taxes and building schools, the people invest money in the education of the pupil. . . . Thus the pupil must know how to correspond to these sacrifices of the people by obtaining good marks and being exemplary. . . . We invest in pupils who have good marks. . . . Those are heads where the soil is fertile. . . . The mediocre pupil will only be an agent for the diffusion of mediocrity.[1]

By 1980, after the first two out of a total of four literacy campaigns, the illiteracy rate for the population over fifteen years old had been brought down to 72.2 per cent from 93 per cent at independence. Though this was a major achievement, the 1980 census still revealed marked differences by gender and region. There were similar inequalities based on gender and region among those who had completed primary and secondary school cycles.

Table 9.1   Mozambique: illiteracy in 1980 – percentage of the population aged 15 and over

	Total	Male	Female
Whole country	72.7	55.8	87.7
Rural areas	78.1	62.3	91.5
Urban areas	39.4	22.0	60.2

Source: *First Census of Population,* table 7, cited in Frieling (1987)

Table 9.2   Mozambique: levels of education completed, 1980

	Whole country			Rural areas			Urban areas		
	Total	M	F	Total	M	F	Total	M	F
Total no. (000s)	11,673	5,671	6,003	10,135	4,865	5,269	1,539	805	734
Primary (%)	4.1	6.5	1.8	2.7	4.5	1.0	13.3	18.3	7.8
Secondary (%)	0.8	1.1	0.4	0.3	0.6	0.1	3.6	4.8	2.2

Source: *First Census of Population*, table 8, cited in Frieling (1987)

The figures for Maputo City highlight the imbalance in education levels between the capital and the rest of the country. Illiteracy rates were 36.3 per cent for men and 57.5 per cent for women (all age groups). However, in the fifteen to twenty-four age group, many of whom had probably benefited from education since 1975, the figures were 7.7 and 24.7 per cent respectively. Some 30 per cent of the population had attended or were attending literacy courses, almost 16 per cent had primary education and 4.5 per cent secondary education. However, the majority of these had only finished the first level of secondary education – the fifth and sixth years following four years of primary school.

Since 1980, the proportion of girls enrolled nationally at primary level has risen slightly – from 42.5 per cent to 44 per cent in 1986. By this time, all provinces except Zambezia had at least 40 per cent female enrolment. However, total enrolment fell between 1980 and 1986, suggesting that girls have had more opportunity to go to school under war conditions than boys. At secondary level, the proportion of female enrolments has remained constant at 30 per cent, though total enrolments have more than doubled.[2]

In 1983, a major reform programme was launched: the National Education System. This was designed before the onset of destabilization, and aimed to restructure the formal school system. A further year was to be added to bring the total length of education to twelve years by having a seven-year primary cycle. Another goal was to raise the intake level and lengthen the training period for new teachers. However, 1983 also marked the beginning of severe destabilization. Although these reforms have been pursued, their implementation has been hampered by economic problems and the war.

After independence, the curriculum was altered by changing the content of some subjects – for example, history and geography – and by introducing new subjects such as political education and 'social areas'. Before the overhaul of the whole system from 1983 the Institute for the Development of National Education was established to provide materials for schools, guidelines for training personnel in different areas including adult education, and a unified system of national education.

This work has been hampered by economic problems, work pressure on staff, often doing more than one job, and logistical problems with supply and distribution of books and materials. The assistance of several external donors including Sweden, Norway and Canada, with publishing educational materials has relieved some of the pressure, but shortages of books have continued.

There has also been a tendency to impose new curricula and policies without sufficient preparation of teachers and administrators. Often, centrally initiated changes were superseded by others without proper assessment or follow-up. This also led to some popular dissatisfaction with the quality and results of the education which the state has provided.

According to Manuel Golias, an Education Ministry official working in teacher training, there are also difficulties with the image of society presented in the material.

Although we know it is important to teach children that the roots of their culture are in the village, and in the preservation of values and the importance of agriculture, if you look at the primary and secondary level, we find that these aspects are not much stressed. The curriculum is designed by teachers who unconsciously reflect the view that city life is best, even if they come from the rural areas.

Nicaragua

In Nicaragua after the 1979 revolution, the goal was radical educational transformation. In 1983, the Minister of Education defined the role of education in the new Nicaragua as 'developing the new person . . . to contribute to the transformation of the new society'. This process had already begun with a mass mobilization in a literacy campaign which brought the illiteracy rate down from 50.2 per cent to 12.9 per cent by 1981 (see page 245). The goal for the formal system of education was to provide a system from pre-school through to adult education which would give everyone access. As a 1987 document summed it up, 'more education, better education and a new [kind of] education'.

The base from which this system grew was limited, especially in rural areas, though nothing like as deprived as that which faced Frelimo in Mozambique at independence. During the Somoza period, most educational facilities and investment were concentrated in the urban areas, where the rate of illiteracy was given as 28 per cent compared with about 76 per cent in rural areas. The agricultural export economy was not regarded as needing a skilled workforce and little priority was given to schooling for the majority of the population. In rural areas only about 6 per cent of the children who entered the first grade completed the primary cycle, and half these entrants dropped out after the first grade. Private schools in the towns served the needs of the élite. On the Atlantic coast, state provision of education was limited, with teaching exclusively in Spanish (see page 120). Much secondary level education was in the hands of foreign missionaries.

Corruption and repression were rife, not only in education but throughout society. Perhaps one of the most symbolic images of the Somoza regime is still to be seen in the capital, Managua, today. The town, sprawling along the side of Lake Managua, has only a handful of buildings over one storey and is without any identifiable centre. This is because much of the central district in Somoza's time collapsed in the massive 1972 earthquake: Somoza and his clique embezzled most of the international aid given to rebuild the city and so its central area remained in ruins. The anger this sparked in the population and the community organizations which sprang up to help those without homes were crucial in the build-up to insurrection.

The best known educational policy of the Sandinista government was its literacy crusade, launched almost immediately after the seizure of power. There was also a massive expansion in the formal schooling system, with an emphasis on building rural schools. From 1979 to 1983, 2,000 new primary schools were built, mainly in rural areas, with 4,020 new teaching posts, in addition to 800 new communal schools, created in co-operation with rural communities. Eight *escuelas normales* (for teacher training at primary level) were created, twenty-one secondary schools were constructed with international help, along with two technical agricultural institutes. Primary enrolment rose from 369,640 in 1978 to 534,996 in 1982, and secondary enrolments from 98,874 to 139,959. In contrast to Mozambique, the Sandinistas did not nationalize education: in fact the Ministry of Education (MED) subsidised 126 private educational institutions, as well as the Jesuit Central American University (UCA) and the Baptist Universidad Politécnica de Nicaragua (UPOLI).

The most original feature was the harnessing of the enthusiasm generated by the literacy campaign to create over 18,000 popular teachers in adult education. Many of these teachers had been learners in the original literacy campaign. After short training courses, they continued literacy work and adult education, mostly in the communities where they lived. Some of the original *brigadistas*, the young literacy teachers, who mostly came from the urban areas, also continued to work in adult education, and others became teachers in the formal school system.

Another aspect of adult education, operating mostly in urban areas, was an 'accelerated primary' programme which gave those who were newly literate access to formal education in night classes. These usually covered two primary grades in one stage. This system aimed to give those who achieved literacy access to further training courses.

In the school system, curricular changes were introduced gradually, but the goal was to make education not only more relevant to everyday life but much more closely tied to the world of work. A production or service component was included in courses throughout the school programme. This included some fruitful experiments at secondary level in applying scientific knowledge to practical problems. As Isabel Benavides, dean of the education faculty at UNAN, the National University, explained it:

Before the revolution, we had a very mechanical, learning-by-rote type of educational model. But now the struggle is for methodology to really be geared towards stimulating intellectual development and problem solving. Above all, I think the methodology is aimed at making the pupil an active element in the classroom. But we don't always manage this 100 per cent. It will depend on how well-trained the teacher is.

With the inspiration of the literacy crusade, one of the goals was to make classroom relations less authoritarian. This proved to be one of the most difficult tasks. It was exacerbated by lack of materials and books, so that the temptation to fall back on 'chalk and talk' remained, except that there wasn't always any chalk. There were also criticisms from teachers, parents and students that the revised curriculum content was much too dense and demanding, with the result that teachers were pressured to rush through it.

The government made strenuous efforts to upgrade the quality of the teaching profession. Large numbers of teachers were 'empiricals' – that is, without formal training. They were offered Saturday courses, combined with distance learning materials, to upgrade their skills. Teacher training also tried to provide a methodology and techniques to deal with rural multi-grade schools, which require different skills from those in single grade teaching.

Education in rural areas faced substantial problems, but the programmes of land reform, the development of co-operatives and higher levels of community organization, along with the provision of more educational opportunities, made learning seem more useful and attractive. An important factor in the advances achieved in education was the ability to mobilize people through organizations under the Sandinista umbrella: trade unions, including the teachers' union, ANDEN; women's organizations; co-operatives; and peasants' organizations. These involved more people at a local and regional level in educational issues and also provided forums for discussion. However, people who were not part of any organized structures, particularly in rural areas, found fewer opportunities for participation.

Language dilemmas

In both Nicaragua and Mozambique, the governments have come up against the question of choosing which language or languages to teach in. This problem appears in a more or less acute form in many countries whose borders were arbitrarily set by colonial rulers or as the outcome of wars.

In Mozambique, there is a wide diversity of languages and in some provinces no one language is dominant. This led to a reluctant acceptance of the colonial language, Portuguese, as the official language. A similar decision was made by a revolutionary government in another former Portuguese colony, Guinea-Bissau. Other ex-colonial countries in the region, including Zambia and Zimbabwe and now Namibia, have chosen English as the main language of instruction.

There are educational drawbacks to this policy. The majority of illiterates, especially women in rural areas, know little or no Portuguese. This adds difficulties to literacy work. In the school system, many teachers do not have a strong enough grasp of the language to teach in it effectively. Furthermore, teaching Portuguese in primary school to children who do not speak it at home further isolates school experience from that of the home. There is now some research being done on local languages in the university, but given the complex pattern of languages, especially with widespread population move-ment, and the cost, it seems unlikely that the government's policy on the official medium of instruction will be changed.

In Nicaragua, the language problem relates specifically to the Atlantic coast region. Historically isolated from the Spanish-speaking central and western areas, the area has been physically cut off and economically little developed. This region played a relatively small part in the struggles which led up to the Sandinista revolution. The gulf between the Atlantic and Pacific coasts became a major political problem in the early 1980s.

Although the population groups are quite small, the linguistic map is complex. There are four language groups: Creole-speakers, and three Indian language groups: Miskitu, mainly in the north, and two much smaller groups, Rama and Sumu. By the 1970s, many people, particularly in the Creole and Miskitu communities, were at least bilingual, speaking their ethnic language and either Spanish (the language of education) or standard English, promoted particularly through Moravian missionary education. In rural areas, however, literacy in any language was estimated to be only 20 per cent.

The Sandinistas quickly conceded the principle of bilingual education, and incorporated local languages into the 1980 literacy crusade. However, the need to translate literacy materials and transport them, and to find teachers in each language, slowed up the campaign and lessened its impact. The Sandinista leadership was made up of Pacific coast Spanish-speakers. They were mainly concerned to cement national unity and did not at first grasp the complexities of the problem and its interaction with political opposition, particularly among the Miskitu. As relationships with the United States worsened, and some of the Miskitu became involved with the Contras, there was a tendency to regard English, and Miskitu, as politically suspect.

Since the mid-1980s, when autonomy was conceded to the Atlantic coast and the principle of bilingual, bi-cultural education was established, the question of language became an educational more than a political problem. Aside from the limiting effects of the economic crisis, there were considerable difficulties in deciding exactly which combinations of language should be taught in school. For example, among the Creole population, many people wanted to learn English, but others wanted Creole to become the language of instruction in schools, along with Spanish. Among the Miskitu, while there was a strong emphasis on the status of their own language, some members of the community preferred their children to learn English.

Destabilization

Neither the Sandinistas nor Frelimo were allowed many years of peace and continuity to see the fruits of these new initiatives, or to discover their flaws, before external forces intervened. South Africa opposed Mozambique's radical regime, fearing its potential influence in the region, and Frelimo's support for both the Zimbabwean liberation struggle and the African National Congress (ANC) of South Africa. It gave military and financial support to Renamo, also known as the MNR, (identified by the Mozambican government as 'armed bandits') as a proxy in operations within Mozambique.

Renamo was first formed by the Rhodesian special services during the Zimbabwean liberation war and was revitalized by the South Africans in the early 1980s to destabilize the Mozambican regime. Renamo, leaning heavily on support and 'advisers' from South Africa, and latterly from Kenya, has no apparent ideological goal. It seeks to disrupt all aspects of life, from supply lines to social services, using extremely violent methods. The aim is to discredit the Frelimo government as being unable to protect or serve its own people. Its activities have continued since the Nkomati accord of 1984. This was supposed to end South African funding of Renamo in return for the termination of Mozambican support for the ANC.

In Nicaragua, the United States similarly regarded the Sandinista government as a threat and a radical example for other Central American states. It trained, armed and gave financial support to the Contras, a motley group of opponents of the Sandinistas, led by former Somocista National Guards. This military campaign was combined with a US economic blockade and trade embargo against Nicaragua from 1985, as well as openly hostile acts such as mining Nicaraguan ports.

These destabilization campaigns put tremendous pressure on the economies and social services of both countries. Transformation gave way to a grim fight for survival. The human costs both of the wars themselves and the economic crises they have caused have been enormous, and the setbacks to programmes of educational and social development severe.

Mozambique: disruption and deprivation

For Mozambique, the economic statistics tell a grim story. A 1989 report for Unicef estimates that Mozambique's total GDP losses from 1980 to 1988 were US$13.5 billion at 1988 prices. GNP per capita fell from US$210 in 1984 to US$150 to 175 in 1988.[3] South Africa put pressure on the Mozambican economy by reducing its use of Mozambique's ports and railways by 90 per cent. About 70,000 Mozambican migrant workers in South Africa have been made redundant and returned home, causing local unemployment and loss of remittances to state and families. The resulting unemployment is particularly marked in the southern provinces of Inhambane, Gaza and Maputo (province, not city) from where the majority of the migrants came.

Mozambique has one of the highest infant mortality rates in the world, approximately 200 per 1,000 live births.[4] Those who depend on emergency support because of war and drought number about 1,690,000 and about half the population is wholly or partially dependent on food aid.[5]

From 1985 onwards, there was a considerable drop in the resources allocated to education, which, by 1987, amounted to 2.8 per cent of GDP, down from over 4 per cent in 1983. As the 1989 Frelimo Fifth Party Congress Central Committee report noted, with continuing increase in demand for educational services, this meant 'a decline in the quality of services and a decrease in the already precarious living and working conditions of teachers'.[6] Access to schooling has been in decline because of the war and financial cuts. The government estimates that 250,000 children have been deprived of education.[7] School attendance for the age group seven to eleven years is estimated to be 40 per cent.

According to the 1989 Unicef report,

After an initial post-independence surge, primary school enrolment has been held at around 46 per cent by the destruction of rural schools and the resulting lack of access for many nominally enrolled pupils. Educational quality has also suffered because war costs and related economic decline have forced cuts in books, equipment, furniture, writing materials and maintenance of buildings.[8]

Frelimo's Central Committee reported that by 1989, 45 per cent of all primary schools had either been closed or wrecked. The provinces of Tete and Zambezia, particularly affected by Renamo actions, have been deprived of 80 per cent of their schools. Even in 1984 these provinces had the lowest enrolment levels and female attendance rates, and the highest drop-out rates in the whole country. Only the higher levels of secondary education, from the ninth grade onwards, have continued to expand, though they have been growing from a very low base. This may be because the majority of secondary schools are in urban areas and have been less affected by the war. However, technical secondary schools have shown very large drops in enrolment, mainly because of unemployment among their graduates due to the virtual collapse of the productive sectors of the economy.

Literacy and adult education work has suffered even more. Between 1984 and 1987, there was a 55 per cent decline in enrolment in literacy classes and a 35 per cent fall for post-literacy classes. Now it is estimated that some 38 per cent of people are literate – but the figure for women is only 22 per cent.[9] It may well be that the rate will slip further with so many children failing to receive regular schooling.

The Fifth Congress document comments: 'We are still far from achieving the desired compulsory schooling as envisaged in the National Education System', conceived in a period of relative peace.[10] A SIDA report sums up the crisis:

Behind the figures . . . lie, first and foremost, the bandit disruptions of the system and the society. Mass movement of the population creates instability and demoralization, even for those not directly affected. Starvation and poverty bring hungry participants to school, and irregularly at that. Thousands of schools serving hundreds of thousands of pupils have been destroyed or closed. However, numerous other factors contribute to the situation: the falling real value of teacher salaries, poor working conditions for teachers, the breakdown of teacher upgrading activities, the fall in state expenditure on materials, delays and calamities in the distribution of available materials, and a rigid formal system of time-tabling and examinations, to name but a few.[11]

The war has seriously affected the morale of teachers and the conditions in which they have to work. In the first place, by 1986, teachers and other educational staff had seen the purchasing power of their salaries slip to a half or a third of their 1980 value. Enrolments for teacher training have dropped off sharply (see Fig. 9.1) and, despite government incentives, there has been increasing difficulty in providing teachers for rural areas where security is poor. Attacks may be sporadic but they are disruptive and frequently very brutal. Apart from the destruction of schools, teachers are regarded as important community members and are often more than usually politicized. As a result, they are particular targets of Renamo. Manuel Golias recalls an instance when a village was attacked. The people fled, only to realize that the teacher had been left behind, so they went back to try and save him.

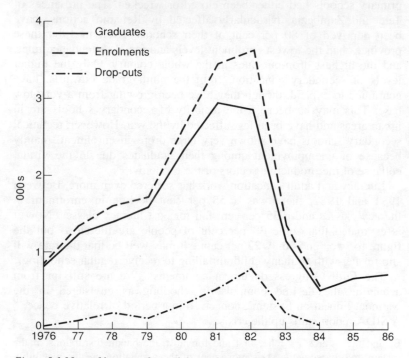

Figure 9.1 **Mozambique: teacher training, primary teachers (one year course)**
Source: Mozambique Ministry of Education (DNFQE)

By 1986, Mozambique's external debt had reached an estimated US$3.2 billion. GNP had dropped in real terms by 35 per cent from 1981 to 1986, overall state expenditure by 58 per cent and education expenditure by 48 per cent. At this point, the Mozambican government finally turned to the IMF. In 1987, the Economic Rehabilitation Programme (PRE) was agreed under IMF and World Bank auspices. This entailed the usual range of stabilization measures – currency devaluation and price rises – though wages were also raised, especially in the higher echelons of the state sector. But there were also staff cuts in the public service and some privatization of production and distribution.

End of a school

Many teachers were displaced in the fighting. One primary school teacher from Gile describes the problems of keeping a school going once the villagers knew they were likely to be attacked by the forces of Renamo:

People had to flee into the bush, seeking to hide from the bandits as best they could, coming into the village only by day. They were very isolated, each one making a shack under the trees for minimum protection from the rain and sun and from the bandits who continued to appear. The parents preferred to keep their children with them, just in case of another attack, but we made efforts to keep the school going. Everything changed. We started later and ended earlier. If anybody got wind of strangers about the area, we sent the children back to their parents immediately. But the numbers of children fell off. Many fled with their parents to Nampula. My class of fifty children dwindled to ten or fifteen. Our salaries were not paid, month after month. We didn't get school books or school materials. Finally we stopped trying to teach and also fled to Nampula.[12]

In the education sector, the government has entered into agreements with the World Bank, and this is already having a marked influence in shifting priorities and goals. One of the main changes has been to allow the establishment or revival of private schools, previously not permitted to operate. The new policies envisage that although the state remains the 'fundamental instrument' in applying educational policy, responsibility for provision should be devolved to non-governmental bodies – including firms, co-operatives, citizens' associations and social or humanitarian organizations which would subsidize community schools on a non-profit basis. Such schools would follow Ministry of Education curricula and, in terms of overall management, would be controlled by the Ministry, but teachers would be recruited by the provider or the community, though approved by the Ministry.

The mechanisms of control and the latitude which such schools would have are still unclear and are being studied by the Ministry of Education. However, the new proposals represent a clear departure from previous ideological and educational ideas, under pressure of economic scarcity and war and from the World Bank.

The effects of these changes have been emerging gradually. The PRE measures probably gave some relief to qualified secondary teachers, by linking pay with qualifications. However, especially at primary level, salaries remain low, and pay rises have not kept up with inflation. In 1990 teachers in five provinces went on strike for a 100 per cent rise. This demand was rejected by the government and resulted in considerable bitterness among teachers.

The dire economic situation has also led to corruption, with some teachers selling examination papers and answers. Many others have set themselves up as private tutors, which is now permitted. However, this promises to do little for educational standards; sometimes these tutors have neither materials nor premises to work from, and hold classes under trees. Teachers' union officials admit that many teachers earn more from private tutoring than from their official jobs.

Another consequence of the new policies has been the decision to charge user fees for state education, so that an increasing financial burden falls on families. This has already been done in health and appears to be markedly reducing the take-up of services. More of the costs of educational materials have been transferred from the Ministry of Education on to consumers. By 1987, although the cost of producing school books was still subsidized, the distribution costs were passed on to parents. At primary level this meant costs of up to 2,000 MT (US$7) a year for each pupil, compared with 40 MT in 1984 (US$1). This system of payment extends to the whole education system including adult education, where numbers of books sold are reportedly very small – either because of low enrolments or because people are going to classes without books. There have also been reports of piles of school books gathering dust in shops, because people cannot afford to buy them. At secondary level, school fees are now being charged.[13]

These developments are most likely to affect urban dwellers and those displaced people and migrants in the urban areas who cannot afford even small charges for their children's education. In rural areas, especially where education has been hardest hit, they will be very hard to implement. Reports suggest that in many areas, textbooks and materials are anyway not available, since provincial traders are not interested in distributing them.

The effects of these policies on access to schooling have to be considered in the wider context of family income and availability of education. The greatest burdens of the war – destruction, disruption of life and economic deprivation – have fallen on the rural population. But the displacement of large numbers of people from the rural to urban areas has put great pressure on the previously more privileged urban education sector. For example, in Maputo City total primary enrolment rose 26 per cent between 1984 and 1986, whereas country-wide it fell 4 per cent. Even in 1986, a small household survey conducted in two suburbs of Maputo – Machava (quite close to the centre) and Xipamanine (at a considerable distance from the centre) – found that 10 to 14 per cent of households questioned mentioned difficulties in letting their children attend school. The reasons were the lack of available places and the long distances between home and school. These were mainly long-standing residents of Maputo, not recent immigrants.[14]

Furthermore, the PRE has hit urban populations hardest, mainly because of rising prices due to devaluation and removal of subsidies.

The effects of 'stabilization'

The impact of the PRE's 'stabilization' measures on households on or near the minimum wage was measured in mid-1988:

	Cost for family of 5 *MT/month*	*% of minimum wage* *(12,500 MT/month)*
Food basket	13,000	104
Rent, electricity, water	14,000	125
Education (books, etc.)	700–1,600	9–20

The average wage in Maputo was 20,000 to 30,000 MT per month, which only just covers these items, and does not allow for clothes or any other basic items.

- the food basket (i.e. rationed food) is no longer taken advantage of in full by the poorer segments of the urban population simply because they cannot afford it any more. Estimates say that as much as half of available rationed goods are left unsold;
- enrolment rates for primary education are decreasing further from the already low level of 47 per cent in 1986/7 as parents keep their children out of school for lack of money to pay for school books, etc; and
- people in rural as well as urban areas stay away from clinics and hospitals where reductions in normal attendance of 50 to 80 per cent are frequent (because of the charges introduced). Already as a consequence of the war, half the children up to five years are short for their age due to malnutrition.[15]

Even if changes in South Africa bring the war to an end in the near future, the costs of simply returning to the situation before the war are enormous, both in terms of the capital cost of replacing destroyed and damaged schools, and the running costs of the system. The hard facts of the situation are outlined in the 1989 Central Committee report:

We should note that over the next decade about half the children aged from 7–11 years will not have adequate conditions to attend primary school normally in terms of the law on the National System of Education and that many other older children will be likewise unable to attend school. During the same period only about 70 per cent of the pupils who complete fifth grade every year will be able to continue their schooling in the regular education system.[16]

In these conditions, the government has had little option but to accept the kinds of changes which the international financial agencies want. The last few years have also seen the re-emergence of political elements within Mozambique who favour these developments and as of 1990, Frelimo ceased to be the sole political party. While the PRE has halted Mozambique's rapid economic decline since the early 1980s, there have been doubts about how appropriate its policies are for a country still at war. At the same time, its high social and human costs quickly became evident. In June 1990, a new IMF 'enhanced structural adjustment facility' was approved, accompanied by a major rescheduling of bilateral debts. The new package did contain some measures to alleviate the economic cost of adjustment for the poor. However, at the same time, drought and war were threatening the country with renewed famine.

Another consequence of the war and economic crisis has been an increasing dependence on external aid. The level of aid increased rapidly after the signing of the Nkomati accord of 1984 and the publicity given to the famine in the mid-1980s. Before this, the regime was not regarded with favour by many of the major donor agencies in the West. Aid trebled to US$649 million in 1987 but it has largely been directed towards relief rather than development. By the end of the 1980s, drought had again intensified the need for emergency relief. In addition, the political changes in the Soviet Union and Eastern Europe have diminished the amounts of aid which are forthcoming for socialist countries in the developing world, including Mozambique.

A further outcome of this very brutal war is the long-term effects on children who have been terrorized or brutalized by Renamo tactics or physically mutilated (see page 238). There are large numbers of such children whom the government acknowledges will be likely to suffer learning difficulties and emotional or psychological disturbances. This is something for which teachers need preparation. Unicef is implementing a programme to help prepare teachers to cope with these added problems in the classroom, and the government itself is to include 'rehabilitation' as an aspect of the training of teachers.

Nicaragua: progress undermined

In February 1990, elections ended ten and a half years in which the Sandinistas dominated politics in Nicaragua. Their education and social policies are undoubtedly their most important legacy, and have attracted much attention and some emulation in other countries of the South. These efforts for change have been constantly undermined by economic crisis and war. By the end of the 1980s Nicaraguan teachers were talking of 'working with our fingernails' and 'teaching with bare hands'. The economic embargo and blockade by the United States and the Contra war had left Nicaragua's economy on its knees, and its population concentrating on day-to-day survival with terrifying levels of inflation, which by the beginning of 1988 had reached a staggering 30,000 per cent a year. By that time, some 50 per cent of the budget went on defence. Although by 1989 the height of the economic crisis had passed, the structural effects of the war and the US embargo left Nicaragua with severe internal shortages, drastically reduced production levels and exports which only covered a quarter of the import bill.

Government deficits were also increased by a number of internal and regional factors. After the fall of Somoza, Nicaragua suffered a substantial flight of capital. It also suffered badly from the decline in trade within the Central American Common Market. Finally, the cutting of trade with the United States from 1985 was a severe blow. At the same time, it implemented a second, more radical phase of land reform, which redistributed more land to previously landless peasants. This helped to boost domestic food production, but, added to the disruption caused by the war, reduced the volume of crops for export.

Some of the deficit thus created was made up by external aid, largely from Eastern bloc countries, though the European Community and Scandinavian countries also provided assistance. However, aid from the United States ceased soon after President Reagan came to office in 1981 and the US administration began to use its influence in the IMF and the World Bank to end any assistance to the Sandinistas.

The external assistance received was still far below the levels needed not only to implement the Sandinistas' social policies but also to sustain the costs of destabilization and war. According to government calculations, the total economic damage, direct and indirect, of the US destabilization policy between 1980 and 1988 was some US$9 billion.

The war and economic problems brought to a halt and in some areas even reversed the major advances made in educational provision in the early 1980s, and like crises elsewhere, often sharpened inequalities and exacerbated existing difficulties. Until 1986, education budgets were sustained at over 10 per cent of government expenditure, but hyper-inflation, currency devaluation and overall budget cutbacks have eaten into the real amounts of money involved. The 12.9 per cent illiteracy rate in 1981 was admitted to have risen to over 20 per cent by the late 1980s. The schools building programme ceased in 1985, and at that time too teachers' real salaries began to decline rapidly. The general economic crisis has also brought the usual gamut of problems external to education, but which none the less limit its effectiveness: transport difficulties, especially for rural areas; cuts in electricity supplies; more hungry children coming to school; more urban children selling chewing gum and newspapers in the streets.

The war has accentuated the disparities both in educational level and general economic status between different regions of the country. The war particularly affected parts of the Atlantic coast and the remote frontier areas, especially in regions I, V and VI (see map 1), already under-developed, with higher than average levels of illiteracy. On the Atlantic coast, many teachers left and some schools in rural areas were still closed in 1989. A further trial for this region was the destruction wrought by Hurricane Joan in October 1988.

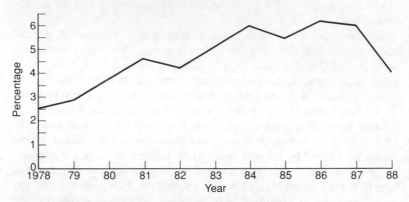

Figure 9.2 Nicaragua: percentage of GDP spent on education
Source: Arrien & Lazo (1989) Nicaragua: diez años de educación

The dangers for teachers in war zones of being identified with the government were exemplified by the fate of numbers of 'popular teachers' who were killed or kidnapped by the Contras. In 1984, when the war was intensifying, 300 popular teachers were killed in the war zone and the popular education network which had been established was 'perforated', according to a Ministry of Education official. 'This worked against us in many areas of the country and we had a lot of losses. Many people feared involvement in popular education because it made them immediate targets of the Contras.' Even in 1989, school teachers in areas where Contras were still operating were threatened with violence if they continued to work.

In Managua, there was some in-migration from rural war zones, particularly in the mid-1980s, straining infrastructure and social services, including education. This trend was discouraged by the government, but the capital's population rose from 24 per cent of the total population in 1980 to 33 per cent in 1986. Some of the recent migrants have returned to their home regions as the fighting diminished, but it is unlikely that all will return to the countryside.

One effect, according to Guillermo Martinez of the teachers' union ANDEN, was to overburden classes,

with 60 kids sitting on the floor in the first grade. The situation of some schools is quite precarious. They work three shifts – morning, afternoon and evening. The night shift is supposed to be for working youth and adults. The truth is that many children also work, so 12-, 13- and 14-year-olds also attend the accelerated primary schools at night. This is the reality. There are children who don't go to school – the national figures are that roughly 150,000 children do not attend school in the primary school age group. And a good percentage of these are in Managua.

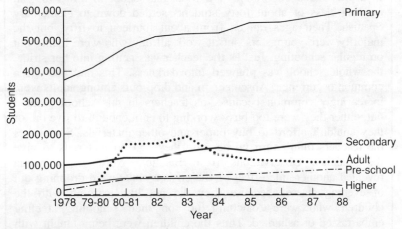

Figure 9.3 Nicaragua: student numbers
Source: Arrien & Lazo (1989) *Nicaragua: diez años de educación*

Adult education, and thus the sustaining of literacy, a key to the Sandinistas' policy, was particularly badly hit in all regions by logistical problems, and by lack of money and materials. Some kinds of adult education through the trade union movement were given in the workplace, but a Central Sandinista de Trabajadores (CST) representative said that educational classes in workplaces had sometimes been suspended because of economic difficulties within the enterprise. The personnel to run literacy and adult education programmes have also been in short supply. For the accelerated basic education programme teachers received an extra payment in kind (*afa* – see page 133) but popular teachers doing literacy work were unpaid and relied heavily on the commitment of young people.

Education officials readily admitted that a decade of Sandinista rule had not yet resolved 'the cultural problem we have inherited of women being relegated to second place'. Social reality, they conceded, cannot be changed overnight. While more women have had access to education, the economic crisis has combined with prevailing social attitudes to limit women's opportunities to improve their economic position. However, as is often the case in wartime, women have stepped into some positions previously held by men. In the education system, the war has accentuated the preponderance of women, particularly amongst paid and volunteer teachers in literacy and adult education. As Douglas Guerero, in charge of the literacy campaign pointed out, this 'has not been induced by the institutions themselves. In part it's due to the war, but it's also an expression of the spirit of women to improve their situation'.

Adult Education – for children

In a dilapidated classroom of a Managua school in mid-1989, an evening class of about forty students settled down to elementary Spanish. Their ages ranged from about fourteen to fifty, but the majority were youngsters out at work all day who were losing out on regular schooling. Just as the teacher was getting into her stride, the whole school was plunged into darkness. This had become a common occurrence. Absenteeism and drop-outs among adults were increasingly common because, as teachers in this school pointed out, either they were too busy working to earn enough to live on, or they couldn't afford to buy paper and other materials. Sometimes the teachers didn't turn up because they had no materials to give the students. Observations from Batahola Norte in Managua revealed another side effect of the crisis. Adults were dropping out of evening classes because they did not like learning with the children who were 'catching up' on their schooling, feeling embarrassed or ashamed. Thus the children were being taught with materials intended for adults, and in some cases by teachers trained only in adult education.[17]

In Ciudad Sandino, a small 'new town' close to Managua, they were celebrating ten years of literacy work (1979–89) with an exhibition. One of the handful of paid staff, a young woman of about seventeen, was full of energy and enthusiasm, but she said that it was very difficult to keep enough volunteers to teach. So many young men, who in the Nicaraguan context are an important component not only of the student population but also of popular teachers and literacy workers, were away on military service. Almost all the teachers at their centre were women, as were the majority of the learners.

The other major cause for concern during the second half of the 1980s has been the situation of teachers in the formal education system. By 1989, teachers' salaries were the equivalent of about US$12 per month (300,000 cordobas in June 1989) for a primary school teacher and US$16 for a secondary school teacher. While teachers command social respect in Nicaragua they are not near the top of the salary league – for example, at the same period a surgeon would receive about US$40 a month and a miner about US$80. One of the consequences of the difficult situation in schools and the low pay was that many teachers left the profession, even to work in the informal labour sector, and some moved to other countries. Their places had to be taken by 'empirical' (untrained) teachers, reaching 60 per cent of total teachers in some regions.[18]

In the late 1980s, teacher drop-out was around 20 per cent a year, higher than the drop-out rate among pupils. This was a backward step, since one of the goals of the Ministry had been to increase the proportion of trained teachers through in-service training to upgrade 'empirical' teachers, as well as by initial teacher training. This drop-out rate from teaching was not only depriving the system of experienced teachers but also wasting resources spent on their training. Furthermore, new teachers were not being trained fast enough to replace the trained teachers who were leaving the profession. There was, for example, a downturn of 20 per cent in total enrolment of teacher trainees for secondary school and above at the National University's Faculty of Education between 1982 and 1987.

This is hardly a climate in which educational innovation could flourish. By the end of the 1980s, most of the Ministry of Education's ingenuity was focused on how to make cuts which would do the least damage. In the mid-1980s the government had already begun to implement austerity measures which cut spending and led to price rises. In 1988 and 1989, a series of measures with many of the characteristics of a 'stabilization' package forced more drastic cuts in government spending.

This *compactación* became an unwelcome household word. The education budget was cut by 19 per cent overall in January 1989 and a further 25 per cent in June. This cut was smaller that that imposed in some other sectors, but it none the less entailed over 7,000 job losses, including 2,400 teaching posts. Some cuts involved not filling posts left vacant by teachers discouraged by the rock-bottom pay and difficult conditions. Most of the other job losses were in support and supervisory staff. It also meant a 29 per cent cut in textbooks, and severe cuts in materials, supplies and maintenance as well as a reduction of training workshops for teachers. No classrooms or schools were closed, but the reality at the level of one village school was that eleven out of twenty-five teachers were 'empiricals' though nine were attending Saturday classes to upgrade their status. In 1988, according to the 25-year-old headmistress, textbooks had to be rented by the students, and in 1989 the students, or their families, had to buy them.

These cuts triggered protests among teachers and a brief strike in some urban centres. President Daniel Ortega met the teachers but said there just was not enough money to pay them more. However, an effort was made to give them some kind of compensation, by extending the provision of the *afa* (beans, rice and sugar rations) beyond the initial emergency period, and offering them free transport and free spectacles. Teachers also received a great deal of support and help from both popular organizations and from communities to ease their situation.

One trade-union official in León, Nicaragua's second city, in 1989 described the education system as 'at a standstill'.[19] Some might argue that it was running backwards. Within the Ministry of Education this brought shifts of emphasis, and some lowering of sights because of the set- backs and acknowledged mistakes of the past years. For example, there was a move to decentralize educational administration, because of growing concern at the gap between the pronouncements at the top in the Ministry and the practice at the level of the school, as well as disparities between educational levels in different areas. This decentralization was partly to ease administrative problems such as salary payments, but it also was intended to encourage more local involvement in education. The autonomy granted to the Atlantic coast was only in its early stages, but that too was an acknowledgement that everything could not be run directly from Managua.

The war and economic crisis has also brought a recognition of the need to consolidate the gains of the early years of the revolution, particularly to reinforce literacy. This was approached from two angles: first, what was known as the 'battle for the fourth grade', an acknowledgement that substantial numbers of children either did not go to school or did not stay long enough to consolidate literacy. This strategy included implementing a revised and 'thinned down' curriculum and trying to ensure supplies of school materials for these grades. The literacy campaign was relaunched, though on a much more decentralized and piecemeal basis (see Chapter 15).

When the economic crisis became severe, community mobilization became not so much a question of participation in decision-making as practical support to keep schools and education projects going. However, this type of economic support, though acknowledged as necessary, was not regarded as ideal: Guillermo Martinez of ANDEN commented in 1989:

We've seen community participation in trying to come up with immediate solutions to the problems resulting from the war – we're talking particularly about materials and infrastructure. We also think that the support and integration of the community is important as an ongoing, permanent and stable factor. The school should go out to the community and the community should also support and be part of the school. [However], the prospects for the short term are such that we will continue to need the economic support [of the community]. When economic stability improves and we are able to deal with these problems, the support and participation of the community continues to be important, but perhaps dealing with other kinds of problems. The state should not only ensure the conditions for teaching and learning but should also be supporting the community. But the community should care for the school because it is a social good and the property of the community.

Jacqueline Sanchez, of the Ministry of Education, also points out that; 'Over the years, since the revolution, many people have become much more demanding as far as education is concerned, and despite all the difficulties, are more critical and expect more of their schools.'

It is very difficult in the circumstances of either Mozambique or Nicaragua to evaluate conclusively the effectiveness of policies which promote education as a means of transforming society, although in the case of Nicaragua, despite the problems, government-sponsored initiatives clearly scored successes, both in educational terms and in terms of social change. However, any such strategy requires far more time and continuity of action and work to bear fruit. In both countries, undoubtedly one of the goals of what the United States euphemistically called 'low-intensity conflict' was to hamper and discredit the revolutionary movements' ability to deliver services to their peoples, and to involve them in changing their lives. Certainly in the case of Nicaragua, this strategy played an important part in undermining the undoubted popular support which the Sandinistas had enjoyed in the first part of the 1980s.

The new UNO coalition government has clearly distanced itself from the Sandinista view of education. First, it has dismissed a number of head teachers appointed by the Sandinistas, and teachers who have objected to changes being made by the government have been transferred to other schools. The new government has also moved to scrap school textbooks developed under the Sandinistas and has imported textbooks from Costa Rica which had been produced with USAID assistance. Only in the National University (UNAN) do the Sandinistas still have overall control.

Solidarity support

In response to the economic crisis provoked by the war and the US boycott, WUS(UK) organized the sending of a container of basic education materials to the Nicaraguan education sector. The money was raised primarily by members of the British teaching unions, AUT, NUT and NATFHE, and the students' union, NUS. The campaign to fill the container was aimed not just at assisting Nicaraguan educators, but also at raising the problems they faced with their UK counterparts.

Since the elections of 1990, WUS(UK) has examined ways of assisting innovative educational projects to continue. One such project is the integrated popular and formal education project in Jalapa near the Honduran border (see page 247). The project aims to eradicate illiteracy in the Jalapa valley with a combination of adult popular education, literacy classes, and work and education courses. The success of the Jalapa project, described by Sandinista education officials as exemplary, depends on the active participation of local grassroots organizations and unions. Even the bank manager takes participation in the project into account when considering loans to co-operatives.

The Ministry of Education, now headed by rightwingers in the coalition, has indicated its intention to concentrate on formal sector education, marginalizing the literacy and popular adult education work which had been so important under the Sandinistas by starving them of funds. Government statements have also made a point of denigrating the achievements of the 1980 Literacy Crusade. Future economic restructuring is likely to include public spending cuts which may also limit further educational expansion.

Debt and the destruction of war have brought major economic setbacks, aside from damage to social services and human suffering. Neither of these countries, poor as they are, can hope to recoup these losses and develop in the future without external assistance. A major question is, will sufficient aid be forthcoming – given the changes in the international political climate – and on what terms?

Sudan: the breakdown of a system

By 1990, Sudan had become enmeshed in almost every kind of economic and political crisis. It falls in the category of a low-income, highly indebted country with its economy practically at a standstill; it is divided by a long-standing struggle between the north and south of the country – the north dominated by Arabic-speaking Muslims; the south, by several tribal groupings, most of whose poeple are either animists or Christians. Since Sudan came into existence as a separate state under British colonial control at the end of the nineteenth century, the north has tended to dominate, to be the seat of government and to take economic and political precedence over the south. This state of affairs has resulted in long periods of civil war beginning soon after independence. A settlement was reached in 1972, but in the 1980s, as the devolution of power to the south became little more than a façade and the economic situation deteriorated, the separatist movement re-emerged.

Throughout the 1980s, Sudan has suffered not only from the disruption caused by its own civil conflict but has also experienced influxes of refugees from surrounding countries – Uganda, Ethiopia and Chad – driven by drought and war. Many of its own people have been displaced by civil war or uprooted by drought or flood.

The origins of Sudan's severe debt crisis go back to the policies pursued from the early 1970s onwards. The government was attracted by the idea of changing Sudan from an exporter of cotton, groundnuts and gum arabic into what was dubbed at the time 'the breadbasket of the Middle East'. It was encouraged in this strategy by the oil-rich Gulf states which were concerned about their dependence on food sources outside the Middle Eastern region. With their financial backing, and some Western aid, Sudan embarked on an ambitious public investment programme focused on large-scale agriculture. However, after the 1973 Arab–Israeli war and the steep rise in oil prices, inflation as well as private consumption began to soar, and from 1976 foreign aid began to fall. While imports increased, exports did not flourish sufficiently to fill the growing gap. By 1977, Sudan had a severe foreign exchange crisis, and by the beginning of 1978 was experiencing shortages of imported goods. At this point the Gulf states and other creditors insisted that Sudan turn to the IMF, and the first of many standby arrangements was signed, with the standard range of measures. The impact on popular living standards was severe, and street riots and strikes ensued. Since then, IMF loans and rescheduling arrangements have become a regular feature of economic life.

These measures have failed to reverse Sudan's economic decline, and problems related to the adjustment policies, the war and drought have intensified. The ratio of per capita debt to per capita income rose from 19.7 in 1973 to a record high of 162.7 in 1985/86. Although Sudan's debt burden eased slightly in the second half of the 1980s, no real turn-around in the economic situation was in sight at the end of the decade. Furthermore, like Zambia, the country is now heavily in arrears with the IMF which in 1990 declared Sudan 'non-cooperative' for failing to repay its debts to the Fund.

Government expenditure has been caught in a squeeze. While revenues stagnate, expenditure has soared – in 1988/89, there was a budget deficit of £S7 billion, fuelling inflation, which reached 80 per cent a year in 1988/89. One of the greatest drains on the exchequer has been the war in the south. Defence and security activities were estimated to be costing more than £S11 million a day. A further drain is the central government subsidy to regional and local governments, which are increasingly in no position to generate revenues from local taxes and production. The government also subsidizes basic goods, including sugar, petroleum and wheat.

Since the crisis began in the late 1970s, spending on education below tertiary level has been at rock bottom and health little better. Only the tertiary sector has maintained a larger share of the cake, an average of over 4 per cent during the period from 1978/79 and 1986/87, compared with 1.04 per cent for general education in the decade from 1978 to 1989 (see Figure 9.4). These allocations are dwarfed by the expenditure on defence and debt service.

Education in Sudan since independence has witnessed a substantial expansion in the total number of schools, pupils and teachers at primary, intermediate and secondary levels. The highest rates of growth were at intermediary and secondary levels (thirteen to eighteen years) though, as in many other African countries, this growth was from a very low baseline. There was an increased awareness of the need for education at all levels, rising levels of literacy – though they are still relatively low – and, while the economy was expanding, a demand for skills. In the 1950s and 1960s education expansion was encouraged by the Sudanization of government jobs as well as growth in economic activity. Since the late 1970s Sudan, like its northern neighbour Egypt, has suffered a brain-drain of professionals to other parts of the Middle East, particularly to the southern Gulf states.

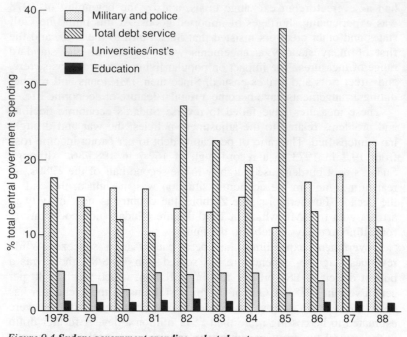

Figure 9.4 **Sudan: government spending, selected sectors**
Source: Derived from *Sudan Economic Survey 1988/89 Appendix 4/2*

Despite this expansion, the low levels of education expenditure mean that many schools, especially in rural areas, are little more than shells. There are still many children of school age who are not in the education system at any level, due to lack of enrolment opportunities, lack of schools, rising educational costs for poor families, high drop-out rates and inadequate government expenditure.

Regional disparities

Although the educational statistics available may be of questionable accuracy, particularly for the war-torn south, they do indicate patterns of difference. In Khartoum and the Northern region, the vast majority of children get to primary school, and over 40 per cent of sixteen-to eighteen-year-olds are at secondary school. However, at the other end of the scale, the southern provinces of Upper Nile and Bahr al-Ghazal have very low enrolment rates, even at primary level. This is partly due to the effects of the war, which has caused massive damage to schools and displaced large sections of the population out of the southern provinces. In Equatoria, which had not, at that point (1986–87), been much affected by the war, enrolments were higher.

However, even before the war erupted again in the early 1980s, education provision in the south was inadequate. Education was very limited during the colonial period, and mainly in the hands of missionaries. During the first period after independence, development was hampered by the first civil war, during which many schools were taken over by the army. After 1972 the semi-autonomous administration made efforts to rehabilitate and expand the system.

Table 9.3 **Sudan: school enrolment ratios, 1986–87 (percentages)**

Region	Primary education (age 7–12 years)		Intermediate education (age 13–15) years		Secondary education (age 16–18) years	
	Boys	Girls	Boys	Girls	Boys	Girls
All Sudan	65.5	45.9	31.3	25.5	19.4	13.9
Northern	98.7	93.8	67.8	69.1	42.3	37.7
Khartoum	77.3	67.5	65.3	64.0	42.9	44.6
Central	82.4	68.8	42.3	35.0	24.5	16.4
Eastern	58.5	39.1	26.1	20.9	15.2	9.9
Kordofan	60.3	35.3	26.6	20.2	17.1	9.7
Darfur	67.1	36.1	18.4	9.6	10.8	5.0
Upper Nile	45.0	13.2	9.3	3.4	5.6	1.2
Bahr al-Ghazal	15.9	6.7	5.9	2.1	4.9	1.5
Equatoria	78.5	52.3	20.1	8.4	14.0	4.1

Source: Ministry of Education statistics 1986/7

Demand continued to outstrip supply. Many schools were established by communities on a self-help basis, with the intention of handing them over to the government. However, the regional government could not afford to take them over, so many of these community schools were overcrowded, under-funded, with too few, and untrained teachers. Discontent with the system, and with the perceived discrimination against the south compared with the north, led to considerable politicization of secondary and tertiary education in the southern regions from the late 1970s onwards. Students protested at the lack of facilities, and teachers at not being paid regularly. Especially in the south, teachers are very badly paid and generally held in low esteem.

Since the civil war began again in the early 1980s, the education system has virtually collapsed in regions like Bahr al-Ghazal, where the fighting has been most intense. Many schools have been destroyed or the students have fled, and these areas suffer from severe shortages of funds, bureaucratic inefficiencies and the difficulties of transport and communications caused by the war. The low enrolments in the western provinces of Darfur and Kordofan probably reflect the effects of the drought which has caused millions of people to leave their homes.

These disparities in regional enrolment levels reflect deeper inequalities in the distribution of income, wealth and essential services. The persistent pattern of inequality in economic, social and educational services has contributed to the widening gaps between regions. It has also encouraged rural–urban migration as rural areas suffered severely from worsening economic conditions during the 1980s.

There are also significant differences in levels of enrolment between male and female students. In predominantly rural areas these discrepancies are most marked, reflecting a low social valuation of education for girls. Although enrolment levels for both sexes have increased, girls' enrolments at all grades remain significantly below those of boys. In the Northern region the discrepancies are not so wide, and overall enrolments are much higher at all levels. In the Khartoum region, female enrolment outstripped that of males at secondary school level, though women make up only a small proportion of students in the technical secondary schools.

The general picture, however, is that girls, especially outside the main towns, have limited opportunities to pursue their education. Furthermore, most schools are segregated by sex, and the building of boys' schools has historically taken precedence over building girls' schools.

It is not just discrepancies in enrolments which are significant, but the ability of children to remain at school and profit from their education. The figures for wastage rates between levels of education reproduce much the same patterns between different regions and between the sexes. Even by the conventional measure of success in education – pass rates in final examination results at each level – these differences are clear. In the Khartoum and Northern regions, in 1986/87 pass rates at both primary and intermediate levels were around 70 per cent for both boys and girls. In the west (Kordofan and Darfur) and the parts of the south for which any figures were available in 1986/87 (for some areas no figures were available because of the war) the average pass rate was below 50 per cent. Girls' results were consistently poorer than those of boys. While examination results alone do not tell us much about the nature of the educational crisis, they are useful indicators of the extent of the problem: undoubtedly school conditions and the situation of teachers have affected their outcomes.

Relatively few students reach secondary school, with a substantial proportion of these being in the Khartoum and Northern regions. During the 1980s, there has been a marked decline in the proportion of secondary students who gain the Sudan School Certificate which enables them to go on to higher education or enter the civil service. Between 1982/83 and 1986/87, in government schools the success rate dropped from almost 80 per cent to 70 per cent; in private and community schools from 40 to 30 per cent; and in technical education from 60 to 55 per cent. Only 5 to 10 per cent of successful candidates get university places, and in the present economic climate employment in the civil service is not particularly attractive. Only for the wealthy is there the option of paying to send their children abroad for university education.

Another major problem for graduates at all levels is the lack of job opportunities: for example, there are now 20,000 university graduates unemployed in Sudan, and for school graduates too there are few opportunities in the formal sector. As in other countries with severe economic problems, there are large numbers of people trying to make a living through informal work.

Unequal educational gains have further increased social and economic inequalities between regions and classes and have contributed to ethnic and political tensions. The costs of war, and the displacement of some 3.5 million people inside the country's borders, have disrupted the social and institutional structures of education.

Notes

1. *Tempo*, 19 April 1981, quoted in Johnston (1989), p.148.
2. Frieling (1987); Table A15; Government of Mozambique (1988).
3. Unicef (1989), pp.18 and 36.
4. ibid, pp.11–12.
5. ibid, p.17.
6. Frelimo (1989), p.10.
7. ibid, p.2.
8. Unicef (1989), p.16.
9. ibid, p.17.
10. Frelimo (1989), p.10.
11. Johnston *et al.* (1987), p.11.
12. Marshall (1988), p.17.
13. Johnston *et al.* (1987), p.16.
14. Frieling (1987).
15. Hermele (1988), pp.19–20.
16. Frelimo (1989), p.10.
17. Archer and Costello (1990), p.53.
18. Government of Nicaragua (1987), p.36.
19. Interview with John Bevan of WUS(UK), 1989.

Education as the arena of conflict: El Salvador, Guatemala, Honduras, South Africa and Namibia

Finally, we come to a group of countries in which state policy on education is not only constrained by external economic and political pressures but also starkly reflects the priorities of a small and exclusive élite. Debt and economic difficulties are less significant than political priorities in determining access to education. In El Salvador, Guatemala and Honduras, education is simply not available to substantial portions of the population, particularly the rural poor and those who are not part of the majority Spanish-speaking culture. In South Africa under apartheid, education has been designed specifically to socialize the mass of the population into accepting an inferiority based on race and class. In the political and military conflicts which have arisen as a result of these inequalities, education is not merely a casualty of war but is part of the battlefield.

Education and repression in Central America

In Guatemala and El Salvador, education cannot be separated from political struggles for a number of reasons. First, the inequalities of the system lead to demands for more and better education for the majority of their peoples; second, the authorities often regard education as a direct threat to their domination so that teachers, academics and indeed books are targets of repression and censorship. All parties in the conflict regard education in its broadest sense as part of an ideological battleground. In Honduras, the levels of conflict are not as high, but the society as a whole suffers a similar pattern of inequality. It is the poorest of the three countries and suffers from inadequate social services, political repression and an economy heavily dependent on the export of one crop – bananas – controlled mainly by foreign companies.

In all three countries, the root of the problem is a highly unequal system of land distribution. This has persisted despite limited land reform programmes in El Salvador and Honduras. One outcome of these severe inequalities, sustained over many years by a small privileged élite, has been that opponents of these regimes have resorted to armed struggle.

El Salvador

In El Salvador, land hunger has been exacerbated by the tiny size of the country in relation to its population. Despite a land reform initiative in the early 1980s, rural society remains polarized. There is also a long tradition of migration, mostly to the United States, as people seek a better life and an escape from poverty and land hunger. Money sent home has become an important source of income for the country – especially from those who live in the United States and send remittances to their families in dollars.

Poverty in El Salvador

The majority of Salvadoreans, 68.1 per cent in 1980, were estimated to live in a state of poverty, unable to meet their basic needs. Social services have now diminished even further because of the war and the crisis since 1979. Since that time, the main economic indicators show an economy in decline. The growth of GDP, which had averaged 5.4 per cent annual growth in the first half of the 1970s and 0.8 per cent between 1975 and 1980, went into reverse, dropping on average 5.7 per cent a year over the period from 1981 to 1988. Per capita GDP fell, on average, 3.8 per cent annually from 1981 to 1984 and scarcely reached zero growth in the latter part of the 1980s. At the same time, inflation began to climb after 1984 and the average minimum wage fell more than 25 per cent in the first half of the 1980s.

The last ten years have brought into the open the struggle between the oligarchy, supported by the United States, and a substantial section of the population, represented not only by the armed opposition FMLN but by trade unions, popular organizations, women's groups, Christian base communities and the liberal intelligentsia. In this brutal war, it is estimated that some 60,000 civilians were killed up to 1989, before the 1989 to 1990 round of fighting which is thought to have claimed over a thousand lives. An estimated 7,000 people have 'disappeared' after being seized by the army and right-wing death squads. Torture has been widely used by both security forces and death squads. Up to a quarter of the population has either been displaced or has left the country since 1980.

Although death-squad activities became less widespread during the period of President Duarte's government in the mid-1980s, they did not cease entirely. After the elections of 1988 brought the ultra right-wing Arena party to power, a new wave of kidnappings and murders began. The most widely publicized was the murder of six Jesuit academics from the University of Central America in November 1989. Both the security forces and the death squads have renewed their campaign of intimidation against trade unions and popular organizations which had begun to regroup and regain influence during the Duarte period. Another major target has been the National University of El Salvador (UES), long regarded by the right wing as a 'subversive' institution. It was closed for four years from 1980 to 1984, with the army occupying the campus, and since then has struggled to continue its academic work.

During 1988 and 1989, according to Amnesty International, the pattern of unacknowledged arrests, abductions and murders of students, academics and other staff has been renewed. An evident aim of the right wing is not merely the intimidation of individuals but also the discrediting of the two major independent universities as educational institutions. Given that the UES mainly caters for the most impecunious students who reach university level, the interruption of its work also affects those who have no alternative access to higher education.

Guatemala: the lowest 'quality of life'

According to a 1982 Unicef study, no other central American country is poorer than Guatemala in terms of the combined indicators of the infant mortality rate, life expectancy and literacy rates. It concluded that Guatemala had the lowest 'physical quality of life index in Central America and the third lowest in the whole of Latin America after Haiti and Bolivia'. In 1985, according to the State Planning Council (SEGEPLAN), 86 per cent of families were living below the official poverty line and 55 per cent were extremely poor.[1]

Despite the development of industry in the 1960s and 1970s, the country is still highly dependent on export crops grown on *latifundia* (large estates) run by a small élite. Ninety per cent of farms are seven hectares or less and 54 per cent are plots of less than 1.4 hectares, described by one writer as 'the size of a grave'. It is impossible for families living on such plots to make a living. They sell their labour to the *latifundia* at harvest time, usually for very low wages.

Guatemala

In Guatemala too, the 1980s marked a high point of repression in a political conflict which has been going on for the best part of thirty years. The government's policy of counter-insurgency against the guerrilla movement in the early 1980s led to large-scale killings of sections of the indigenous Indian population (*indígenas*) and Spanish-speaking (*ladino*) peasants who sympathized with them. The result of this unequal and little-publicized war was estimated at 50,000 dead, the displacement of 300,000 into 'model villages' in 'development poles' (another version of 'strategic hamlets') and some 300,000 refugees outside the country.

Death squads, in which the army and security forces have been implicated, reappeared in the late 1980s, despite the election of a civilian government in 1986. According to Amnesty International, human rights abuses have intensified since a series of abortive coup attempts by the army starting in May 1988.

The targets of these attacks, beatings, kidnappings and murders have been trade unionists, peasants (especially those involved in campaigns for land redistribution and resistance to recruitment into civil defence patrols) and Indians who have given themselves up to the army and been taken to resettlement areas after years of living in hiding in the mountains. Academics and students have also been victims. The University of San Carlos has long been regarded as a hotbed of opposition, and the list of those imprisoned, tortured and murdered is long, even since 1986. Members of the School of Agronomy who have been accused of being too sympathetic with the problems and plight of the *campesinos* (peasant farmers) have been particularly targeted. The Archbishop of Guatemala, Prospero Penados del Barrio, declared that the assassination of seven students by death squads in 1988 showed that the country was living by the 'law of the jungle' despite the supposed democratization of political life.

On 6 July 1988, Buadilio Aguilar Dardón, an 18-year-old secondary school student in Guatemala City was detained on his way to school. He then 'disappeared'. His 'disappearance' occurred in the context of several days of school strikes called by the co-ordinating committee of secondary school students. The students were calling for the restoration of school buildings damaged during the 1976 earthquake in Guatemala and a subsequent tremor in May 1988. The co-ordinating committee reported that students participating in the strikes had been receiving death threats. Because of this, Buadilio Aguilar's family believe that the security forces were responsible for his disappearance.

During the same series of school strikes, the Guatemalan newspaper *El Gráfico* reported that students at the Instituto Normal Central para Varones (Central Boys' School) had been taken into their school by security agents and severely beaten. In interviews with foreign journalists, students at the Institute confirmed this version of events.

Teachers supporting their local community's campaigns have also been subject to death threats. Amilcar Méndez Urizar, a school teacher from El Quiché, a predominantly Indian area, had helped local peasants to file petitions against serving in the ostensibly voluntary civil defence patrols. In 1988, he received a death threat at his home with a skull and cross-bones reading, 'It's just a question of time and opportunity, but we'll get you.' He received numerous other threats and was often followed by men he could identify as members of the local Treasury Police (part of the security police).[2]

Indigenous communities in Guatemala, which make up between 60 and 75 per cent of the total population, form an underclass. They live predominantly in the mountains, in conditions even worse than those of Spanish-speaking peasants. The brutal suppression of the insurrection of the early 1980s was not an isolated incident. During this century, Indians have had their communal lands broken up, forcing the majority to become migrant labourers in the coastal areas for at least part of the year, in conditions often approaching serfdom. Forced labour was not abolished until the 1940s.

Their access to education is even more limited than that of the rural population generally. There are some twenty-two indigenous Indian languages spoken in these communities, and the government has made little effort to support education in these mother tongues. It has, for the most part, imposed Spanish language and culture and discouraged expressions of indigenous cultures. Even where communities have got together to build a school themselves, under an agreement with the government, they have sometimes had to wait years before the government sends teachers to staff it.

When teachers are sent, most of them are *ladinos*, as relatively few teachers from the indigenous communities are trained. The *ladinos* teach mostly in Spanish and have little or no grasp of the languages or culture of their pupils. This is not to say that mother-tongue teaching in these circumstances, where there are a number of different languages, is necessarily the solution at all levels of education. But the underlying issue is the overall lack of respect for indigenous concerns and culture manifested by the government and the *ladino* élite. Among some indigenous groups there is also resistance to any kind of integration with *ladino* society which means denying their own culture and becoming 'Spanish'. In the meantime, the vast majority of Indian children either do not go to school or do not reach the end of primary school. The indigenous peoples have 'always been the instruments of labour and of production, but not the recipients of social benefits from the government'.[3]

Some efforts at literacy work have been made by church groups and by the government, but they only deal with a tiny fraction of the problem. As far as the government is concerned, such efforts seem to be too little, too late: the traumas of many years have created strong suspicion and resistance to any state interventions. According to the 1981 census, 46.5 per cent of the population over the age of seventeen was illiterate. In the rural departments with predominantly Indian populations – for example, Quiché and Alta Verapaz – illiteracy rose to 78 per cent. These percentages are not based on functional literacy but on the most rudimentary writing skills.[4]

Since the counter-insurgency campaigns of the early 1980s, the country has become highly militarized, and those indigenous groups which have returned from hiding or exile after the destruction of their homes and villages have been strictly controlled. The new 'model villages', into which substantial numbers of Indians have been resettled, are closely supervised by the army. Facilities such as schools and health posts have been built in most such villages, but are said to be poorly stocked and staffed. Some families are reluctant to send children to these schools and other children are obliged to work in order to help support their families. Most of these villages have little access to land, are not self-sufficient and rely heavily on food aid and food-for-work programmes. Both Catholic and evangelical churches (particularly those based in the United States) have given economic aid to villages, particularly in the Ixil 'development pole'. It seems that those who become active evangelicals stand a better chance of obtaining housing materials and educational opportunities for their children.

In the Ixcán region of Quiché province, the army has permitted the re-establishment of co-operatives first set up in the 1970s. It intervenes in and supervises every aspect of the co-operatives' running and organization. As Manz observed:

It is not up to the villagers what programs will be organized. The education delegate, for example, cannot promote an adult education programme similar to a late 1970s programme that included subjects such as the political and social history of Guatemala; Indian movements, leadership training; human rights, legal rights; agrarian structure, etc.[5]

In the rural areas, the 'civil patrols' have the job of hunting insurgents and controlling the new settlements. There are severe penalties, especially for *indígenas*, for avoiding this service. Ironically, one requirement to become a civil patrol commander, directly accountable to the army for keeping the community in line, is literacy.

Honduras

Honduras has not experienced levels of upheaval and violence comparable to Guatemala and El Salvador in the 1980s. However, its involvement in the conflict in Nicaragua, acting as the main host country to the Contras, has attracted a good deal of US aid and military personnel and has led to the increasing militarization of society. The education sector has not been isolated from these trends. The authorities have increasingly interfered in school curricula, repressed student and teacher organizations, and promoted new organizations favourable to the Nicaraguan Contras. The teachers unions, the largest and most influential of which is COLPROSUMAH, were among the most combative trade unions in the country until the early 1980s. Since that time, it has suffered repression from the government and military authorities. In 1982 the Honduran government effectively took control of COLPROSUMAH by giving official recognition to a small splinter group. The move, condemned by the International Labour Organization, led to a dispute which lasted through the decade. The genuine elected leadership of COLPROSUMAH was denied access to the union's headquarters and to the union's funds and dues, which the government passed to its puppet union.

Students' organizations were legalized in 1979 but banned again in 1987 after the murder of student leader Marion Adalberto Rosales. The conflict within the student body has reflected the growing political importance of the Contras and their supporters, who have formed their own student organization, Nicaragua Democratic Youth–Democratic Students Front (JDN–FED). It was a member of this group who was alleged to have shot Rosales. Despite the ban on student activity, in 1989 there were strikes and demonstrations against the government's new educational measures, which included raising the minimum pass mark and the elimination of courses in sociology, economics and political economy from the curriculum.

Economic crisis, conflict and schooling

The political repression and discrimination in access to education based on class, region and ethnic origin which characterizes these countries has been sharpened by economic recession. All three countries have at one time or another during the 1980s had recourse to the IMF for standby loans. In El Salvador and Guatemala, the disruptions of war have added to the problems.

El Salvador

The cycle of repression, political violence and civil war in El Salvador has had complex outcomes in economic terms. The war, and the relative success of the FMLN in hitting economic targets, has led to marked reductions in both agricultural and industrial production. These problems of themselves have increased inflation and indebtedness. For example, the country has not only suffered from unstable coffee prices, but also from a decline in production. Many factories are working at only a fraction of capacity.

However, in contrast to Nicaragua, where the economy has come close to collapse, in El Salvador both the additional costs of the war and increasing indebtedness have been counterbalanced by very large injections of aid from the United States. Since 1980, the economy, which has always been dependent on exports of a small range of agricultural products, especially coffee, has become highly dependent on US aid. This has equipped the army and paid much of the direct cost of the war. The combination of aid and money sent home from workers abroad has buffered the economy against world market pressures and prevented its collapse.

Aid has also allowed the government to maintain a minimum of services and infrastructure. For the United States, this has been part of its purpose as an aspect of counter-insurgency policy: to prevent the mass of the population defecting to the FMLN and its allies, and to deal with the social and economic costs of about half a million displaced persons.

El Salvador: aid feeds war effort

In El Salvador, official aid receipts almost trebled between 1981 and 1987, when the total reached US$426 million (US$86.4 per capita). Three-quarters of this aid came from the United States. From 1981 to 1985, US aid to El Salvador totalled US$1.7 billion, of which some 30 per cent was direct military aid; 44.1 per cent was economic assistance to prop up El Salvador's ailing economy, hard hit by the war; 10.5 per cent was food aid; and only 15.4 per cent went to development and governmental reform. By 1988, total US aid since 1981 had risen to some US$3 billion, with the pattern of allocations remaining much the same.[6] Education made up 22.5 per cent of development aid in 1985 and 17.5 per cent in 1987.[7] From 1989, the changing international political climate and the bad press following the murder by elements in the army of six Jesuit priests in December 1989 has led the US Congress to question more closely the level of support being given to the government of El Salvador.

Despite this assistance, and a temporary improvement in coffee prices, by 1989 the economy had not revived significantly and the country still had a substantial debt problem. In 1986, the Duarte government introduced the *Programa de Estabilización y Reactivación Económica* (PERE), which included devaluation, price hikes and temporary restrictions on imports. Soon after coming to power, the Arena government instituted a new round of 'stabilization' measures in 1989, including privatizations, currency devaluation and price hikes, particularly for public transport, which provoked a wave of popular discontent.

The education system reflects the polarization of society. Despite an expansion in access to education in the 1970s and reforms carried out in the 1960s and again in the late 1970s, the fundamental patterns of inequality have remained and have been accentuated by the war. Since 1980, education has been severely affected by the war, at times almost paralysed by it.

School closures have seriously affected educational provision. In 1979, 444 schools were closed; in 1981, 877; in 1983, 763; and in 1984, 653. The displacement of large numbers of rural dwellers to urban areas has increased overcrowding in urban schools. According to government figures, almost 60 per cent of all displaced persons in

1987 were concentrated in four departments: San Salvador, Morazán, Usulután and San Miguel. Almost 60 per cent of those displaced were reported to be under the age of eighteen. Of some 200,000 children displaced by the war, it is estimated that about 80,000 are not in school.

The situation was made worse by the 1986 earthquake, which exacerbated the housing shortage and destroyed or damaged numerous schools. For some schools in San Salvador, the government's subsequent 'repairs' consisted of simply knocking down walls which were damaged, leaving the school a mere shell.

El Salvador has a school population aged four to twelve of two million, but only 600,000 of these are served by public sector schools. Enrolments at both primary and secondary levels fell sharply in the early 1980s before beginning to rise steadily from 1984 onwards. Drop-out rates in rural areas are high, due to poverty and war. During the period of massive repression in 1980, rural drop-out rates were 40 to 50 per cent in each of the first six grades and 20 to 30 per cent in urban schools. By 1986, when the repression was more selective in character, urban retention levels were much higher, though 10 per cent or more of students were still dropping out in first, fifth and sixth grades. Rural drop-outs remained on average around 20 per cent, and 45 per cent at sixth grade.

Although government figures show adult illiteracy rates continuing to fall to below 30 per cent, the real rates are thought to be far higher than this. If functional illiteracy is taken into account, the total could be as high as 60 to 70 per cent. In the years since the present conflict began, resources devoted to the eradication of illiteracy have been grossly insufficient. During the period from 1980 to 1984, literacy programmes were reaching between 1.1 and 1.9 per cent of the illiterate population aged ten and above. The very limited results of these programmes have been ascribed to the lack of security for teaching personnel, especially in rural areas, and the suspicion and fear of potential learners.[8]

The intense conflict in the years from 1980 to 1982 led to many resignations among teachers, while many others asked for transfers. According to the Salvadorean Commission of Human Rights, between January 1980 and January 1981, 136 teachers were assassinated. Many teachers belonging to the teachers' union ANDES became actively involved in the struggle for political justice as well as for their own economic interests. Consequently many activist teachers have been forced to leave the country after threats to themselves and their families. The total numbers of teachers fell in the early 1980s and only began to pick up after 1983.

For those who remain, quite apart from political pressures, conditions in public sector schools are often discouraging. Official figures give average class sizes as forty to fifty, but it is reported that in the rural areas there are often seventy to eighty children in a class.

Even in urban schools, physical conditions are often difficult. According to one teacher in an urban school, 'there is no chalk, the blackboards are worn out, there aren't enough desks and the classrooms are not appropriate – some don't have glass in the windows so in winter teaching is practically impossible'.

Parallel to the state education sector are growing numbers of private schools and universities. Enrolments in the private sector have grown from under 14 per cent of total enrolments in 1984 to nearly 20 per cent in 1988. The private schools are for the élite, mostly in urban areas. The best of them have produced a small number of highly educated and skilled people. The majority, however, are not of very high quality, but the fees are beyond the reach of most Salvadoreans. This is also true of some thirty private universities which have sprung up in recent years. This means that at school level there are two worlds of education. The Dean of the Faculty of Humanities and Science at the University of El Salvador argues that,

because of the conflict which El Salvador is going through, the education system has been divided into two. One is the private sector, at the service of the governing and dominant class, which is to all intents and purposes closed to people who do not belong to the upper class. The other large sector is the public sector in which there isn't any exclusivity.

Expenditure on education has diminished as a proportion of public expenditure, falling from 20 per cent in 1979 to 13.7 per cent in 1984, then rising to 17.8 per cent in 1988. Defence spending for the same years was 12.7 per cent, 24.2 per cent and 28.2 per cent respectively. In 1981, there was a reorganization of the educational structure involving decentralization of funding to regional 'nuclei'. However, since the scheme was implemented in very unfavourable political circumstances and at a time when overall resources for education were shrinking, its impact was limited.

In public sector schools in the late 1980s, shortages of government funding were bringing pressures to charge fees. A communal representative explains:

One of the problems is that there are teachers who do not have a salary fixed by the Ministry of Education and sometimes this salary is made up from fees paid by the parents since the Ministry argues that they don't receive a sufficient subsidy to pay the teachers. So we see that if you have a school that goes up to the ninth grade, the Ministry covers the costs up to the sixth grade but the other years are paid for by parents.

A teacher from an urban school in the Soyapango region gave her perspective:

As the economic crisis has got worse, the attention the government has given to education has got less to the point where instead of opening schools they are closing some of them, because – so they say – they can't pay the teachers' salaries. The war situation has also had an influence in the deterioration of education because there are places – especially in the rural areas – where there hasn't been any normality in schools for years.

Guatemala

In Guatemala, economic growth went into reverse in the first half of the 1980s. GDP per capita, already low, slumped to the level of the early 1970s, with negative growth rates persisting from 1981 to 1987. Guatemala turned to the IMF for assistance with its debt problems in 1983 and agreed a standard package of stabilization measures, including government expenditure cuts and the privatization of several public sector enterprises. Open urban unemployment increased five-fold between 1981 and 1986, and 45 per cent of the working population did not have a permanent or full-time job. For those with jobs, salaries remained at the 1980 level until 1985, while inflation rose. For example, the price of the main staples, beans and maize, increased three-fold in 1985. Among the most vulnerable sections of the population, these trends have been accompanied by high infant mortality and morbidity, poor housing, high levels of illiteracy and children working from a very early age.

The combination of economic crisis with government discrimination and neglect is reflected in the education system. In 1986, there were an estimated 10,000 teachers without jobs and 800,000 school children without classrooms. The proportion of GDP devoted to education is the lowest in Central America: 1.4 per cent in 1986, down from 1.8 in 1980. This is lower even than El Salvador with 2.5 per cent, and 4 to 5 per cent for other Central American countries in 1986.

In 1987, the coverage at primary level was 62.02 per cent. The situation is more acute in the rural areas when only 32 per cent of the population aged seven to fourteen years are enrolled at school. At secondary level (*nivel medio*) the coverage in 1987 was 20.97 per cent. Added to this are the high repetition and drop-out rates. In Indian communities particularly, whole families sometimes migrate in search of employment. This affects the education of children as well as literacy classes and other types of non-formal education for adults.

Guatemala has relied heavily on external aid, especially from the United States, though this was suspended for a time under the Carter administration because of Guatemala's human rights record. However, it has since been resumed, with a strong emphasis on political stabilization. The level of US aid is not on the scale of that provided for El Salvador, but it has still risen six-fold since the beginning of the 1980s to US$82 million in 1986. USAID, the World Food Programme, and the UN have funded food donations to the army-controlled model villages set up after the uprising in the highlands in the early 1980s.

Honduras

In Honduras, the pressures of a growing debt crisis built up in the late 1980s. A 1988 loan agreed with the World Bank was suspended when the government resisted devaluation of the national currency, the lempira. However, other austerity measures have been imposed which have checked spending on education. The most obvious problem is the shortage of school places to meet demand, particularly at secondary level. Large numbers of teachers are unemployed, not because they are not needed, but because the government does not provide funds to employ more teachers. In 1989, the Minister of Education, Elisa Valle de Martinez, acknowledged that there were some 6,000 teachers out of work. She added that 80 per cent of the annual education budget was spent on teachers' salaries. While many schools did not have a full complement of teachers, the Ministry was unable to create new posts for lack of funds.

At primary level, official figures claim a gross enrolment ratio of over 90 per cent, but drop-out levels continue to be very high in rural areas. Some 40 per cent of primary schools are 'incomplete': that is, they do not cover all six grades. The vast majority of these incomplete schools are in rural areas where classes are also large – the teachers' union COLPROSUMAH claims that in some rural schools there are up to 120 children in a classroom. Teachers have to cope with multi-grade classes with little in the way of materials and books. As one rural teacher recounted: 'Most of us have to teach six grades on our own in one room. In my case, I've got a 16-year-old in the first grade.'[9] In some cases, schools are closed for two or three days a month while the teachers travel to the capital to collect their pay.

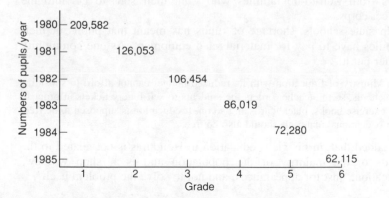

Figure 10.1 **Drop-outs from a primary school cohort 1980–85**
Source: NUT/WUS (1988) *Less Arms, more Education*, p.18

At secondary level, about 36 per cent of the age group (fourteen to nineteen years) is in school. In line with the pressures towards privatization within the economy as a whole, the state is increasingly ceding its role as provider of education, especially at secondary level, to the private sector. Private schools, however, are only to be found in the urban areas, which further lessens the chances of secondary schooling for rural children. The table below shows that private and semi-official schools far outnumber state-run schools at secondary level. But the number of students per school in the state sector is considerably greater than in the private sector.[10]

Table 10.1 **Honduras: Public and Private Schools (secondary schools) 1985**

Status	No. of schools	Total no. of students
State	80	80,021
Semi-official	20	19,358
Private	212	75,379

Source: Department of Education, CONSUPLANE, Honduras

In the private sector, there is little control over fees and curricula, and standards are very variable. In this very poor country, private school fees are beyond the means of much of the population. However, for families who can afford to pay the fees, the poor record of state schools makes private education seem attractive, even if in reality its quality is poor. There is also a small sector of very expensive élite schools which teach in Spanish and English, used mainly by upper and upper-middle class families who aspire to send their children abroad to university. The 1980s have also seen the development of four military schools run by the army but privately financed. They offer a few scholarships but are mainly attended by boys from well-to-do families who want their sons to get into the officer corps.

In state schools, shortage of funds has meant that pupils or their families have to pay for materials and equipment. As one community leader put it:

The Ministry of Education with its reduced budget cannot afford to subsidize the schools, so the teacher orders the students to sell lottery tickets in order to buy exercise books, blackboards and so on. If education is supposed to be free, then educational materials should also be free.

He added that, in his view, education in Honduras is not geared to the needs of the majority of the population and is a 'shop window' education: 'just for appearances, and not to solve the problem itself'.

South Africa: education and the ideology of apartheid

Change is at last on the horizon in South Africa, but its outcome and the effects on its neighbours are not yet clear. However, any new government will be faced with the legacy of a distorted education system and the need to find new strategies – as well as major financial investment – to change it. In Namibia, the newly independent government is already facing this challenge. The effects of forty years of apartheid ideology and hundreds of years of racial discrimination on South African society have been reflected and reproduced in its education system. Education has become part of the political battleground, and its transformation into a non-racial system can only be part of a much broader transformation of society.

Since the National Party came to power in South Africa in 1948, the education system has been one of the principal instruments through which the apartheid system has been sustained and perpetuated. At an ideological level, the purposes of segregated education systems were spelled out in the Bantu Education Act of 1953, which created an education proclaimed to be 'appropriate' to the limited prospects for black people under apartheid. Meanwhile, Christian National Education was designed to fit white people to remain rulers and to enhance their belief in their moral and racial superiority.

In practice, this meant the maintenance of separate and unequal schools giving whites and blacks two different types of education, with great differences in quality and access. Provision for the two other groups defined under South Africa's system of racial categorization, the 'Coloureds' (people of mixed race) and Asians, was also separate. Though marginally better in quality than that provided for the black population, their education fell far short of that which was provided in privileged white schools. Grossly disproportionate amounts of money per pupil for each system reinforced these differences. In 1960/61, expenditure per capita for black education at all levels was 12 rand, compared with 158 rand for each white pupil (calculated in 1988 rand).[11] Economically, these systems fed into largely distinct labour markets. Until the 1970s, at least, whites retained a virtual monopoly on skilled labour by means of a system of job reservation.

On the economic front, changes in the economy and labour needs since the 1970s have been among the factors encouraging modification of this rigid system. None the less, the changes in 'Bantu education' have not fundamentally altered its status as education for inferiority and subservience. Since the 1970s, however, fewer and fewer black, Asian or Coloured people have been willing to accept this separate and unequal provision.

Because of its pivotal role in sustaining the apartheid system, education has always been a central political issue, and is perceived by all parties to the conflict as a terrain over which political struggle occurs. In the 1950s, one focus of black resistance was the Bantu Education Act, along with the other legal structures of apartheid. However, civil protest was pushed underground in the 1960s after the Sharpeville massacre and the banning of the African National Congress (ANC) and other anti-apartheid organizations.

Education was also at the centre of the revival of resistance to apartheid in the 1970s. The most striking instance was the 1976 Soweto uprising which was sparked off by secondary school pupils' opposition to the authorities' insistence that they learn certain subjects in Afrikaans, viewed by most black people as the language of the oppressor. (In contrast, the Coloured population of Cape Province regard Afrikaans as their language and have used it to express their radical sentiments.) In this battle, secondary schools and their students were on the front line. This set the tone for the 1980s, when, despite successive draconian states of emergency, both secondary schools and universities have played a major part in challenging the government. By the mid-1980s, confrontations were not confined to major urban centres, but were occurring in most parts of the country.

Since the Soweto uprising, some reforms of the system have taken place, in response partly to this political pressure but partly also to the changing nature of the South African economy. All but the far right have acknowledged the need to develop a more skilled workforce, since whites can no longer fill the demand. The Department of Education and Training (DET) has consequently implemented some changes, including reform of language policy, development of training facilities (though many of these are financed by industry and capital, not by the state) and a marked increase in investment in the African school system.

In the 1980s, sections of the ruling party have also adopted a strategy of attempting to co-opt or at least pacify the small black middle class. This has principally meant providing more access to consumer goods and services, such as education, while continuing to deny any section of the black population access to political decision-making, or fundamentally changing the economic order.

Given the extreme paucity of provision in the past, to close rather than merely narrow the gap between white education provision and that of other racially defined groups would require an investment well beyond anything that was envisaged before the 1990s. Leaving aside the question of a total reform of the education system, it is estimated that to provide all children with roughly the same standard of provision as white children have now would entail at least doubling or trebling the education budget.

DET expenditure on black education has certainly risen very significantly during the 1980s, with per capita expenditure for all educational levels rising from 176 rand per pupil (1988 rand) in 1980/81 to 595 rand in 1987/88, though much of this increase had been taken up by the rising bill for teachers' salaries. By the second half of the 1980s, total spending on African education had exceeded that for whites for the first time, though Africans make up 70 per cent of the population and whites only 17 per cent. In the homelands, black education is even more under-funded than under DET jurisdiction. The per capita expenditure in homeland schools in 1987/88 was lower than that in DET schools – with Kwazulu, for example, spending only 412 rand per pupil. Between 1988/89 and 1989/90, there was a further nominal increase in expenditure on all African education departments (including so-called independent homelands) of 20 per cent. However, with inflation running at nearly 13 per cent, the increase in real terms was much lower.[11]

The fragmented structure of South African education

A major difficulty in assessing how far these changes have actually affected conditions in South African schools is the way in which the education system is structured. There are no less than seventeen ethnically based departments of education, eleven of which deal with the black population. These are the Department of Education and Training (DET), responsible for providing education to African children living in 'white designated areas'; the departments responsible for education in the so-called 'self-governing states' or bantustans/homelands (Kwazulu, Lebowa, Gazankulu, Kangwane, Kwandebele and Qwaqwa); and finally there are Ministries of Education in the so-called 'independent states' of Transkei, Bophuthatswana, Ciskei and Venda, whose 'independence' is recognized only by the South African government. Most of these homelands are not even single stretches of territory, but are formed from a series of pockets of land interspersed among white areas. In addition, there are four departments for white education based on provincial divisions, plus separate departments for Coloured and Asian education.

Table 10.2 **South Africa: expenditure on education by race (millions of rand)**

	Africans	Coloureds	Indians	Whites	Total
1975	131 (17%)	89 (11%)	39 (5%)	536 (67%)	795 (100%)
1976	156	103	44	646	948
1977	191	133	56	816	1,196
1978	110	144	61	877	1,192
1979	245*	179	75	1,000	1,498
1980	305* (18%)	175 (10%)	83 (5%)	1,116 (67%)	1,679 (100%)
1981	298	247	123	1,361	2,029
1982	557*	294	155	1,688	2,695
1983	755*	405	196	2,056	3,413
1984	1,224	451	225	2,032	3,932
1985	1,460	571	259	2,456	4,755
1987/88	3,400 (42%)	1,007 (12%)	404 (5%)	3.320 (41%)	8,131 (100%)

* Excluding 'Homelands'

Source: Survey of Race Relations

These figures also have to be seen in the context of a rapid rise in demand and enrolments, despite the fact that black education is neither free nor compulsory, and expenditure is not keeping up with need. Black population growth is not particularly high compared with other African countries – 2.39 per cent annually from 1980 to 1986 – but this still means a growing demand for school places. In the late 1980s, this demand has been much increased by the partial return to school of those who were out of school or sent away to rural areas during the school boycotts and political turmoil of the late 1970s and early 1980s. The increase in secondary school enrolments in DET schools has far outstripped the rate of population increase.

Despite some expansion of the system, classes are still very large, on average forty or more, and facilities are overstretched. In 1988 and 1989, increasing numbers of secondary school students found them- selves excluded from school on a variety of pretexts, including failing their matriculation exams and political activism (see Chapter 13).

According to Sheila Sisulu of the South African Council of Churches, the DET's strategy has largely involved shifting resources from place to place rather than substantially expanding the system. While they build schools or refurbish classrooms in one place, they are cutting teachers' posts in another, despite evident need. Since 1987–88, the state has, for the first time, been responsible for providing stationery and textbooks, which previously parents had been expected to pay for. However, experience around the country suggests that materials arrive late in the school term or not at all.

After years of political repression, the education system has little credibility with those it is supposed to serve. Even for those who reach the last year of secondary school, only about 50 per cent pass the matriculation exam, and only a handful achieve the higher grade of 'matric exemption' which is required for university entrance. The exam itself has been the subject of considerable dispute, with accusations that not only is the marking inconsistent and some of the markers corrupt, but that the DET and the homelands education authorities frequently 'move the goalposts' by altering the pass levels year by year.

The segregated nature of the educational system remains the same as ever, with only a few private schools taking pupils of all races. For example, with the white population growing at less than 1 per cent per year between 1980 and 1986, many white schools have suffered dramatic falls in enrolments. Since 1979, 196 primary schools and seven secondary schools have actually closed. These facilities have not been for the most part made available to children of other races. New legislation will allow for a local vote on desegregation of individual areas. However, a change would be subject to the agreement of over 70 per cent of parents.

Two days after the unbanning of the ANC in February 1990, the minister in charge of black education, Stoffel van der Merwe, announced that more money would be made available to the black education system. He said it would take some time to redress the imbalance in spending on black and white children when five times as much is still spent on each white child as on each black child. However, he told a press conference that for deeply ingrained historical and cultural reasons, to integrate black and white school systems now would risk chaos in the education field as well as political and economic instability: 'One would probably increase the potential for conflict in the white community if eventually white education is controlled by anyone else but white people themselves.'[12]

Furthermore, the reforms which had been implemented up to 1990 did not emerge from discussions between the communities concerned and the government but have been imposed from above. Even specific changes which are beneficial at the educational level may be regarded with suspicion because of the political context in which they were made.

Unequal access

The political conflict in black secondary schools, especially in urban areas, has attracted attention to their very considerable problems. However, segregated education has failed to provide even basic primary education for many black South Africans. The majority of all black pupils are enrolled at primary level: 78 per cent of all enrolments in the DET's jurisdiction (compared with 56 per cent of all white enrolments). Drop-outs in the first years of primary education remain very high. Only 77 per cent of children enrolled in the first grade (Standard Sub-A – SSA) in 1985 survived into the second year (Standard Sub-B – SSB), little better than the 74 per cent of 1966. It seems that drop-outs at this early stage have remained a serious problem, particularly in rural areas, though there has been some improvement in the retention rates over the whole primary cycle (SSA to Standard Five).[13]

In 1986, official figures put the proportion of black South Africans over twenty without any education at all at 37.4 per cent (not including those in 'independent' homelands). With the addition of the large numbers of children and teenagers who have had only a few years of schooling, rates of illiteracy of well over 50 per cent seem entirely credible (see Chapter 16).

During the 1980s, however, there have been very marked changes in the levels of secondary school enrolment, even allowing for political disruptions. Between 1980 and 1987, overall enrolment in primary and secondary school increased by 42 per cent. However, the increase in SSA enrolments was 24 per cent, only just keeping up with population growth, whereas in the final matriculation year (Standard Ten), the increase was 327 per cent.[14] While the absolute numbers reaching this level are still relatively small, the rapid growth in secondary school enrolments does reflect the relative expansion in the availability of skilled and semi-skilled jobs, especially in urban areas, which has already been referred to.

South Africa is a large and complex country where conditions in one place cannot be generalized to those in another. For example, drop-out rates are not spread evenly on a regional basis. The problem of primary school drop-outs is particularly serious in rural areas and on white farms within the jurisdiction of the DET. Though whites make up only 17 per cent of the population, they control the most fertile farming areas.

Within the designated white areas live the black workers and their families who provide the labour on commercial farms. In educational terms they have remained in a kind of limbo. On white farms, the children of resident farm workers receive schooling only if the farmer is prepared to build a school and take ultimate responsibility for its management. Until recently the DET provided 50 per cent of the cost of building (75 per cent from 1988 onwards) and water supply, but no other infrastructure, and paid the teachers. There is no compulsion on the farmer to provide education at all. As a result, by the time the DET did a survey of farm schooling in 1986, only 3 per cent of the total of 5,782 farm schools offered education for more than seven grades, and 21 per cent did not offer education beyond four grades. Only forty-nine farm schools had secondary classes, of which no more than five went up to Standard Seven (nine school grades) and nation-wide there was only one full secondary farm school.

Consequently, many farm children have never been to school. Of those who do attend, many do not go until the age of eight or nine because the schools cannot fit them in. Classes are crowded, with 40 per cent of schools having a teacher–pupil ratio of 45:1 or higher, and many schools have multi-grade classes.

The DET has proposed a number of measures to upgrade farm schools. However, while they remain in the hands of farmers, and while agricultural workers are completely dependent on their employers not only for their jobs but also for housing and education, there can be little hope of real improvement or of community involvement.[15]

In the past, children could be compelled to work on the farm, thus effectively denying them schooling. This has now been made illegal. But with this kind of education, these children's prospects are poor. Angie Romorola of the National Education Crisis Committee (NECC) recalls interviewing children on white farms about how they saw their future. Farmers often warned them of how violent and unpleasant life in urban townships could be, and said it was better to stay in the country. But as one child said, unless you can find another sort of job (not on the farm), education is no use for farm work. Here, he said 'we're all just like mealies [corn cobs] in a sack'.

In the townships within white-designated urban areas, opportunities to go to school are greater, at least at primary level. But the combination of poor school facilities, extreme political tensions in schools and in townships, constant repression and security force interference, recent exclusions of children from school and scepticism about the value of 'Bantu education' all contribute to high drop-outs and low achievement, especially at secondary level. In many areas, there were sustained disruptions of schooling, especially during school boycotts in many areas in the early 1980s. In Natal, the severe disruptions caused in the townships by conflict between supporters of Inkatha and the United Democratic Front (UDF) have meant that many children have lost years of school.

Indian and Coloured schooling has, on the whole, been better than the African system, but again, in the 'white' rural areas there are pockets of severe deprivation. For example, in rural Cape Province, especially in the famous wine-growing areas, there are groups of Coloured workers who still live in semi-feudal conditions similar to those found among black workers on white farms in other parts of the country.

The 'homelands' are, for the most part, over-populated, over-grazed, and impoverished. Apart from their resident populations, over the years they have served as a 'dumping ground' for people forcibly removed by the South African government from 'white' areas. These areas are dependent on South Africa economically, and are run by local political élites dependent on South African support, frequently with corrupt administrations. The standard of living is low, and services limited. The original goal of South Africa's bantustan policy was to create segregated reserves of cheap labour for factories, farms and services in the adjoining white areas. Today there is still little local employment except in the 'homelands' administrations. Migrant remittances from those who work in white areas are a major source of income. The government's policy of dividing the different ethnic groups among the African population has in some cases encouraged particularist nationalisms, nowhere more so than in Kwazulu, where the 'Zulu nationalism' of the Inkatha movement has contributed to a polarization of black society in Natal, with highly detrimental effects on the education system and on the lives of young people (Chapter 13).

The school systems, decentralized to puppet 'homelands' governments, are of even poorer quality than those provided by the DET. However, administrative separation from South Africa has not necessarily meant that homeland education departments are entirely autonomous. The DET, says Taylor,

exerts a strong indirect influence on the other ten African departments, all of these having been established by the DET or one of its predecessors before being granted 'independence'. Not only were the structures and systems of these departments inherited from Pretoria, but the genealogy of their staffing policies derive from the same origin. The DET also plays a leading role in the drawing up of syllabuses and work programmes, the setting and marking of exams, and the approval of textbooks and other materials. The majority of African departments adopt these curricular policies and materials directly; any changes which may be effected are of a minor quantitative nature.[16]

At the same time, the decentralization of educational responsibilities to the homeland governments means that Pretoria and the DET can disclaim responsibility for problems in the homelands.

Another issue, as yet little studied or confronted, is that of gender differences in access to education and achievement at school. So far, general levels of awareness of the consequences of gender discrimination are still very low, especially in the formal education sector. On a broader front, even the popular movements are only now beginning to raise issues connected with gender and women's rights – despite the long-standing existence of women's groups which have campaigned on a variety of anti-apartheid issues. In terms of the future of formal education, priority has been given to achievement of non-racial education, and neither questions of female access and achievement, nor the gendered content of educational materials, have been given much attention. In the non-formal sector, however, some groups have tried to address these issues.

According to Angie Romorola, gender inequalities are very well entrenched. Whereas women are frequently family breadwinners (in contrast with women in white South African society), they are otherwise expected to be subordinate to men. The apartheid system has historically led to the disintegration of family and kin structures, but has not replaced it with anything else.

In formal education, the pressures of life under apartheid have had contradictory impacts on women. Girls are often pulled out of school to look after younger children, especially in urban areas, since there is no childcare for many children under school age. The state offers small subsidies to pre-schools, but the system is poorly developed except for some voluntary projects, and in the townships both parents frequently work. Another problem is the pressure on young women to marry and have children by the age of eighteen to twenty. Until the age restrictions were introduced in secondary schools, it was not uncommon for boys to continue at school as long as it took – even until twenty-two or so. For girls, this was less acceptable.

However, official figures suggest that more girls have tended to stay at school to secondary level than boys, both in the homelands and in DET areas. In general, this is probably because the pressure on boys and young men to go out to work is much greater. Where there has been serious political conflict, schoolgirls have often been involved in protests and boycotts. However, there is rather less chance that girls will be detained or go on the run from the security forces, a factor which has increased male drop-out levels. In recent years, teenage girls in townships like Soweto have been deterred from attending school, however, by the growing levels of violence directed against them, including numerous cases of rape, both by males from their schools and by outside gangs.

An escape from these adverse educational conditions for the more affluent sections of black society is to send their children to the growing number of private schools, mainly in urban and suburban areas. Many of these schools are more liberal in tone and educational curriculum, and have higher academic standards and a better environment than township schools. However, these are only within the reach of the better-off and those who can win a scholarship or bursary. Clearly this offers no solution for the majority of students from low-income families, while for most rural children no such alternatives exist.

A kind of halfway house for urban secondary students is the proliferation of Saturday and evening schools to help students pass their matriculation exam. Some of these, certainly in Johannesburg, are located in the city, far from the townships, and involve a long journey. On the whole these attract students with some money to spare. Other classes of this kind, sometimes called 'street academies', exist in the townships and cater to youngsters who have dropped out of school or want extra tuition outside school. But in poor families, many youngsters spend Saturdays earning money or helping at home, which prevents them attending such classes. These institutions are simply coping with low pass rates in the matriculation exam, an immediate manifestation of a broader problem of apartheid education which they can do nothing to solve.

The government itself has encouraged individual rather than collective advancement by turning much of the initiative for vocational and technical training over to the private sector – with local and multinational companies selecting candidates for higher-level training and providing scholarships and bursaries to this end. Since the mid-1980s, there has also been a sharp growth in the numbers of foreign aid donors giving various kinds of scholarships, either for study abroad or training in South Africa.

In the last few years, South Africa, though a rich country compared with its northern neighbours, has none the less been hit by international economic trends, including declining gold prices, as well as by pressures of sanctions. Furthermore, a large proportion of the budget has been spent on both internal security and the war with Angola. Inflation has been above 11.5 per cent since 1983, and reached 18.6 per cent in 1986. Between 1981 and 1986, real average personal disposable incomes fell by over 17 per cent. At the same time, economic recession has led to sharp increases in unemployment, especially among young black people, and there has been a growth in black migration from impoverished and drought-stricken rural areas since the ending of influx controls in 1986. The living conditions of many of these migrants in illegal squatter settlements is often precarious. They also have difficulties in sending their children to school because they do not have the correct papers.

WUS and educational assistance to South Africa

WUS International and WUS(UK) have a long history of supporting the efforts of the black majority of South Africans to overcome the educational discrimination which is an integral part of apartheid. This support takes a variety of forms.

WUS provides scholarships and bursaries in front-line states for South Africans forced to flee into exile. Young people and students were still fleeing during the summer of 1990, in fear of harassment, detention and violence, particularly in the Natal region.

WUS provides a limited number of scholarships in the United Kingdom, primarily for South Africans in exile, but it is also prepared to consider emergency applications from inside South Africa. Following the unbanning of the ANC and other organizations and the release of Nelson Mandela, the focus of the programme has become much more developmental, supporting group training (Access) and postgraduate study.

In the United Kingdom, WUS also promotes and co-ordinates placements on the Southern African Campus Scholarship Scheme. These are 'solidarity scholarships' run and financed by students, staff and institutions in the United Kingdom. More than eighty higher education institutions now participate in this scheme.

Inside South Africa, WUS supports the provision of scholarships and bursaries, primarily, but not exclusively, in the fields of education and medicine. Support in 1990 has enabled several thousand black students to continue into higher education.

WUS also supports more than thirty educational projects inside South Africa, ranging from literacy work to specialized research projects.

Attitudes to education

Like most other oppressive systems, apartheid education has had an impact on individuals, families and communities which goes beyond economic disadvantage and even political disenfranchisement. A system which is openly and avowedly inferior does not encourage those who participate in it to have a high self-esteem. In the case of South Africa, this kind of self-esteem has to be sought in deliberately resisting the implications of what is taught rather than accepting them.

The education system is designed to imply that the whole of black African society is inferior and marginal, morally and intellectually; that blacks have no history worthy of recollection; that their culture is at best no more than 'picturesque'. These ideas have been built into curricula and materials. Over the last few years, some of the gross distortions of early generations of textbooks have been removed. However, history, geography, literature and indeed all social sciences are still, for the most part, filtered through the assumptions of white society.

One result is the profoundly ambivalent attitude to education of most black South Africans. Responses range from feelings of helplessness to anger – the latter increasingly common. Most people are keen for their children to be educated but despair at the kind of education they receive. Many students have little faith in the value of what or how they are taught and largely despise school. They also know that the chances of a job at the end of it are small. Yet increasing numbers struggle to pass matriculation exams.

My teacher

My teacher
My teacher's like a battle tank
Roaring at the enemy
The enemy is us
And the roaring is the lesson
He keeps us in a prison camp
Torturing us every day
And he will keep on torturing us
Till our minds are worn away.

Poem by a 13-year-old student, writing in a frequently banned student magazine, Cape Province, mid-1980s.

The role of black teachers in apartheid education is even more invidious. Teachers can be punished for deviating, either politically or administratively, from the system imposed on them, and this can include the loss of their jobs. So they are required constantly to compromise. The poor physical conditions under which many teachers have to work may be difficult enough, but their problems are compounded by the gulf which has developed in many schools between teachers and pupils, and the low regard in which teachers are held. Their training and the pressure to conform to state rules and regulations have over the years made them appear to their pupils, and many parents, as agents of the regime. Physical attacks on teachers by students are not unusual.

In recent years, the DET has begun to offer carrots as well as sticks. About one-third of black teachers in DET secondary schools have no secondary teaching qualifications (see Figure 10.2). While teachers without full qualifications are poorly paid, qualified teachers are now relatively well off. So there has been a scramble among unqualified teachers to obtain upgrading. However, they are not always offered study leave or proper in-service training to achieve these qualifications, and so they tend to use school hours to do their own work rather than concentrating on their students. Absenteeism among teachers is also common, encouraged by the present chaotic conditions in many schools.

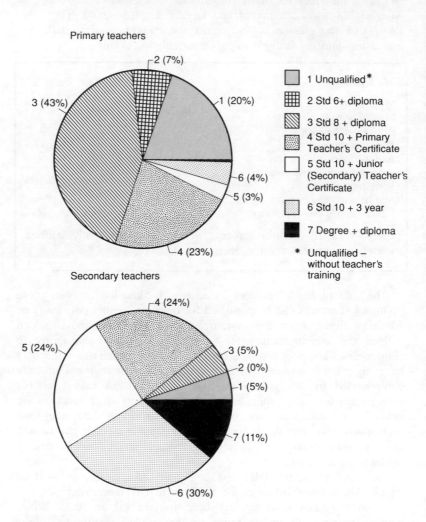

Figure 10.2   Qualifications: South Africa: black teachers
Source: DET (1987) *Annual Report*

Challenging the system

While the education system has been a major target for opponents of apartheid since the 1953 Bantu Education Act, it was not until the 1980s that more concrete attempts were made to formulate ideas for another kind of education system. In the 1970s, the prevailing demand among political activists and their academic sympathizers was for freedom first and education later. This view has since been altered to contend that the struggle for education is part of the struggle for freedom and that some demands which affect the education system should be fought for while apartheid is still in place.

One of the turning points was the schools boycott movement in the early 1980s, initiated by the black student movements, which left many thousands of black children from seven-year-olds to teenagers effectively out of school for several years. Some parents moved their children to rural areas to avoid the disruption and continue their schooling. As concern grew about this situation, particularly in the heartland of Soweto, parents came together in community groups with students and progressive teachers, and agreed upon an organized return to classes.

One outcome of this initiative was the formation of the National Education Crisis Committee (NECC) in 1985. The return to school was accompanied by a new call for 'people's education', focusing on demands for an end to racial discrimination in education, democratic community participation in decision-making in schools, and a more relevant curriculum purged of racism. Clearly, this is a programme which could command considerable support, but its development has been impeded by several problems. The first, and most significant, was the re-imposition of the state of emergency in 1986. The NECC's leadership were all detained, and the organization was banned, along with many other anti-apartheid organizations. This effectively strangled its activities for several years. Furthermore, most parent–teacher–student bodies in the community were suppressed. Those groups which were able to continue operating were restricted in their mobility and contacts.

So, until recently, the ideas behind the movement have largely remained at the level of slogans and their deeper implications have not really been worked out. However, since the unbanning of the ANC, UDF and other anti-apartheid groups, the NECC has regrouped. Although the political future remains unclear, the new circumstances have allowed much more room to manoeuvre than in the past. The challenges are none the less great, and the organization has still to define its role. As one of its leaders put it, the NECC is 'almost drowning in possibilities'. State power, and consequently that of the education authorities, may have been eroded, but it still controls formal education.

The NECC's first initiative, echoed by Nelson Mandela on his first day out of gaol, was to urge all children to return to school. This was viewed as crucial to end the long period of disruption in schools and to deal with the problems of student demotivation. The leadership of the NECC is well aware of the contradictions in urging children back into the overcrowded classrooms of a system still based on apartheid principles. However, while acknowledging the need to 'normalize' education, it aims to challenge the assumptions of the DET, not least their refusal (up until March 1990) to shift black children from overcrowded township classrooms into empty places in white schools. Another area on which a challenge has been launched is on the standards of administration and marking of the discredited matriculation examination.

There are many kinds of difficulties confronting an organization which is trying to make a start on restructuring education, but without access to formal power. Not least of these are disagreements within its own ranks. For example, students, both at secondary school and university, for whom activism rather than strategic thinking has been the prime consideration in the struggle, have to be persuaded to co-operate. Furthermore, numbers of other organizations, large and small, have been involved in a variety of 'alternative' educational projects, and the question arises as to how much autonomy these should retain. There are also numerous problems arising out of the broader political situation: as of 1990 these include the possibility of reintegrating all or some of the homelands into a national education system; the outcome of the bid for national political status by the Natal-based Inkatha movement, with attendant violence which has severely disrupted life in the Transvaal as well as Natal; and the length of time it takes to dismantle the apartheid system completely.

Finally, the whole idea of people's education will need elaboration, and how it can be implemented will depend on these political developments. One of its greatest challenges will concern the future role and status of teachers. The alienation of large numbers of teachers, and their uneasy relationships with students and communities are problems which will not vanish overnight. A recent step forward was the announcement in October 1990 of the formation of a broad-based teachers' organization – the South African Democratic Teachers' Union – which brings together a number of teachers' unions previously separated on racial, geographical and political lines. This may initiate a wider discussion of the role of teachers in a new South Africa and begin to change entrenched attitudes. Certainly the resolution of these problems will be crucial for the development of a more democratic and less authoritarian education system. As one observer noted, there is a need to develop democratic practice in the classroom as well as outside it, if people's education is not to become simply 'a process of looking for a new set of right answers'.[17]

Namibia – a new beginning?

South Africa's education policy in Namibia mirrored its policies at home. It created segregated education systems with eleven departments of education divided on regional lines in addition to departments for whites, Coloureds and Rehoboth (German speakers). Afrikaans was the dominant language of instruction.

Statistics are poor and not easily comparable, but those which do exist show stark contrasts in conditions between different education authorities. For example, in Ovamboland, the northern region, worst hit by the war, drop-out rates at primary school are highest. Of the children who started school in 1983, 50 per cent had dropped out after four years. The differences were also evident in the age range of primary school pupils. In the white sector, 94 per cent of primary school pupils were aged twelve or below. In Ovamboland 60 per cent of primary pupils were aged fifteen or above. In other black education authorities (Caprivians, Hereros, Damaras) the main age range in primary schools was eleven to fifteen. Very few Namibians reached the end of secondary school. The system was highly authoritarian, with detailed control of curricula and how teachers used them. While there did not seem to be an overall shortage of teachers, their distribution was very uneven between regions, and their qualifications varied widely.

As in South Africa itself, the authorities had increased spending on education over the last few years, so that qualified teachers are fairly well paid, and except in the poorest regions, school building stock is in reasonable repair. In recent years, there has been considerable private sector intervention in secondary level education and vocational and technical training, mainly by the large mining companies.

This, in outline, is the situation facing the government of the newly independent state. Because of its mineral wealth, Namibia is not a poor country by African standards, but the challenge will be to channel that wealth towards internal social and economic development, rather than into the pockets of multi-national and South African mining interests. Meanwhile, large numbers of Namibians are extremely poor and many more are still dependent on remittances from workers in South Africa for a living.

The South West African People's Organisation (SWAPO), formed in 1959, became involved in educational provision as well as in fighting the South African occupation. With the help of the United Nations Institute for Namibia (UNIN) and other agencies, SWAPO developed a network of schools which served the large refugee population in camps in Angola and Zambia. These schools were for children but adult education and literacy classes were also provided. The movement has therefore had considerable experience of educational provision in exile.

Access courses for Namibians

WUS(UK) has run two special scholarship programmes in the United Kingdom for Namibians forced to leave their country before independence and take refuge in the front-line states. These courses have allowed two groups of mature students whose education was inadequate and disrupted to study science from pre-GCSE to degree or HND level.

The two groups on the four- and five-year study programme had been denied any science education at all in pre-independence Namibia. WUS(UK) also organized crash courses in exam techniques, English language and study skills for these students.

Members of the group progressed from pre-access courses to study science in higher education. Most studied mining and geology, areas vital to Namibia's future.

As independence approached, all the Namibian students on these courses went home to take part in the election process. Around half returned almost immediately, while half deferred their studies for a year.

On coming to power, SWAPO announced an ambitious programme of educational expansion, to provide ten years of schooling for all Namibians with English as the official language of instruction. This programme is likely to take time to implement. As in post-independence Zimbabwe, enrolments will probably expand very rapidly. If that is the case, in the short run the education system may have difficulty in servicing this new demand. First, there is the problem of how to integrate the fragmented educational administration; and second, how to put into effect a new curriculum to replace the South African one.

Aside from the logistics of creating new books and materials to replace the present South African-produced materials, there will have to be a major push to upgrade and retrain teachers. Although many teachers opposed the apartheid regime, their only training has been in the rigid and authoritarian methods of education used in black South African schools, with no freedom or initiative allowed to the teacher. Retraining would, therefore, need to include some rethinking of the role of the teacher. Another hurdle will be the use of English as the medium of instruction. While SWAPO's decision to opt for English as the official language reflects a wish to avoid conflicts between different indigenous languages, relatively few people who have not been refugees know English well, and this will have to be taken into consideration in teacher training. Imposing English at all levels of the education system may not turn out to be either practical or appropriate.

The history of educational neglect in Namibia has left many adults, especially in rural areas, without any schooling. The demand for literacy and adult education is likely to be considerable. The Namibian churches, which played an important role in resistance to the South African regime, and in providing basic education before independence, seem likely to play an important part in this non-formal education.

Notes

1. Painter (1987), p.3.
2. Amnesty International (1989), pp.18–19, pp.25–6.
3. Interview by John Bevan of WUS (UK) with a priest who had worked with indigenous Guatemalan communities.
4. Painter (1987), p.8.
5. Manz (1988), pp.40–9, pp.119–20, p.142.
6. Jiménez *et al.* (1988), p.53; US General Accounting Office (1989), p.13.
7. Jiménez *et al.* (1988), p.55.
8. Antonio Orellana (1985), p.36.
9. NUT/WUS (1988), p.24.
10. Bueso (1987), Tables 5 and 13.
11. NECC (1989), Papers.
12. *Independent*, 6 Feb. 1990.
13. Taylor (1989), p.56.
14. *Indicator SA* (Summer/Autumn 1989), p.90.
15. Graaf (1989); *Indicator SA*, Spring 1986 and Summer 1988.
16. Taylor (1989), pp.28-9.
17. Gultig and Hart (forthcoming), p.32, quoting O. van den Berg (1989), 'Towards a relevant curriculum': keynote address to the Teachers' Association of South Africa, Durban.

Plate 1 For the Mozambican street child, 'home' is little more than a few plastic bags. The effects of the world recession hit the poorest hardest: in Mozambique, they are compounded by war.

Plate 2 In South Africa poverty cannot be disentangled from politics: a woman protests against conditions in the economically deprived rural 'homelands'.

Plate 3 Girls from poor families stand the least chance of getting an education. Young women like this displaced Sudanese girl are often expected to stay at home looking after younger children.

Plate 4 The Marotholi theatre group in Lesotho uses drama to involve the community. Together they learn to express ideas and demands and resolve grievances. Here a woman tells a friend about her husband, a migrant worker in the mines. Later he returns after a strike in the mines with the news that he has lost his job.

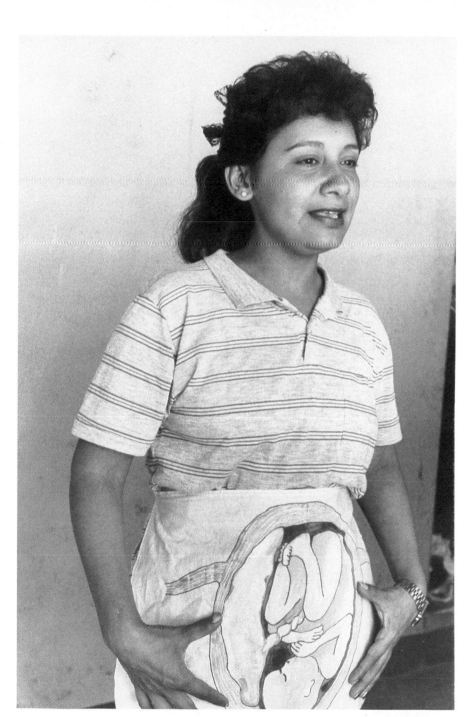

Plate 5 Health education for women in Nicaragua has overcome the barriers of illiteracy by using imaginative teaching aids: here an apron supplied by a Scandinavian aid agency graphically illustrates one stage of pregnancy.

Plate 6 A new children's library opens in Managua. In the years following the 1979 revolution, many Nicaraguans felt, for the first time, that education could play an important part in their lives.

Plate 7 Mozambican fourth-grade pupils in Zambezia province make do with logs instead of desks or chairs in their classroom. This province has been particularly hard hit by the war, which has made progress in education virtually impossible.

Plate 8 The privileged position of the white population of South Africa is evident in the lavish facilities their children enjoy at school.

Plate 9 Children from southern Sudan selling vegetables in Hillat Kusha, an 'unplanned' area of Khartoum North built on a rubbish dump. Most of the inhabitants have fled the war and famine in the South, and their children have little chance of education.

Plate 10 Primary school children in a village school in Honduras. Pressure on families to pay for books and stationery is increasing as government budgets are restricted.

Plate 11   A young Salvadorean sells flowers at a traffic light in San Salvador.

Plate 12   Adults attending evening primary school in Messica, Manica province, Mozambique. Women often have great difficulty in attending these classes regularly because of the time-consuming demands of looking after their families.

Plate 13 For children working on white-owned farms, little schooling has been available. As one child said, education is no use for that kind of farm work: 'We're all just like mealies in a sack.'

Plate 14 A rural school in Namibia before independence. While teachers were officially supposed to teach in Afrikaans, few pupils understood it.

Plate 15 'Female students unite and fight triple oppression' reads this student banner. Integrating women's rights into the struggle for people's education remains a challenge.

Plate 16 A school in the 'homeland' of Bophuthatswana. Per capita expenditure on education in the 'homelands' is even lower than for blacks in the rest of South Africa, while the demand for education is rising rapidly.

Plate 17   Some groups of refugees have succeeded in organizing their own education programmes. These refugees, who have returned to El Salvador from camps in Honduras are running their own school. The Salvadorean teachers union ANDES has been instrumental in promoting literacy programmes in refugee camps in Honduras, as well as supporting returning refugees.

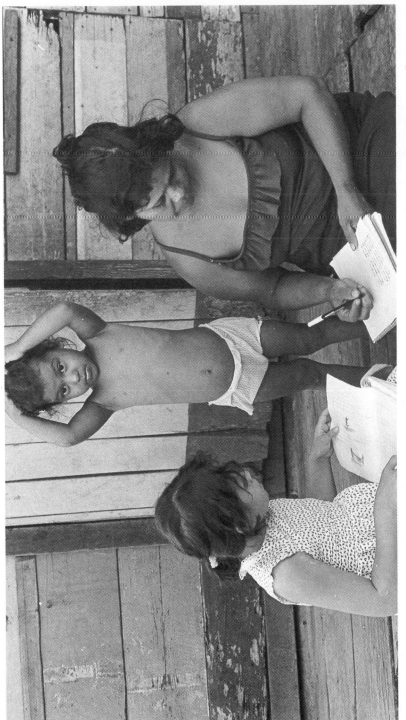

Plate 18 A child teaches her mother to read and write in Bluefields, on the Atlantic coast of Nicaragua. The Nicaraguan literacy crusade helped to promote new ideas about methods of teaching literacy and challenged the idea that only 'professional' teachers are effective.

Plate 19 Villagers organized their own open-air literacy class in this FMLN-controlled area of Morazan province, El Salvador. The teacher has only attended the first grades of primary school, and different age groups are taught together.

PART THREE

Learning and Teaching in Marginal Communities

The effects of a national economic and political crisis on family and community decision-making about education have not been comprehensively researched. They have generally been considered less significant than questions relating to health and food and have not been of great interest to most macro-level planners. However, it is impossible to understand how vulnerable groups respond to the various crises which confront them without considering how decisions taken at government and international levels affect their educational opportunities. The examples are chosen to reflect a range of experience across regions and issues, focusing on communities which are marginal or have become so.

Each case examines people's views on education and their responses and initiatives. Discussions are with parents, teachers, community leaders, community groups and students themselves. In this sense the views are partial and subjective, but this can often tell much more than than statistics alone.

CHAPTER 11

Family income and education in Central America

Schooling in the rural areas

Rigoberta Menchú, a young Quiché woman from Guatemala, became a political leader during the repression of the early 1980s. She dictated her memoirs to a Venezuelan anthropologist. She spoke in Spanish, which she had only just learnt, in order to communicate more widely the oppression she and her people have suffered. But she did not learn in school or from books, only from listening. In her childhood, formal education played no part. By the age of eight she was working with her parents in the coffee harvest on a coastal *finca* (estate) and for the rest of the year helping to keep the family alive in the mountains. There was no question of going to school, partly because she had to work to help the family survive, and partly because her father, whose favourite child she was, saw the schooling provided by the government as alien to their culture and as destructive. As a teenager, she became a Catholic catechist, but taught others about the scriptures by memorizing texts read out by one of her brothers who had learnt to read from friends.[1]

In Guatemala, El Salvador and Costa Rica, marginal families survive by working as internal migrants, harvesting commercial crops for big farmers. This makes it very difficult for children to have any steady schooling. In Guatemala, this pattern of migration is especially common among the Indian populations of the highlands who come down to the *fincas* on the plains for wage labour. Conditions are often very harsh. Large groups of families live in *galerias* – open-sided barns with no beds or sanitation. Schooling and health care are rarely available – children have to work – and rations, if provided, are limited. It is common for children to die of malnutrition or from the excessive use of agricultural chemicals on the plantations.

In most Central American countries, the official age for children to start school is six to seven years for primary school and eleven to twelve years for secondary school. But in fact the age at which rural children enter school, and how long they stay, varies according to a number of factors. First, whether there is a school nearby – and in the large countries like Guatemala, Honduras and Nicaragua, 'nearby' can mean sixteen to twenty kilometres away. The second consideration is whether the child's labour is required either in the home or in agricultural work. The difficulties faced by marginal communities have been increased by economic crisis and war in the last decade. They face low wages and lack of work, exacerbated by the fact that many peasants have lost access to land, which has often been sold to big land-owners.

Even in Costa Rica, where more small farmers still remain, there has been increased pressure to sell out to large land-owners. One interviewee talked of the experience of the peasant community to which he belonged. It had been formed many years ago with much effort and sacrifice on the part of the various families to clear land in the forest, and build houses. But in recent years, economic difficulties have forced many of them to sell their land to big owners who already possess tracts of unused land. Then, without a source of income, these families have to travel around seeking wage labour.

Settled rural communities in the poorest regions also have increasing difficulties obtaining education for their children, and coping with the resulting financial burdens. A local representative described a school in a village twenty-four kilometres from Santa Rosa de Pocozol, in the mountainous San Carlos district of Costa Rica:

[One problem for the teacher] is the distance. To reach the community there is only a bus service three times a day, apart from that you have to walk. Another problem is that the pay [s/he] receives from the government does not cover transport, food or housing or teaching materials. Because of all this, the teachers and some parents' representatives felt obliged to go to San José and ask help from the Ministry to obtain help for the school, and this is how they obtained the desks for the school in this community. The school itself was built mostly with community funds and very little help from the government.

Another difficulty is the erratic attendance of children at school because they have to help with jobs around the house, work to help their parents economically. Another thing is the continual migrations of families in search of work – all this is detrimental to an adequate education.

Community representatives from two rural communities in Los Chiles, another poor area in the north of the country, had similar complaints. Money and resources were inadequate, especially for materials and equipment in their schools; school buildings were in bad condition; and there were not enough teachers. They also mentioned the lack of parental resources to pay for children's needs, and the reluctance of some parents to keep their children at school, especially into the secondary cycle. At secondary school in Costa Rica, though enrolment is still free, the costs of materials are very high for poor families.

Although the state still provides the majority of resources, it seems that these communities also have to make considerable inputs towards all aspects of school life – contributions to school meals, fundraising activities – raffles, bingo, and cultural events – as well as school maintenance costs.[2]

In Nicaragua, the growing economic difficulties families experienced increased the perennial problem of irregular school attendance among rural children. As Jacqueline Sanchez of the Ministry of Education explained, the situation in the countryside is quite difficult because when there is a lot of agricultural work, depending on the season, children have to help their parents. So there are attendance and punctuality problems. We haven't completely convinced the parents of the priority of having their children study. This isn't just a lack of comprehension, it's also to do with the economic situation. Virtually all members of the family have to work.

Earning a living: female-headed households in urban areas

In the urban areas in most Central American countries, there are large numbers of female-headed households. In Costa Rica, in 1984, 23 per cent of urban households were headed by women. In El Salvador, the proportion is higher, about 27 per cent country-wide. In Nicaragua, up to 30 per cent of urban households were female-headed in the mid-1980s. Only in heavily rural Guatemala are the numbers of women heads of household rather smaller. Substantial numbers of these women have migrated from rural areas. In contrast to many African countries, women are just as likely to move into cities as men.

While some women are left widows either by war or natural causes, many are abandoned by their male partners (rates of formal marriage are low in urban areas in all these countries). They are left with the entire responsibility for feeding, clothing and educating their children. They have to play a number of roles – mother, father and breadwinner.

Women who have become breadwinners face difficulties earning enough money in a time of recession. Since the 1970s, increasing numbers of Latin American women have been drawn into the workforce. However, during the economic crisis, when more women were seeking work, high unemployment reduced their chances of finding formal sector jobs. In Costa Rica, for example, the economic crisis of the early 1980s brought a rise in open unemployment from 5.9 per cent in 1980 to 9 per cent in 1983. By 1987, the rate for men had improved to 4.7 per cent but the rate for women remained at 7.9 per cent. Women's wages are one-third lower than men's in El Salvador and Costa Rica. In Nicaragua, there are still differences, on average 10 to 20 per cent, between male and female pay rates. In all cases their value has been eroded by wage freezes and inflation.

Most women in this situation work in the informal sector, but this deprives them of any legal protection available to formal sector workers and of social security benefits. Women also suffer from a lack of well-defined property rights and access to credit, which might help them to prosper.

Typical informal sector work for women in Central America is low paid and insecure: domestic service, street hawking, particularly of food, and home-based artisan work, or sub-contracted piece work.[3]

This point was taken up by a teacher in a rural school. She confirmed that the economic situation had led to increased drop-out rates.

The parents find that it's necessary to use the children to increase their income, so their schooling is restricted. As a teacher you try to visit the parents and explain to them that it's a shame for the child to give up studying, but you don't always succeed [in convincing them].

She added that she tried to stay after school hours to help the children who were falling behind because of absences: 'you need to bring these children up. But some other other teachers can't do this because they find they have to do another school shift or work to meet their own needs'.

Survival tactics: urban poverty and schooling

Acute poverty, sharpened by economic pressures, limits the choices which families have about how to use their income. The following studies on urban areas, where access to school is generally greater, suggest that absolute poverty leaves little room for choice in the matter of education. For those who have a little more freedom, other factors come into play. These include the availability of free education, the distribution of work and household income between family members, opportunities for employment, and parental attitudes to education.

El Salvador

The late Segundo Montes, the Jesuit social scientist who was among six priests from the University of Central America in San Salvador murdered by elements of the Salvadorean army in late 1989, wrote of society in El Salvador:

Economically, in the upper class [the family] is predominantly a unit of consumption and training on the basis of inheritance or of the highly paid employment of the head of the household; in the middle [class] the woman may also be integrated into the paid workforce . . . but the children are mainly consumers, being trained to take their place in qualified jobs. On the other hand, in the lower classes, all [family] members are called on to be more producers than consumers, and their meagre earnings are scarcely sufficient to allow them to survive and maintain themselves at the same economic level.[4]

El Salvador is a much more highly polarized society than either Costa Rica or Nicaragua. The levels of deprivation are greatest in the rural areas, especially in those areas disrupted by the war. However, Ministry of Planning figures for 1985 estimated that even among the urban population, the proportion of families living in absolute poverty was 30 per cent, compared with 9.9 per cent in 1977. Open unemployment reached 34 per cent in the mid-1980s, with many more under-employed. The real value of wages at the low end of the pay scale had halved between 1978 and 1987.[5]

Table 11.1   **Central America: GDP per capita, cumulative percentage change, 1981–88**

Guatemala	−19.5
El Salvador	−15.2
Honduras	−14.1
Nicaragua	−27.4
Costa Rica	−8.7

Source: CEPAL (1988) *Balance preliminar de la economía latinoamericana*

A study conducted in five slum areas of San Salvador in the mid-1980s by a local housing foundation gives some idea of the predicament and priorities of families living close to the survival line. It was based on interviews with 903 heads of household, almost half of whom were of rural origin. Less than 10 per cent had been born in the neighbourhood where they now lived. Some 400 had moved to this area since 1980. The average size of family was given as five, and half the heads of household interviewed were women. Seventy per cent of all household heads could read and write, but of these 75 per cent had not passed grade six at school. In 25 per cent of the families no member was studying and a further 25 per cent had only one member studying. A substantial number of children were clearly not at school.

A study of average household income and expenses among the families interviewed gives an indication of why this is. The majority of household heads (and probably other family members) worked in the informal sector for a low income. Food made up more than 70 per cent of outgoings for the average family. Combined with costs of housing, transport, water, light and aid to other families (necessary in order to receive help in return), this took up the whole of disposable income. The authors comment: 'the data indicates that income does not cover all necessities, including . . . clothes, medicine and education, which seem to remain outside the family budget and which are only covered eventually in the course of the year'.[6]

Clearly, some families use loans or remittances to bridge this gap. Others choose to prioritize one of the 'other' needs – education or health care. Where there is strong community solidarity and organization, the chances of keeping children in school are obviously better. As one Salvadorean interviewee pointed out:

In some of the schools, particularly the primary schools, there are teachers who belong to organizations which identify themselves with the people, like some of [the teachers] who belong to ANDES. In that case there is an agreement with the parents and more understanding.

Interviews with teachers and community representatives confirmed this picture. A teacher in the Soyapango region described the difficulties of families in her zone where many of the children are from poor urban districts.

Today there is more unemployment than before and parents have more difficulties in sending their children to school, and when they do, it's only for the first years, after which they put them to 'learn a trade'. Also before, the people were able to rely on some social services, but with the war, these are less and less available while government funds have been cut a lot.

She added that the cost of necessities like clothing had increased year after year and this also influenced parent's decisions to take children out of school.

She said that she had noticed in her school that increasing numbers of children were dropping out and gave the example of four children who had left her fourth-grade class in the previous month. Some of the mothers said they couldn't afford the costs. The parents of one girl had migrated to work in the United States, and she was left on her own with her teenage brothers and sisters. The teacher also found that major problems were created in the classroom by the fact that many children came to school tired and hungry. Many lived in houses unfit for habitation, much less for studying.

School fees, as noted earlier, are now commonly charged. According to a community representative,

this affects the family economy, especially if the parents have five or more children at school. With the difficulties caused by the lack of employment, parents end up having to take pupils out of school before the end of the school year because they can't pay the fees and the exam fee.

Mexico

Most studies on the ways in which low-income families have coped with economic crisis have only dealt incidentally with education and have not examined in detail the costs involved. Two studies from Mexico during the first part of the 1980s, when the debt crisis there became severe, suggest that low-income groups are very resourceful in coping with crisis, but something always suffers. Education is a likely, though not an inevitable, casualty. Both these studies deal with groups which are probably not as poor as those in the San Salvador study, and who, therefore, have more room to manoeuvre. Furthermore, Mexican society, while under great economic pressure, is not in the same state of upheaval as that of El Salvador.

Sylvia Chant examined the patterns of income distribution in a low-income community in the industrializing Mexican city of Querétaro. This research was carried out in the early 1980s at the beginning of the debt crisis but during a period of sharp changes in employment and social structures in Mexico which had been going on since the 1970s. Here most families owned their homes, and were better off than those who only rented. There was a mix of male-headed households, female-headed nuclear families and female-headed extended families. It emerged very clearly that women's earning power was much less than that of men. In the case of work in manufacturing industry and services, women earned on average half the pay of men; only in the restaurant and catering sector were women's earnings slightly higher than those of men.

Schoolchildren and full-time child workers contributed 38 per cent of the income in single-parent households and 40 per cent in female-headed extended households but only 10 per cent in male-headed families. However, Chant points out that families may also suffer disadvantages with a male breadwinner who routinely keeps a substantial proportion of his earnings for his own use, while refusing to allow his wife to work. In one case,

the husband of a woman called Lourdes earned 4,000 pesos a week repairing car wheels in a workshop. He often did not come home on pay-day, preferring instead to join his workmates in local bars and brothels so that the following morning she considered herself fortunate if she received 2,000 pesos from his wage packet.[7]

When the mother is responsible for the education and health care of the children, she may find herself having to pay these expenses out of meagre 'housekeeping'.

Another survey of a working-class community in the Mexican city of Guadalajara examined the changing patterns of work and family income over the years 1982 to 1985, during which time Mexico's debt crisis was intensifying. Over this period, La Rocha noted a marked increase in the numbers of working women and in the numbers of both boys and girls working under the age of fifteen (the usual age at which both sexes leave school in this community). Some boys were working full-time in waged employment, and more daughters were doing full-time unpaid domestic work, while others of both sexes were working part-time while at school. This, la Rocha suggests, was 'a deliberate strategy to cope with economic crisis'.[8]

The measure of that crisis could be seen in the decline in family income, which in real terms fell by 7 per cent over the three years. Male head of household earnings fell by 35 per cent, so much of the difference was evidently made up by other family members' work. There were some changes in the deployment of this reduced budget. Food consumed about the same proportion of reduced overall income, while the proportion spent on clothes and shoes increased, due to rising prices. There were, however, marked declines in proportions spent on education, which fell from 6 to 4 per cent, and on health care, which fell from 2 per cent to nothing. Since the children went to state schools which were still free of charge, the main expenses were food and transport – with the main cut being made in food bought for school lunches.

Displaced in Guatemala City

In Guatemala, internally displaced Maya people not only have great difficulty in surviving economically, but are often under pressure to suppress and conceal their cultural identity. Isobel is a Quiché woman displaced and living in Guatemala City since the mid-1980s, when her village was burned to the ground. Since then, she and her fellow villagers have been constantly on the move. Several members of their community, all catechists, have been killed by death squads. Isobel and other members of her community live in Guatemala City without papers, so they cannot send their children to school, nor can they work legally. Anyway, in a city with some 40 per cent unemployment, little work is available. They survive by making handicrafts and the women sell them in the streets, though they risk detention, and possibly their lives, by doing this. In order not to be identified, Isobel has had to give up wearing traditional dress, very important for Maya identity, and she wears western clothes. Being illegal has meant becoming invisible.[9]

Costa Rica

In Costa Rica, the patterns of school drop-outs in marginal urban areas seem more complex, perhaps because the education system is better established. Both boys and girls are more likely to stay at school into the secondary cycle than in El Salvador.

In the following survey, the children do not seem to drop out of school simply because of lack of money, though this is certainly a problem at secondary level, but for various reasons which suggest scepticism about the results of education. It also suggests that significant numbers of children who do not complete primary school are functionally illiterate.

La Ciudadela 15 de Setiembre is a township in the province of San José, built in the early 1960s with funds from the Alliance for Progress and USAID to house people from slum areas closer to the centre of the city of San José which were being redeveloped. Further houses were constructed in the late 1970s. The community had to organize and fight to get basic facilities such as drinking water, light, transport and schools. The area is now considered poor, marginal and overcrowded, with interviewees from the community identifying drugs, unemployment, alcoholism, prostitution and poverty as the major problems. A number of local organizations work to provide opportunities for adult education and literacy, though these do not seem to be well co-ordinated.

A sample survey of 220 totally and partially illiterate adults aged fifteen to forty conducted in the community showed that 77 per cent had dropped out before the end of primary school and lost the ability to read or write. Over a third had left school before the age of ten. Over half gave poverty as the reason for leaving. Among the school-age children of these illiterates, over one-third were not at school; reasons for leaving included dislike of going to school, health problems and taking up apprenticeships. Only 12 per cent cited economic problems. In almost half the households, the decisions on children's education were taken by the mother. It seems that resistance to formal schooling in youngsters growing up with illiterate and semi-literate parents is a serious problem. It may also reflect the view that the kind of education given in schools is irrelevant, and does not help people from poor communities.[10]

Children on the streets

In most of the cities of Latin America, children can be seen on the streets at a very young age as vendors and shoe-shiners, in street gangs, as prostitutes. Some still live with or have contact with their families, others live on the streets and few have seen the inside of a classroom for more than a few years if at all. Central American countries are no exception.

El Salvador

Six-year-olds can be seen selling on the streets in El Salvador. Juvenile crime, drug addiction and prostitution of both males and females at a very young age are rife. These children are out of school and on the margins of society, and are very vulnerable to violence, both in their own homes and in the street.

There are increasing numbers of young children working, especially in San Salvador. One woman in San Salvador market has her young sons working with her. Her husband is 'travelling' and she can't afford to send them to school – to buy shoes, books and so on – though she would like to. A 1983 survey of 355 children working in San Salvador found many of the children had chronic illnesses – intestinal infections and bronchitis – and over 70 per cent of them were not at school. Most of these had never attended at all, and those who did were far behind in their grades.[11]

Another problem is the numbers of orphans, displaced and abandoned children created by war and the 1986 earthquake in El Salvador. Several interviewees said that there were many children who, having lost a father or mother, had been forced to leave school and go out to work. Even worse, there are children who find themselves completely alone and wander the streets, begging. There are not enough centres to help such orphans, and those that exist have been overwhelmed. Most tragic, there are children who have caught diseases such as polio, who live in the streets and have to beg in order to eat.

Some organizations, particularly church groups, are helping children with shelter, medication, school materials and food. This work will help alleviate the suffering of these vulnerable children, but far greater efforts and resources are needed. According to the Dean of the Faculty of Sciences and Humanities at the University of El Salvador, the government does nothing to help with the education of the displaced population, which is left to voluntary agencies, for the most part church groups.

Nicaragua

Despite far greater efforts to improve social services and support for the poor in Nicaragua, by 1989 substantial numbers of children could be seen on the streets of Managua selling chewing gum, cigarettes, matches and other goods. There are said to be more of these child street vendors than there were a few years ago – a reflection of the intense economic problems. Certainly, many of these children have families and, in marked contrast to El Salvador, many of them at least manage to study for a few years. At the end of the 1980s, the evening shift (accelerated primary) in urban schools was usually filled with youngsters who were working during the day. However, as Jacqueline Sanchez of the Ministry of Education pointed out, in marginal urban communities 'there are problems teaching kids who have to juggle work with study – they won't have the energy'.

These under-age workers are not a new phenomenon in Nicaragua, and the Sandinista government seemed to accept as a reality, though not a desirable one, that children under fourteen do work. The authorities' main goal was to try and ensure that those who work have some protection and also some opportunities to study, both at school and in literacy classes. A survey on child workers in Managua in 1984, before the economic crisis deepened, looked at a sample of 450 children aged eight to fourteen who worked. It also interviewed some of the people who were responsible for them – parents, heads of household or guardians. The size of the problem has grown since then and the study made no claims to precision, but it gives some idea of these children's situation.[12]

Out of the sample, 144, or one-third, were girls. It is not clear whether this represented the overall balance of males to females in the workforce under fourteen. A substantial proportion came from families who had migrated from the countryside. In 48 per cent of cases, the person responsible for the children was their mother, rather than either both parents (37 per cent) or the father (7 per cent). For some of these children, access to school had also been inhibited by lack of documentation; for example, birth certificates. Some two-thirds of the sample were studying while working, though well over half of these were above the age for the grade they were in. In the group aged eight to ten (the average age of the children was twelve) only 25 per cent of the total and 15 per cent of the girls were judged to be literate by a test conducted by the survey team. Just over half of this age group and 67 per cent of the girls were completely illiterate. The remainder were all functionally illiterate; that is, they could only read or write with great difficulty.

However, by the age of fourteen, 86.5 per cent (82 per cent of the girls) were literate. The relatively high levels of literacy among this age group may reflect the effects of the rapid increases in school attendance after the revolution, with these children getting at least a few years of schooling. Certainly the sample showed a greater propensity to attend school in the thirteen to fourteen age group. Obviously the accelerated primary programme has been a considerable help for these children, allowing them to study while continuing to work. Unfortunately, it is impossible to tell how many of the eight to ten age group have gone on to study and become literate. However, judging by the economic crisis of the late 1980s, the number of youngsters not getting an education may have increased, both because of increased pressure to go out to work, and also the lack of resources for adult and accelerated primary classes.

However, the study also suggested that it would be misleading to lump together all under-age workers. For example, those who were apprentices and workers in the service sector had much higher school attendance and literacy rates than shoe-shiners, street vendors and unpaid family workers. In the latter categories were to be found the highest proportion of illiterates, of those who had not been to school, and of those who had only reached fourth grade or less by the age of fourteen. These children work long or irregular hours making it difficult to fit in schooling, and nothing in their work would encourage or reinforce literacy.

Conditions in the classroom

The economic crisis, inflation, low wages and unemployment all make it more difficult for children to get to school and stay there. But for those in class, conditions often inhibit effective learning. Furthermore, low pay, poor conditions and constant shortages make teachers' lives very difficult.

The view of many educationists at present is that, other things being equal, class size is not a crucial determinant of success in learning. However, this generally assumes a class size of fifty or under, and reasonable conditions. In some places in Central America, classes can be between sixty and 100 at primary level. In the region, many educationists argue that the multi-grade schools with a single teacher, which are to be found in many rural areas, are highly unsatisfactory. Certainly, classroom management and lesson planning for this kind of teaching requires skills not often possessed by the average under-trained primary teacher.

None of this does any good to the teacher's mental or physical health or ability to cope with the job. Neither, in many cases, does the school environment. In several countries, the shortage of classrooms and the condition of those which exist has been made much worse by war, earthquake and hurricane. In El Salvador and Nicaragua, many schools in conflict zones have been damaged or closed, and in El Salvador, Nicaragua and Guatemala earthquakes and hurricanes have destroyed schools.

Very often in rural districts and poor urban districts, teaching and learning take place in dark classrooms, poorly ventilated and sometimes with water coming in when it rains; sometimes without enough desks for the children or any chair or table for the teacher. In El Salvador, the government recently inaugurated a school in which no desks had been provided, and from the first day children received their lessons sitting on the floor. According to one interviewee it is not uncommon to see children shivering from the cold of the floor and because they have not eaten before coming to school.

In Nicaragua, another problem has been shortage of water and electricity. In the countryside, the government has made efforts to improve the supply of drinking water and electric power, but there are often shortages. According to one rural teacher:

Sometimes we have to send the children home because there isn't any water. The cuts are supposed to be on Wednesdays and Saturdays but sometimes we go 15 days without this service and we collect water in tanks because we can't stop the school for so long.

Malnourished, tired children do not learn well, and find it hard to concentrate. If they are malnourished over a long period, they are also vulnerable to disease, which means time away from school. In Guatemala, the Education Minister in the Cerezo government, Eduardo Meyer, quoted a survey carried out by his Ministry which showed that in 1986, eight out of ten pupils who attended primary school arrived with empty stomachs.[13]

Although school feeding programmes may well miss out the children most in need – those whose families cannot afford to send them to school – for many children, school is the one place where they receive a square meal. Withdrawing such programmes, as has apparently occurred in some areas in El Salvador, removes an important nutritional prop. The following evidence from Costa Rica suggests also that the provision of a school meal may encourage the poorest parents to keep children at school, and that the withdrawal of this benefit may tip the scales in the decision to take them out of school.

Costa Rica offered the one of the best feeding programmes in the region for pre-school and school children. The Centros de Educación y

Nutrición (CEN) operated child feeding centres in the middle of the day, and the Centros Infantiles de Nutrición y Atención Integral (Cinai) offered food and education to children all day long. There were also school meal programmes for primary schools. However, these programmes have been reduced in the last few years by cutbacks in government expenditure. The budget assigned to these programmes has been cut, so that the quality and quantity of food for the children has declined. In addition, many of the staff working on the programmes, mainly the cooks, have been sacked. Food is sent to the education centres, but in many of them there is no cook.

In many cases, the parents and the community have organized to pay the salary of a cook so that the children can be fed at the centres. However, the communities or parents do not always have the money to pay the cook's salary, in which case the children are left without food. In this situation, some parents prefer to take their children out of school, especially if they have to travel long distances to get there. As one community representative in a poor neighbourhood explained:

If there is no meal provided at school, many parents are of the opinion that it's better for the child to be hungry at home, than go hungry to school. Before, the school meals represented an alternative for households with very low income, because they knew that even if the child couldn't eat at home, at least if s/he went to school they got a meal.

For people in these marginal situations, education may be in the abstract desirable but in practice it cannot always be highest on their list of priorities. Family survival may dictate other strategies, or choices as to how many children can go to school and for how long. In some communities, first choice is given to boys. For example, in the rural area of Quiché in Guatemala there are strong cultural barriers against education for women, whether as adults or children. As a community worker in Guatemala explains, 'The woman is denied access to education not only because she has to go outside her own communities [to receive it] which the men do not allow, but because she believes that her place is in the home.'

However, the attitude to women's education is not the same everywhere in Central America. For example, in Costa Rica it has become accepted that both girls and boys should go to school. In fact, in poorer communities, especially in the rural areas, more boys than girls leave school, especially at secondary level, in order to work. In other words, the 'opportunity cost' of keeping boys at school is greater than it is for girls. The major problem for young women outside the main urban centres is the difficulty of making any use of their schooling.

In societies which offer minimal prospects of advancement for people in the poorer sections of society, the incentives to make the sacrifices to keep children at school are not great. And there is a further, ideological dimension to this problem. Where the government not only fails to provide anything approaching full educational coverage and the formal education system is simply not relevant to most people's lives, this may act as a deterrent to participation. A clear case of this alienation can be seen in Guatemala. An Indian interviewee from a village in Chimaltenango describes the combined effects of poverty and the alienation of learning in a 'foreign' language:

When kids reach fourth or fifth grade, many parents take their children away from school, either because they cannot afford the necessary textbooks and exercise books, or they need them to help their work. That's why most adults are illiterate, because as kids they get taken away from school. The other main problem is that the language we speak mostly in this area is Cakchiquel. Sometimes the teachers only speak Spanish so the poor child doesn't understand. Because they don't understand, the teachers think they are stupid and so the child gets really frightened.[14]

Financial problems in the education system as a whole are increasing the marginalization of those with the least resources to fall back on. The shortage of government funding leaves schools with a choice between being without resources or seeking them from communities. Long-term private sector investment or even charitable donations are not often to be found for the day-to-day running expenses of a village or slum school. So teachers and parents' associations have had to fall back on the help of their communities to collect funds through activities such as raffles and sales, or, alternatively, to ask for a monthly quota or fee to try to cover the basic material resources needed. The communities may not object to contributing, but for families whose economic situation is already marginal, to ask them to take on any added financial burden is to make their position worse. As one interviewee in Honduras remarked, 'There are people who can't even buy tortillas, much less contribute to buying a desk'.

Notes

1. Burgos-Debray (1984), *passim.*
2. Surveys in La Tigra and San Jorge, Los Chiles.
3. García and Gomáriz (1989), vols 1 and 2, *passim.*
4. Montes (1986), p.315 (translated from Spanish).
5. Montes (1988), p.518; 'El Salvador: Conyuntura Económica' (1987).
6. Fundación Salvadoreña . . . (1987).
7. Chant (1985), p.25.
8. González de la Rocha (1988), p.214.
9. Based on *Out of the Ashes* . . . (1985), p.22.
10   Arzamendia Candia (1985).
11.   Acker (1986), pp.61–2.
12.   D'Ciofalo (1986).
13.   Painter (1987), pp.3–4.
14.   Painter (1987), p.8.

CHAPTER 12

Family, community and education in Africa: rural Zimbabwe and Khartoum, Sudan

Conditions in the Kezi and Umzingwane Districts, Matabeleland South Province, Zimbabwe

Matabeleland South is a predominantly rural province of Zimbabwe, where only 2.6 per cent of the population are classified as urban dwellers (compared with a national average of 25.7 per cent). It lies adjacent to the border with South Africa. In the period of white government, the opportunities for rural black children to complete primary school were limited and girls had even fewer chances than boys. There were very few secondary school places for blacks, and for these there was intense competition. In a marginal area such as Kezi district there was only one secondary school, and in Umzingwane, two. Since education was not free at any level, sending children on to secondary school usually meant a major financial sacrifice on the part of parents. As it was, for every 100 black children who entered primary school, only twenty completed the primary cycle, only six entered secondary school and four got as far as Form Four.

Although the war of liberation was less intense in this part of the country than in the northern and eastern provinces, the period after independence from 1980 until 1987 was plagued by instability caused by the political conflict between the ruling ZANU(PF) and the opposition ZAPU parties. Dissident armed groups attacked villages and farms in rural Matabeleland, and the Zimbabwean army's response to these attacks led to destruction of infrastructure and the harassment of local people. In these circumstances, it was impossible either for people or government to turn their energies to development. Kezi was particularly hard hit, with numbers of young men jumping the border into South Africa to escape the bitter political strife. Qualified teachers left the rural areas for the safety of the towns, and families also moved away from trouble spots, causing a sharp drop in school enrolments.

Since 1987, the region has faced the daunting task of restoring its infrastructure and embarking on new development. But throughout the 1980s, prolonged periods of drought have caused shortages of food and water, and seriously affected agricultural production. In the worst period, Kezi region was particularly hard hit, with over 70,000 people reportedly in need of drought relief. Though in 1989 drought was not a problem country-wide it was still causing problems in Matabeleland, as well as in parts of Mashonaland, and in Manicaland. Although there was sufficient food nationally to supply these regions, shortages remained in drought areas because of insufficient transport to get food to needy areas.[1]

The government, with the assistance of some external agencies, implemented feeding programmes and drought relief assistance from 1982 onwards. However, the effects of the drought were severe. In Matabeleland South, there was a considerable increase in cases of malnutrition, and children were reportedly fainting with hunger at school. The Organization of Rural Associations for Progress (ORAP), a Zimbabwean non-governmental rural development organization, began running school feeding programmes in twelve schools in the worst-affected areas of Kezi. This helped to improve school attendance and normalize children's health status. In 1984, when both the 'troubles' and drought were affecting life in Matabeleland, a report summarized the main reasons for drop-out at primary level as follows: parents leaving the area; unconfirmed transfers (where a school had a record of a pupil leaving to go to another school, but the pupil was not registered at the new school); the security situation; financial difficulties; lack of interest or discouragement of pupils. Also mentioned, for girls in Grade Three upwards, were pregnancy and early marriage.

Education, family income and economic problems

Table 12.1   Zimbabwe: Matabeleland South – School enrolments, government and non-government schools, 1987

	Matabeleland South			National total		
	M	F	(F % of total)	M	F	(F % of total)
Primary						
Grade 1	12,795	12,248	48.9	187,470	185,523	49.7
Grade 7	13,452	12,130	47.4	171,898	154,004	47.2
Secondary						
Form 1	8,587	7,183	45.5	114,416	88,483	43.6
Form 3	3,879	2,441	38.6	73,467	50,636	40.0
Form 4	3,558	2,057	36.6	69,524	44,391	38.9

Source: Annual Report of the Secretary for Education 1987, tables 2 and 3

Despite all these disadvantages, the greater availability of schooling since independence has had evident benefits, in terms of enrolments, and how long children stay at school. There is little doubt, here as elsewhere in the country, of people's interest in seeing their children well educated.

But in poor rural communities, these changes have also had their costs. The poorest parents, especially those wholly or largely dependent on the vagaries of rain-fed farming, find the demands made on parents to contribute to the cost of schooling difficult to meet. For those with only limited amounts of land and livestock, and without any in-flow of migrant remittances, a drought year or a year of bad harvest means there is no surplus income with which to pay fees. Producer prices of maize (the staple crop) have been kept above the rate of inflation, but prices of food and other goods to consumers have risen rapidly, sometimes more so in isolated areas where the cost of transport is high. So if families become net consumers of food, rather than net producers, they are vulnerable to these inflationary trends. Another problem is the timing of demands for school fees, which may fall, for example, before harvest, when there is no money coming in. This can cause short-term problems leading to indebtedness, arrears of fees (where permitted) or temporary withdrawal of children from school.

Some people have lost access to land or livestock because of extended periods of drought and civil disturbance. During the 1980s, increasing numbers of men have gone to look for work in the towns or over the border in South Africa or Botswana. In Zimbabwe, as in other countries of the region, women form the backbone of the farming population. They often shoulder most of the responsibility for food production as well as for domestic work and finding money to feed, clothe and educate their children. Country-wide, it is estimated that about one-third of rural households receive remittances from husbands or relatives in urban areas or working in countries to the south, though in the communities described here, relatively few families appear to rely on them. Among the poorest families are those headed by women who do not receive any remittances.

In Matabeleland South, a number of initiatives have been taken, mainly by women, to form local mutual support groups. These have subsequently been supported by ORAP to form extended 'family units' (*amalima*) which, through group savings and productive activities, give support to community members who have fallen on hard times. One form of support is help in keeping their children at school. The information which follows comes from discussions within these groups and interviews with teachers and pupils at schools in Kezi and Umzingwane districts, particularly those schools with which these groups co-operate.

The costs of education

Women of the Mazwi group in Matobo (Kezi district) outlined how they were being squeezed by drought and unemployment:

It is difficult to get money to educate our children because our husbands are not working. For the past years, this district has not received rains. Without water there is very little we can achieve to raise the school fees which are so high and at the same time try to supplement the food shortage. The drought has also taken its toll on our livestock which we could have sold to raise the school fees. This is beyond our means.

Some of the women in the Mazwi group had husbands working in South Africa who occasionally sent money for school fees. But three had husbands who had disappeared to South Africa, leaving them to fend for the family. Another family unit, at Donkwe-Donkwe, was supporting two women whose husbands had disappeared during the political disturbances, and no one knew what had happened to them.

Women themselves try numerous activities besides crop production to raise funds for education. These include brewing beer for sale, selling chickens or goats, weaving baskets, making bread, fencing fields, and illegally crossing the border to South Africa to buy goods for re-sale – a highly risky exercise. Other options are temporary wage labour and cattle herding on neighbours' land. For the most part the amounts of money they earn are very small.

Primary school charges are considered manageable for all but the very poorest families, or those with a large number of children of school age. There are no fees at primary level, but families have to pay into the school building fund – Z$10 a year – and Z$3–4 for sports funds, school functions and a general purpose fee. The big expense is school uniforms, which are compulsory and cost Z$30–45. In addition, parents are expected to pay for pencils, rubbers and rulers.

At secondary school level, however, there is a widespread feeling that fees are too high – and they are still rising. As the secretary of the Donkwe-Donkwe group remarked, 'It's becoming beyond our efforts . . . . It's not because we want them [the children] to go out and work but it's the lack [of money for] the school fees which forces us to withdraw them.'

Teachers and parents' groups gave the following estimates of secondary school fees and charges in 1989:

	Z$
Fees, building fund, sports fee and general purpose fund (per annum)	124 –174
Uniforms	60 – 70
Extra payments for practical subjects (mentioned by teacher at Tshelanyemba Secondary School):	
Agriculture	6
Fashion and fabric	8
Building	12
Exams:	
Zimbabwe Junior Certificate	20
'O' levels: Z$29 per subject (information from Nswazi school)	

Teachers at Nswazi Secondary School commented that these fees, especially the examination fees, were much too high for rural people, especially for those on incomes of Z$100 a month and below. Over 60 per cent of pupils had not yet paid their fees for the year. Policies vary from one rural district council to another as to whether children can stay at school if fees are not paid, though the government has said it intends to standardize the rules.

Some parents have been forced by economic hardships to take their children out of school, and few children are able to complete their 'O' levels because most parents cannot afford the examination fees: sometimes they can only afford two or three subjects, while five passes are needed to get an 'O' level certificate. It is common for youngsters to drop out at Form Three just before taking 'O' level – at the age of fifteen or sixteen. At the secondary school in Silobi, the headmaster said that at one time there were seventy-nine students in Form Three who were ready to register for 'O' level the next year but only thirty-one actually wrote the exam. Most had dropped out because their parents could not afford to pay the exam fees.

Parents with a number of school-age children obviously find things difficult. A member of the Donkwe-Donkwe group said that she had five children still at school – two at secondary level and three at primary level. 'To meet the cost, this has forced me to brew beer which is illegal.'

One 18-year-old from Nswazi – still in Form Three – explained his predicament.

I come from a broken family. At present I live with my mother and stepfather, and my stepfather is not willing pay my fees. My mother buys vegetables for re-sale and during the school holidays I also sell vegetables to raise money for my school uniform. The money which my mother raises is not enough to cater for school fees and food. For the past two terms, I have not paid school fees and I have been sent away from school several times. [He was also unable to write his mid-year exams because school fees had not been paid.] It looks like next year I will not able to continue my education because of lack of fees.

Gender and education

In a survey conducted in Highfields township in Harare just before independence, the main reason given by women as to why they dropped out of education, whether at primary or secondary level, was financial (before independence, fees were charged at all levels in black education). It was also linked to the priority given to boys. For example: 'My father did not believe in educating daughters. After primary school, he said he only had money for my brother to go to secondary school.' And again, 'We were a very poor family. My father only had enough money to educate my brother up to Form Two. I only went as far as Standard Three [five years of primary school].'[2]

Social attitudes to female education may be changing in Zimbabwe, but they are doing so slowly, especially when it comes to priorities between boys and girls in rural areas at secondary level, when money is tight. Very considerable strides have been made, even in poor regions of the country, in provision of primary education, and access to it. In terms of gender, both in areas with high and with lower drop-out rates, girls' enrolment at primary level is about equal to that of boys.

In 1984–85, the nation-wide transition rate to secondary school was almost 84 per cent for boys and 79 per cent for girls. A study of Chipinga, a mainly rural district in the east of the country, showed an overall transition rate of 74.6 per cent, but it varied between zones from 39 per cent to 94 per cent. It is likely that such unevennesses would be found in other rural areas, such as those in Matabeleland South. In secondary school, the enrolment figures for girls continue to decline in relation to those of boys. In 1987 in Matabeleland South, girls made up 45.5 per cent of enrolments in Form One (nationally 43.6) but by Form Four this had slipped to 36.6 per cent (nationally, 38.9).[3]

Discussions with parents and teachers in the two districts revealed an interest in educating daughters, but at the same time some built-in prejudices in favour of boys. Some mothers emphasized the importance of educating children of both sexes. Women in the Mazwi group said: 'Our society is changing and we have realized that education is important for our children, whether boys or girls, and we struggle for all of them.' They added that their daughters were the mothers of tomorrow and they need to earn money to look after their families 'and even to look after us as our sons are deserting us for South Africa'.

In practice, however, others admitted that when it came to choices in poor families as to which children should go through secondary school, the boys tended to be chosen. The headmistress of Bezha Secondary School said that economic pressures were severe and the school had an estimated drop-out rate of 30 per cent a year. Early in secondary school, she said, is when parents 'begin doing things in favour of boys', and pick 'the most intelligent' to continue. Teachers also noted that parents sometimes made heavy demands on girls to do domestic and farm work as well as going to school. They were expected to fetch water, which can mean walking miles, or to work in the fields.

Some observers have also remarked that there is often gender discrimination by teachers in the classroom. Boys receive more attention and are often given priority in the distribution of scarce school materials and books. In secondary schools in Matabeleland South, about 75 per cent of teachers are male.

The question of schoolgirl pregnancy was raised several times. This is a major issue in Zimbabwe and is often aired in the media. But there is a general tendency, echoed in the interviews, to blame the girls, without questioning the role of the males involved, whether young boys or, as is not uncommon, male school-teachers. The fear of girls becoming pregnant also acted as a deterrent to keeping girls at school. In the Donkwe-Donkwe group, it was said that while education was important for their daughters, 'the great problem is school pregnancy. We struggle to raise school fees for them [daughters] but they disappoint us. This influences us to give priority to boys'. A similar point was made by people in the Sezhube group. Girls are also withdrawn from school to make early marriages, sometimes under economic pressure from their families.

Among women of the older generation questioned, most were keen on some kind of literacy or skills training but not happy with what was at present available. They may not be representative because they are women who are active in community affairs. But a number made the point that, although initially people had attended literacy classes (part of the national literacy campaign – see Chapter 16), they became discouraged by lack of books and materials. They added that as the teachers were unpaid volunteers, there was a high turnover and frequent absenteeism. Such teachers clearly did not succeed in inspiring these learners. In a number of cases, people said that literacy classes had now closed. Another difficulty mentioned – and not often taken into account in literacy work – was that many older people have eyesight problems. Furthermore, the years when literacy classes had been established in the area (1983 onwards) were also the years of political instability, when 'people were generally harassed if found at any gathering'.

Women involved in the 'family units' saw the importance of education for themselves. Basic literacy meets immediate economic and practical needs: 'We are required to sign for our ID cards, passports and voting, and we can read the Bible in Church. But, above all, most of us are engaged in small businesses like sewing or poultry, and these need proper management if you are to succeed.' This might include opening bank accounts. For others it was important, especially with families scattered in other parts of the country, to be able to read and write letters.

Some of the women agreed that literacy and skills training gave them more chance to take control of their own lives. If they could earn money independently, some felt that it improved their relationships with their husbands, resulting in more co-operation and understanding, and greater partnership in dealing with the many problems which confront families. The very fact that a woman is earning money which she controls means she is likely to have more bargaining and decision-making power in the household.[4] None the less, there were those who sounded a warning note that advanced or higher education for women could cause conflict in a marriage, as the man 'feels low and unrespected'. Man's accepted role is as the head of household, even if in many cases he is frequently absent from that household. Clearly, many women have internalized this reluctance to embarrass or annoy their husbands by pushing for high levels of education.

Community financing and initiatives

At Tshelanyemba Secondary School, parents have contributed to the construction of school classrooms, toilets and teachers' houses, providing local building materials, moulding bricks and paying builders. They also participate in the meetings of the Parent–Teacher Association (PTA) and have income-generating projects to raise money for the school. They keep poultry, rabbits and an orchard, from the proceeds of which they help to buy desks and other school equipment. They also make a small contribution of Z$2 per child for school functions. Parents who cannot afford to pay towards the building are expected to offer labour instead – for example, by making bricks. This seems to be the usual range of community contributions to education, though evidently the dynamism and effectiveness of PTAs vary from area to area.

There have also been other kinds of community-based initiatives which give support to the poorest families. 'Family units', supported by ORAP, began in different years, triggered by the economic crisis caused by drought and political instability. ORAP has helped them to organize themselves and supported them financially and in acquiring equipment for income-generating projects. They are modelled on long-standing forms of communal solidarity between extended family groupings, mainly but not exclusively composed of women. Income-generating and community development projects have developed around the country since independence and are very much encouraged by the Ministry of Community and Cooperative Development. Both ORAP's work and that of other groups has also received support from a variety of foreign aid agencies.

It is a measure of the perceived importance of education and, for some, the financial difficulties entailed in keeping children at school, that a major priority among these groups is sustaining the education of children. The group in Donkwe-Donkwe grew out of the crises of the mid-1980s. As they explain,

1984 was a particularly hard time for most of us in this district because of the drought problems and the political instability. There was a severe food and water shortage which resulted in many families withdrawing their children from school because they could not afford to pay school fees and at the same time buy food. . . . Because of these problems, we then decided to mobilize ourselves into collective traditional family units to pool our ideas and small resources and solve our problems together.

Among ourselves we identified three needy members whose children had been sent away from school because of lack of school fees. . . .We then decided to raise funds to sponsor these destitute cases. For a start, each member contributed Z$5 and we managed to raise about Z$100. With this, we initiated a project on gardening and poultry. Other members were involved in traditional crafts like basketry and wood carving. The proceeds from these efforts went towards school fees for two of the destitute pupils and the other child was assisted by outside funds from ORAP.

They are members of ORAP and are encouraged to organize their work 'through dialoguing in meetings until we understood the situation and our problems'.

The types of projects they undertake are similar to those which individual women mentioned as ways of earning extra money, combined with collecting small sums of money in the unity club. ORAP sometimes helps with particular projects – for example, by providing wire netting, cement and chicks for a poultry project. Some of the 'family units' do not deal with the question of school fees but concentrate on more general forms of support. The Ihlanganyela group (Sibomvu area) started in 1986 and makes school uniforms for the local primary school, with ORAP support. But they also act as a mutual aid society for daily needs – mealie meal (maize meal), salt and cabbages, and clothing – to help members who experience misfortunes, such as a death in the family.

The groups had a variety of income-generating ideas, but the main factors inhibiting project development were said to be lack of water and lack of capital funds. In Mbizo area, one group said they had twice started chicken-rearing projects and had been forced to give up by the water shortage. Another group complained of constant queues at the local water borehole. Trying to generate off-farm income on a regular basis is difficult without initial investment capital, which a number of groups in the survey were clearly struggling to raise. However, it is certainly easier for groups to raise such funds than it is for individual women, or families. ORAP provides some capital inputs to projects, but the demand seems to outstrip supply.

Women in this area, as in other parts of Africa, are under increasing pressure to expand their monetary contribution to the household, in addition to their other roles. Certainly in Zimbabwe and Zambia, the need to meet school fees is a new and rising cost for which they often find themselves responsible. In these circumstances, skills become very important. Women in the groups expressed the wish to have much more practical training, to increase the possibilities of income generation. The Sezhube group suggested an education centre where training in agriculture, building, sewing and home economics could be offered. Others suggested that if an electricity generator were to be installed in the local school, it would be possible to have evening classes. Others wanted to learn book-keeping and management. Apart from this demand for new kinds of education, women in unity groups in Bonjeni district stated that their relationships both with other community members and with their own families had been changed for the better since the clubs had started.

In school

In rapidly growing rural schools, equipment and facilities have not kept up with demand. In some secondary schools, ten children were sharing one textbook, and because of the shortage of building materials, especially cement, there were not enough classrooms, even where the community was prepared to build them or pay for the building. Consequently, in good weather some classes are held under the trees with no desks, while in bad weather they all squeeze into one classroom. A secondary school teacher described the situation as follows:

Most rural schools are poorly equipped, but they are expected to undertake the same examinations as urban schools which are better equipped. For instance, we have no proper laboratory, apparatus or chemicals but the students are expected to sit for a science practical at the end of the year.

The government is introducing curricular changes to give a more practical orientation to secondary education. However, the changes have not become fully effective in these rural areas as yet, though there appears to be local enthusiasm for this kind of development. A teacher at Tshelanyemba school observed:

Although there have been some fundamental changes in the educational system with the introduction of technical subjects such as sewing, building, agriculture, carpentry and so on, the implementation of these subjects leaves a lot to be desired. There are serious bottlenecks in nearly all schools, including this one, because of the poor supply of equipment and lack of water which make it impossible to carry out many practical tasks as intended. Thus the pupils' motivation diminishes.

Drought conditions have stymied all kinds of school agricultural projects.

However, he added that he did not want to be too critical – there were some successes. He told the story of two girl pupils doing a building course. They were doing well but their parents could not afford to keep them at school any longer. The school talked to their parents and managed to arrange a contract with a local businessman for the pupils to build a store. Thus they were gaining practical experience while earning the money to pay for their fees. Heartening though this may be, especially in a male-stereotyped occupation, the question is whether they will be able to find regular work once they leave school.

According to some mothers, a bureaucratic hitch has increased the problem of late starting at school, quite common in rural areas, where many pupils are above the age for their grade. They cited the difficulty in obtaining children's birth certificates which are required to register children at primary school. Some of the women said they had registered and paid for their children's birth certificates as far back as 1982, but despite going all the way to Bulawayo had not yet received them.

There are also numerous practical difficulties for staff: teachers are often not paid on time and are often absent, chasing up their salaries during working hours. Another irritation mentioned was that during examinations, completed papers are supposed to be delivered to the regional office daily, from each rural school, whether it is remote or close by. Transport is often difficult to find and no transport allowance is given to the person who makes the delivery.

For the most part, teachers' living conditions are not attractive: often several teachers have to share a room or a very small house. A student said that teachers come and go frequently because of poor conditions. Other teachers confirmed that qualified staff were often lured away by the attractions of schools in town or more privileged private schools. One group of teachers noted that many non-government schools were unregistered – in fact fourteen out of eighteen in Matobo district council area and eight out of twelve in Umzingwane. This, they said, meant that headmasters were not paid at the proper rate. This diminishes the headmaster's authority and, as another teacher pointed out, encourages corruption, such as embezzlement of fees, something which was complained of nation-wide in the Ministry of Education's annual report in 1987.[5]

A large number of teachers are still unqualified. At primary level, only a relatively small proportion of teachers in government schools are unqualified (7.2 per cent country-wide in primary schools and 18.9 per cent in secondary schools) but in the non-government or government-aided schools almost half the teachers are classified as untrained: 50 per cent in primary schools and 45 per cent in secondary schools. In Matabeleland South, there are very few government schools and in the non-government sector at primary level, 49 per cent of teachers are untrained (59 per cent of the women teachers) and at secondary level, 53.5 per cent (women teachers, 49 per cent).[6]

Community attitudes

There was a general feeling among interviewees that health and general social conditions in the rural areas had improved since independence, and there was universal praise for government efforts to promote health education, especially among women. Village health workers, mainly local women, some of them trained through the literacy programme, seemed much appreciated. Some women were also very pleased to have pre-school education for their children, though this still seems to be at the early stages of development, both here and in other parts of the country. There was also general approval of the developments in agricultural extension services, in which women's role in farming has certainly been taken more seriously than in many other parts of Africa.

The people interviewed, mainly women, but also men and boys, of different age groups, all saw benefits flowing from education, both of children and adults. These included greater independence, hygiene and health, improved lifestyle, the importance of literacy, communal unity and better family life (including men contributing financially to the education of children). However, in practical terms, the effects of slow economic growth, combined with the setbacks from drought and political conflict in this region, seemed for many people to frustrate the efforts and sacrifices made to achieve education. Two points came across very strongly. First, parents were upset and angry at high rates of failure in examinations. Children, they said, were learning but not benefiting from it, which made it all the more unlikely that they would get jobs and thus relieve the parents of the financial burden of keeping them. In turn, pupils often felt discouraged and demoralized by failure. Some people blamed unqualified teachers and poor school conditions. Others thought the curriculum was inappropriate. Many stressed the importance of changing the curriculum to emphasize more practically oriented courses, both in schools and adult education and literacy courses. They wanted to learn skills that people could use, preferably in a local, rural context.

However, others went on to say that the kind of education received was irrelevant anyway: you couldn't get a job even if you passed the exams because economic opportunities were not there. 'You don't receive the fruits of the labour [of education].' Unemployment loomed as a stark problem for those leaving school. One alternative mentioned for young men was to go to South Africa or Botswana in search of work. But as far as finding work locally was concerned, prospects were not good. Even those who do get good 'O' level passes, noted the Mazwi group, cannot find jobs or vacancies in training institutions.

This could lead to youngsters getting involved in crime and drugs, some said. A school student added that even school graduates in the rural areas with five 'O' levels 'are loitering around without jobs, except for those who did practical subjects like agriculture or building – they have formed co-operatives'.

Some ambivalence therefore emerged about the results of education; while everyone thought it was a good thing in general, they were not always happy with the practical outcomes they see in Zimbabwe today. Interviewees clearly linked the success of education with improvements in their overall economic situation, especially economic development in their own region. Drought and water shortage were viewed as the most serious immediate problem and one which the government could do more to alleviate, especially by building dams and boreholes. Another recurring theme was the need for better transport and communications, and the opening up of markets for local products.

They were willing to contribute to education, but felt that the government needed to do its share towards broader development, and also that given their economic circumstances, secondary fees were unreasonably high. Some demanded that education should be free in both school cycles. The Mazwi group of women took this view:

'Yes, we certainly have an obligation to participate in education and development. We as women play an important and decisive role in development. But we need assistance from our government and other development agencies.'

Khartoum, Sudan: pressures on urban education

Drought or war in rural areas puts heavy pressure on towns and cities, as people migrate in search of work and relative security. In Khartoum, the economic crisis and the influx of people from other regions have caused a decline in the quality of education provision and growing inequities in access.

Interviews conducted in late 1989 with education officials and teachers and in schools in two Khartoum communities revealed some of these problems. As-Sahafa (Bloc 21) is a largely low-income district in the southern part of the old city of Khartoum. Halfaia is a more economically mixed community on the edge of Khartoum North, where the inhabitants include farmers, merchants and salaried people.

The cost of public education for low-income groups is becoming 'unbearably high', according to the interviewees. First, families have to pay for textbooks, exercise books, pens, pencils and other school equipment. Because of the deteriorating physical state of many schools, pupils are sometimes officially required to provide their own desks and chairs. Lack of funds for running and maintaining schools has forced headmasters and school administrations to levy additional fees for repairs, books, cleaning and new construction. In poor neighbourhoods, fewer people are able to pay these costs. This, in its turn, contributes to worsening conditions in the school.

In addition, parents face the rising costs of clothing, transport and meals and health care for children. The consumer price index (1980 = 100) reached 650 in 1987, and 965 in 1988. Consequently, poor families are increasingly concentrating on survival rather than education for their children. Some have been forced to take their children out of school, sometimes sacrificing the education of girls for that of boys. Others look for additional jobs to pay for these growing obligations, and many have sunk into severe indebtedness.

The interviews suggested that poor families who were increasingly unable to meet the rising costs of educating their children faced fewer and fewer chances that their children would get as far as tertiary education. People saw the unequal distribution of educational opportunity as increasing. Wealthy people can afford to pay for their children's education and the poor cannot. Those without reserves of savings are increasingly unable to earn enough money to meet these costs. The cost of higher education has increased during the 1980s, which is a deterrent, even for those who manage to get through the school certificate exam. Completion of schooling and access to higher education becomes a direct function of income, rather than of the student's ability.

Drop-out rates, primarily for financial reasons, are said to be much higher for children of poor families. Many drop out before their education can give any benefits in terms of income and employment. It was also pointed out that the majority of poor families have more children of school age and therefore are faced with the considerable cost of keeping a number of children at school at the same time.

With the inability of the state to spend enough on general education, and the deterioration of schools, richer families with fewer children are increasingly resorting to the burgeoning private-sector, fee-paying schools. Another way in which money can purchase better opportunities, even within the state education system, is the widespread employment of private tutors after school to supplement the poor learning conditions at school. Ironically, it is often the schoolteachers themselves who supplement their incomes by doing this kind of work. Even those with modest means try to get tutors for their children, but for the poorest families it is not affordable.

Teachers also commented on the difference in educational achievement levels between poor and richer children. Malnutrition and general weakness were said to affect children's ability to study. They also noted the decline in contacts between parents and children, because the parents have to spend most of their time providing for basic material needs and have little time to spend with their children, leaving them unsupervised and unhelped. They also found that this led to the loss of contact between parents and the school administration, which they saw as as a contributory factor in drop-outs, truancy and involvement in crime.

While in urban areas there is still an interest in getting children through the educational system, some teachers and officials said that in rural areas people do not care much for education, especially in illiterate families. However, this seems to stem at least in part from feelings of social discontent and alienation, and the firm conviction on the part of these families that it is the government which has deprived them of their rights to education.

The worsening economic conditions, drought (especially in western Sudan) and the war in the south, have driven great numbers of people to migrate to Khartoum and the central regions. One result of this is growing homelessness in big cities, and increasing numbers of children who are either separated from their families or whose families cannot support them. There are some 25,000 street children in Khartoum. About a quarter of these children are from Khartoum itself, half from the drought-stricken western regions of Darfur and Kordofan and about 20 per cent from the south.

Table 12.2   **Sudan: street children in Khartoum**

Age	Below 8 years	8 – 11 years	12 – 15 years	16 and above	Total
Total number of street kids	1,425	5,200	12,300	6,075	25,000
% of total	5.7	20.7	49.2	23.3	100

Source: Al-Engaz Al-Watani, no. 44, 7 Nov 1989

For people from the south in particular, coming to the north means crossing a linguistic, cultural and religious divide. For them, the north has many of the characteristics of a foreign country. Children have problems at school because the language of instruction is Arabic. Few of them know more than minimal Arabic, since in the south, particularly in Equatoria province, English or vernacular languages are mainly used in schools.

Notes

1. Radio Zimbabwe, July 1989.
2. Muchena (1980), p.33.
3. *Annual Report of the Secretary for Education* (1987).
4. For an example of this argument from Zambia see Commonwealth Secretariat (1989).
5. *Annual Report of the Secretary for Education* (1987).
6. Ibid.

CHAPTER 13

South Africa: the politics of marginality and educational provision

In South Africa, poverty is primarily the result of segregation on racial lines, although there are economic and social divisions within the black community. In townships like Soweto, there are some people who have managed to get rich by legal or illegal means, but for the most part people are impoverished not only in the economic sense but also by their lack of human and political rights – by being categorized as inferior. In the younger generation, fewer and fewer are prepared to accept this idea of inferiority, but it is hard to escape from its corroding effects in daily life.

An aerial view of Johannesburg and the surrounding black townships (which house more people than the city itself) still offers a visual map of apartheid. On the one hand, there are the tower blocks of the central business district, and like cities in other industrialized countries, the affluent outer suburbs. In these almost every house has its green square of lawn and its blue sparkling patch which is the swimming pool. On the other side, at the outer limits of the city, are the townships, with their endless lines of box-like houses on a back-cloth of red-brown dust which often seems to overwhelm the efforts of householders to create gardens and greenery.

By the end of the 1980s, certain districts had become known as 'grey areas' – inner-city areas like Hillbrow, from which many of the previous white inhabitants have moved. So the tall apartment blocks are largely populated by black and Coloured families, whose presence is not strictly legal. Such areas exist around other cities too, and the inhabitants of such grey areas have been periodically harassed by the authorities. But even when they are permitted to continue living in the area, up to 1990 they have been non-people as far as the provision of facilities is concerned, since these are still designated as 'white' districts. In Hillbrow, for example, with a rapidly falling white population, many 'white' schools are on the verge of closure, with enrolments no more than 30 per cent capacity. Meanwhile, unless their parents can afford private education, black children have to be bussed many miles to township schools, which are turning students away.

Table 13.1   **South Africa: school enrolments**

Area	Year	Std 1		Std 3		Std 6		Std 10	
		M	F	M	F	M	F	M	F
Northern	1981	21,321	20,875	13,491	14,221	6,510	8,059	2,055	1,828
Transvaal	1987	20,841	20,151	16,099	16,405	10,743	11,574	2,776	3,278
Jo'burg	1981	11,725	11,348	9,578	10,389	6,809	8,937	2,489	2,743
	1987	9,948	9,184	9,903	9,996	11,354	12,650	2,804	2,974
Natal	1981	13,503	12,983	8,555	8,380	3,394	3,657	459	732
	1987	14,465	13,504	11,056	10,888	4,937	5,738	1,128	1,173
Kwazulu	1981	62,514	58,930	46,181	44,515	23,873	27,287	4,610	5,081
	1987	81,580	77,041	67,606	66,791	42,542	47,435	11,863	14,847
G'kulu	1981	10,830	10,182	7,309	7,630	3,148	3,312	1,239	963
	1987	17,245	15,691	13,161	12,501	7,971	9,272	3,261	3,728
Lebowa	1981	39,202	36,359	31,588	30,884	16,848	17,794	4,686	3,532
	1987	45,535	42,113	40,762	39,414	32,621	34,168	16,425	17,739

Notes:
1 These are official statistics.
2 Kwazulu has by far the largest homelands education system, and it is also growing very fast.
3 There is a general trend for girls to remain at school longer, and to outnumber boys, in some areas by Standard 3, in most by Standard 6. Boys tend to drop out early to work, and throughout the 1980s because of political conflict.

Sources: DET *Annual Report*, 1981 and 1987

Soweto

More than three million people live in the area called Soweto (an abbreviation of South Western Township). It was established, like other townships, as a separate area to house black workers employed in the white city of Johannesburg and the mines of the Vaal Reef. As people have been migrating to this area in search of work for many years, there is a mix of people of different origins: Xhosa, Pedi, South Sotho, Zulu, Ndebele and Tswana-speaking people. Many of Soweto's inhabitants have lived there all their lives and consider it home, although there has been significant in-migration in recent years, especially since the ending of influx control in 1986. There are now areas of Soweto inhabited by squatters, migrants from the countryside, a situation exacerbated in recent years by drought in some rural areas. There are also squatters living in the back-yards of 'legal' homes.

Though there is now a small middle class, the vast majority of Sowetans could be described as working class. An estimated 60 per cent are either unemployed, or work in the informal sector, as traders, or brewing or selling liquor to make a living. Living conditions are generally cramped and difficult, with severe overcrowding of the standard two- and four-room houses, in which fifteen to twenty people sometimes live. Workers commute daily by bus, train or taxi to Johannesburg, twenty kilometres away.

Soweto has been severely affected for fifteen years by conflict with the security forces. Political resistance and levels of political activism are high, especially among the youth. This was dramatically evidenced by the Soweto uprising of 1976, which was led by school students. Distrust of all agents of government, particularly the police, runs high. In 1985, people in Soweto created street committees to deal with local crime and daily problems, and refused to accept police intervention. These efforts at self-organization were suppressed by the reimposition of the state of emergency in 1986. At the same time, certainly until the end of 1989, the security forces maintained a heavy presence, and tensions were increased by less visible factors such as the use of informers and *agents provocateurs*.

Social tensions appear to have reached an all-time high: many areas are dangerous for their own inhabitants, and crime and gangsterism have been on the rise. This was exacerbated by the breakdown of community organization under the state of emergency. Public facilities in most major urban townships are also under stress from growing numbers of poor rural migrants.

'Leaving your brains at home': attitudes to the education system

It [education] makes one to see him or herself before the mirror as inferior. You have to see yourself as the poorest of the poor because, according to the South African government, that is the way God has made you. Our education does not make you question this pre-supposed status.

Judy Moloi, a parent from Emdeni, Soweto.

Parents, teachers and students from several districts of Soweto gave the following picture of education and their attitudes to it. The survey was conducted in the second half of 1989, before President de Klerk came to office, and addresses educational issues which were of particular concern in Soweto at that time. There was a virtually unanimous view that the existing education system was unequal and exploitative. A high-school student and a member of COSAS (the Congress of South African Students) recorded that,

For apartheid to sustain and maintain the status quo, unequal distribution of knowledge especially in the educational (academic) sphere was a prerequisite. But what does this mean to the alienated black majority? Since its inception, Bantu education met with resistance among black people. The history of resistance can be traced back to the 1950s. Since then [the issue of] education has escalated in our country up until today when the education crisis remains a burning issue.

Parents complained of the under-funding and poor quality of the education their children received, from the system of separate and unequal education authorities to the poor facilities in schools and the high drop-out rates. The system is designed to 'socialize our children to be labourers', one parent remarked. Some pointed out that they had to pay taxes to a government which ruled without their mandate for their children to be taught to feel inferior.

What is more, several interviewees said, the Bantu education system is highly authoritarian at all levels. It 'does not allow you to question authority'. They pointed out that all education measures, from the 1953 Bantu Education Act to recent Department of Education and Training (DET) measures on access to schools, and the development of 'finishing schools' (see page 209), were imposed without consultation. Some people stressed that there had always been resistance by the black community to Bantu education. But attempts to protest about this or any other aspect of government policy have been regularly suppressed by the security forces. Some parents and teachers were particularly concerned at the disruption this caused to schooling, as well as the arrests and detentions which are commonplace. During the states of emergency in the 1980s, large numbers of school-age children were detained, causing, among other things, severe disruption to schooling.

Teachers were particularly aware of the rift that the political situation in the schools had caused between teachers and students. One teacher said that the basic causes of conflict in schools and the alienation of pupils and parents lay in the apartheid system of education which controls finance, administration and legislation. But 'the burden has been shifted from those primary causes to . . . parents, community and students. [The problems of] education today are blamed on [these] secondary causes'. Another teacher pointed to the ideological distortions in the curriculum, especially in the presentation of South African history. Yet another said that nearly all subjects have no relevance to everyday application. Education is viewed as separate from society. 'It is an institution which promotes its own course.'

One high-school student tersely summed up this problem: 'The textbooks and the teachers are the ones to do the thinking for the students. It's a system of leave your brains at home and come to school.'

The state of schools

Schools in Soweto are in a poor condition as a result of the combination of years of under-funding and damage caused during confrontations with the security forces and by internal school violence. Both teachers and pupils talk of learning in classrooms with no windows, or broken doors, a considerable ordeal in Johannesburg's cold winters. Pupils frequently have to clean classrooms, and they or teachers have to buy their own cleaning materials.

Until 1987, black students had to purchase all their own school materials, though these were provided free in white schools. However, despite a DET announcement that textbooks would be provided for all black students, the reality seems to have been rather different. According to teachers and pupils in Soweto, books either did not turn up, or were the wrong books or arrived very late. A parent said that at her daughter's junior secondary school (Tladi Junior Secondary School in Mofolo North) in 1989 it was six weeks into the term before any books or stationery were delivered. Equipment, especially for teaching science, is in short supply, as are science laboratories. What are called science laboratories, said a teacher, are just like any other classrooms, without equipment or material for experiments.

Exclusions, expulsions and drop-outs

Since 1987, there has been a considerable increase in secondary school enrolments, as pupils returned to school after the years of boycott and disruption. This has put pressure on school places, as the system is not expanding fast enough to cope. The DET's response has been to impose restrictions on how long pupils can stay at school, ostensibly to relieve pressure on school numbers. However, the way in which this has been implemented has caused great resentment in the black community because a number of the criteria for exclusion are clearly political, and others are regarded as extremely unfair. Furthermore, since the department has left it to individual school principals to enforce these rules, the rift between students and school authorities has been further deepened, with students' anger and hostility sometimes manifesting itself in physical attacks on staff.

The exclusions were also the subject of angry comment by many of the interviewees. A group of Vaal parents pointed out the injustice in barring black children from DET township schools which were said to be 'full' while schools in white areas stand empty.[1] Some of the white schools which have been closed for lack of pupils have even been converted to non-educational uses. At the end of the 1980s, the following were the main criteria for excluding black students from schools:

- *Zoning*: students enrolling are supposed to come from the zone in which the school is situated. If they are coming from primary school, they should come from the primary school in the same zone. If they are coming in at a higher grade, they should have been resident in that zone in the previous year. This excludes the increasing numbers of squatters and migrants moving into the urban areas, who do not always have the requisite documentation for their children. It can also lead to the exclusion of pupils who had been sent by their parents to rural areas to study for a year or two away from the troubles and who are now trying to return to urban schools.

- *Over-age students*: many students are considerably over-age for the grade they have reached, due to periodic drop-out, grade repetition, because of exam failure, late starting of school, or because of political upheavals. Official statistics indicate that in 1987, before the age rule came into force, some 17 per cent of primary school students (up to Grade Five) were over thirteen years of age. Interviewees frequently mentioned twenty- to twenty- two-year-olds seeking to continue in high school. Ages for grade limits have been fixed at eighteen for Grade Eight and twenty for Grade Ten, when in the past people were accustomed to youngsters continuing in school for as long as it took to finish.

- *Exclusion for political reasons*: those who have been in detention find it almost impossible to get back into school. Children on the run, or in hiding from the security forces, have no chance of schooling. A few organizations have tried to help small numbers of these youngsters, but because of the risks of collecting them together this has had to be on a piecemeal basis. Some supplementary school programmes have been set up by churches, voluntary organizations and trade unions for ex-detainees who cannot get places in DET schools. One student activist said that people he knew who had dropped out of school had been discouraged from returning by their teachers, who blame poor performance on activism in the school's student council.

- *Matric failure*: failure of the matriculation exam has also been a major issue in school exclusions. The matriculation failure rate in DET schools is high: in most years 40 to 50 per cent of entrants. Only a tiny proportion succeed in attaining the higher level 'matric exemption' which allows candidates to apply for a university place. One of the few ways of passing, or improving on poor grades, has been to stay at school and take the exam several times. The new rules deny students the change to repeat the exam at school.

In Soweto, the DET's apparently *ad hoc* solution to 'full' schools was to set up a dozen 'finishing schools' where those who fail matriculation are sent to repeat the exam. Interviewees alleged that the teaching is poor (DET teachers are used, teaching an extra afternoon shift), the afternoon sessions too short to cover the syllabus, and the atmosphere of the classes is discouraging. Other students repeat exams through adult education institutes, or private tutorial colleges, or street academies. Others just give up.

The resentment over these exclusions is made worse by the fact that the exam itself is regarded as problematic. It is widely believed that the system is stacked against black pupils, both because of the poor conditions in which they learn and because of the way the exam itself is set and marked. Most interviewees said that the standard of marking is inconsistent from year to year and subject to subject. Others claim that marking is farmed out to unqualified people and that the results are manipulated to exclude black students from universities.

There is also a tension for many black students between their ideological rejection of the whole system of Bantu education, and the practical need to get through the matriculation exam with reasonable results in the hope of getting a job or a university place. This is a change from the situation of the 1950s and 1960s when no such jobs were open to black people. Now there are a limited number of white-collar and professional jobs available.

Many of the interviewees knew secondary school pupils who had dropped out of school. A number said this was for economic reasons – their families could not afford school uniforms and materials – or because the pupil had to work to help the family. Undoubtedly, high unemployment and relatively high levels of inflation in the last few years have reinforced this tendency. But in South Africa, many drop-outs are caused by factors internal to the education system. Students often become disillusioned with education, seeing it as pointless and alienating, and feel that the system is stacked against them. The frequent use of corporal punishment by teachers was cited as another reason for leaving.

For female pupils, there are other issues, though not all interviewees acknowledged that there were differences between schooling problems for girls and boys. The violence of the surrounding society is reflected in the schools, especially at secondary level. There is the violence of the security forces, often entering schools in confrontations with students, while teachers routinely use corporal punishment on their pupils. There is also violence among students, with sexual harassment both by teachers and peers, and the violence of street gangs coming to schools. This problem, the result of breakdown in community organization due to repression, and lack of student respect for teachers and educational authorities, seems to have reached serious proportions in Soweto. In a small survey of students from a number of Soweto secondary schools in 1989, the majority thought that girls at their school were harassed or even assaulted. Though the majority thought that outsiders were responsible, others said the harassment came from other pupils in the school, or from male teachers.[2]

The issue of teenage pregnancies was frequently raised. Most interviewees did not attempt to analyse the reasons but treated this as a 'fact' about girls. As in the Zimbabwean survey, the implicit view, especially among adults, was that girls bore the responsibility for their predicament. In South Africa, as elsewhere, girls are thrown out of school if they become pregnant and are unlikely to be able to return. One student, however, did give a different kind of explanation, saying that economic instability had destroyed harmonious family relations and eroded parental authority. Thus it would be an illusion to expect that in these circumstances 'a parent [i.e. mother] can settle down and have a [talk] with her child on sex education'.

People's education

The call for 'people's education' first emanated from Soweto, from the parents' groups and the quickly suppressed student-parent-teacher organizations of the mid-1980s. In 1989, there had been little opportunity to put any of the ideas generated at that time into practice, so that the interviewees' ideas about the future shape of education in a new South Africa were necessarily hazy. None the less, most of the people interviewed had strong ideas about what should be changed, seeking particularly new kinds of relationships between teachers, parents and students.

Among the students interviewed, education was undoubtedly considered, in theory, a good thing, but tainted by their experience of Bantu education. Those at high-school level who have been involved in student activism tended to espouse strongly the slogan of people's education. But for most of them it is an abstract idea, because in practice most students' experience at school is of unremitting authoritarianism.

Views varied on what people's education should be, seemingly according to the degree of political involvement of the individual. A few interviewees, especially teachers, were doubtful about the whole idea. A number of respondents said that they thought the concept of people's education was not well understood. Students shouted slogans but didn't really know what they meant, they said. Others said it was was confined to a relatively small group of academics and intellectuals. Another observed that the idea of people's education was a Sowetan phenomenon, not widely understood elsewhere. A student went further, remarking: 'It seems that the majority of our people in Soweto including teachers don't understand what [people's education] is. It seems it is an idea understood by university students and academics. But it [people's education] must also train the teachers who will implement it.' Another suggestion was that materials on people's education should be disseminated in languages other than English so that it would be comprehensible to more people.

Of course, the state of emergency in force from soon after the formation of the National Education Crisis Committee (NECC) inhibited wide dissemination of these ideas. None the less, most of those questioned had their own views on what people's education should achieve, mostly arising from their evident discontent with the present state of education for black people. For some, the main goal of a new education system would be the transmission of skills in post-apartheid society, to open up new opportunities for black South

Africans. One teacher wanted a more religious basis to education. A more common theme was the need to develop education which taught students to be critical and think for themselves and to end the authoritarian relationships between government and schools. As one student pointed out, the present system treats teachers, pupils and principals 'like small children'.

Some people thought the community should provide financial resources for the school system as well as 'moral support'. Two parents thought control of education should be by the community instead of the state, while others wanted the community to be consulted. One woman thought that communities could advance people's education because the majority of the community is 'illiterate in the formal sense, but very rich in informal education. In this way the communities can help if the informal knowledge they have may be integrated with formal education to make a whole'.

The experience of recent years has created great concern over the role of the community in education, and the importance of changing the relationships between parents, teachers and students. At the time of the interviews (1989), it seemed to have been the parents who, at least in some areas, had some success in mediating over disputes and negotiating with both schools and pupils. Some parents' groups had tried to negotiate with the DET to settle local disputes, but without much success. A number of students spoke with respect of the role of the Soweto parents' committee in ending the school boycott in 1985. Their replies suggested that in retrospect they thought the parents had been right to demand a return to school.

Parents were also acknowledged to have played an important role in dealing with a crisis connected with gang intrusions in high schools in the Diepkloof area early in 1989. They formed the Diepkloof Concerned Parents Committee which endeavoured through meetings and consultation to lower the tension in the schools in the area where there was great anxiety over safety of students and teachers, as well as a very high level of anger and discontent among school pupils at the DET's handling of the school exclusions.

Although several students saw the necessity of ending the existing hostility between teachers and pupils, few were willing at the time to accord most teachers even grudging respect. Students, parents, and even some teachers themselves characterized teachers generally as 'passive', or 'spectators', afraid of the DET and generally compromised in their behaviour. Respondents in the survey did not always blame individual teachers for this situation, but rather the system under which they worked and in which they were trained. As far as the state and the DET are concerned, their role has been to implement the Bantu education system. As we have seen, in the 1950s teachers did object and were suppressed. But since then, they have not recovered the political initiative.

A Meadowlands student said:

I think the teachers are part and parcel of apartheid, because most of them don't want to be involved in organization. The teachers are the ones who should fight for us, especially history teachers because the students are not taught about black history but instead they are taught the history of the Boers [Afrikaners]. Teachers must make home visits to understand their [pupils'] learning environment.

This perception that teachers were often uninterested or uninvolved in their pupils' home life and problems was echoed by a number of interviewees, and many stressed the need for a more sympathetic relationship between teachers and students.

Parents often charge teachers with being unqualified or incompetent, but the question arises as to whether this is an educational system in which they want a 'qualification'. According to some of the teachers themselves, their training and conditions in the classroom inhibit initiative and independent thinking and encourage caution, passivity towards their superiors and an authoritarian attitude to students. One teacher argued that teacher training college does not provide any preparation for the realities of black education.

In the college when you are trained, you are taught to teach an ideal pupil in an ideal environment, you became an ideal teacher. What you are taught in college is out of this world. As a teacher you are subordinate to the principal, you have no say whatsoever.

A primary teacher put it this way: 'Under the DET the teacher has no right to question those in authority. Teachers are just given circulars and are not part of decision-making. Principals are like police who enforce the rules of those on top.' However, as another teacher put it, 'teachers mustn't allow themselves to be treated like jellyfish'.

Teachers were viewed as having been marginal in all the struggles over education, from the Soweto uprising to the 1980s boycotts, the formation of the NECC and the one-off classroom boycotts of recent years protesting about specific issues. The common perception is that they fear victimization by the DET if they become involved in protests. The fact that high-school students in the forefront of struggles were rarely supported by teachers (with the exception of fairly small groups of progressive teachers), has meant that they have incurred the hostility of activist students. This is in addition to the poor relations stemming from the authoritarian regime in the classroom. This problem has been further exacerbated by the recent school exclusions, for which students have often blamed their teachers.

At a political level, action has been taken to create unity between teachers' unions, which had been fragmented on a regional, racial and political basis. However, some of the more conservative teachers' unions – for example, Tuata in the Transvaal, to which many Soweto teachers belong – has not joined the new South African Democratic Teachers' Union. It has a large membership, but is largely inactive on political issues. According to most teachers interviewed, it does nothing except collect union dues. According to a primary teacher,

It fails to challenge DET corruption – like promotion through nepotism. I am afraid to mention names directly because I will be victimized by the Department [DET]. But I know many examples of inspectors [seen as the enforcing arm of the DET] promoting their sons and daughters to become headmaster or headmistress. Tuata is failing to challenge all this. Politically, Tuata is naive.

Northern Transvaal

In the course of the 1980s, discontent with the education system has spread far beyond the confines of Soweto and other major conurbations. Even small towns and rural areas, both in regions where education is controlled by the DET and those under 'homeland' governments, have seen student activism. Awareness of educational conditions in the rural areas has also increased among the urban black community, because many parents sent their children to stay with relatives or friends in the rural areas to keep them from the disturbances and allow them to continue their studies. As a result, they became aware of the poor quality – and quantity – of schooling in many such regions. In rural areas like Northern Transvaal, the limitations affect not just the availability and proximity of schools, but also the subjects offered at secondary level, in particular in the sciences. None the less, little systematic research has been done on conditions in rural schools, particularly in the homelands, and their plight has not until recently received much attention from those who are active in promoting change in South African education.

In Northern Transvaal, a large proportion of people cannot make a living out of farming, but depend on migrant remittances and a variety of other work. Many were either forcibly relocated there by the government, or, having lost jobs and therefore residence in white areas, were forced to move there. Their land is poor and they live in precarious circumstances. Recent drought conditions have aggravated the problems of agriculture. Consequently, those who receive migrant remittances or work in nearby towns are likely to be better off than farmers. However, in recent years the down-turn in the South African economy has meant considerable unemployment among migrants. For example, in Lebowa homeland, in Northern Transvaal, according to South African official labour statistics the number of employed migrants dropped from 445,816 in 1981 to 258,572 in 1985.[3] In the poorest communities, a recent survey showed that people spend up to 70 per cent of their meagre income on food, and children are often malnourished.[4]

The three areas covered represent a profile of rural and semi-urban life and education in Northern and North-eastern Transvaal. The first area is Shiluvane, a rural district some 36 kilometres from the small northern Transvaal town of Tzaneen in the 'homeland' of Gazankulu. Its population consists mainly of landless poor peasants, the majority of whom are women and children. The bulk of men are migrant labourers employed in various towns throughout the Transvaal. Those who remain with their families constitute a cheap labour force for white agricultural and industrial projects bordering on the Gazankulu and Lebowa homelands. Others work for various departments of the homelands government, which also employs a small black middle class of clerks, teachers and nurses.

Nkowankowa is a small township thirteen kilometres from Tzaneen. Much of the population is employed as wage labour in industrial projects in the township and in Tzaneen. There are also numbers of civil servants working for the homelands government and a handful of small businessmen, especially in the retail trade.

Finally, Mankweng township, forty-eight kilometres from Pietersburg in the 'homeland' of Lebowa, has a rather similar population composition, though it has in addition a university community of students and academics from the University of the North at Turfloop (only for black students).

The general problems of the education system identified by Soweto residents – of discrimination, inequality and under-funding – were also mentioned by interviewees living under these homelands governments. A large proportion of schools are so-called 'community schools' with buildings and facilities mainly financed by the community. There seemed to be even fewer opportunities to express grievances here than in Soweto. The Gazankulu government, according to a Shiluvane student, suppressed expression of grievances in schools. He added that the banning of student representative councils had caused strikes and disruption in schools. In Nkowankowa, the only student organization allowed was the Student Christian Movement. For teachers, the only union is Tuata, on which opinions were much the same as in Soweto – that it was ineffective.

An older woman from Shiluvane observed that the Gazankulu government favoured 'useless school committees composed of ignorant and uncaring people who think that their duty is to spy or inform on teachers and care less about the progress of teachers and students'. Another separate study of secondary schools in the Mapulaneng district in Lebowa found that in community schools, the school committees frequently have little or no say in what goes on in the school and no control over the use of funds which they provide for buildings and other school facilities. The money is often handled by the local chief or by the school principal, with ample opportunities for embezzlement. In this case, it was found that they were not accountable for the use of the funds to the school committee, a situation made more difficult by the fact that many members of the committee were not literate or numerate. Circuit inspectors who are supposed to examine school committee minutes and financial statements rarely do so.[5]

A government clerk in Shiluvane said that government corruption and nepotism are rife. Bursaries and facilities such as school buildings, libraries, laboratories and transport for students are provided only to the children of the elite. A high-school teacher in Nkowankowa township claimed that matriculation examiners were often ignorant of the syllabus and of the subject they were marking.

The physical state of schools, especially community schools, was said to be very poor. Finance for buildings and maintenance comes from local businessmen and the community. Classes in community schools are particularly overcrowded. One reason for this, cited by a teacher in Nkowankowa whose estimate of the average teacher–pupil ratio was 1:60, was that teachers were hired in terms of the number of classrooms available in the school (usually insufficient) and not in terms of the overall number of pupils. Another reason he gave was that the principal's salary depends on the number of students in the school, and as a result the principal takes as many students as possible, regardless of whether there are sufficient classrooms or teachers. There were said to be many unqualified teachers.

The study of Mapulaneng secondary schools suggested that a significant number of the teachers interviewed felt they did not get the support they needed from parents. It was suggested that migration played an important part in this, since some pupils had one or both parents working in the cities, and, as one teacher put it, the student was 'bringing himself up to be a delinquent'.[6]

In our survey, student drop-outs were attributed to much the same range of factors as in Soweto, including political exclusions and pregnancies among female students, though not violence and threats of violence. There was a rather stronger emphasis on economic reasons for leaving school. A former teacher in Mankweng said she knew of pupils ranging from the ages of eight to the early twenties who dropped out. Among the eight- to fourteen-year-olds, she said this was usually due to poverty or lack of parental care. At this stage the drop-outs, she said, were mainly boys. However, in the adolescent group the majority of drop-outs were girls, whereas those in their early twenties were, again, mostly males. The reasons given for dropping out in adolescence and beyond were pregnancy, disillusionment with school, financial problems and police harassment. But the teacher pointed out that, in addition to pregnancies, there were other differences in the pattern of male and female drop-outs. Girls were sometimes forced to stay at home and look after younger brothers and sisters due to the lack of crèche facilities in black areas for working mothers. However, she added that both girls and boys were sometimes forced to leave school and look for work to alleviate their families' financial problems. A male high-school student had a different perception – he thought most teenage drop-outs were boys because they were more involved in politics than girls and more likely to be detained or forced into hiding.

Levels of political activism and awareness seemed more patchy than in metropolitan areas, with some schools remote from centres of resistance. Some people did not know anything about people's education but those who knew were generally positive, stressing the need to get rid of the apartheid education system because it is 'unequal, exploitative and wasteful'. Answers differed, however, on what changes were needed. One teacher trainee thought 'the education whites get is OK', while another student stressed that people's education would 'empower people with know-how'.

Opinions seemed more divided than in Soweto on the role of the community in the present educational crises. A Mankweng teacher thought that the idea of people's education had furthered community participation in education, whereas in rural Shiluvane, one respondent said that parents, as well as teachers, were too passive.' A high-school graduate from Mankweng cited recent instances where parents tried to unite with teachers and students to solve schooling problems. Teachers, as in Soweto, came in for a considerable amount of criticism for 'fence-sitting and lack of initiative'.

A former teacher from Mankweng blamed teachers for the present problems in education. She pointed out that generations of black teachers, like the white missionary teachers before them, had taught black children to be docile and not militant. She recalled that as a child she had been made to dance with her school mates for the celebrations when South Africa was declared a republic in 1961, 'thinking that it was the liberation our fathers were fighting for'. She said that when she was at school boys were brainwashed to be servile, and quoted a rhyme;

A Boy wanted
[Boy is used by white South Africans to refer to a black man of any age]
Wanted a boy who is manly,
Kind and polite
A boy you can always rely upon
To do what is right.

She remarked bitterly that 'speaking the truth today will put me in gaol because the truth they want is something that is not right'. Girls, she went on, were brainwashed into believing that they should grow up to be sweet and humble wives who should unquestioningly accept the oppressive rules meted out to them by their husbands. Although she conceded that things were changing and that some teachers were now waking up from their 'deep slumber' to challenge these kinds of indoctrination, there were still relatively few teacher-activists. This, she said, was due to their social background and experiences.

Missing out on school in Natal

Of all the regions where schooling has been disrupted by political conflict in South Africa over the past few years, Natal in the late 1980s presented some of the most acute problems. In this region there have been increasing levels of internecine violence between the Zulu nationalist Inkatha movement of Chief Buthelezi and followers of the United Democratic Front. Since late 1989, Buthelezi has begun to challenge the role of the ANC, and has tried to create a mass-based movement which would give him a leading role in national politics. In pursuit of this goal, Inkatha has begun to challenge the ANC and its supporters in other parts of the country, particularly in the major townships of the Transvaal, resulting in widespread fighting and bloodshed.

In Natal, schools have been among the sites of these conflicts, both for teachers and pupils. The research so far available on this conflict suggests that these political labels may obscure other kinds of social conflict, caused by rural-urban migration and the divide-and-rule tactics embodied in the government's bantustan policies. John Gultig and Michael Hart characterize Kwazulu as follows:

. . . with 44 separate pieces, [it] is the most fragmented of the bantustans. It makes up 38 per cent of Natal's land area but has 55 per cent of its population, and Natal itself has a population density twice the national average. . . . The fragmentary nature of Kwazulu makes it doubtful that any significant development can take place within it. The majority of Kwazulu's econ-omically active population (280,000 migrant workers amd 384,000 commuters in 1981) are employed outside the bantustan and a third of the population is landless. With only approximately 60,000 wage earners within Kwazulu (mostly employed by the Kwazulu government) migrant remittances exceed Kwazulu's internal revenue creation. Furthermore, like the rest of South Africa, there is relatively permanent unemployment of young entrants to the job market and especially of people from the more remote rural areas.[7]

There is considerable instability and mobility of population in the Natal region today, and the city of Durban is one of the fastest growing conurbations in the country. It seems that Inkatha supporters are frequently migrants from rural areas, whereas UDF supporters tend to be more established urban dwellers. As tensions between the groups exploded into violence, residential instability has been further increased as people try to move away from areas of conflict. Refugees moving into areas which have previously been peaceful have sometimes sparked new communal tensions. The political leadership, especially of Inkatha, has undoubtedly taken a hand in the conflict, but after more than three years of street warfare, the initiative seemed largely to lie with the street gangs on both sides. For the population at large, one set of researchers' observations suggested that 'in some cases those who saw their communities divided into Inkatha and UDF factions had no idea what these labels meant, other than names for those living on one side of a boundary or another'.[8]

What is certain is that the conflict has seriously affected the opportunities for schooling for children both in DET and Kwazulu schools. The region represents the administrative lunacy of apartheid and homelands policy. Kwazulu is a series of forty-four fragmented areas scattered among 'white areas' in which there are also black townships. The educational situation is therefore very complex administratively and often chaotic, since the DET controls schools in 'white' areas, while a few miles away or less are schools controlled by the Kwazulu administration.

Education has become a central battleground in the struggle for power and control between the government, Inkatha, and the UDF and its allies. DET schools are by and large in a better physical state, and teachers are better paid than in the homeland schools, but this has been achieved by the application of exclusion measures similar to those described for Soweto. Kwazulu schools are generally overcrowded – they do not enforce restrictions on class size – and badly equipped. The educational budget for 1987–88 was one of the lowest even among the 'homelands'. Some students trying to get into Kwazulu schools were reported to have been refused places, either because the school was actually very overcrowded or because they were suspected of UDF sympathies.

According to surveys conducted by the Educational Project Unit (EPU) at the University of Natal in 1988, the scale of the 'de-schooling' problem was substantial both because of exclusions and because of local conditions. Interviewees frequently spoke of being too frightened to go to school, for fear of being caught up in clashes between rival groups. Many families had moved from their homes to escape the violence, and their children could not find school places in the district to which they had moved. Other families said they could not afford the school fees.[9]

In the schools, daily life could be very tense. Gultig and Hart's survey of schools in the Pietermaritzburg area (Edendale and Vulindlela) gave examples of matriculation exams being disrupted by invading Inkatha vigilantes, of school hours being cut to 9.30 a.m. to 12.30 a.m. because students felt it unsafe to travel at the normal times. 'The most dramatic deschooling of pupils occurred after the Inkatha attacks of March 1990. Schools in Taylor's Halt, Kwashange, Kwamnyandu and Maqonqo were emptied. Teachers left these schools and refused to return as did many of their pupils who had become refugees in Edendale. These events have forced approximately 60,000 pupils and 1,000 teachers out of their schools. Almost all the pupils interviewed stated that they were afraid to return to their schools and former homes because of the presence of Inkatha and the police.'[10]

A rare study of the role of women in this conflict suggests that different age groups were drawn in for different reasons. Older women began to play a part mainly because of their role as mothers defending their children, endangered both in school and out of it. Women, as mothers and as teachers, became involved in confrontations with the security forces and in trying to protect their families and communities against vigilantes. One woman teacher recalled her reaction when policemen engaged in unprovoked tear-gassing and beating of pupils. When one instructed a black subordinate to go back and hit children who were running away, 'I then opened my arms and physically forced these policemen to go back. There were about fifteen of them. I was so angry, I told them they could shoot me or leave as I wanted them to do. . . . After that . . . they instructed all the police to withdraw'.[11]

For younger women, especially girls still at school, the situation was found to be rather different. Girls were often excluded from student organizations because of their greater responsibilities at home, parents' fears for their safety and negative attitudes of their male comrades and schoolmates. The survey quoted the following remarks by an interviewee which sum up both the common male view of women's 'irresponsibility' and the pressures on young girls trying to cope with the demands of school and home, especially in an atmosphere of fear and danger.

Meetings are called by the SRC [Student Representative Council] and only the boys are invited to those meetings. When you question why the girls are not there, the boys will say it's because the girls can't keep important things to themselves. Even if they fight it (*sic*) in the classroom, they [girls] still have to go home and do the household chores that are specially set aside for girls. In fact, girls are often complaining about it, you know, that they have to study just as much as boys but the boys get very few chores to do around the home. I mean, girls will sometimes end up even ironing the boys' shirts for school.[12]

According to the survey by the Education Projects Unit, relations between teachers and students were poor. Teachers were said to fear students who had lost respect for them, but were also afraid of being labelled as UDF members if they questioned the content of the syllabus. Teachers working in Kwazulu schools were expected to sign a loyalty oath to Kwazulu which was effectively a loyalty oath to Inkatha.

Initiatives have been taken by independent groups, particularly from the churches, both to try to calm the situation and to help provide alternative schooling for at least some of those who have been out of school. Since the unbanning of the ANC, its leadership has also tried to intervene. However, the problem is clearly on a large scale and cannot be resolved without a solution to wider political and economic problems. There cannot simply be a return to the status quo; as in the rest of South Africa, the 'normalities' of apartheid education will no longer be accepted.

Notes

1. Narsing (1989), p.10.
2. Ibid, p.27.
3. Ritchken (1990), p.3.
4. Operation Hunger (1987).
5. Ritchken (1990), pp. 14–15.
6. Ibid, p.39.
7. Gultig and Hart, (forthcoming), pp.5–6.
8. Education Projects Unit . . . (1988), p.17.
9. Ibid, p.18.
10. Gultig and Hart (forthcoming), pp.13–14.
11. Black Sash affidavit M, 6 Sept. 1985, quoted in Beall *et al*. (1989), p.42.
12. Interview with S, 9.12.86 in Beall *et al*, op. cit. p.44.

CHAPTER 14

The dilemmas of refugee education: Central America, Sudan and Southern Africa

Internal and international conflict has forced millions to flee their homes in search of safety. Under the United Nations Convention on Refugees, host countries are under an obligation to provide education for refugees, but their needs are likely to take second place in the light of the education crisis. Education is especially valuable for refugees: it helps them overcome the trauma of exile and provides a route to participation in the refugees' new society. For refugees living in camps and for communities living in exile, education is an important focus of activity, keeping alive cultural activities and helping overcome the disruptions caused by dis-placement from their own country.[1]

Table 14.1a **Refugees and displaced persons, Central America, end 1988**

Country	Refugees	Undocumented	Internally displaced
Costa Rica	40,800	250,000 *	n.a.
El Salvador	500	20,000	400,000 *
Guatemala	3,000	220,000 *	100,000 *
Honduras	37,000	250,000 *	22,000
Mexico	53,000	128,000 **	n.a.
Nicaragua	7,000	n.a.	350,000

Notes:
* Government estimates.
** UNHCR estimates based on figures given by NGOs.

Source: UNHCR *Refugees* March 1989 p.20.

Table 14.1b **Mozambican refugees, mid-1989**

Country	Refugees UNHCR-assisted	Undocumented
Malawi	693,021	26,979
Zimbabwe	75,700	100,000
Zambia	24,000	

Source: UNHCR, Fact Sheet 3 (2) Oct. 1989

Refugees: a question of definition

On Sundays, groups of young Salvadoreans gather to play football on the dusty open ground which lies between several poor neighbourhoods in Mexico City. There is no evident difference between them and the groups of young Mexicans. They share many of the same problems as other poor inhabitants of this vast, polluted and sprawling city. But they are different in one sense. Many of them have no legal status in Mexico, but conditions in their own country have made it difficult and often very dangerous to return. So they live in the limbo of the 'undocumented'.

Who is a refugee? According to the internationally accepted definition applied by the United Nations High Commission for Refugees (UNHCR) and by many governments, a refugee is an individual with a well-founded fear of persecution in his or her own country. However, in view of experiences in many parts of the world today, there are arguments for a broader definition based on the overall internal situation in the country of origin where war, repression and economic crisis may combine to make living conditions impossible, even when individuals are not directly threatened with death, persecution or imprisonment.

The situation of undocumented Central American migrants is a good example of the difficulties arising from defining refugee status narrowly. At least 250,000 Central Americans are living in Mexico, possibly double that figure. Most are Salvadoreans and Guatemalans. The largest single community living outside official camps is Salvadorean. Many have no legal status in Mexico, having been classified by the Mexican government as 'economic migrants'. Certainly many of the problems they face are similar to those of illegal migrants, particularly difficulties in gaining access to services, education and health care. But they also suffer the effects of being forced out of their own country by war, death threats, murders and repression on the one hand, and the severe economic problems caused by the war on the other.

Even for those whose status is recognized, and who live in refugee camps or as part of the host society, the label 'refugee' creates its own kind of marginality. This is exacerbated if the family or individual is also poor, lacks knowledge of the language of power, and is culturally alienated or isolated. Attitudes to refugees are often ambivalent, particularly if the host country is suffering serious economic problems. They are frequently exploited as cheap labour, particularly if they do not have legal status, while refugees in camps may be resented because they have access to services which the local population does not have – for example, health care, education or piped water. Sometimes differences in language or culture cause tensions, though in other cases local people may accept and even welcome refugees.

Although the UNHCR is the major international agency dealing with millions of refugees around the world, its powers are very limited because it depends on funds from member states and good relations with host countries to maintain access to refugees. The UNHCR deals with the results and not the causes of refugee outflows. It can only call attention to the host country's legal obligations; it has to ask permission from that government to operate in its territory and has to obtain funds for its work from donor governments. In recent years, the organization has suffered serious budget cuts.

Defining the educational needs of refugees

Problems and constraints in providing adequate educational services to refugees vary according to differences between the refugee groups, their circumstances and the curriculum which is offered. In developing a general policy on refugee education, some key dimensions are:

● short-stay versus long-stay populations;
● intention to integrate into the host country versus intention to return or resettle;
● politically organized versus unorganized populations;
● camp-settled versus spontaneously settled populations;
● host governments hospitable versus hostile to refugees;
● cultural and linguistic homogeneity versus heterogeneity of host society and refugees.

Each of these dimensions may overlap with others and each has different implications for the type of education possible and desirable.

From: *Refugee education: the case for international action* (1986).

Governments often regard refugees as a 'security' threat, either because they attract cross-border attacks or because they are regarded as politically subversive. For example, in Zimbabwe, Mozambicans in camps in the eastern provinces close to the Mozambican border have suffered government-imposed restrictions on their freedom of movement. According to the authorities, this is for their own safety because of the frequency of Renamo incursions into these areas. The Honduran armed forces regard Salvadorean refugees as 'subversives', so their camps are kept under constant guard and their movements severely restricted. On numerous occasions the army has actually raided the camps.

The provision of education for refugee groups poses particular problems related to their language and culture and the unpredictability of their future. Should educators make a priority of helping them to adapt to their new environment, or are they to be educated in preparation to return home? How important is it to sustain their own language and culture? Who should teach them? Should the education of children be a higher priority than education for adults? These are only a few of the questions which arise. Clearly, the answers depend on the particular circumstances of the group, but in general education for refugees should sustain the group's language and culture and should acknowledge and respect the group's experiences. Education should be provided by the host society, but with supplementary provision in the mother tongue if that is not the language of instruction. Education has both to help refugees adapt to the new society and to keep alive the prospects of returning home.

Access to education is a major problem for many refugees, especially for those who do not have legal status. Even those who are settled in camps often have very limited educational opportunities, because of lack of funds or lack of interest on the part of the host government, and because of lack of trained teachers.

For camp refugees, the dangers of dependency and passivity may be outweighed by possibilities for community solidarity and organization. For example, in Honduras, the Salvadorean teachers' union, ANDES, was instrumental in establishing literacy programmes and other educational opportunities for refugees there. In Sudan, many groups of Eritrean and Tigrean refugees have established their own schools and organized their own educational programmes. In Namibian refugee camps in Angola and Zambia, education was given a high priority by SWAPO, which sought to make up for the lack of educational opportunities which Namibians had suffered at home.

Of course, the educational needs of refugees vary not only according to their situation as refugees but also according to their social and economic origins. To take one example, the social profile of Salvadorean refugees in Central America shows differing characteristics both geographically and over time: those who fled to Honduras were predominantly peasants, many of whom fled on foot as the militarization of rural areas increased from 1980 onwards. In Costa Rica and Nicaragua, there was a higher proportion of middle-class professionals. In Mexico, the first wave of refugees was mostly peasants, but by the mid-1980s there was a much higher proportion of urban skilled and semi-skilled workers, as well as middle-class professionals. This reflected the increasing political and economic difficulties in the urban areas of El Salvador. Refugees of middle-class origin are less likely to be illegal and also less likely to live in refugee camps. Their educational needs will be different from those of an illiterate peasant family. In contrast, the vast majority of refugees from Guatemala are indigenous people from rural areas; equally, refugees from Mozambique are overwhelmingly from rural areas.

We look here at aspects of formal and non-formal education in camps and for undocumented refugees living in the community. The main focus is on Mexico, Costa Rica, Zimbabwe, Zambia and Malawi, all hosts to major refugee populations. Not only do government policies differ, but so does the character of the refugee populations. In almost all these situations, however, educators face a number of dilemmas about language, culture, the future needs of refugees, who is to teach them and how.

Salvadoreans in Mexico City

One woman working at a centre for refugees in Mexico City recalls how she fled from El Salvador with only the clothes she stood up in after her husband was killed by the security forces. She has three sons and she is putting them through secondary school. 'I can't read or write, and I don't care about that, but I am determined that my children should be educated.' However, the hurdles facing mothers like her, alone with their children, are considerable.

A small sample survey of Salvadorean refugees in Mexico City showed that the majority of those questioned had come into Mexico without visas or permission. They had not sought to obtain papers subsequently because of the expense and the documentation that was needed. Of the minority who had entered legally, mainly on tourist visas, almost half had not attempted to renew their permission to stay, because they lacked the necessary papers required by the Mexican authorities. They had, therefore, lapsed into illegality.[2]

Some undocumented refugees have found other Salvadoreans with whom to live, or live in Mexican communities which are sympathetic and accept them. Others, however, feel less secure and take precautions which can isolate them from the community. As the study showed, among a small sample of Salvadorean men without legal status, most said they took precautions such as not going out late at night, avoiding places where the police are often found, not revealing their nationality and not talking in public (when their accent would reveal their origin), not socializing with neighbours, and moving house frequently. Some try to pass for Mexicans, particularly when looking for work. Obviously this is not a favourable environment for children to grow up in.

In Mexico, the marginality of undocumented refugees has made them particularly vulnerable to the increasing pressures within the Mexican economy. Jobs in the formal sector are hard to find, and most refugees, except the relatively small number of professionals, work in the informal sector. They are often street hawkers or domestic servants, or they work on building sites, often for fly-by-night contractors, with poor wages and dangerous conditions.

The price rises which affect all the poor in Mexico are made worse because illegal immigrants can often only get access to services such as health or education by paying for them. As the director of one refugee support group, Movimiento Amplio para Refugiados de El Salvador (MAPRES), points out:

Levels of nutrition for children are low. You can't say that leaving El Salvador and coming to Mexico necessarily means an improvement in this respect. Children are particularly vulnerable because they don't have easy access to mother and child health care or to education. In many cases, families have to pay [for these services]. For those who do not have employment and therefore income, this is a problem. The economic crisis and inflation have hit most those with the least protection, the most vulnerable, like the undocumented refugees – the Mexicans still have some protection from the state.

For Salvadoreans without papers, there are problems sending their children to state schools, even if the child was born in Mexico. For those who have been to school in El Salvador, graduation certificates are not recognized by the Mexican education authorities. It seems that some children do get places at primary level, if the school is prepared to be flexible, but sometimes payments have to be made. At secondary level, access is much more difficult. There have been some schools set up for Salvadorean children in the Federal District, but they only make up a small proportion of the places needed.

At secondary level, they charge fees which are hard for a poor family to afford if they have several children at school. The schools themselves also need constant financial support. This is a difficult decision for aid agencies which fund them, because it can be argued that these schools are simply privileging a small group of refugees without serving the needs of the community as a whole. WUS (El Salvador) offers small bursaries to keep children at school, but like the other projects which assist undocumented refugees, they only meet a tiny fraction of the need.

The refugees are scattered over the huge sprawl of Mexico's Federal District, which makes co-ordination and assistance by organized Salvadorean groups and other agencies much more difficult. Organizations like CORES (Casa de El Salvador) and MAPRES provide some training courses (for example, MAPRES has started a dentistry training programme). These are designed to help people to find work while in Mexico, but their main aim is to improve people's skills for when they return home. These and other organizations also provide some basic health care, vaccination of children, psychological support and counselling and, also important, a meeting place and informal advice centre.

Their economic and logistical difficulties are considerable, however. They have problems reaching people, and problems with obtaining any consistent external funding. Many of the refugees, especially women, also find it difficult to go on training courses, partly because of distances, but mainly because of the pressure to work. As one member of the MAPRES women's committee explained: 'For women the greatest difficulties are time and economic problems. Take my case – I was doing a training course but I had to give up because I didn't have time and I needed to work. Women can't study full time: they have too many other tasks to do – they have to work in order to survive and the work they do is very badly paid.' This vicious circle often encourages or reinforces the tendency for women to put all their efforts into the education of their children.

Cultural identity is also a matter of concern. At the Casa de El Salvador, a group of women run courses for young children to give them some idea of their own culture and history. As one said, 'It's important for them to learn about Mexican culture if they have to live here, but these kids have never seen El Salvador and we don't want them to grow up without knowing about their own country.'

Nicaraguans in Costa Rica

Costa Rica, despite its image of tranquillity, has been affected by the turmoil in neighbouring countries. It has become a country of refuge for Nicaraguans fleeing the war against the Contras and Salvadoreans who were political refugees from the civil war. In the early 1980s, the numbers of Nicaraguans were relatively small and they were mostly housed in reception camps, where many of them have remained ever since. The population of Salvadoreans is much smaller, and most have either integrated to some extent or have returned to El Salvador.

However, the flow of people from Nicaragua increased to a flood by the second half of the 1980s as a result both of the economic and military crisis in the country and also as a result of the destruction wrought by Hurricane Joan. By mid-1989, it was estimated that there were some 40,000 'undocumented' Nicaraguans in Costa Rica. Most came from the poorest regions of Nicaragua, especially from the southern Atlantic coast areas, where the increased social benefits of the Sandinista period had been least felt. The level of illiteracy among these refugees is high, and their health status is poor, with infant mortality at 57 per 1,000, three times higher than the Costa Rican national average. Many of the young men left Nicaragua to avoid military service; others left because of the economic crisis as well as the war.

The legal refugees, numbering some 8,000, are under the auspices of UNHCR and are entitled to the relatively generous benefits – including free health and education in the government school system – provided by the Costa Rican government. The problems of the refugees, legal and illegal, both mirror and exacerbate the economic crisis of Costa Rica in the 1980s. Because of rising unemployment, even legal refugees find it increasingly difficult to get work permits, and relationships with local communities, and with the authorities, have become strained at times. UNHCR, under increasing pressure to cut back budgets, has concentrated on providing technical and vocational training for post-secondary levels rather than university level. The main problem with this has been that refugees, especially women, who graduate from these courses have difficulty finding employment and getting work permits.

The attitude both of the government and the populace to unofficial refugees appears somewhat ambivalent. The children of undocumented refugees usually have access at least to primary schooling and to health care. In the north, where most of the undocumented Nicaraguans are found, primary schools have been fairly flexible in taking children whose parents do not have proper documentation. At secondary level, however, it is much harder for them, and they certainly cannot take the exams which would allow them to go on to university. Without documents, they also do not qualify for scholarships.

However, the extra demands on the education system in terms of resources have caused concern and some resentment, especially when substantial numbers of Nicaraguan refugees are settled in poor regions of the country where education facilities are already insufficient. As we have seen, economic constraints on education budgets have made it impossible to build more schools or hire more teachers. For example, there is a major concentration of refugees in the area of Los Chiles, an already poor district with considerable educational problems. In many primary schools in this region, well over half the children are Nicaraguan, and for some schools the proportion is as high as 90 per cent. In addition, as one education official pointed out, those Nicaraguan children who get to primary school have particular difficulties – first, because their families frequently move around to seek work, and second, because the teachers employed in these schools are not particularly well qualified and certainly are not equipped to deal with children whom the Costa Ricans regard as coming from a different social and cultural background. 'These children are marginalized in our communities and educational institutions, not counting their lack of [legal] papers.'

Certainly in the northern region, it is not unusual for local people to blame the newcomers for increasing social and economic problems, and for arms and drug-smuggling. Refugees are also said to have brought with them diseases such as malaria which had been virtually eradicated in Costa Rica. While this may be true, it is also a way of labelling refugees as unwanted outsiders.

For illegal refugees, the only work available is often the result of land-owners and others taking advantage of their status to pay rock-bottom wages, sometimes below the legal minimum. Thus they undercut the employment of local workers and increase resentment on the part of Costa Rican workers. At the same time, the work is sporadic and refugees often have great difficulty in maintaining their families. Families move around looking for work in the sugar and coffee harvests, the only kinds of employment in which all the family can work, restricting children's access to schooling.

Unlike other refugee groups which have relatively strong social or political ties, their reasons for leaving Nicaragua were more diffuse and not all connected with opposition to the Sandinista government. Observers have noted the relative difficulty in some of these groups of initiating any collective community projects, such as literacy work, though there are some literacy programmes, sponsored both by the government and by other agencies. Social cohesion is generally said to be based more on family than community. Some who opposed the Sandinistas also associated any collective project with the Nicaraguan literacy campaign, which they regarded as indoctrination.

Guatemalans in Mexico[3]

Guatemalan Mayas who fled their countries in tens of thousands during the government's counter-insurgency campaign in the early 1980s mostly went to Mexico. At first, they lived mostly in camps in Chiapas, close to the Guatemalan border. Others managed to settle among the generally sympathetic local population in the south of Mexico. Many of these refugees were ill and starving by the time they reached the Mexican border: they were 'hunted like animals' by the Guatemalan army and had been forced to live in the mountains on leaves and wild fruits, not daring to make fires for fear of detection.

Once in Chiapas, people began to organize among themselves and received limited assistance from UNHCR and the Mexican refugee agency COMAR. However, their situation, as far as the Mexican authorities were concerned, was problematic: the Guatemalan army made raids over the border to attack the camps, worsening already strained relations between the two countries. The Mexicans also claimed that because the region in which the camps were located was densely populated, competition for work and resources would eventually create tensions with the local population. The authorities decided that the Guatemalans should be relocated much further north away from the border area, in camps at Campeche and Quintana Roo, where there was a relative shortage of labour. In 1984, after considerable resistance, some 20,000 refugees were persuaded or pressured to move to the new area. People had managed to develop some organization in Chiapas, where they felt they were still close to their own country, something which for most of them was very important. In the new camps, COMAR made efforts to make the refugees self-sufficient in basic food, but the land is poor. Substantial numbers have to work outside the camps to survive, since provision of rations has gradually been diminished.

Education programmes have started up in the new camps, initially with Guatemalan teachers who were themselves refugees. A very large percentage of the population is illiterate, reflecting the high levels of illiteracy among Mayan populations in Guatemala. According to one of the teachers in Maya Tecum, one of the camps, 'Nationally there is 65 per cent illiteracy in Guatemala but it is higher amongst *campesinos*, higher still amongst indigenous *campesinos* and it reaches almost 100 per cent amongst indigenous *campesino* women.' In Maya Tecum Module 2, 60 per cent of the population is Ketchi, 35 per cent Quiché and 5 per cent *mestizo* (of mixed origin). In Maya Tecum as a whole, COMAR recorded 37 per cent of refugees as speaking only Maya languages. Among the Ketchi speakers, illiteracy is highest and very few people speak Spanish, because the region they come from is very remote and has resisted Spanish incursions. Among the Quiché, intrusion by Spanish speakers has been much greater and therefore more people know some Spanish.

This situation posed a dilemma for the teachers as to which language or languages they should use for teaching. People's experience of education in Spanish in Guatemala was generally negative. They regard Spanish as the language of the oppressor, and a good many refugees are still mono-lingual, which would make learning in Spanish harder. However, the teachers opted for Spanish. There were several reasons for this. First, the lack of communication between different Mayan language groups poses a serious problem. In the camps where different groups have to live together, the lack of a common language creates difficulties. The other argument for learning Spanish is that it is likely to remain the language of power in Guatemala for the foreseeable future, and if Maya people cannot use it they have to rely on intermediaries and are extremely vulnerable to exploitation. The third problem for the teachers was a practical one: 'We didn't have the material or human resources to produce books in different mother tongues.'

Another barrier to teaching reading and writing in indigenous languages is that some are not fully written. Some Guatemalan groups working with refugees have tried to develop alternative strategies to reinforce the use of languages which are not written by using tape cassettes and visual images in order to stimulate discussion.

Professional teachers, literacy promoters from the communities and learners have had to evolve methods of dealing with these problems, while preserving and promoting the value of indigenous languages and culture. Learning Spanish had to become a liberating, instead of an oppressive, experience. In Spanish too, methods had to be devised to cope with the problem that many people could speak little Spanish when they began, so that it was impossible to use the syllabic method advocated by Freire and now widely used in Spanish-speaking countries. Instead, they used a phonetic system, building up sounds, reinforced by pictures. In this way they could identify words in Spanish and their own languages. The content of the materials was designed to reinforce rather than to denigrate their own cultures and to try to rebuild confidence in their own way of life which had been torn apart by the conflict.

The outcome of the adult literacy programme, which began in Maya Tecum in 1984 and initially lasted ten months, was revealing of the communities' priorities. Learning Spanish, particularly for the Ketchi speakers, seems to have been a liberating experience which allowed them through discussion with others to 'relive our past'. It helped them to see the past as part of a collective experience, rather than just individual suffering. For this group, oral Spanish and the ability to communicate was much more important than learning to read and write. Particularly among the Quiché speakers, however, there was a much higher drop-out rate.

The assessment of the overall impact of the literacy campaign up to 1989 is that, although it has been successful in teaching a large number of people to communicate orally in Spanish, the literacy work itself has has less impact. According to the teachers, the illiteracy rate in the camp is still about 70 per cent and most of the adult literacy work has now ceased, in favour of concentrating on the education of children. Those who were most opposed to the closure of literacy programmes were Ketchi women who were very eager to learn.

The reasons for the limited success of literacy work are complex. It seems that the demand to learn reading and writing, as opposed to speaking Spanish, is patchy. Furthermore, the camp environment does not help to reinforce literacy in those who have learned – it is still a predominantly non-literate environment and such books as are available are for children. Refugees have suggested that they should try to obtain books on subjects which would help with their work and bilingual dictionaries which would help them learn more words in Spanish.

However, according to Archer and Costello, the economic situation in the camps in Campeche and Quinto Roo has also contributed to the problems with literacy work. Although COMAR and UNHCR aim to make these camps self-sufficient and have reduced their support accordingly, in reality the refugees are working poor-quality land which is unable to grow enough food. Workshops and income-generating projects in Maya Tecum have not flourished. In a much more competitive atmosphere than prevailed in the early years of exile, individual families and groups are benefiting, rather than the broader community. One of the results is that a substantial number of camp-dwellers take work outside the camps. Consequently, fewer people have time or are available to join in any adult education projects.

Children in the camps, however, are more likely to go to primary school than they would have been in Guatemala – up to 80 per cent of children in Maya Tecum attend. However, there are somewhat negative attitudes to education in some parts of the community, combined with the fact that the Mexican education authorities had not, as of 1990, recognized the schooling given in the camps by Guatemalan teachers, many of whom do not have formal teaching qualifications.

Primary school graduates therefore cannot get into secondary schools unless they are taught by Mexican teachers, and there are few vocational training programmes. As one worker with a Guatemalan voluntary group observes, 'Their future is very problematic – they don't have any amusements or entertainments. Some go and work in the cities and pick up bad habits. Some also develop identity problems about being Guatemalans.' Thus, youngsters often have problems of a different order from those of their parents. He emphasizes the need to deal with these psychological difficulties as well as providing for the physical well-being of refugees.

Refugee education in Sudan

As of 1989, there were some three-quarters of a million refugees in Sudan, mainly from Ethiopia, Eritrea, Tigray and Chad. About half of this number are in refugee settlements and reception centres. They had fled from drought and war, and now make up 30 per cent of the population of Sudan's eastern province. The Sudanese government provides education for children in official refugee settlements. Some refugees who have settled in Sudanese communities go to the local schools.

For most of these children there is a basic language problem – they do not speak Arabic, which is the language of instruction in school. Also the Sudanese teachers are not always sensitive to the cultural differences they encounter in refugee schools. The general standard of education reflects the low quality of Sudanese education generally (see page 136). As a result, the government has had to forbid anyone under fifteen from attending the literacy classes which have been set up in many of the settlements. Teenagers often prefer to go to those classes, taught in Tigrinia, than to the official school classes.

There are also groups of refugees who have been consigned to a kind of bureaucratic limbo. They are the inhabitants of 'transit camps' which were intended as initial reception centres, but where people may remain for several years. In these camps, there is no official provision for formal education at primary level. In some cases, this has led to children attending literacy classes intended for adults, which teach through the use of self-study materials and discussion groups, which are not appropriate for teaching young children.

For refugees living in towns, the various liberation movements have established their own schools, which have their own curricula and teach in mother tongues, though Arabic is also taught as a subject. However, these schools have to rely largely on unqualified refugee teachers and pupils cannot sit Sudanese school examinations. This means that it is difficult for them to go on to any form of higher education. For the most part, however, children in either type of school do not get beyond primary level. After that, for girls, there is the pressure to get married, and for boys to go out to find work.

Foundation courses at junior secondary level (in English) for refugee youngsters who have missed or dropped out of school are run by the Sudan Open Learning Unit. The unit has also developed three levels of literacy learning materials, including a post-literacy component (in Tigrinia) which is being widely used in eastern province refugee camps and with groups of spontaneously settled refugees. WUS(UK) has recently started literacy work using these materials with Tigrean women in Tawawa settlement, near Gedaref, where there is a high proportion of female-headed households.

Support for refugee education

WUS(UK) supports a number of small-scale innovative projects for refugee education. For example, in eastern Sudan, the Eritrean Relief Assocation runs primary schools for refugee Eritrean children. In 1986, WUS(UK) sent an Eritrean educationist to review the schools programme and to run a series of in-service workshops for the teachers. In 1989, the organization arranged a second series of training workshops for refugee teachers, as well as sending funds for books and furniture for the schools, which are built by the refugee community.

In Djibouti, WUS(UK) established an education programme for Ethiopian refugees. Between 1983 and 1985, WUS selected teachers from among the refugees in the camps, trained them and helped devise a curriculum and develop teaching materials. Local counterparts were trained to take over the project's management. An educational resource centre was also set up.

A visit two years later found the schools running successfully but identified needs for further teacher training, particularly in the area of producing learning materials. The original textbooks were falling apart, and the teachers did not have the experience to produce their own materials. An educational consultant visited Djibouti in late 1988 for two months to help the teachers learn how to supplement textbooks with their own materials.

Mozambican refugees in Southern Africa

The kind of schooling to provide for refugees depends not only on local conditions and the type of refugee population but also on what prospects they have of returning home in the relatively near future. In the case of Mozambique, people did not flee out of fear of their own government but of its opponents: the armed opposition movement, Renamo. Thus the government has a closer relationship with the refugees and more interest in their welfare than in other situations.

The largest camps for Mozambicans are in Malawi, Zambia and Zimbabwe, though there are differences in the relationship between the Mozambican government and the host state. In all camps, some kind of education is now provided, though conditions are often very difficult.

The fact that people expect to go home encourages the learning of Portuguese, not a language used in the host communities. Language has become a major issue not because of political conflicts with host populations – certainly in Malawi and Zimbabwe there are common languages across borders – but because of questions about the future viability of the refugees' education when they return home.

Host governments have different policies, with Malawi and Zimbabwe allowing tuition in Portuguese, the employment of Mozambican teachers, and recently, the use of the Mozambican curriculum. In many respects, this seems very desirable compared with the Zambian policy of using the Zambian curriculum in vernacular languages and English, with local teachers. But the logistical problems are considerable. First, books have to be supplied from Mozambique, where disruptions of production and transport problems have hampered delivery. Some textbook printing has been funded by foreign aid agencies, but the mechanisms for distribution have been very slow. Second, many of the Mozambican refugee teachers are not familiar with the new curriculum being introduced grade by grade under the 1983 National Education System (see page 116). However, recently the Mozambican government has sent trainers to Malawi and to Zimbabwe to conduct in-service training for refugee teachers, in an effort to remedy this problem.

There are only primary schools in the camps, and when children graduate, they cannot go on to secondary schools outside Mozambique without special language training. Here the Zambian policy has an apparent advantage in that children are able to go on to Zambian secondary schools. However, in practice, their English is rarely good enough for this to be possible.

In Zambia, the Mozambican government has little input into the provision of education. The programme is designed along Zambian lines, with Zambian teachers. At Ukwimi agricultural refugee settlement, for example, there are two schools, one of which also takes some Zambian pupils from a local school which was closed down. On the whole, since these are new schools and have some external support, they are better equipped than some local schools in terms of desks, cupboards, bookcases and tools, though there is still a shortage of teaching materials and textbooks. Parent–teacher associations have been set up along the same lines as those in Zambian schools. They are mainly concerned with self-help and fundraising and, to a lesser extent, with curricular and instructional issues. However, there have been difficulties in mobilizing people for this kind of voluntary work, as they tend to be too busy working for their own families' needs.[4]

The presence of large numbers of refugees has imposed severe strains on local social services and job availability. In Malawi, a country undergoing a severe economic crisis and cuts in social services, the refugees in some districts outnumber the local population, who themselves have insufficient land. For the most part, the Mozambicans have been allowed to settle legally among the local population, and have done so without friction, but the pressure on resources is overwhelming.

School overcrowding is very severe, with reports of between 120 and 200 children in one class. Only about 35 per cent of school-age refugees are estimated to be in school. Not only is there a shortage of classrooms, but also a desperate shortage of Mozambican teachers. There are only 373 qualified teachers for a total of 60,267 pupils. They have been assisted by some untrained refugees working as teachers. But by 1989, these volunteers were apparently becoming discouraged by the lack of remuneration. Among the professional teachers, many are only qualified to teach the lowest grades of primary school, but because of the shortages have to be used throughout the primary system.

Zimbabwe began to ask for help from the international community in the mid-1980s as the refugee influx grew and the local systems could no longer cope. By the late 1980s, there were also signs of tensions between refugees and local populations, especially in the east of the country where Zimbabweans have been killed during Renamo attacks. Apart from the growing numbers of refugees in the four official camps, there are also large numbers of Mozambicans who are not legal refugees but who cross the border for longer or shorter periods of time in fear for their safety or looking for work. This reflects a long-standing pattern of migration, with even Mozambicans who have been in the country for many years having no regularized status. Of the recent entrants, most, like their predecessors, work as agricultural labourers; some of their children get into local primary schools in the eastern provinces, particularly since those from the border areas of Mozambique close to Zimbabwe speak Shona like the local inhabitants.

Literacy programmes are not very developed in these refugee camps. In Zimbabwe, the local non-governmental adult literacy organization ALOZ (see page 260) has started literacy work in the camps, but this programme encountered difficulties because the Mozambican education authorities have been slow to supply a curriculum and so literacy work has been done in Shona rather than Portuguese.

The longer the refugees stay, the greater the pressure for provision of post-primary education and vocational or technical training. Not only is there the dilemma of language, but also the shortage of funds makes training programmes, whether for school children or adults, very difficult. In Zambia some programmes have been started, with external assistance. But here, refugees have trouble finding work, even if they have received some training, because of the severe economic recession in the country. Their movements are also restricted by the government, so that it is difficult for them to travel round looking for work.

The development of educational facilities has generally been slow as the authorities struggle to provide accommodation and basic living needs. There are considerable differences between the amounts of external assistance available in each of the host countries, especially from non governmental organizations. In both Zambia and Zimbabwe, a number of non-governmental organizations are actively working with Mozambican refugees, whereas in the most overburdened country, Malawi, there are very few. In Zambia, the World Lutheran Federation has a large programme and in Zimbabwe, Redd Barna (Norway), Save the Children Fund (SCF, USA) and the Otto Benecke Foundation (Germany) are all involved in providing skills training.

Living with nightmares: education and the effects of trauma

The administrator of the Mazoe River Bridge Camp in Zimbabwe identified a number of social problems which particularly affect young Mozambicans in refugee camps: boredom and frustration leading to delinquency, mental problems and alcoholism; a large number of early marriages; and at the same time, a high rate of marital breakdown. He also noted the need for constant attention and affection for old people and careful handling of orphans and unaccompanied children in their foster homes. Some of these problems are the result of camp life itself: the demoralization and uncertainty about the future. But some of the difficulties relate to the experiences which refugees had before or during their flight from home, from loss of family members or the break-up of the family unit. The psychological traumas which result seriously affect people's ability to learn. It has been reported that some Mozambican refugee children have arrived virtually catatonic and sit for days staring into space.[5]

The Mozambican government has now introduced into their own curriculum a requirement to include 'rehabilitation' – presumably to help people deal with both their existing predicament and the possibility of returning home. However, for poorly trained or untrained teachers there are great difficulties in dealing with severely traumatized youngsters who have witnessed, and sometimes been involved in, horrific violence and brutality. Helping them to come to terms with these problems, and to deal with schooling, is a major task.

In Mexico, some small groups have begun to evolve types of participatory group therapy and non-formal education techniques designed to deal with the suppressed trauma that often afflicts refugees, especially women heads of household, left alone to support their families. Many suffer not only from the horrors and losses they may have experienced in the past, but also the daily anxieties of an insecure existence, sometimes in an alien culture. Education, for adults and for children, has to deal with these traumas and the blockages they cause to learning and to self-expression and self-assertion.

Renamo: control by atrocity

Eye-witness accounts of Renamo's methods suggest that the organization makes little or no attempt to justify its actions to local inhabitants, but relies on force to achieve compliance. Renamo does not try to win communities' support by providing services, but simply destroys government facilities. According to one report, Renamo has characteristically divided its operational areas into three categories:

- Areas in which the main aim is to extort a tax in kind from the inhabitants, who are often also made to act as porters for these goods to Renamo bases. These demands are enforced by threats and use of violence.
- Control areas, in which the inhabitants, and groups abducted from other areas, are forced to work for Renamo, and are not allowed to leave the area on pain of death. A form of slave labour is used to work on plantations and for porterage.
- Destruction areas, where villages are targeted for destruction with a particular focus on schools and health posts. In these attacks, whether or not there is resistance from Frelimo troops or villagers, anyone caught is usually killed or abducted.

For young people, the prospects of life under Renamo control are horrific. Some refugees who had lived in the control areas said their villages had schools, but that children over the age of ten or eleven were taken off to forced labour, either as porters or plantation workers. For the children at school, one refugee alleged that the children were taught to read and write but were also encouraged to act as spies for the Renamo police. Others said the main school activities were working in the fields or building houses. Older boys were also taken to join Renamo forces, and often themselves became involved in killings of civilians. Girls and young women were said to be frequently forced to provide sex for Renamo forces. Fleeing from destruction, control and even tax areas is difficult and dangerous, as anyone discovered is very likely to be killed or mutilated.[6]

In Mexico City, there are several groups working with women which now acknowledge the importance of education in the broadest sense, to prevent them internalizing their stress and anxiety which can emerge as physical illness. However, those involved point out that it is difficult to get funding for such projects because most aid agencies concentrate on the refugees' most immediate needs for food, housing, clothing and general education.

The following short study from Costa Rica gives some idea of the kinds of psychological problems encountered in both women and children and their impact on educational achievement and general self-confidence. Salvadorean refugees in Costa Rica do not live in camps, and substantial numbers have now returned to El Salvador. In contrast to the Nicaraguans in Costa Rica, they have legal status, and are relatively well organized. The Salvadorean teachers union, ANDES, and local Salvadorean organizations provide pre-school education, help for families and individuals with social and psychological difficulties and workshops for women to develop skills.

This report was written by a Salvadorean woman who has worked in an institution for Salvadorean refugees in Costa Rica which not only provided a crèche for children but also offered psychological help to children, adolescents and their parents, and those refugees working in the centre.[7] The centre catered for children from babies to eighteen-year-olds, to help the broken families and female-headed households in this refugee community, where children had to be left while the mother went out to work.

She found a range of problems among these children: from aggression, withdrawal and self-isolation, low self-esteem, bed-wetting and nightmares, to lack of concentration and learning difficulties. For example, there was one little boy of three years who could say only seven or eight words very imperfectly. He was the youngest of three children, living alone with their mother in Costa Rica. Their father had remained in El Salvador for the previous two years and the family had always clung to the idea that he was coming 'soon', although this reunion in fact was constantly postponed. The mother said that their father had been very demanding with the children and had punished them if they had not been quick to learn what he taught them. It was he who took on this teaching role in the home. However, the youngest child learned to speak after the break-up of the family. The mother had not taken on the teaching role previously assumed by the father, because if she had, she would have had to face up to the reality that he was not going to come back. Consequently, she did little to encourage the child to speak, with serious effects on his development.

In this case, the effects of the war in El Salvador and the consequent break-up of the family caused not just physical separation, but also the abandonment of particular roles and responsibilities within the family. Until the boy's problem was diagnosed and he was given some individual help to develop his ability to speak, he had been placed in a group of one- and two-year-olds, further inhibiting his progress.

Research suggests that over 20 per cent of Salvadorean refugees and displaced people in all categories had experienced the killing or disappearance of a family member before they fled their homes during the first half of the 1980s. A smaller proportion lost family members during the flight. Children often continue to relive these events and devote a great deal of time and energy trying to make sense of their experiences. This can lead to a withdrawal from the world around them and consequent learning difficulties.

Take the case of one nine-year-old girl, T., from a *campesino* family, who was repeating the first grade of primary school for the third time. When she was seven, she had enrolled in First Grade in El Salvador. However, harassment forced the family to move into the city, where they stayed with friends. They had serious economic problems and the mother sought refuge in Costa Rica, intending to send for the rest of the family. The father remained with the children in El Salvador. According to the children, he would go off to work for several weeks at a time without returning to them, and finally he went off to work and did not come back. After three months they were told he had been killed in a confrontation with the security forces. Their mother brought the children to Costa Rica where T. was enrolled in First Grade for a second time. However, she was forced to repeat the First Grade yet again because, as her teacher observed, she had serious learning difficulties. The only thing she did was to draw, 'as if she was in another world'. Her drawings, which were later used to help understand her state of mind, showed her obsession with the experiences the family had been through. They frequently dwelt on death, with which she was evidently trying to come to terms and were all in dark colours – black, mixed with grey and brown. Her efforts to deal with her memories and feelings meant she shut out the world around her, and was therefore incapable of absorbing what she was taught at school. Although the staff at the centre were able to identify her problem, it is not easy to solve and she continues to have learning difficulties. It is all too easy for teachers simply to dismiss such children as unintelligent or deliberately difficult.

The author also saw a good deal of the pressures on women as mothers and heads of the family. She points out that in Central America, men often abandon their wives or partners and children, either leaving the area to seek work, or leaving them for another woman. The economic crisis and the increase in refugees from political conflict has further increased the numbers of women left alone to cope, both with feeding the family, and also making all the decisions about the children's education and upbringing. Some are still suffering the grief and trauma of the death or separation from their partner, and the loss of their own culture and environment. Consequently there are many women bearing this emotional burden who are suffering mental or physical illness, which in its turn has its effect on the development of their children.

The uncertainties about the future and the question of when and whether to return can also create family conflict. The views of the children may be different from those of the parents. One adolescent explained his feelings:

I don't understand them [his parents]. They have always said that they decided to leave El Salvador for the sake of us children – they were afraid that something might happen to us, but now they're thinking of going back, despite the fact that the situation is still not sorted out or resolved. I do want to go back, but I don't think its any better [there]. Here in Costa Rica life is different, at least we can stay alive.

The researcher adds that the wish to return among children born in Costa Rica was less strong, at least while the war was going on, while adults often felt guilty at having 'settled down' in Costa Rica.

Going home

The issue of refugee return or resettlement was discussed in 1989 at a conference of Central American states. Some government representatives argued for more funds to be given for dealing with or resettling refugees. The refugees were seen as part of the battle for aid. Others argued that even in the absence of a political settlement, returning home was the only resolution to the problem. Some Salvadoreans, for example, who have been living under harsh and restrictive conditions in camps in the east of Honduras agreed to return to El Salvador before the latest round of fighting. However, some refugee groups have campaigned first to be allowed to return to their place of origin, not to go where the government sends them, and second, to return in groups, not as individuals. All this is to try and prevent harassment and victimization of individual returnees by the authorities.

In El Salvador, communities who have returned *en masse* are relatively well organized and have embarked on community development projects, including health, housing, education and production. They have had assistance, not from the government but from aid agencies, especially church organizations, including the Catholic, Episcopalian and Lutheran churches, and the International Red Cross.

Returning to poor rural areas, these refugees have come back with more skills than when they left. Through literacy work, organized primarily by the Salvadorean teachers union ANDES in the camps, most people have become literate. Their children have been to school. They hope to work with those who have remained to pass on what they have learned. Those who have returned in groups and are kept under some supervision by international organizations are less at risk from the security forces, even if a settlement is not reached. Their situation contrasts favourably with that of Guatemalans returning to their homes. There have been repeated allegations that Guatemalan returnees have been detained by the army on arrival, and that some have not survived. Others have been held for weeks or months at the army bases to which they are forced to report. Those allowed to return to their home area often find their land has been seized and given to others. Many are sent to model villages in 'development poles', where they are closely monitored by the army and the civil patrols.

In Namibia, refugees have returned home in the far more favourable climate of independence, though resettlement will undoubtedly be a long process. Here the problem will be to expand education and social services to meet the needs of the deprived local population, and of the returnees. Refugees in the SWAPO camps have had more access to schooling and literacy programmes, as well as scholarships, than have people living in the more deprived parts of Namibia.

Schooling for children in SWAPO camps was compulsory, and adults were expected to be involved in educational programmes, whether for literacy or further training. With help from external agencies, the United Nations Institute for Namibia has trained hundreds of civil servants for a future Namibia and the Namibian Extension Unit has provided distance learning opportunities in basic subjects, such as maths, English, health care and agriculture. This has not been easy, given the shortage of resources and the very low levels of skills and training among the Namibian population as a whole, but these efforts have all been designed to contribute to the development of an independent Namibia. Despite the length of their exile, refugees, and certainly their leaders, focused their educational strategy on preparing for a future in Namibia.

Notes

1. This section is based on research by Etel Romano of CSUCA, and by the author, with material on Guatemalan refugees in Mexico generously provided by David Archer and Patrick Costello, and from secondary sources shown in the resource list.
2. Oviedo Mendiola (1989).
3. The material in this section is drawn from research done by D. Archer and P. Costello, *passim.*
4. Mkangaza (1989).
5. Seminar . . . Zimbabwe (1990), 'Preliminary report', pp.7–8.
6. This account was taken from Gersony (1988).
7. Romano (1989).

PART FOUR

Breaking the Culture of Silence: Organizing for Literacy

Most of the literacy initiatives we describe here have arisen out of economic crisis and political struggle. Some have been initiated by governments, others by non-governmental groups. In their generative ideas, if not always in their practice, they aim to contribute to changing society and giving those who are economically or politically dispossessed some control over their own lives. In this sense, most are opposed to some degree to the established order. Circumstances and ideology have dictated different strategies to achieve literacy and various other educational and political goals. A variety of problems, revelations and surprises have resulted.

Breaking the Culture of Silence, Organizing for Literacy

CHAPTER 15

Central America

The silence is not of our making. Historically and socially, men and women are social beings. We need to relate to each other, to talk, to pass on our experiences and knowledge. So why do we keep quiet? Who benefits from our silence? Who would be afraid if we spoke up?

(Literacy worker from Chaletenango, El Salvador).[1]

In Central America, literacy and popular education have been strongly linked with political struggles. Demands for education have been regarded as an important part of agendas for change. The past decade – despite, or perhaps as a consequence of, deepening economic and political crisis – has seen a rapid growth in popular organizations, many of which espouse the idea of popular education. A certain amount of 'fictionalization' is to be expected. The reality of popular participation in projects is often rather different from the goal which exists in the minds of its initiators, but undoubtedly substantial strides have been made in understanding both the problems and the promise of such work.

Nicaragua after the literacy crusade

The initial literacy crusade in Nicaragua in 1980 has been one of the main inspirations for other literacy and popular education initiatives in the region. It capitalized on enthusiasm for the new government and its goal was as much political education as literacy *per se*. Despite the overall success of the campaign, its results were none the less more patchy than the national figures would suggest, if only because the illiteracy rates in many rural areas were well above the national average.

Apart from the numbers of people it reached, there was another aspect of this campaign which was considered important in the longer term. Young people from urban areas who became *brigadistas* (literacy workers) were confronted, for months on end, with the poverty of the rural areas. They experienced the conditions not in an abstract way, but through the communities and families they got to know. This was certainly an important consciousness-raising exercise. Many of these *brigadistas* went on to become popular teachers, whose work became the backbone of continuing literacy and adult education, particularly in rural areas, after the end of the campaign.

The future of literacy work, and indeed policies on education in general, have now been thrown into question by the victory of UNO in the polls. But the plan which was to be pursued by the Sandinistas in the renewed national literacy campaign is interesting, both in terms of strategy and of materials. The intention was for a much longer-term campaign than the 1980 crusade, which would have fallen into three sections:

- The first was to run from September 1989 to 1991. Its primary aim was to contain illiteracy, to reduce it to the 12.9 national average achieved in 1980, and make up the ground lost since then.
- The second phase, planned to run from 1992 to 1994, was the reduction stage: 'Without setting a specific target, we want to push illiteracy down from 12.9 per cent.'
- The third stage, from 1994 to the year 2000, was the phase of elimination of illiteracy, defined as below 3 per cent.

There are several significant differences of approach from the crusade of 1980. The original campaign worked on a mixture of widespread enthusiasm, international solidarity and a good deal of trial and error. According to Douglas Guerero, who was in charge of planning the renewed campaign:

The 1980 crusade was full-time and five months long. The country's economic situation just now does not allow us to repeat this. And this strategy of doing it in three stages means we don't have to do it as intensively. We have a lot more technical experience than we had in 1980. What we have now is less material resources.

The campaign was to be much more decentralized, with regions choosing their own pace according to their needs and capacities. Another difference was in the content of the literacy manual (paper and printing paid for by Swedish aid), which focuses less on directly political topics than the 1980 material but more on daily life, health, family, children and communal organization. The 1980 manual had a nation-building function, raising political consciousness and consolidating the Sandinistas in power. It also used the rhetoric of war and battle campaigns. This undoubtedly was successful in mobilizing and appealing to those who were involved in the anti-Somoza struggle. However, in areas where people had participated little in the struggle, it was as likely to have an alienating effect. This time, consciousness-raising was on a different level, attempting to take an approach with a broader appeal.

According to Guerero, the new materials focused more broadly on the rights and duties of the citizen and 'the practical elements of daily life – getting organized and solving the problems of the community. These are themes which are acceptable to any Nicaraguan'. Certainly there was more emphasis on skills, reflecting both Nicaraguan experience and a tendency among many groups in the region to move away from emphasizing exclusively the political conscientization process while largely ignoring people's daily needs and demands for practical skills.

Although in most of the country the new literacy drive had scarcely begun before the elections, in one northern district, Jalapa, the renewed literacy campaign began in 1988 as a kind of pilot project. It illustrates how the more piecemeal approach was developed. The demand for a renewed literacy campaign came from within the region itself. Among the groups which had been active in advocating the campaign were the agricultural co-operatives which felt that they would benefit if their members were able to keep records and accounts.

This is an agricultural region in the north, bordering Honduras, which has experienced serious problems with infiltration by the Contras. The first seven target communities of the new campaign in October 1988 to February 1989 were people moved by the army or displaced during the fighting, some of whom had been angry at the way in which they were relocated. In these communities, the level of illiteracy was estimated at 25.6 per cent. In the corresponding period from October 1989, the campaign moved on to a further nineteen long-established communities. A separate target group for on-going literacy work was out-of-school youngsters who work in the tobacco plantations, described as very tough and very difficult to convince of the value of literacy.

As in the 1980 campaign, the literacy teachers or *brigadistas* were youngsters from the agricultural college and secondary schools. In the first phase, they were volunteers, in the second, the campaign counted as part of the work-study component of the regular school curriculum. Otherwise there were no payments or rewards, apart from a T-shirt and some prestige in the community. What was different was that this time 70 per cent of the *brigadistas* were female.

There was very little money for the campaign, and the young teachers lived with families who could often scarcely afford to feed them. They also suffered from the lack of all kinds of materials – paper, pens, blackboards, chalk. Those whom the students taught then went on to become popular teachers themselves, on the model of the earlier campaign.

Despite the problems, the campaign seems to have been effective not only because of the *brigadistas'* enthusiasm, but also as a result of organization at the local level. The campaign involved the regional Ministry of Education and a variety of other Sandinista-linked organizations, including the women's organization (MOMLAE, previously AMLAE), the peasants' union, the co-operatives organization and the Sandinista Youth Movement.[2]

A further change was evident in the approach to the question of the Atlantic coast, where differences of language and culture, political dissidence and isolation from the rest of the country make for a very different kind of environment. Johnny Hodgson, a Creole, and formerly a member of the Atlantic Coast Autonomy Commission, recalls the effects of the first campaign:

Learning to teach

One of the key aspects in the Freirean approach to teaching and learning is that it is intended to break down the authoritarian barriers between teacher and learner. This is far from an easy task for either side, because so many assumptions exist about both roles. As Freire has pointed out, it cannot mean the collapse of the two roles into anarchy – though this is sometimes the outcome.

Antonio Pineda, who has worked in literacy since 1980, mainly in the poor and isolated region of Río San Juan in the south of Nicaragua, suggests how he sees the interaction taking place. In Río San Juan, the original literacy campaign had relatively little impact, and a new campaign was launched in the mid-1980s which was far more successful and led to the area being declared free of illiteracy. He believes strongly in learning to read as 'a second liberation' (the first being political).

The world has to recognize the importance of books, and methods [of teaching] are also important, but most important is how the teacher reaches the heart of the person taught. The very best books with gold-leaf engraving can be very pretty and the teacher might have the very best methods in using this book, but how is that teacher going to get the *campesinos* and workers to understand the contents?

The teacher, he says, must not talk over people's heads and must understand their problems, by being part of the community and 'making people fall in love with the idea of coming to study'.

This he admits is not easy and is a matter of attitude rather than teaching methodology. One way is through working with a community; for example, joining in the building of a bridge, a church or a health centre. Another is through getting to know the children, which is a way of 'getting to the heart of the community'. He also points out that most teachers think basically that they are superior to the peasants.

The *campesinos* know many things and we teachers are perhaps embarrassed to ask. Because we are teachers, we have our degree. But there are teachers – and I have seen this – who have to sleep the night on a river bank because they don't know how to cross. I've seen teachers who get lost up in the mountains, while the *campesino* looks at the sun, looks at the sort of vegetation and knows which way to go. So when the *campesinos* and workers know they are called on to be our teachers then later on, you can teach them and they will accept that.

While Pineda himself expresses a deep and almost romantic attachment to life in the mountains, he is well aware of the practical problems: 'It's very hard. The problem is how to transmit this to future teachers: there are many who really don't want to be humble like this.'

The impact of the original literacy campaign is sometimes said to have been a disaster, especially politically, but the effects were different in different communities. In the north, in the Miskitu and Sumu areas like Rio Coco, the political problems were increased by the campaign.

Some Miskitu who worked in the campaign now say that they actually altered the official literacy materials so that they expressed opposition to the Sandinistas. However, according to Hodgson, in the Creole areas, like the town of Bluefields, the campaign gained quite a lot of support and contributed to settling problems with the Sandinistas. Until recently, secondary school pupils in Bluefields were still doing literacy work with adults as part of their schooling. However, he agrees that the original materials had considerable weaknesses in conception, particularly the idea that it was enough simply to translate existing materials designed for Spanish-speaking learners. 'For example, they teach you in Miskitu. But just teaching you Miskitu while the things they are teaching you about are not the things that identify the Miskitu people, then that's not going to mean much to you.' In other words, the cultural content is just as important as the language itself.[3]

Honduras: peasant union initiatives

The Nicaraguan literacy experience has had numerous imitators. One of the more bizarre examples is that of the campaign launched soon after the original Nicaraguan campaign by the Honduran government. The intention was to pre-empt any pressure for a 'democratizing' literacy campaign. The government campaign was poorly planned and, despite substantial financial aid, mainly from the United States, had little impact. It also relied on a form of coercion to achieve its aims. Every person who could read and write was supposed to teach someone who could not, and if they did not do so, they were to be fined. Clearly, attempts at mass mobilization on this negative principle are unlikely to be successful.

Further official efforts at out-of-school education have mainly been through the medium of radio programmes for distance learning. According to one source, who had recently listened to some of these programmes, they were essentially material designed for children and had not been properly adapted to the needs and interests of adults. According to a Honduran social worker, the Adult Education Section in the Ministry of Education has extremely limited resources. Anyway, she added, this work is not a political priority for the government.

Other initiatives have been taken by the Catholic Church, but the most striking example of a campaign which has achieved significant successes in recent years is that of the Honduran peasant's union, the Central Nacional de Trabajadores del Campo (CNTC). One of the difficulties of national government-sponsored literacy campaigns is that learning has to be based on communities which, unless in a revolutionary situation, may be difficult to organize or mobilize. Another approach is for organized groups such as trade unions or co-operatives to initiate their own programmes for their own members. The CNTC was formed in 1985 through an amalgamation of several peasants' organizations. It is an organization of substantial size, working in fourteen out of eighteen regions, with 23,000 members. The literacy programme thus has a ready-made constituency among their membership throughout Honduras. The participants are peasants, although access to classes is not confined to the membership.[4]

Literacy, however, has not been presented as a goal in isolation from other aspects of life: one of the key aims of the union has been to mobilize around demands for effective land reform, and they have deliberately linked their literacy programme to wider economic and political issues in the countryside. In some places, literacy groups have been involved in land seizures and have been harassed by the security forces. Recently, however, the literacy campaign has been recognized by the Ministry of Education, which gives literacy workers a minimum of protection.

The programme, launched in 1986, followed a step-by-step approach. Its organizers first worked with specialists in literacy education before the execution of the project was handed over to the CNTC itself. The organizers stress the importance of the fact that the programme is run by the union itself and not by outside experts, though they acknowledge the importance of the expertise and funds which have been given by outside agencies and individuals, from Latin America, the United States and Europe.

They began with a pilot project in the region of Cortes, where the union has a strong base. The preliminary stage was to go and find out about the communities in which they might work. In the course of investigating community needs and interests, they chose appropriate 'generative words', reflecting local concerns to use as the key words in building the literacy manual; for example, children, family, women, health, education, land and agriculture, and areas of direct concern to the union such as co-operatives and land reform. They also took photographs to illustrate those words. These were shown to the various communities, and changes were made according to their suggestions. According to one of the literacy monitors: 'The words chosen came from the *campesinos* and reflected their lives . . . and we liked that a lot.' The literacy materials were then put together from these elements. Publication of this material was externally funded by a Swiss agency and is of quite high quality, using large numbers of photographs.

Literacy promoters (called monitors) are drawn from, and chosen by, the local community. However, there are basic criteria governing that choice: that they are members of the community and have some status within it; that they can read and write and are numerate, or have some formal education; and that they are keen to do this work and have good relations with the community.

The monitors receive a brief though quite intensive initial training lasting about three weeks, largely through workshops and discussions. It seems that the monitors often want more training than they actually get. They work on a voluntary basis, and in the union's view, the dedication they show is the key to the success of the work. New promoters are drawn from the literacy groups themselves, so that the development of new promoters comes out of the literacy work itself.

The main problems in the pilot phase were, first, that drop-out rates were quite high among learners, though not necessarily so in comparison to other literacy projects. Drop-outs were said to be because of work, illness, poor sight, lack of light (at evening classes), living a long way from where the classes were held, and lack of interest. The problem of light was remedied when the Swiss development agency, which had also paid for printing materials, provided 300 gas lamps.

Interestingly, they found that in the first stage at which only reading and writing was taught, people got more discouraged than after the introduction of basic maths, in which people seemed to do very well. The conduct of learning is by Freirean methods of dialogue around generative words, syllabic exercises and analysis and discussion of images. The later post-literacy materials are designed both to impart skills and information and to generate changes in ideas and consciousness.

There have been other problems internal to the character of the organization. The union is dominated by men, at all levels, especially the leadership, although the literacy advisers who put together the materials were mostly women. In the early stages of the campaign, few women enrolled, and were often actively discouraged from doing so by male members of their families. As a result, separate classes have been held to encourage women to join, and enrolments have apparently increased. However, the fact that this was not taken into account in earlier planning stages indicates something of a blind spot in practice among the leadership at various levels.

Another difficulty has been the lack of support for the monitors, whose work is often difficult. This is mainly due to the shortage of personnel, who have to travel long distances to give that support, though efforts have been made to remedy this. Despite the help the CNTC had with printing, all the other materials for the learners have to be financed by the union. In many cases, local schools and communities have helped out, though there are still shortages. However, the union notes that the richest resources are those which are created within the project itself: the stories, histories of local experience, songs and poems which learners and monitors have created, which form a fertile basis for creating post-literacy materials.

El Salvador: literacy under fire

Economic and political circumstances, as well as the educational and cultural environment, influence people's eagerness for literacy and numeracy. El Salvador's governments have made a number of attempts to initiate literacy campaigns. They have had little success because of the civil war, especially in the 1980s, and people's fears and suspicions of government-sponsored projects. But this does not mean that people are not eager for literacy and education.

The example of the liberated zones in El Salvador in the mid-1980s was a case in point. While the fighting was continuing, a literacy programme was started up in the 'controlled zone' (that is, controlled by the FMLN) in Chalatenango province between 1982 and 1984. At first, the local popular organizations set up under the FMLN began to establish schools. These had virtually no materials and taught all ages, children and adults, fighters and civilians, sitting under trees or on river banks where soft sand substituted for a blackboard. Such was the demand for education that it was regarded as 'one of the people's expectations of the revolution' not to be deferred until after victory was achieved. It was also a deliberate policy to demonstrate the break with the kind of education provided by the state, challenging both its goals and the relationships between students, teachers and the community. But it was also a response to necessity because many schools had been destroyed or teachers had fled to escape the conflict.

A more organized literacy campaign was developed in the controlled zones through a group of teachers who belonged to the teachers union, ANDES. They were influenced by the mass campaigns run in Nicaragua and Cuba, but because of war conditions could not follow exactly the same methods. They were also strongly influenced by the work of various Christian base communities which had been active during the 1970s, especially the groups of priests and nuns who had worked with communities in Suchitoto and Aguilares. These groups had tried to put into practice their belief that, for dispossessed people, education meant 'reclaiming their own history', and thus challenging the established order.

ANDES also took up the idea promoted by Freire and others that there should not be a body of professional teachers to 'teach' literacy, but that literacy workers should come from the local community and essentially learn as they taught. However, they found that learners, with a pre-existing idea of a teachers' role, would not always accept young literacy teachers who were barely literate themselves. The co-ordinator of the literacy campaign at that time recalls: 'People had their [preconceived] ideas. They wanted 'a teacher' or at least an adult. For the children it didn't matter but the adults wanted a 'proper' teacher. When they went to the school and saw a young lad with a primer in his hand, they didn't have confidence in him.'[5]

The role of the popular church

In Latin America, changes in the outlook of the Catholic Church began in 1968 with the Second Conference of Latin American Bishops in Medellín, Colombia, which focused on the social and economic plight of the peoples of the region. Along with the Vatican II proclamation, this formed the basis for a more politically engaged attitude to social problems: the Church became effectively split between those who strove for social justice in this life, and those who either actively supported the existing political order or who refused to become openly involved in challenging it.

In Central America, the development of the 'popular church' was particularly strong in El Salvador, where a number of priests began to work mainly with peasant communities to create Christian base communities, and to train peasant leaders in *centros de promoción social*. The effectiveness of their work was enhanced, ironically by the army and the political élite who labelled these priests as 'communists and third-worldists'. This conflict explains the virulent campaign launched by various right-wing governments in El Salvador against these priests and their sympathizers. The most notorious incident was the murder of Archbishop Oscar Romero, but his death was just one of many.

Another difficulty was to convince people who had never benefited from education that they were capable of learning. A popular teacher said she found that once people took the decision to learn,

they want to learn everything in the shortest possible time. Their interest had been strengthened as their level of political consciousness made them realise that for centuries they had been denied the right to education. But in their heart of hearts they still don't believe they are capable of learning. But [now] necessity has obliged them to come to classes despite this scepticism.[6]

The necessities were those of the war. Those who were involved in fighting needed to be able to read instructions on equipment, and numbers on guns or shells, to be able to read written commands or issue them. For those not directly involved in combat, the work of popular committees entailed tasks made easier by the ability to write or count. When communities had become scattered by the fighting, it helped to be able to write and read letters. The need to be numerate for practical reasons encouraged the popular teachers to include it with the initial literacy work, rather than, as was the more common strategy at that time, to leave numbers and basic maths to the post-literacy phase.

The lack of available materials encouraged teachers and learners to use the environment around them, and also to draw on the knowledge of illiterate people; for example, in the uses of plants as medicines. On the other hand, the lack of materials could be a serious problem. Some teachers were very keen that children should use drawing as a means of expressing themselves, but sometimes they were reduced to using wrapping paper, or had no paper or pencils at all.

The campaign was frequently interrupted after 1984 by ferocious bombardments of the region by government forces. It became more common for teachers to have to interrupt both classes and training workshops because of the need to go underground to avoid bombs, which could make scheduling training for teachers very difficult.

Many of the professional teachers involved were women. As in a number of countries in the region, a large percentage of the teaching force, especially at primary level, consists of women, and this is reflected in the ANDES membership. Women were also involved as popular teachers. The training of voluntary popular teachers was intended to be by the 'cascade' method, but this was no easy task. The intention was that those who had been on the course should become 'multipliers' by conveying what they had learned to others. As the co-ordinator of the campaign admitted: 'In reality what happened was that they passed things on just as they had been told them, and one of our preoccupations was how to succeed in making [the popular teachers] into multipliers rather than simply repeaters.'[7]

Outside the controlled zones, there have also been developments in various kinds of non-formal learning, particularly in urban areas. In recent years, especially since the time of the Duarte government, popular organizations, trade unions, women's groups and others have increasingly become involved in provision of education, both for children and for adults. This aims not only to provide for those who do not manage to stay in the formal school system but also to provide education which is liberating rather than encouraging conformity with the existing system.

For example, mass organizations such as the trade-union federation FENASTRAS has its own schools, not just for trade-union work, but also teaching children to read and write, and study history, geography and so on. Obviously, these schools do not provide qualifications which are recognized in the formal state education system, but they have much influence. Church and Christian base communities have also been involved in a wide range of educational initiatives. A remarkable number of women's organizations have emerged from the crises of the 1980s. Some focus particularly on trade-union work, human rights and political mobilization, but a number have become involved in popular education and development work.

Gender issues are little mentioned in the record of experiences in the Salvadorean-controlled zones. Whether they were ignored or overridden because of war and crisis conditions is not clear, but certainly rural women's lack of access has been a feature of many experiences of literacy work. One of several women's groups which was formed in the late 1980s is the Asociación de Mujeres

Salvadoreños (AMS), which has a particular interest in developing literacy and training health promoters in alternative medicine. Because of the war, it has been very difficult to work in many parts of the countryside. Most of the women's groups have centred their work in urban areas. But as more areas have become accessible in the last few years, AMS has been trying to reach women in rural areas.

The University of El Salvador (UES)

The 1980s have been an extremely difficult decade for the University of El Salvador. It has faced political and military interference, closures, campus invasions by the military, and the assassination or disappearance of numbers of staff and students, as well as severe earthquake damage and shortage of funds. None the less, the university has embarked on an innovative scheme to alter the nature of its academic programmes and change the relationship between its staff and students and the community.

In the medical and dentistry faculties, a number of new courses have been created in primary and preventive health care, nutrition and mother and child health. The students do not just learn by sitting in the classroom but are expected to work in the community. This is not simply a form of community service, but aims to change the attitudes of existing professionals, and to motivate both rural and urban communities to become more involved in their own health care. In dentistry, an agreement was signed with the Ministry of Health to allow students to work in government health units. However, as one university professor explains, this is not easy. 'The people who work with the government health service have a different conception and try to change the ideas and methods of work of the students, saying that they won't be good dentists. It's a constant battle of ideas.' Some of the senior faculty do not like it either, and a number have resigned. Replacements have had to be sought from outside the country.

In another initiative in 1987, students from the Department of Psychology ran an eight-month literacy campaign in two poor neighbourhoods close to San Salvador – Credisa and Amatepec. Although an assessment of the results suggested that the planning of the project and training of students as literacy teachers was weak in some respects, the students made considerable efforts to encourage people to learn, including spending a lot of time visiting their homes and talking to them about their problems. Whatever the weaknesses in the programme, it certainly broke the separation of academic learning from practical work which usually prevails in universities.

Guatemala: language and power

In Guatemala, a major issue in literacy work is that of language. Attitudes to the question of which language should be used in literacy work have varied among indigenous groups, and between communities, depending how much contact they have had with *ladino* (Spanish) culture. One argument is that while Spanish remains the language of power, those who are obliged to deal with, for example, land-owners and government officials are at a disadvantage if they do not know Spanish. There are many stories of indigenous people losing their land because they have signed documents they did not understand, having been misled or deceived as to their contents. Political activists like Rigoberta Menchú have also found that when they travel around the country and speak to indigenous communities other than their own, the language differences make it necessary to use Spanish as a lingua franca. For that reason, some groups have conducted literacy work in Spanish in indigenous communities. This was the practice of the peasant organization, Central Unidad Campesino (CUC) until recently, when they switched to using indigenous languages. The argument for this latter strategy is, first, that it helps to preserve Maya cultures; second, it is seen as part of a strategy to build up an indigenous base in local and community politics which could more effectively resist *ladino* oppression.

Opposition to the government and the dominant culture and language has sometimes led to a rejection of literacy projects, particularly if they are run by outsiders. One indigenous group, the Mam Cultural Association (ACUMAM) has, for some years, operated a radio station in its own language, with some external support. At first they did not want to use the radio for literacy programmes: they wanted it to promote their own culture and language and to provide useful information and advice on daily matters, including agriculture. Only recently has a literacy programme been developed – in their own language, and not in Spanish.

Women in indigenous communities are least likely to know any Spanish, or to have any formal education at all. A representative of a Guatemalan non-governmental development agency, IDESAC, said: 'Women are refused access to education not only because they have to leave their own communities [in order to obtain it], which the men do not allow, but because it is believed that women's [role] is solely in the home.' The upheavals of recent years may have brought changes in attitudes in some communities. However, it is more likely that initiatives in any aspect of education for women will be more effective if they are in indigenous languages and within their own community.

Government-sponsored literacy projects as well as literacy projects run on *fincas* (commercial estates) by land-owners have shown poor results. This is despite the fact that the government campaign was supposedly based on indigenous languages and employed apparently

'Freirean' techniques, in terms of the learning method and consultation with communities. The campaign was directed particularly at indigenous groups whose illiteracy rates are estimated to be much higher than those of the society as a whole. However, the brutal treatment of these communities, especially over the last decade, means that they do not trust any government initiatives. Teachers from the communities did not want to volunteer and as a result, most of the teachers were *ladinos* without knowledge of the local language, so that both the language and participatory aspects of the programme did not work.

The failure of official literacy projects in Guatemala seems not only to be the result of cultural resistance, though this evidently is a strong element, but also of a related problem – a different set of priorities. Guatemala's indigenous communities have mostly oral cultures. Literacy is therefore far from being the first demand in many communities. Other issues take priority: land, housing, health, cultural preservation. Alberto Colorado, a Guatemalan working in Mexico expressed it this way.

Popular education has a problem. The question is – is it necessary to learn to read or write as part of popular education or not? I think not, because in many cases there are groups who do not need to read or write in order to have a great consciousness to transform the world – later the need [to read and write] arises, once the consciousness is there. Reading and writing are not the first priority, maybe number ten. This is our experience with Guatemalan peasants. Consciousness creates a demand for many things – land, water, housing and literacy.

He adds that interest in literacy has not been encouraged by the negative image of government campaigns. 'They were trying to teach people things they didn't want and which didn't interest them. That's why Freire's method is not the mechanics of teaching, it is a method of analysis – and afterwards people learn.'

Costa Rica: the uses of literacy

Costa Rica presents a contrast. This is a largely literate society, at least officially. Illiteracy levels are low nationally – under 7 per cent – though there are still substantial regional and local variations. For example, the 1984 census showed that in particular districts, the rates for the population over the age of ten were still relatively high: for example, Turrubares in San José province, 18.6 per cent; Los Chiles in Alajuela, 19.4 per cent; and Talamanca in Limón, the highest percentage in the country, 22.2 per cent. Furthermore, some authorities on adult education estimate that a very much larger proportion – up to 50 per cent of the population (over fifteen) – is functionally illiterate.[8]

This is, however, a society where a minimum ability to read and write is considered the norm and in practical terms is useful for the majority of people. Therefore the pressure on illiterates to learn and the negative connotations of illiteracy are greater. Various kinds of out-of-school education, skills training and night classes are offered both by government and non-governmental organizations. But there has been a good deal of criticism of government-sponsored literacy and adult education as not having moved away from the methods used in primary school. Adults, it is said, are often taught as if they were children, with materials which are not geared to their needs. Despite experiments in neighbouring countries, Freirean methods and principles are little used.

In a rural district of Costa Rica, where illiteracy at about 14 per cent is still quite high relative to the national average, a group of people involved with the local agricultural producers' association had very positive attitudes to literacy. They regarded it as helping them to cope with their environment.

The main difficulties which they identified for those who are illiterate or innumerate in Costa Rican society were practical ones. The inability to read signs makes it difficult to find your way around, especially in the city. To be unable to read instructions on labels, recipes and prescriptions can be dangerous. People also felt the disadvantages of not being able to read or write a letter, making access to information difficult. A more recent worry mentioned by a number in the group is the inability to sign a cheque or hold a bank account or read bills. A number of people suggested that it prevented or inhibited participation in community organizations: you couldn't become a secretary or a treasurer, for example.

But apart from practical matters, a number of people either stated directly or indicated that it was humiliating not to be able to read or write: 'You have to ask other people to write or read a paper for you and that makes [you] ashamed'; 'You have to stick to agricultural work and in that you're worse off or worse-treated.' It also made people feel marginalized or helpless: 'If you don't know how to read and write, it's like not having eyes.'

Notes

1. Toledo Hermosillo (1990), p.99 (translated from Spanish).
2. Government of Nicaragua (1988), 'Memorias . . .'
3. Interview with Johnny Hodgson by Jane Freeland, 1990.
4. This section is largely based on the account of the literacy campaign given by the CNTC in CEAAL, *Formación de educadores populares . . .* (1989), pp.39ff; Archer and Costello (1990), p.59ff.
5. Toledo Hermosillo (1990), p.86, (translated from Spanish).
6. Ibid, p.80, (translated from Spanish).
7. Ibid, p.89, (translated from Spanish).
8. For example, author's interview with Tito Quiros, University of Costa Rica, 1989.

CHAPTER 16

Southern Africa: contrasting experiences

Zimbabwe – losing momentum

The Zimbabwean national literacy campaign was conceived originally as a mass mobilization, a 'third liberation struggle', as the then Minister of Education put it. At independence, an estimated 40 per cent of the population over fifteen years old was illiterate, and 15 per cent was 'semi-literate'.[1] The campaign was intended to raise political awareness, as well as improve the literacy figures. In terms of rhetoric it sounded rather similar to the model established by Nicaragua, or perhaps Tanzania.

However, the campaign seemed to run out of steam before it really started. First, it was postponed for almost a year until 1983, when the first euphoria of independence had worn off and when economic problems were beginning to pile up. Second, the Prime Minister made the decision to transfer much of the responsibility for the campaign to the Ministry of Community Development and Women's Affairs (MCDWA). The reasons for this were not clarified. It may have been felt that the Ministry of Education was overburdened with the demands of a very rapid expansion in formal education. Furthermore, the MCDWA may have been regarded as the appropriate ministry because of its community links and structures at local level. However, the division of labour, with the Ministry of Education retaining control over training and materials and the MCDWA responsible for running the campaign, was unsatisfactory – the more so because the MCDWA had very limited staff resources. Planning was sketchy and did not initially include any strategy for post-literacy education.

The lack of dynamism at the top seems to have been reflected in the very patchy public response. In the years after independence, some of the structures of local community participation which had existed in parts of the country during the liberation war had withered away or become marginalized. New forms of community organization had not yet taken root, and this left the campaign with a 'top down' structure. This was despite the involvement of some very able and committed local literacy facilitators, many of whom were ex-combatants. Almost all mass campaigns of any length suffer from high drop-outs, but in Zimbabwe this resulted in the closure of many literacy classes and discouragement of learners. Furthermore, assessments of the campaign have suggested that in the public eye, especially the male public eye, the MCDWA was not regarded as 'serious' and literacy was labelled as a woman's preserve and thus downgraded.

The national campaign was in the main mother-tongue languages, Shona and Ndebele, so learners would not initially have been discouraged by learning in a language of which they had a poor grasp. However, some learners, especially in urban areas, would have preferred to learn English.

A key problem seems to have been the use of volunteer teachers who, especially in rural areas, had little back-up. In the absence of widespread local enthusiasm they became tired and discouraged by long periods of working without any material reward. Furthermore, the whole programme gave the impression that it was not receiving the highest priority and therefore the rewards in terms of status in the community were not necessarily very great. As a result, not only learners but also the teachers dropped out in large numbers. A total of 80,000 literacy tutors were trained on two-week short courses up to mid-1985, but at that date only 11,000 literacy groups were functioning, so probably about 11,000 teachers remained active.

Another impediment in the remotest and most deprived parts of the country was lack of transport and fuel allowances. This made it difficult for the district literacy co-ordinator to keep in touch with the groups and to distribute the materials. A frequent complaint was that books did not arrive or were in short supply.

Not only were there very great variations in enrolment regionally, but also there were different responses from men and women. On the whole, women seem to have been more enthusiastic, but the timing of classes often made regular attendance difficult for them. The attitude of men to the campaign was not generally positive. They seemed to regard it as a second-class form of education ('women's education'), and were also reluctant to admit that they were not literate. They either resisted enrolling or dropped out in large numbers, which influenced those who had adopted a 'wait-and-see' attitude.

There are now attempts to instil new life into the literacy programme, but it has suffered from not being a very high priority with the government. In terms of both human and economic resources, it has tiny allocations in comparison with formal education, into which most of the government's efforts and investments have gone. The economic constraints of the mid-1980s have also had their effect, deterring new spending. Payment of tutors is now beginning, but of course it is much more costly than using volunteers and probably limits the numbers reached.

There are also some voluntary literacy programmes which have played a significant role over the years. The largest and longest standing group is the Adult Literacy Organization of Zimbabwe (ALOZ). This organization started during the colonial period but has developed considerably since independence. It offers literacy programmes in English and, unlike the national campaign, in which it was not directly involved, is open to the influence of Freirean participatory approaches.

Mozambique: the problems of reaching women

In Mozambique, literacy has been regarded by the Frelimo government as of key importance. However, the task – to make a dent in an illiteracy rate of 93 per cent – was much more daunting than in the Nicaraguan case. The government therefore decided on a series of prolonged campaigns, rather than a once-and-for-all mobilization, which was probably not a practicable option in the post-independence economic crisis. Teaching was in Portuguese and priority groups were identified.

In the course of four consecutive campaigns from 1978 to 1982, overall enrolment declined sharply, and with the exception of two provinces, Manica and Maputo, drop-outs from the fourth campaign were between 65 and 89 per cent. The onset of the war with Renamo and the increased rigidity and centralization of the literacy campaigns' administration partly explain the decline. The government also experienced difficulties in bringing about changes in the economic structure – particularly in the introduction of effective agricultural co-operatives. This undoubtedly caused organizational problems, particularly in rural areas, and poor economic prospects also contributed to falling interest.[2]

However, there were also specific problems which affected women, who were least likely to be literate. The use of Portuguese as the language of instruction contributed to the difficulties experienced by the literacy campaigns in rural communities. Despite centuries of Portuguese domination, rural women had rarely learnt the language. Men were more likely to have had some contact with Portuguese through trade or migrant labour. The nature of the campaigns themselves excluded large numbers of rural women, even though the official women's organization played a role in mobilization. The campaigns concentrated mainly on 'organized' sectors of the community, including formal sector workers who had literacy classes in the workplace, and co-operatives.

Figure 16.1 shows that, especially in the early campaigns, many women did enrol, and just under half of those who completed the course passed the final literacy test. However, by the fourth campaign enrolment levels and success rates had fallen sharply, with a very small number of women nation-wide completing the course. Eagerness to learn was dampened by various factors, notably: too much work to cope with two hours of literacy classes a day plus homework; the constant and distracting demands of childcare; and male disapproval.

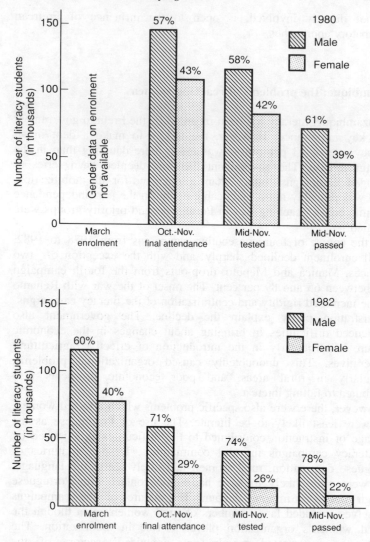

*Figure 16.1   **Mozambique: Second and Fourth Literacy Campaigns, 1980 and 1982.***
Source: Lind (1988) *Adult Literacy: Lessons and Promises,* p.77

According to studies of the campaign and of post-literacy adult education, other, less visible hurdles affected women's learning. Some feared that the demands of studying would lead to conflict at home, and possible rejection by husbands. Others lacked confidence in their ability to learn. A woman who dropped out of an adult education course after repeating the third year said: 'When I close the book, my head also closes. I don't think I'll go any more. I'm just going to irritate the teacher. Not even a little bit stays with me – nothing enters.'[3] On the other hand, women who succeeded in becoming literate seemed to gain confidence, even if the impact on their lives was otherwise small.

Popular education and literacy in South Africa

In South Africa, the idea of people's education has grown up in reaction to the discriminatory Bantu education system. Unlike most of the other movements described so far, it grew out of groups organizing within the formal school system. The 1980s also saw the emergence of numerous 'alternative' education projects, both for children and adults. These projects included literacy work, support for matriculation students, and help for out-of-school children. They have become increasingly politicized but some of the exponents of people's education are doubtful of those which provide 'alternative' non-racial schooling in the private sector for black children. They regard this as élitist, since it allows just a handful of black children to escape the state system.

There has also been much debate over the use of the term 'empowerment' in the context of education. Those with a more radical approach argue that empowerment can easily be interpreted as simply individual success and mobility – escape from the toils of the system – which runs counter to a policy of challenging the system itself. The National Education Crisis Committee (NECC) has also suggested that a good deal of the money going into 'alternative' education projects is being misspent. Eric Molobi said:

Never in the history of our country has so much money been pledged to help in the education crisis. There is simply a plethora of new funders and new programmes. Some of these are fly-by-night operations, set up by con-men who rip off our people while pocketing the money from overseas donors. The fashionable concept of 'alternative education' has become a misnomer, acting as a blank cheque to wealth and status. Even big business uses it in its own programmes, some of which are outright dubious in intention and operation.[4]

Despite these reservations, the need for further development of literacy and adult education is very clear. Large numbers of black South Africans, and to a lesser extent, Coloureds, have not gone to school or have not stayed at school more than three or so years. The statistical basis for deciding how many people are actually 'illiterate' is not reliable, since census data was based on self-assessment by individuals, which is thought to have led to serious underestimates in official figures. Certainly most independent estimates are well above the 33 per cent illiteracy rate in the black population which appears in the census figures. The likely figure seems between 50 and 60 per cent.

A study done in the early 1980s at the University of Cape Town argues that estimates should take into account the fact that literacy is a process which goes beyond reading and writing. It should also include numeracy and language learning – especially in a country where the languages of power, Afrikaans and English, are not the first languages of much of the population. The author also points out that the levels of learning in many primary schools are so low that the Unesco criterion of four years of schooling to achieve literacy is probably too short in this case.[5]

The problem of illiteracy and semi-literacy is on a large scale and widely dispersed. As members of the English Literacy Project (see below) point out, 'What people really want is not so much 'literacy', a concept which is not understood, as basic education which many people have not had.' This need is not confined to older people: the number of teenagers who have very few years of schooling, or severely interrupted schooling, is also large. In urban areas, squatter families do not get a minimum basic education and there is widespread need in rural areas. At present, the adult basic education available to meet this need is certainly not on a scale commensurate with the problem, especially in rural areas. As members of the literacy organization Learn and Teach point out, the literacy organizations are only 'scratching the surface of the problem'.

The Department of Education and Training (DET) does provide literacy and adult education classes on request from communities. However, these are concentrated in urban areas, based in DET schools. The methods of teaching and learning suffer from many of the same problems as formal schooling. The teachers are primary school teachers who are paid extra to take literacy classes in afternoons or evenings. Most deliver lessons, as one observer put it, as if they were teaching children in Standard 1. The textbooks used are designed for schoolchildren rather than adults. The courses are overloaded and heavily geared towards to getting a certificate. Given the general feeling about schools as oppressive places, and distrust of state education, many people are put off or drop out. In the 1980s, the skills shortage has encouraged some private employers to create workplace adult education programmes for their employees, but these cover only a very small number of black workers.

The scale of the problem is such that some people have argued that it cannot be solved without a broader political change in the nature of South Africa's government. Others, however, while acknowledging that they can scarcely solve the problem, have considered that it is important to lay some groundwork and perhaps contribute to changing the terms in which the debate about education is framed. They also regard it as important to support individuals and groups in their efforts to break from the repressive education system which encircles them.

A number of groups have emerged which attempt to meet these needs. Only in the past few years has there been an attempt to make links between groups and share ideas and experiences. Co-operation has been made all the more difficult because most such organizations have been under varying degrees of official scrutiny and the state of emergency has greatly hampered communications and co-ordination. Their scope and effectiveness has varied according to conditions in particular regions, so that there is uneven development.

Many organizations work out of Johannesburg, where some departments in the University of Witwatersrand have also been active in educational research and the promotion of adult and continuing education for black people. In the University of Natal too, some groups have been actively involved in promoting community education. However, in Natal, academic, church-based and secular groups have been hampered by Inkatha–UDF conflict as well as state repression. In the Western Cape, a relatively liberal atmosphere and support from the University of Cape Town and the University of the Western Cape have allowed the development of adult education work to quite a high level, including among poor Coloured communities and farm workers.

The University of the Western Cape, established as a 'Coloured' university, no longer restricts access on a racial basis and has made considerable efforts to alter its curriculum and style of teaching in order to provide a more relevant education for its students. In addition, it works in adult and out-of-school education with trade unions and other organized sections of the community.

In contrast, the Eastern Cape, like the Orange Free State, has experienced high levels of repression, making any kind of progressive organization very difficult, with little support from universities and other established institutions.

Some of the largest and longest-standing literacy organizations still have an approach which emphasizes skills acquisition and does not attempt to question the broader environment in which learning takes place. However, there are a number of groups now which have taken a much more politically engaged view of adult education, though they do not all share the same political positions. Among these, the broadest reach has been achieved by Learn and Teach, which started in 1974, providing literacy classes in English, mainly to domestic workers. Since then, they have increased their coverage to include rural areas and work in mother tongues and English as a second language. They also train literacy workers for other organizations, and have developed their own literacy materials.

Adult education and conscientization have also become issues within the trade-union movement. The trade-union federation, COSATU, is very concerned about educational issues in theory, but in practice they seldom reach the top of the agenda because the organization is constantly responding to urgent political crises. Within particular unions there has been considerable interest in education work as a form of consciousness-raising. Some literacy groups, like the English Literary Project (ELP), work specifically with unionized workers. Although there is the advantage that these workers are organized and many are interested in learning, the ELP has found that there are great logistical difficulties in keeping learning groups together. 'People get tired and have lots of disruptions – having to work overtime, problems with travelling, and with family commitments.' In Johannesburg, where they do most of their work, travelling is a major problem, since people often have to commute long distances to work from the segregated townships. Another problem is with employers, who are by no means always sympathetic. '[They] don't always allow us access to the work-site, or they try to appropriate literacy programmes as their own initiative and take credit for them, while still not giving their employees time off to go to classes.'

According to members of the Learn and Teach literacy organization, the vast majority – 80 per cent – of their learners and literacy co-ordinators are women. In rural areas where women are 'not working' (that is, they do not have waged employment) they very often start groups themselves. In urban areas, more men attend, but are still a minority. The experience of literacy workers in Natal is much the same; that among women in rural and peri-urban areas, the demand for literacy is far higher than among men, not only because more women are illiterate but because 'it's much harder for men to admit illiteracy or lack of competence in English than it is for women'. They have found that women without wage employment 'want to do something – they want mainly to help their children. They are well aware of the deficiencies in their kids' education and want to be able to improve that situation'.

Many people working in adult education argue that a nation-wide campaign is needed to deal with the high levels of illiteracy in South African society, where being illiterate or semi-literate is certainly a major disadvantage. By the end of the 1980s, with political change in prospect, the NECC had begun to turn its attention to the issues of literacy and adult basic education and their relationship to the idea of people's education.

Notes

1. Lind *et al.* (1986), p.3.
2. Lind (1988), *passim.*
3. Marshall (1988), 'Literacy, state formation and people's power: education in a Mozambican factory', quoted in Urdang (1989), p.231.
4. Eric Molobi, NECC Keynote address, Conference on Education and Training for South Africans and Namibians, Michigan State University, 1986.
5. Wedepohl (1984), p.3.

PART FIVE

The Future of Education in the South

By the end of the 1980s there was a recognition that the debt crisis, political conflict and environmental degradation had seriously affected the poorest countries and communities, and that educational provision was one of the casualties. However, there continues to be considerable debate as to what future strategies for education should be. This section examines the main educational issues and their relationship to broader economic and social questions. Finally it discusses the role of external aid in the field of education.

The Future of Education in the South

CHAPTER 17

Basic education for all: prospects for the nineties

> To serve the basic learning needs of all requires more than a recommitment to basic education as it now exists. What is needed is an 'expanded vision' that surpasses present resource levels, institutional structures, curricula, and conventional delivery systems while building on the best in current practices.
>
> *(World Declaration on Education for All: Article 2)*[1]

These brave words are part of the declaration issued by the World Conference on Education for All held in Jomtien, Thailand, in 1990. For the poorest and most conflict-ridden countries, the prospects of achieving primary education for all by the year 2000, as the declaration envisages, seem remote. Much depends on improvements in the economic sphere. At present, economic recovery is evident only in a handful of stronger economies and those which have received heavy injections of external economic assistance.

New options may be created by the changing international political climate. Dramatic changes have taken place in East–West relations and in the political and economic complexion of Eastern Europe. The dissipation of Cold War rivalries may help in finding a solution to some regional conflicts in Africa, Asia and Central America. However, the demands of Eastern Europe and the Soviet Union for aid from international financial agencies and from Western governments raise questions as to whether countries of the South will see much-needed flows of aid and trade diverted. Furthermore, those countries which previously received much of their assistance from the Soviet Union and the states of Eastern Europe are now seeing those flows drying up, or severely reduced.

The so-called 'peace dividend', created by the expected reduction of military expenditure in the North, could allow for the growth of international aid on concessionary terms. However, it cannot automatically be assumed that more funds will be channelled to developing countries. At present, this is little more than a pious hope. It seems just as likely that, for example, the United States will utilize most of the funds released to meet domestic demands. The dramatic changes in Europe have also tended to shift world attention away from the South. The peripheral status of most nations of the South may therefore be reinforced by these changes.

This is the context in which education systems in the South face the 1990s. While there are rays of hope, and some new beginnings in the offing, particularly in Southern Africa, the general outlook is a difficult one. It will require a great deal of effort, and a conscious alteration of priorities on the part of international agencies, governments and non-governmental organizations to bring about real changes in the prospects for education for the poorest people in the South. For many of them at the moment, the priority has to be bare survival.

The World Declaration on Education for All, though acknowledging in its final draft the existence of the international debt crisis and the need to resolve it, made little attempt to relate this to the broader economic and political context in which education occurs. Many of its recommendations are to be welcomed, as is the possibility that more attention and funds will go to education in the South in future, but a great deal was left unsaid.

Funding education

The case studies in this book, covering countries with a wide spectrum of political goals and economic problems, give some indication of the variety of factors which can influence the effectiveness of basic education. These factors are by no means confined to the working of the education system itself.

A key question is funding and the role of the state in providing it. In many countries rapid population growth compounds the economic pressures on state resources, and these are likely to intensify unless economic growth and development is restored. In the countries examined, the burden of financing formal education at both primary and secondary level is falling increasingly on family, community and non-state institutions. In many cases this is not the result of any ideological commitment to shifting educational financing out of the state sector, but is rather due to the effects of economic recession and lack of funds earmarked for basic education. The 'privatizing' of funding of education has taken place, not through the development of private schools, but by mobilizing private resources for education within the public sector.

This trend, the examples show, puts considerable pressure on the poorest families, who are also experiencing falling or stagnating income levels. Inputs to education may take the form of time spent in unpaid labour, especially on the part of women, in lieu of money. This too has its cost.

In relatively prosperous countries with relatively well-established education systems, the effects of community funding in the form of fees and charges on children's participation in schooling may be insignificant. However, the examples of Costa Rica and Zimbabwe show that at secondary level, where fees are higher and rising, and where real incomes are not rising to match, high fees can deter poor families from keeping children at school when they could go out to work. In least-developed countries, where the poor can hardly afford to feed their children, even very small fees at primary level are a deterrent.

Community involvement in the creation of new schools can have very different outcomes according to context. Where communities build schools which are intended to be part of the state system, they can only be effective if the state can then afford to sustain the running costs. If a poor community builds a school, it is unlikely to be able to sustain its recurrent costs. If external funding cannot be provided, the school will either fall into disuse, or will be of very low quality. Discrepancies of provision can also arise where the state is not in a position to make up the difference between what a wealthy community can put into a school and what a poor community can afford. Therefore, if equity of provision in basic education is to be an important consideration, community financing cannot be regarded as a simple panacea for the problems of funding education.

If communities are to participate in the processes of education, they should have the opportunity to contribute more than money and labour power. The World Declaration on Education for All talks of the need for communities to act in 'partnership' with government. Whether this is feasible depends very much on the relationship between government and society. The question of democracy in education cannot be addressed in isolation from the broader question of democracy in society. In an authoritarian state, this 'partnership' is likely to be highly unequal. As the case studies have shown, in practice, communities can often supply funds and services without taking part to any extent in decision-making about the process of education. Very often parents' participation is designed to promote the success of their own children, or their own prestige, rather than to benefit the community as a whole. Parents are largely being mobilized as a resource for the continued provision of a service already pre-packaged. In societies where social and educational inequalities are deep-rooted, parents or communities may not have access to sufficient information to make effective decisions on what changes need to be made. In other cases, where people are sufficiently organized to make demands on the state, these are not always welcomed by those in power. None the less, where the ideology of government has been to increase community involvement in decision-making in the school, the results can be fruitful.

'The community' is often invoked as the key resource which will take education forward into the twenty-first century. However, this assumes that the community is an easily identifiable and homogenous entity. As some of our examples have shown, this is far from the case. Many communities, especially in urban areas where there has been a good deal of in-migration, are diffuse and unorganized. In societies which have experienced severe social disruption as a result of war, government policies or economic crisis, even less can be assumed about the nature of the family and the community. Communities which are cohesive may be held together by family or tribal and ethnic loyalties – but these may equally be divisive. Furthermore, most communities have economic and gender hierarchies and may not easily accept equal access to education or other activities by all their members. Until such divisions, rivalries and power structures are understood, educational and development initiatives which succeed in one place can go badly wrong in another.

Another catchword popular in recent discussions of education is 'decentralization'. Again, the effects of decentralization depend on the political, economic and organizational context. Socio-economically more advanced regions and élites tend to benefit the most from decentralization and devolution. The decentralization of the administration of education, for example, is by no means always intended to give communities more say in education. It may, as the examples of South African and Namibia demonstrate, be part of a divide-and-rule strategy.

Thus, the effectiveness of community participation in education, partnership with government, and decentralization of control cannot be considered in isolation from the political and economic context in which they occur. One of the indicators of effectiveness is the extent to which they give a voice to those whose views usually remain unheard – because they are poor, illiterate or female.

The quality of education

Teachers: the vital link

If new education strategies are to be developed, one of the key elements in their success must be the teacher. An ill-qualified, disaffected teaching force, working in poor conditions and constantly short of money, will not be effective in implementing change. Teachers tend to receive much of the blame for failures in the education system and little appreciation for their role. Where teachers organize to defend their economic positions, or their human rights, they tend to be regarded as troublemakers. In ideal terms, teaching is often held to be a vocation but in reality is regarded in many societies today as the lowest form of professional work.

In the countries examined, the situation of teachers ranges from unsatisfactory to catastrophic in terms of conditions, salaries and training. This leads to low morale, drop-outs from the profession, or preoccupation with earning income outside teaching, leading to absenteeism and poor performance. Teachers in rural areas face the most difficult conditions. In urban areas, however, where there are high levels of poverty, overcrowding and violence, teachers face different forms of stress.

Even in countries where many teachers have been committed to the social and political goals of the government, commitment can wear thin when it is impossible to live on the meagre salary. Raising teachers' pay to a living wage seems, therefore, to be a necessary prerequisite of progress, though it is far from being sufficient.

In international circles, considerable concern has been voiced over the quality of basic education in countries of the South, questioning whether, if children do go to school, they actually learn anything. In country after country, we have seen the difficulties of teaching and learning in a school which is falling down, or has no facilities or teaching materials. The examples show that these problems have been exacerbated by cuts in education budgets, and lack of foreign exchange for building materials, transport, paper and other necessities. However, advocating better-quality inputs into education seems often to conflict with the broader economic strategies which countries are asked to pursue: tight budgets, cost-cutting and strict control of wages. Economies of scale can be made, bureaucratic inefficiencies in ministries of education can be remedied, but these measures alone, for most indebted countries, will not bridge the financial gap.

Other kinds of 'efficiency' measures which have been advocated by international agencies and academics include utilizing facilities and teachers more intensively through multi-grade classes and double shifts. However, in many of the countries examined here, these practices are already in operation. This leaves little room for further savings, and furthermore, as they are at present practised, their outcomes are often far from satisfactory.

These intensive methods need not necessarily be detrimental to learning if, for example, teachers are properly trained to work with multi-grade classes and have suitable learning materials. However, as comments by teachers of multi-grade classes in Central America indicate, taking a class of eighty children of different ages under a leaking roof without books or materials is not a happy experience. Equally, the use of double shifts is not necessarily harmful, though, for example, the Zambian experience suggests a good deal of absenteeism and late-coming by pupils and teachers, and some difficulty in covering the work in shorter periods. The system can work if teacher morale is high and there are enough materials to go round. Flexibility in the timing of schooling, both during the day and over the course of the year, may help in avoiding drop-outs. However, in order to make these strategies work, far more investment is needed than is currently available in teacher preparation, in facilities and materials.

Changes and greater flexibility in methods of training teachers are crucial. Simply using more untrained teachers, in countries where large numbers are already without qualifications, may be cheaper but is unlikely to contribute to the quality of the system. In some of the poorest countries where there is a severe shortage of teachers, new forms of initial training may be needed. One option is for trainees to spend more of their time in the classroom, as in Zimbabwe's recent teacher training programmes, though that experience emphasized the need for strong trainee support and well-prepared distance learning materials.

In countries which still have large numbers of untrained teachers, in-service training may be more effective than college-based initial teacher-training, especially where resources are limited. It has been increasingly used to upgrade untrained or under-trained teachers, or for specific purposes, such as the introduction of new syllabuses. Various methods have been used, from on-the-job training in a school setting to distance learning and participatory workshops. There has been some cross-fertilization of ideas on training methods and approaches from non-formal education. Some academics argue that 'participatory training methods', as used in popular education, are 'labour- and time-consuming, neither fast, efficient nor inexpensive'[2]. While such methods may not be the best way to tackle training in technical skills, they can be appropriate for tackling more general methodological problems and issues relating to teacher attitudes. In the same way, distance education techniques are not appropriate for all types of learning.

However, these methods all work best where the trainers themselves are highly effective; where the trainees have access to well-constructed materials; and where the trainees in the classroom are given a good deal of encouragement, back-up and support. The effectiveness of these methods depends not only on good management, but also on the availability of funding to make initial investments, and to ensure that materials, transport and good communications are available.

Furthermore, effective training depends on the overall morale of the teaching force. Motivation may come from a sense of dedication, political or moral commitment to students or to the education system as a whole, or it may come from more mundane sources such as the achievement of a higher qualification. Training of this kind is least effective where teachers are not valued or where physical conditions make it very difficult for them to do their jobs.

The role of the professional teacher has been challenged in recent years from different points of view. Implicit in many of the recent discussions of the role of teachers is the idea that, especially if they are organized and unionized, they represent undesirable 'vested interests'. On the other hand, the current view of the 'professional' teacher has been criticized by those who, like Paulo Freire, argue that teachers should cease to be authoritarian figures who dole out pre-packaged knowledge. However, while challenging the present notion of a 'professional' teacher, this argument does not necessarily advocate using untrained teachers. It rather argues for a very different kind of training. In non-formal education, there has been an increasing awareness of the need for an understanding of and respect for other kinds of knowledge which students may have and how they can be harnessed.

Content and scope

The preoccupation of both governments and international agencies with structural adjustment policies has intensified what has been called 'the search for the golden fleece of low-cost quality' in basic education. The World Bank views efficiency – namely the passage of a pupil through the school system and its examinations – as largely predicated on the 'correct' package of school inputs: teaching, materials and curricula. A good deal of emphasis is placed on management of the school system. Undoubtedly, it is important to have both efficient and dedicated personnel in ministries of education and in schools. However, one of the effects of cutbacks in government spending has been to further deplete these cadres, which are already small in many countries. They have been undermined during the period of economic constraint by poor salaries, increases in corruption and the sheer difficulties of actually doing their jobs.

This approach also rests on the view that social background is less important than 'inputs' by the school itself. In practice, the social and political dimensions are crucial in terms of both access and school achievement, particularly when examining the inequitable effects of economic crisis and adjustment. The quality of education is not confined to the technical quality of inputs, but also relates to the content and scope of education. This is influenced by wider social, economic and political factors: the power relations both within the school and between the school, community and government. The case studies suggest that the alienating effects of education in highly oppressive societies are as much a reality as people's eagerness to learn. This affects not only whether children go to school but whether they drop out and what they achieve. While people may be eager for a 'good' education in the conventional sense of transmission of knowledge and skills, they are often acutely aware of the political context in which this education takes place.

To take two examples:

• Well-produced and easily available textbooks are an important asset, but if their contents are irrelevant to the experiences of students, denigrate their culture or ignore their language, they are unlikely to stimulate interest or assist achievement.
• In strictly pedagogical terms, there may be effective ways of choosing the language of instruction or coping with the demands of bilingual societies. But when language becomes part of a political struggle, a narrowly educational approach will not be effective if it does not take account of how language relates to political and cultural identity.

There is also a psychological dimension to political repression and economic deprivation which has an impact on education. Adults who have not been to school, or who have dropped out early and who feel they have little or no control over their own lives, often face an added hurdle to learning. A sense of powerlessness and a lack of self-confidence makes many people, particularly women, believe they cannot learn and inhibits them from taking advantage of whatever opportunities may be available.

Access to school for girls is still a major issue in many countries. Enrolment and success at school are affected by factors outside as well as inside the classroom. For a girl, going to school can bring an early experience of the conflicting demands of school and home, which also characterize the lives of adult women with families and jobs outside the home. Undoubtedly, this affects their performance at school. Social norms and expectations may deter girls or women from pursuing their education, as they internalize the roles ascribed to them. Power relationships between men and women in the family, and male assertion of control over women's sexuality and fertility, also have a bearing on how women can profit from education. Finally, the economic crisis has increased pressures on the poorest women and, from a young age, has intensified demands on their time, further reducing their opportunities for education, whether in school or out of it.

War and political repression can leave a legacy of educational deficit, or a 'lost generation' with little or no education. Where resistance has been accompanied by high levels of social organization and motivation towards education, the basis for a reformed education system may exist. But educational reform, it has often been shown, will have little impact without broader social and economic reforms. Moreover, in order to capitalize on these developments, resources – material and human – are much needed, and education of all types has to compete with many other urgent demands for reconstruction and development.

Another legacy of conflict is large numbers of refugees and displaced people. Their plight raises many questions about what are 'appropriate' forms of education. Much depends on their prospects of returning home. Should education aim to equip children and adults to live in the country of exile, and to accept its norms in terms of language, culture or skills? Or should it focus on sustaining the language and culture of their homeland? Cultural identity and related issues often become of more than usually explicit importance in education among refugee groups.

In logistical terms too, the problems of providing education for long-term refugee groups increase rather than decrease over time. As the World Council of Churches Refugee Service notes: 'Once refugees have completed primary school, for example, they want secondary schools. Once they have completed a basic training course, they are ready for more advanced training.'[3] Solutions to these problems, and to the question of dealing with widespread mental health problems which arise among people traumatized by the experience of violence and of exile, cannot be sought purely within the bounds of the education system.

The numbers of children who have not attended school, or who have received a truncated or ineffective education, has risen in some countries over the past decade and has remained at a high level in others. Thus, in future, the need for continuing education for teenagers and adults is likely to grow – both for basic literacy and, increasingly important, for post-literacy education and skills training. This will require more flexible approaches to education than those which prevail in most formal education systems today. While the rhetoric of 'popular education' still runs ahead of practice in most cases, the concepts it embodies and some practical examples have at least offered new definitions of what constitutes 'education', as a process which is not divorced from people's daily experience. It also questions authoritarian teacher–pupil relations and the 'human capital' school of thought which values only those skills that have a direct bearing on the labour market. In the more effective experiments, education and development projects can broaden the concept of 'skills' – often seen in international agency reports as limited to developing technical and commercial abilities – to something which comprehends the cultural, social and political aspects of education. This could form part of a process which would help to introduce more flexibility into formal education, difficult though this is likely to be.

Yet none of this can happen while out-of-school and continuing education is treated as a poor relation, an appendage to the 'real' business of education. One long-term alternative is a much closer integration of childhood and continuing education, which need not necessarily involve the types of specialization currently practised in Northern educational systems.

Outcomes of education

A major problem with current educational thinking is that there is an implicit assumption on the part of most educationists in the South as well as those in the North, that the models of education developed in the major industrial states are superior to all others, whether or not they are appropriate to any other kind of economic or social order. Nowhere is this more evident than in the debates over higher education in the nations of the South.

One of the solutions to the problems of financing basic education which is often advocated is the transfer of funds from tertiary education, where costs per student are often very high, to primary education, where returns to education per student are said to be highest. The justification is that higher education in the poorest countries is élitist and therefore benefits only a tiny part of the population. While there may be an argument for some shift of resources, this raises the question of the value of higher education in relation to basic education.

As suggested earlier, basic education provides a foundation without which higher education cannot flourish. It might be more useful to look at the purposes served by higher education and its relevance to the society's needs. Could it be more closely integrated into the economic and social needs of the country? Certainly, the production of 'professional' élites whose first goal in life is to leave the country is unsatisfactory and a waste of resources. However, as in the case of basic education, beginning the discussion from the point of view of how expenditure cuts can be made blocks a longer view of what these institutions are intended to achieve.

Access to higher education is an important aspiration in societies in the South, and no nation can be truly autonomous unless it has its own autonomous cultural and educational institutions. Even the most underdeveloped countries need an appropriate pool of highly skilled people, intellectuals and a locus for critical analysis of their history, economy and society. If societies in the South are to elaborate their own models of development, rather than simply to copy Northern models, these need to be developed in their own higher education institutions, where curricula can reflect histories and cultural values appropriate to their own societies. The cost of study abroad can be far greater than that of maintaining domestic institutions and, in the absence of government funding, can exacerbate the perpetuation of local élites, denying higher education to all but the most wealthy. The example of the University of El Salvador shows how, even under extreme conditions of repression and under-funding, the university can be a focus for service to wider social goals. The issue is not so much to save money on higher education as to ensure that the university serves the community and nation's development, and allows the burgeoning of ideas in an atmosphere of autonomy and academic freedom.

Experts frequently recommend that education systems should provide training in skills directly relevant to employment and the development of the national economy. However, generally speaking, narrow definitions of 'human capital' as labour skills have not led to desired results. Furthermore, economic crisis and recession creates a vicious circle for educational planners: as the recession deepens, more and more graduates are without jobs. But planners seeking to alter the structure of education to match economic trends are faced with the dilemma of whether to plan for prolonged recession, or to assume that economic growth will soon return.

Education is not simply linked to economic growth but also to the broader political and social development of society. In countries like Zimbabwe, questions are being asked about the model of education being employed, derived from a European system, designed to serve a small and privileged élite. Should its competitive, exam-oriented and rather academic approach be changed? The response, there and in many other countries, has been to try and move towards a vocational approach to schooling which teaches skills relevant to economic needs. However, this type of educational provision is costly and furthermore, Zimbabwe, like many other ex-colonial societies, does not place a high value on manual skills, least of all when these relate to farming. Thus it is not only a question of assessing the economic demand for particular skills, but also of questioning the society's assumptions about both work and educational achievement.

There are also questions about what a particular society expects education to achieve. If social equity or a more democratic society is among its goals, this cannot be achieved by education alone. This is a challenge which the Namibian and South African education systems will be facing, with a legacy of sharp inequality and authoritarianism. Educational reform will not solve the problem, though it is one of the key ingredients. Education is inextricably bound up with people's aspirations for change, and with the nature of the political system. Carnoy and Samoff observe that: '. . . education serves as a primary terrain of conflict over the form of the state. Precisely because the nature of the state determines the character of education, the schools become sites for conflicts about the character of and control over the state'.[4]

The right to basic education is not merely a question of successfully completing a requisite number of grades and examinations. The criterion of success needs to be broadened from that of simple 'efficiency', to include the contribution education makes to building critical thinking, participation and co-operation and therefore to development of a democratic civil society. An expanded vision of basic education should conceive it not just as a human right for each individual, but also for people as social beings, something which is often omitted from the individualist, competitive model of education.

Notes

1. 'World Declaration on Education for All: Meeting Basic Learning Needs', Jomtien, Thailand, 9 March 1990, Article 2.
2. King (1988), p.127.
3. World Council of Churches, *Refugees* no. 101E, p.7.
4. Carnoy and Samoff (1990), p.380.

CHAPTER 18

The debt crisis and international responses

Substantial and long-term increases in resources for basic education will be needed. The world community, including inter-governmental agencies and institutions, has an urgent responsibility to alleviate the constraints that prevent some countries from achieving the goal of education for all. It will mean the adoption of measures that augment the national budgets of the poorest countries or serve to relieve heavy debt burdens.

(World Declaration on Education for All, Article X)[1]

Despite almost a decade of stabilization and adjustment programmes, many of the debtor nations of the South have yet to regain the economic performance levels reached in the 1970s, let alone to show signs of growth. Even the less severely affected countries are growing only slowly. Macro-economic indicators for some countries in Latin America and sub-Saharan Africa improved slightly in the mid-1980s, but subsequently deteriorated again. Although most of the industrialised countries have recovered from the effects of the global recession, overall indebtedness has not significantly decreased. In many developing countries, especially in sub-Saharan Africa, it continues to grow apace.

In 1990, optimistic World Bank growth forecasts, compiled before the onset of the Gulf crisis, assumed domestic economic policies which adhered to IMF guidelines and increased external aid. These were tempered by the admission that, even assuming these favourable conditions, in sub-Saharan Africa per capita incomes, already close to minimal subsistence levels, were unlikely to grow at all in the first half of the 1990s, while in Latin America, despite modest overall economic growth 'the number of poor people is unlikely to decrease in this decade'.[2]

Thus, the World Bank's *World Development Report* acknowledged the magnitude of the problem of poverty in the South. It also placed more emphasis than in the past on remedying the social costs of adjustment. However, much damage has already been done to social infrastructures.

'It is not just that development has been stopped or even retarded in the Third World. The hope of development for a better future has been lost.'[3] A concerted and far-reaching approach to resolving the debt issue would make a major contribution to restoring this hope and reviving debate on major development issues. There are clearly several aspects to any solution of the debt problem:

- What to do about existing debts – the so-called 'debt overhang'
- How to arrest and reverse the net flow of funds from South to North
- Finally, the key long-term question – of how to prevent further debts on this scale being accumulated in future.

Until the late 1980s, moves towards debt relief were for the most part scattered and uncoordinated. For governments of the North a very important concern has been to protect the international banking system, though this concern often operates to the detriment of debtor countries. A few years ago, the idea of any creditor writing off debts was unthinkable. Now some commercial banks have made provision for bad debt from their profits and have written-off some portions of developing country debt and renegotiated others. This has occurred particularly in Latin America, where most debt is owed to private banks. The US Brady proposals of 1989 acknowledged officially for the first time that commercial bank debts will not be repaid in full. However, by mid-1990 only Costa Rica and Mexico had made agreements with commercial banks which 'forgive' a part of their debts. In 1990, President Bush proposed a free-trade zone with Latin America and measures to reduce Latin American and Caribbean official debt to the United States, though this is only a small proportion of total debt. However, such reductions were to be available only to countries 'that adopt strong economic and reform investment programmes with the support of international institutions'.[4]

Since 1988, the major European governments, led by the Nordic countries, and more recently including Britain, France and Germany, have 'forgiven' portions of official debt owed by sub-Saharan African countries, or converted it to grants. However this scheme does not apply to officially guaranteed commercial credit. The IMF and the World Bank, too, have finally acknowledged that the most indebted countries in sub-Saharan Africa have almost no chance of 'growing out of debt'. The IMF has extended its fund which helps re-finance maturing debt obligations on more concessionary terms, and the World Bank has eased its loan terms for low-income countries.

Options for debt relief

- *Rescheduling*: this does not contribute to relief of the debt problem in the long term, since it simply defers the problem to an unforseeable future.
- *Debt for equity swaps*: these allow foreign private creditors, companies or banks to use debt payments in local currency to buy up companies or financial enterprises in the debtor country. These deals present the debtor countries with a national sovereignty problem by introducing foreign investment on terms over which they have limited control. Furthermore, in many of the poorer

debtor countries, few enterprises are attractive investment prospects. These debt swaps are declining in popularity. In Latin America the only enthusiastic taker was Chile, while Mexico and Argentina have limited their use. Even at their height, they covered only a small proportion of total debt.

● *Debt swaps for development*: some multilateral organizations, such as the World Wildlife Fund (WWF) and Unicef, have initiated swaps which contribute to development. WWF used a swap to finance a national park in Costa Rica and an Amazonian forest reserve in Bolivia. In this case control of the asset and its administration remains with the nation concerned. Unicef participated in a similar scheme by which the Midland Bank agreed with the Sudan government to transfer funds owed to the bank to Unicef for use in water projects in Sudan. These projects are a constructive approach to debt and could be extended. However, they are unlikely to cover more than a small proportion of debt payment, and offer development opportunities only on a piecemeal basis.

● *Debt buybacks*: these allow the debtor country to buy back its debt at a discount on the 'secondary' financial market. However, observers point out that if countries cannot in the first place afford to pay the interest on their debts, they are unlikely to be able to afford to buy back the principal, even at a discount. In some cases, loans at concessionary rates of interest have been made available to buy back debt on the secondary market at as little as 18 cents per dollar, leaving the debtor with a smaller debt at a lower rate of interest. The commercial lender ensures immediate recovery of a portion of the principal and surrenders any right to further payments of interest and principal. The concessionary lender can seek agreement to conditions on the debt swap model; namely, that the debt service saved should be redirected to agreed development programmes, paid for in local currency. These schemes only apply to commercial debt for which there is a secondary market, which limits its applicability. Furthermore, the pace of implementation of buybacks needs to be slow to avoid putting inflationary pressures on the local economy.

The above strategies seem unlikely to tackle the major part of the debt, especially for the most indebted countries, and those which are very poor and offer few inward investment prospects.

A more drastic solution is simply to write off these debts – what is sometimes called 'debt forgiveness': There are variations on this: from writing off the whole debt, or converting it into a grant; to 'forgiving' interest payments; or setting a cap on the level of interest which could be charged. But even this would not solve the problem without co-operation between the various major creditors. So far this has been done on a limited scale.

- *Increased IMF and World Bank support to severely indebted countries*: A particularly worrying aspect of the growth of debt in Africa has been the increasing proportion of debt owed to multilateral financial agencies, especially the World Bank and IMF. These are debts for which there is no official provision for rescheduling, renegotiation or roll-overs. UNCTAD has suggested that debt relief should be extended to multilateral aid given on concessionary terms. However, this forms only a minority of both the IMF's and the Bank's loans. Only in Africa do low-interest International Development Association (IDA) loans make up some 60 per cent of total loan value (1989). The IDA provides assistance to the poorest countries (defined as those with an annual GNP per capita of US$480 [1987] or less). The terms of assistance, including interest rates, are more concessionary than IBRD loans, which have higher interest rates and shorter repayment periods.

- *Unilateral action on the part of one or a group of debtor nations*: This can range from suspension of interest payments to repudiation of debts. The first option has been taken by a number of countries which have simply been unable to pay interest on their debts on time. Another variation is to limit interest repayments to a certain percentage of exports. This was the strategy pursued by former President Alan García Pérez in Peru. The outright repudiation of debt (interest and principal) is only possible for governments whose power base does not depend on wealthy groups with substantial funds in Northern banks. These investments are a likely target for retaliatory action on the part of creditors.

Two basic questions may be asked of proposals for alleviating debt:

- How far does the proposal go in practical terms in sharing economic responsibility for debt? This includes not imposing adjustment measures mainly designed to secure the assets of creditors. At this level international co-ordination is needed and agreed principles for the solution to various types of indebtedness.
- In any specific case, who will benefit from the measures taken? Do they promote equity as well as economic growth? Examination of specific national needs and problems is very important in this context.

Although the recognition that many countries of the South cannot pay their debts is a step in the right direction, it falls far short of the scale of action necessary to get these countries out of the debt trap. Piecemeal relief does not signify that all parties to the debt crisis, including Northern governments and banks, have accepted that they bear a responsibility for it. Whether or not this responsibility is acknowledged has implications for future arrangements to avoid indebtedness.

The radical view is that to prevent countries of the South falling back into indebtedness requires a major reorientation in international trade and aid policies. This would mean altering economic policies in Northern countries – for example, more aid with fewer conditions less tied to purchase of the donor country's goods and services. It would also involve changes in trade policies, including preventing protectionist tendencies.

If debtor economies were to develop and grow, this would lessen the need for assistance, which is the goal of structural adjustment policies. However, while the economies of the South remain so dependent on world financial and trade trends, it is hard to see how this can occur without changes in the international financial order. Even in countries held to have 'successful' adjustment programmes, it is unclear whether these bring sustainable, long-term growth. First, macro-economic formulas do not take account of the variety of economic situations in which they are imposed. For example, in poor countries with an under-developed entrepreneurial class, private capital resources do not exist to take over large-scale, public economic enterprises or social welfare functions from the state. Another alternative is to allow foreign capital or institutions to fill this role. The long-term effects of opening up weak economies to foreign investment have not generally been favourable, particularly if social equity is taken into account.

Pressures towards total trade liberalization and indiscriminate promotion of exports, especially of traditional primary products, are also open to criticism. The United Nations Economic Commission for Africa has argued that these measures increase the vulnerability and dependence of debtor countries. In the volatile world market for primary commodities and with strong protectionist tendencies in most industrialized nations, attempts to develop export-oriented agriculture can entail considerable risks, particularly if there are numbers of other indebted countries also trying to compete in the same markets.[5]

The Commission has pointed out that internal reforms are also urgently needed, particularly land reform and reduction of defence spending. However, these are not welcome suggestions for many regimes and élites: indeed, many of the current internal conflicts revolve around precisely these issues. Moreover, the international financial agencies are much less ready to challenge governments on these issues. Although they are willing to make considerable inroads into national sovereignty by laying down macro-economic policy and pushing for increased privatization at all levels, they are far less eager to challenge these other aspects of the social order.

The so-called 'conditionality', or strings attached, both to adjustment programmes and to aid, leave the recipient nation little room to choose its path of development. If it does not fulfil stringent conditions attached to aid, new loans or debt relief, these are forfeit. The World Bank and the IMF are showing some signs of increasing their flexibility in applying conditionality, but the basic terms and how the success of adjustment programmes is measured remain much the same.

Arguments are now being put forward for a much less rigid approach to conditionality, if not for its removal. If conditionality is to be imposed, Griffith Jones argues, it should not be based on narrowly defined financial performance criteria but on criteria which focus on growth and development towards greater equity – which might include targets for spending on health, nutrition and education, as well as an agricultural sector which can respond to needs for food as well as for exports.[6]

It is now widely acknowledged that public expenditure cuts, low wages and inflation which have resulted from most structural adjustment policies have had serious long-term social and political consequences. This has been recognized in Europe, with both the EC and individual European states contributing to schemes which aim to meet the 'human costs' of adjustment. However, the interventions so far have for the most part been picking up the pieces after the adverse effects of structural adjustment policies have already manifested themselves. They have not challenged the assumptions of the adjustment process. Moreover, the strategy of compensatory programmes frequently seems to be giving with one hand what is being taken away with the other (through budget cuts, trade imbalances and debt service). The country concerned also remains dependent on whether or not the international community actually produces new money in sufficient amounts to support the social sector – which experience shows is not guaranteed.

Aid: a narrowing focus?

All these factors have influenced the character of current aid giving, not only by the international financial agencies, but by other donors which increasingly follow their guidelines.

Throughout the 1980s, as the mountain of debt has grown, economic constraints have tightened. As Richard Jolly of Unicef noted: 'At least in the 1970s and even the 1960s there was an element of competition between the former imperial countries that Third World countries could play off. There was not the standardization of economic approaches now produced by the World Bank and the IMF which produces common fronts. There was also the opportunity of getting other support from the Soviet Union or East Europe.'[7]

The World Bank now invites bilateral donors to support structural adjustment programmes, and also sectoral loans conditional on structural adjustment measures being taken by recipient governments.

Thus, bilateral donors are made party to the macro-economic 're-organization' of recipients' economies. This has increased what is known as 'cross-conditionality' – that is, when leading donors – for example, the World Bank or the IMF – set performance requirements for loans which are then replicated by other donors. In the field of social policy, including education, there has also been a notable homogenization of assumptions about the goals and purposes of aid among major donors, along the lines set down by the international financial institutions.

Because of the decision-making structure of these multilateral financial agencies, with voting strength based on financial contributions, the poorest countries are not in a good position to influence policy. The poorer the recipient country, the more difficulties it has in getting aid money, and the more its own priorities tend to be marginalized or amended in favour of priorities laid down by donor agencies. M.J. Kelly, discussing educational aid to Zambia, notes two kinds of problems. First, where the Ministry of Education does not have strong research and development units, and therefore finds it difficult to set clear priorities itself, '[It] has been obliged to fall back on reactive adjustment to the proposals of donor agencies'. Second, he argues,

when virtually all available resources are tied to inescapable salary payments, [there is a tendency] to accord a higher priority than they deserve to proposals that seem likely to attract additional funds, particularly if these will support ongoing activities. This leads to the aberrant situation where the priorities of a donor, or what are perceived to be those priorities, are espoused by the ministry as its priorities. Put in cruder terms, the danger is that priority may come to be equated with the availability of financial resources – priorities lie where funds are assured.[8]

In practical terms, one of the effects of economic crisis on aid flows over the decade has been to erode their monetary value through inflation, as well as through the rising costs of imported materials. Aid programmes and projects have also suffered from the infrastructural failures which afflict debt-affected countries: particularly lack of locally available materials, and transport problems. There are also increasing shortages of experienced personnel, particularly in the public sector, as senior staff leave because of low pay and frustration. Where recipient governments are expected to provide counterpart financing, projects are sometimes held up when they cannot provide the necessary funds. Where the economic crisis has been compounded by drought and military conflict, a substantial proportion of aid has gone not to development but to short-term drought relief, food aid and to sustaining existing services.

The search for cost-effectiveness has also influenced the mechanisms for project implementation. The World Bank, for example, as well as some bilateral donors, is keen to 'initiate a broadened dialogue with non-governmental organizations', both in donor and recipient countries. In addition to 'contributing to the Bank's thinking on development', 'non-governmental organizations can be cost-effective in the delivery of social services'.[9] So far, the number of World Bank projects involving non-governmental organizations – local or external – is small: 202 between 1973 and 1988. Many European non-governmental organizations already receive part of their funding from their own governments and from the EC.

However, a paper outlining the role of non-governmental organizations in literacy work, presented at the World Conference on Education for All in Thailand in 1990, suggests that by no means all of them are happy about being viewed by multilateral agencies and governments as a 'cost-effective' alternative to state welfare services. The paper, in summary, made the following points:

● Non-governmental organizations are not a cheap source of labour: some of the interest that is being shown by the larger funding agencies towards them has been, frankly, an economic one (non-governmental organizations have lower overheads). With restricted funds in most places, this has become an attractive alternative, but non-governmental organizations have no interest in being the means by which the state begins to abandon its responsibilities.

● Non-governmental organizations are not simply delivery systems, either for the government or the various multilateral agencies.

● Non-governmental organizations have their own agendas: they aim to promote alternative structures of society. 'In some countries, they claim to represent broader social support than the state institutions in literacy or adult education.'

● Non-governmental organizations are linked to popular movements: they are often linked to broader social movements, such as human rights movements, movements for democracy, women's movements, peace movements, and struggles by indigenous peoples for their rights.[10]

This implies not only a different 'constituency' but an approach to literacy and education which is different from the formulations of the World Bank and a number of other large agencies. There is evidently considerable resistance in some non-governmental organizations to the notion that they might be co-opted into multilateral or bilateral programmes as part of a strategy to deal more cheaply and easily with the economic crisis. However, many non-governmental organizations do continue to engage in dialogue with government aid agencies, in the hope of influencing their policies.

Notes

1. 'World Declaration on Education for All: Meeting Basic Learning Needs?, Jomtien, Thailand, 9 March, 1990.
2. *World Development Report; 1990*, p.16ff.
3. S. Griffith-Jones, in Hewitt and Wells (1989), p.77.
4. *Guardian*, 28 June 1990.
5. United Nations Economic Commission for Africa (1989), *passim*.
6. S. Griffith-Jones, in Singer and Sharma (eds.) (1989), p.14.
7. Richard Jolly, in *Literacy and Liberation* conference report, WUS(UK) (1990), p.8.
8. M.J. Kelly (1987), pp.85–6.
9. World Bank *Annual Report 1989*, p.95.
10. NGO round table presentation to the World Conference on Education for All, Jomtien, Thailand, 1990.

CHAPTER 19

Changing patterns of international aid to education

Education is one of the most complex fields of aid-giving – if only because of its diversity and the differing interpretations placed upon it by donors. 'Educational aid' can vary from a health education component in a water project to the provision of high-technology equipment or expertise for a university physics laboratory. It is, therefore, quite difficult to assess exactly how much assistance has gone to education overall. Official figures mainly reflect the levels of aid to formal education. Another question is whether these figures represent the amounts of money which actually go into recipient countries' education systems. In the case of international agencies and bilateral donors, it seems that a substantial proportion returns to the

Table 19.1 *Long-term trends in aid from all sources: major Western donors*

Country	Net Volume Overseas Development Aid (ODA) (Aid as % of GNP) US$m at 1987 prices/exchange rates		
	1975–76	1980–81	1987–88
USA	7,997 (0.26)	8,480 (0.27)	9,376 (0.20)
France (incl overseas territories)	4,101 (0.62)	5,257 (0.52)	6,572 (0.73)
Germany	3,345 (0.38)	4,598 (0.45)	4,473 (0.39)
Netherlands	1,300 (0.79)	2,005 (0.80)	2,118 (0.98)
UK	2,156 (0.39)	2,305 (0.39)	2,077 (0.30)
Japan	3,062 (0.22)	5,463 (0.30)	7,700 (0.31)
Canada	1,425 (0.50)	1,407 (0.50)	1,986 (0.48)
Sweden	1,041 (0.82)	1,105 (0.60)	1,381 (0.88)

Notes:
1987–88: Average aid as % of GNP = 0.35 from Development Assistance Committee countries
Their share of world aid = 84.1%.
Eastern bloc countries' share of world aid = 9.1%.

Source: *1989 Report*, Development Assistance Committee, OECD, Paris, Dec. 1989.
Table 1.

donors through payments to expatriate staff and consultants, fees paid to donor country educational institutions by students from recipient countries, and contracts for educational materials and other educational inputs which go to firms in the donor countries.

Official aid

The main sources of aid to education are the World Bank, bilateral government-to-government agencies, such as the Overseas Development Administration UK (ODA) in Britain, and non-governmental organizations in Western countries. Smaller amounts have, in the past, also come from Eastern bloc countries. Education is not among the first priorities of aid from the EC. Very little work has been done in formal basic education, though rural development projects, in conjunction with non-governmental organizations, often have an educational component. Among the other international organizations, UN agencies, especially Unesco, perform a mainly advisory and research role, and provide technical assistance to national education systems.

In the 1960s and 1970s, it was generally accepted that primary schooling was the business of governments and was not usually a priority area for aid donors. In some cases, particularly in Africa, expatriate teachers remained with support from overseas governments, and assistance was given with curricula and textbooks. There was also substantial assistance to school building programmes. Generally the emphasis was on funding capital costs and definitely not the recurrent costs of basic education.

The World Bank is the largest single donor, accounting for 15 per cent of total international support to education.[1] The World Bank first discussed the importance of basic education (primary schooling, non-formal education and literacy) in a 1974 policy document, which signalled a shift of emphasis from its previous stress on higher and technical education. At the time, this view was not widely held in international aid circles. However, it coincided with the Bank's espousal in the 1970s of a 'basic needs' strategy. This led to the inclusion of some non-formal educational components in development projects on health care and agriculture. However, the basic needs approach adopted by the Bank stressed income-generation for the poor rather than any kind of redistribution of wealth. Its projects rarely reached the poorest layers of people who had most need of basic education, health care and services.

The proportion of World Bank lending for primary education increased from about 5 per cent of lending for education between 1970 and 1974 to some 28 per cent between 1986 and 1989. Lending for secondary schooling and teacher training has remained static at around the 10 per cent level of total lending for education.[2]

Table 19.2   **World Bank lending for education (US$ millions)**

	Annual average 1980–84	1985	1986	1987	1988	1989
Sub-Saharan Africa						
Education						
US$m	102.1	119.0	114.7	104.9	178.2	88.2
% total	5.4	7.5	5.6	5.0	6.1	2.2
Agriculture						
% of total	29.0	21.9	21.2	24.8	19.2	19.2
Non-project						
% of total	14.7	10.3	20.3	14.6	26.0	32.5
Latin America and Caribbean						
Education						
US$m	70.9	195.8	10.0	84.9	88.3	140.0
% total	2.3	5.3	0.2	1.6	1.7	2.4
Agriculture						
% of total	25.6	12.0	40.9	23.2	26.7	2.8
Non-project						
% of total	2.0	11.8	14.8	20.4	5.3	25.5

Source: Derived from World Bank *Annual Report 1989*, pp. 106, 130

In the 1980s, the Bank's increasing involvement in structural adjustment programmes has intensified the search for 'efficiency'. Lending for education, as in other sectors, is mainly intended to 'assist with redeployment of existing funds' rather than to pay for additional resources, and there is an increased emphasis on the use of funding as 'leverage' to achieve policy changes in the recipient country.[3] There has also been some tension within the Bank between the practitioners of macro-economic strategy and research staff whose findings have led them to call for increased funding for education, particularly in the poorest countries.

Recent World Bank loans to primary education focus, for the poorest countries, on refurbishing schools and building new ones – in other words, largely making up for setbacks caused by the economic crisis. Others envisage wholesale refurbishment of educational sectors, emphasizing particularly efficiency, management techniques and cost-effectiveness.

At the World Conference on Education for All in 1990, World Bank President Barber Connable said the Bank was to increase its role in educational development in the South. He announced that 'the Bank will double its educational lending over the next three years to an annual level of US$ 1.5 billion'.[4] Relative to the organization's total resources, assistance to education has up to now been a small component. Since the 1960s, there has also been a shift in the regional pattern of funding, with Asia receiving only 17 per cent of total World

Bank educational funding in the 1960s, and 44 per cent in the period from 1985 to 1989. Africa's share meanwhile dropped from 37 per cent to 15 per cent. As a proportion of total assistance in Africa, education has not gone above 7.5 per cent, and in Latin America and the Caribbean levels have been even lower, scarcely exceeding 5 per cent (see Table 19.2).

Connable's announcement thus signalled a shift of emphasis in World Bank policy. The 1990 World Development Report continued to stress the need for market-oriented economic restructuring, but argued that it should be part of a two-part strategy. The second part is the provision of 'basic services to the poor', including primary education. It is acknowledged that the pursuit of this strategy involves a politically sensitive 'trade-off between the interests of the poor and the non-poor', and the allocation of more income and public spending to the poor. However, raising one of the key issues in many of the countries discussed in this book, the redistribution of land, the report argues that in many cases such reforms are too politically difficult. Education is therefore presented as a substitute for, rather than an adjunct to the reallocation of resources on which economic and political power is based. 'In most countries, the two-part strategy . . . which sees investment in education as the best way of augmenting the assets of the poor, is more likely to succeed.'[5]

USAID's policies on education follow fairly closely the lines of current World Bank policy, stressing management, efficiency and re-allocation of costs, along with upgrading teachers and development of educational materials. USAID tends to be heavily involved in countries where the United States is concerned to support the regime. USAID has relatively few education programmes in South America or in sub-Saharan Africa. But in Central America, it has programmes in El Salvador, Guatemala, Honduras and Costa Rica, as well as in several Caribbean states. In Guatemala, this has included, since 1984, a programme in co-operation with the government to develop bilingual education for indigenous Mayan peoples. This, while in itself not an undesirable goal, has to be seen in the context of US-supported 'pacification' policies which aim to control the indigenous populations (see Chapter 10).

While USAID has followed the World Bank in increasing its emphasis on primary education, this trend has been slower in West Germany and the United Kingdom, which have developed a reputation for high-level technical and scientific assistance to education. This in turn has affected the kind of projects which they are approached to fund by governments seeking aid.

In the United Kingdom, where overall aid levels have been falling over much of the past decade (see Table 19.1), education has remained at about 10 per cent of all bilateral aid. In the past, assistance has been concentrated on financing expatriate teaching staff and trainers for vocational and technical training, supporting higher education and providing capital funds for equipment. Within the ODA Education

Section, there has recently been some change in attitude towards a more 'poverty-oriented' approach: with more interest in training for informal rather than formal employment, in primary education, training of local staff, and a recognition of the need to pay more attention to the needs of women and rural people.[6] However, this has yet to be reflected in the profile of existing ODA projects, and would require substantial redeployment of resources to be effective.

In West Germany, education is not regarded as the first priority for official aid. At present, precedence is given to environmental protection and food security. The profile of its educational aid is rather similar to that of the United Kingdom, with a strong emphasis on technical, vocational and university education. Only a small proportion of funding goes to basic education, though it was thought that this might increase somewhat after the World Conference on Education for All. The main emphasis in the primary sector so far has been on practical and science subjects in schools, developing mother-tongue teaching and the integration of education into rural development.[7] As in the United Kingdom, the Federal Ministry for Economic Co-operation is in favour of linking its educational aid to World Bank sector loans for education.

The Scandinavian countries, in contrast, have on the whole focused educational aid towards basic education, though the Swedish International Development Authority (SIDA) also brings students to Sweden for training, and sends Swedish personnel to provide technical assistance. However, an increasing proportion of SIDA's education budget (58 per cent in 1988) goes to primary education. It is also willing to be involved in ongoing support for primary and secondary education. Scandinavian agencies often fund the costs of producing textbooks and equipment for vocational schools, as well as supporting teacher training. According to SIDA's guidelines, 'there is little point in drawing a distinct line between capital costs and running costs'. However, like most other bilateral agencies, it will not finance teachers' salaries.[8]

The role of non-governmental organizations[9]

The roles played by non-governmental organizations in education are more diverse than those of governments and multilateral agencies. Their influence in the development field has been not so much through the relatively small-scale funding they provide (roughly one-tenth the size of OECD countries' total overseas aid) as through their contribution to debates on development and on education, and pioneering of innovative ideas and techniques. They divide along a number of axes, some of which affect their role in educational projects. Some centre on a particular group as recipients – for example, refugees or children. A number of major US voluntary organizations stress individual child sponsorship, as does World Vision and, to a much lesser extent, the Save the Children Fund, which is switching its policies away from this approach.

Scholarships

Scholarships in further and higher education are necessary because of the lack of adequate higher education provision in most Southern countries, especially for refugees, whose access to education in host countries in the South is often very restricted. But scholarship assistance has to be seen in the wider context, and organizations working in this field are increasingly giving priority to training within the region, rather than in expensive Northern institutions. However, scholarships in the North may be necessary for reasons of security of the individual. This applies particularly to refugees and has been an issue on the programme for South Africans administered by WUS(UK). Such scholarships may also be necessary because training is not available in the region – WUS(UK)'s programme for Central American refugees is for post-graduate study in development-related areas not available in Central America – or where the donor country is the host country for the refugees – WUS(UK) runs a programme for Ethiopian and Eritrean refugees in the United Kingdom.

A new programme initiated by WUS(UK) addresses the training needs of non-governmental organization development workers in Africa and the Middle East. The World Conference on Education for All (Jomtien, Thailand, February 1990) laid great emphasis on the involvement of grassroots, community and voluntary organizations in the provision of basic education. Non-governmental organizations are already key actors in the delivery of non-formal education, including 'conscientization' programmes (particularly for women), health education, environmental education and vocational training for the disabled.

WUS(UK) has brought together a coalition of British development agencies which work through local partner organizations or branches in the South. The 'NGO Training Programme' offers opportunities for some fifty people a year to study on short specialist courses in Britain. An important aspect of the scheme will be the chance for these non-governmental organization activists to meet one another, share ideas and experiences, and build contact networks which will continue to aid their work once they get home.

The British agencies in the consortium behind this scheme recognize that women do not get a fair share of training oppor-tunities so the scheme provides a 60 per cent quota of training places for women and provides childcare allowances to help women to be able to take advantage of the opportunities available.

Many agencies target specific marginal groups; for example, rural women or minority ethnic communities. Several major agencies use volunteers in the field as opposed to paid professional staff. Some of these provide schoolteachers or trainers in agriculture or vocational work. For example, in Zimbabwe today, because of the shortage of local secondary school teachers, WUS Canada and other agencies send teachers to work in schools there. In the case of WUS Canada this is part of their general practice.

Strategies for development and political orientations differ widely, and non-governmental organizations work in a much greater variety of contexts, from very small groups and individual communities right through to projects at national level. While there are some non-governmental organizations which work in formal education, the majority confine themselves to the non-formal sector, with literacy and skills training as the most important components. For example, the German non-governmental organization Welthungerhilfe, which concentrates mainly on agricultural development, does not initiate literacy campaigns, but finds that literacy sometimes becomes an issue during the project, especially if it involves community organization. In that case, it generally funds local organizations to do the literacy work. Many non-governmental organizations do not define education as a separate aspect of their work, treating it as part of development projects with women in agriculture or health care, or with street children, in income-generating projects or as part of water and sanitation schemes. Others use various kinds of participatory education in building up community organizations or co-operatives. Consequently, it is difficult to separate out, either in financial or conceptual terms, precisely what their educational input has been. The concepts and experiences of 'education' viewed from this kind of development perspective are in many cases markedly different from those to be found in organizations primarily working in the context of formal education.

The relationships between non-governmental organizations and both their own and host governments are often complex. Many non-governmental organizations receive substantial funds from their own governments, depending on how closely their political perspectives match those of their government. This varies from country to country: for example, in the United States, it has been common practice for USAID to employ private voluntary organizations as implementing agencies. In the United Kingdom, voluntary sector organizations generally keep more distance from the ODA and the government, though the ODA is now interested in increasing co-operation and joint funding. In West Germany, some 50 per cent of funding for voluntary sector agencies comes from public sources. In Canada and Sweden, non-governmental organizations tend to work quite closely with the state aid agencies.

Non-governmental organizations may, however, choose to distance themselves both from their own governments and the governments of the countries in which they work, preferring to work in the interstices between state and community. In situations of violent conflict they may opt for working with dissident or liberation movements. In these situations, government aid agencies often work at arm's length through non-governmental organizations or, like SIDA, have a separate department which deals with humanitarian aid to liberation movements.

There are now also substantial numbers of non-governmental organizations active in development work in the countries of the South. Some of these may be little more than paper organizations to receive funds from external sources, and essentially represent the interests of these external donors. But some are active and effective popular organizations – for example, in Central and Latin America and in South Africa. In these regions, trade unions and church organizations play a particularly important role. A number of major Western non-governmental organizations now work mainly through such local organizations.

Given the very contentious nature of development work in many regions, especially in South Africa, the Horn of Africa, the Middle East and Latin America, political considerations are never far from the surface. Aid agencies are often faced with difficult choices. Though they may try to avoid being identified with a particular political grouping, in conflict situations neutrality is rarely possible. Education, especially literacy and non-formal work, is unavoidably contentious where governments or influential political groupings regard all forms of development work or popular education as threatening.

Both local non-governmental organizations and their external partners can face harassment and even serious physical dangers if they work with groups whose goals are opposed to those of the state and its backers – whether liberation movements, women's groups, trade unions, or community or refugee groups.

A good example of how conflicting views can influence the policies of development and aid workers can be seen in church and missionary activity in Latin America. Some groups within both the Catholic and much smaller Protestant groups active in the region have opted for a commitment to popular Christian-based communities and to the struggle of the poor and under-privileged in these highly polarized societies. The types of educational projects they support reflect these policies. On the other hand in recent years there has been a proliferation of fundamentalist and pentecostal Christian groups, especially in Central America. Many of these are heavily influenced and often funded by US-based fundamentalist churches, closely associating themselves with the goals of US policy in the region.

Political crisis, debt and adjustment have also had their impact on the kinds of work which non-governmental organizations do. If the communities with whom they work become more impoverished, there is a constant pressure to pick up the pieces by responding to immediate needs. For organizations with strong development goals, this may be necessary in the short run but it is not considered desirable. These pressures may also create equivocal situations in which they are drawn into work – for example, in education or health – which has hitherto been regarded as the province of government. This may be interpreted as acceptance of the 'privatizing trend' prevalent in multilateral and some bilateral agencies, even when the agency in question does not favour this trend.

The crisis in state funding of education in the 1980s, for example, has put new pressures on non-governmental organizations involved in non-formal and community education. Should they give financial support to schools where the state is unable to provide it? Should they support individuals or communities to pay fees imposed in state schools because of the economic crisis? Or should they concentrate on 'picking up the pieces' by concentrating on out-of-school education for those who have been unable to go to school? Relatively few agencies are willing to become involved directly in funding formal education. First, the sums involved tend to be large, and recurrent funding is a long-term burden that few non-governmental organizations could afford to take on. Many agencies are also opposed in principle to funding formal education, which they regard as the proper province of the state, and are opposed to the cuts which have been made.

However, some agencies have exceptions to this rule. Oxfam (UK) for example, states, 'we would avoid compensating directly for cuts in state support for formal education', but it is involved in some compensatory programmes for particular marginalized groups. These include, for instance, very poor rural groups and indigenous and tribal peoples excluded from education provision (through bilingual education programmes). WUS(UK), in like manner, sometimes assists with the formal educational needs of refugees, particularly women.

Christian Aid also has reservations about giving support where communities themselves are paying for education, especially at secondary school level. It comments: 'Where a community invests a lot of its own resources in a formal secondary system, that can serve to push a few individuals up the ladder, not change structures.' However, assistance to allow families to keep children at school may be given indirectly through local organizations. As we have seen in the case of ORAP in Zimbabwe, which receives support from a number of international non-governmental organizations, part of the work of their 'family groups' is to help families pay for education.

Wars often make non-governmental organizations focus on emergency aid, but they may also induce them to assist in the formal education sector. The Portuguese development group Oikos points out that in the countries where it works – Angola, Mozambique and Guinea-Bissau – 'debt and war are the main causes of problems' in education, and it is currently preparing to support the reconstruction of some school buildings in Mozambique. Organizations working with refugees also become involved both in training programmes, and sometimes in the education of refugee children, where state programmes are not open to them.

As Klaus Wilkens of the Federation of Protestant Churches (EKD) in Germany points out, acute poverty, hunger and social need can create another kind of pressure, which is especially evident among the churches in Latin America, to depoliticize their work.

With the burden of the social costs of structural adjustment programmes and so on, the churches feel obliged to help the poor, for example, in Peru, through feeding programmes, but at the same time efforts in the field of development – to make the poor aware of their situation and help them to articulate demands and organize themselves – are hampered. We are told by government to take care of the poor, not to interfere in politics.

He adds that many church groups do not want to legitimize government policies by accepting this role but are under great pressure to do so.

Mixed motives: the politics of aid

Most governments and non-governmental organizations in the South are in need of aid, some more desperately than others. But in many cases, this need is also mixed with reservations. Long experience of foreign intervention and the use of aid as a political weapon leads to suspicion of the motives of the donors. A sceptical view of aid is most common among those opposing repressive regimes who have long watched aid and trade bolstering the power and credibility of these regimes.

In South Africa, assistance to education programmes which will assist individual mobility has been regarded with suspicion by the more radical sections of the liberation movement. They regard these programmes as attempts to buy off an educated class of blacks and to divide the black community. If, occasionally, suspicions are misplaced, they are hardly surprising in the light of past experience with those major Western states, especially Britain, and until recently the United States, which have retained strong links with the apartheid government.

In Central America, similar suspicions are entertained, especially in Guatemala, El Salvador and Honduras where there is a long history of US aid geared to 'combating communism' rather than promoting social justice. European donors are generally less subject to these suspicions. None the less, the need for assistance and solidarity, especially among local non-governmental organizations, is considerable. Honduras, for example, has long experience of interventionist aid at a number of levels, from USAID and the Peace Corps, to the activities of fundamentalist Christian groups with strong connections to the right-wing establishment in the United States. A Honduran social worker with a community education programme summed up the situation from the point of view of local non-governmental organizations:

International aid is certainly important, as long as it is not tied to international interests. If one is offered funding tied to external interests and not the actual needs of the country it is not acceptable, but (at the same time) we are faced with the problem that we are not economically independent.

Central American views of US aid policy

The following views were expressed by Central Americans invited to a symposium on the impact of US assistance to Central America, organized by the US government's General Accounting Office, the Central American Institute for Public Administration, and the Latin American Faculty of Social Sciences, in August 1988.

Most participants agreed that not much progress had been made to achieve economic stabilization and structural adjustment. They felt that the United States distributed economic assistance as a tool to achieve its security objectives instead of as a means to achieve long-term, regional economic stability. They charged that US aid is: (1) administered according to 'universal truths' that ignore individual country circumstances; and (2) channelled bilaterally rather than through multilateral agencies in order to control its application. Some felt that the United States has undue influence over the IMF, the World Bank and other multilateral organizations and that, as a result, these organizations have policies which emphasize short-term stabilization policies at the expense of gradual economic development and long-term solutions.

The majority of participants felt that economic *malaise* in the region continues due to a perceived 'double policy' on the part of the United States; that is, the United States seeks to attain economic stability in some countries while destabilizing others. Further, they felt that it is impossible to stabilize an economy without first addressing the basic needs of the poor majority, who bear the brunt of economic instability.[10]

The divergent philosophies embodied in aid strategies for education and development are highlighted by a Mexican popular education organization:

Participation, self-management, the commitment to the community and solidarity in educational work have been limited by the paternalist practice, which sees its role as giving aid rather than empowerment, imposed by the development agencies which have worked in the region. As a result, in many cases the communities look to the association to solve their problems and provide for [their needs].[11]

Thus one view is that aid agencies are in the business of problem-solving, mainly through the provision of expertise and material resources. The other view is that aid should help people not just to adapt to and cope with economic and social change or crisis. It should support people's efforts to gain control over their own lives and to organize in demanding a voice to influence change both at a local and national level.

The language now used by many aid agencies to describe their goals also invites critical scrutiny. Diverse political messages are embodied in the use of apparently similar terms. The terms 'empowerment' and 'self-help' have become widely used in aid and development circles, but their meaning in practice can vary considerably. For example, does empowerment simply mean giving the individual the opportunity of social mobility, or does it mean giving communities the tools and abilities to fight for a better life? Both meanings appear in the development literature and in the reports of governments, international agencies and non-governmental organizations. Self-help can simply mean mobilizing people to work without pay, or it can mean political mobilization and self-organization. This kind of ambiguity applies particularly in discussions of women and development, notes Kandiyoti:

Behind the rather bland and uniform sounding recommendations to equip and empower poor Third World women, there may lie a wide range of frankly contradictory objectives from simply making women more efficient managers of poverty, to using their claims and organizations as a political vehicle for far-reaching redistributive measures, both within and across nations.[12]

Future priorities for aid in education: levels of aid

- Aid to education needs to be increased. The World Conference on Education for All suggested that to provide the most minimal education for all school-age children by the year 2000 would require an additional input of aid of over US$1 billion a year. This still assumes some cost-cutting, transfer of costs to users and recouping a good deal of the cost of education from general taxation on the part of national governments – measures of questionable feasibility in many of the poorest countries.
- Increased aid to education cannot be at the expense of other social and environmental needs. As we have argued throughout this book, education can only flourish when it takes place in a healthy environment in the broadest sense.
- The increase can, however, be at the expense of military assistance to recipients, military expenditure in the donor countries, and international aid which is mainly geared to improving the trade position of the donor country, or to wasteful

'white elephant' and prestige projects which bring no benefit to the majority of the recipient country's population.

- Donor nations should maintain aid flows at least at the UN target of 0.7 per cent of GNP.

- The World Declaration on Education for All left individual countries to come up with national plans for the future of education. This is certainly better and more flexible than a 'global strategy' to be imposed on all. But the conditions imposed by donors may limit the kinds of plans which will be judged acceptable for funding. Conditionality which limits policy options available to recipients should be lifted.

- Basic education for all (access to school, and to continuing educational opportunities, including literacy, for adults and out-of-school children) should be a key goal for national governments and the international community. Its implementation needs to be sensitive to the local social, economic and political context.

- Equity cannot be achieved in basic education unless it is integrated into the broader context of social and economic reform – particularly land reform, and access to basic services (housing, clean water, basic health-care facilities) and a living wage in employment or self-employment.

- Vulnerable groups which require particular attention in developing a strategy for basic education were identified in the World Declaration on Education for All after some prompting from the non-governmental organization lobby: they included women, refugees and cultural and ethnic minorities. However, it is a long step from statements of principle to the active participation of these groups in the construction of projects. It is also important to take account of these groups' needs and interests, not only in projects designed specifically to meet their needs (for example, women's literacy programmes, or bilingual education for linguistic minorities) but also in regional and national education programmes, in which, because their voices are not heard and they are rarely consulted, their interests are not taken into account.

- While women and children have been identified as particularly vulnerable to the human costs of adjustment, gender considerations have in practice not been taken into account in designing adjustment packages. The specific needs and problems of women facing economic hardship, both in the family and outside it, must be taken into consideration and remedied, if equity in basic education is to be achieved.

- Most educational programmes, whether in the formal or non-formal sector, which cater for poor and vulnerable groups will find difficulties in becoming financially self-sufficient. Therefore funding, whether from national or international sources, needs to be long-term.

● There is a good deal of innovative work in both formal and non-formal education being carried out by governments and non-governmental organizations. Often, their experiences are unknown to others working in the same field. More co-operation and exchange is needed to avoid the tendency even within one region constantly to repeat experiences. This is true, both of international aid agencies and of national organizations and governments in the South.

Notes

1. Connable (1990), p. 11.
2. World Bank (1990) *The Dividends of Learning*, p.21.
3. Interview with William MacGreevey, Central American Desk, World Bank, Washington, DC, 1989.
4. Connable (1990), p. 11.
5. World Bank, *World Development Report 1990*, p.3ff.
6. Interview with Roger Iredale, Chief Education Adviser, ODA, London, 1990.
7. Interviews at the Federal Ministry for Economic Cooperation in Bonn and Deutsche Gesellschaft für Technische Zusammenarbeit (GTZ) in Frankfurt, 1990.
8. SIDA (1986), p. 7.
9. Information on specific organizations in this section is derived from their published reports, from interviews conducted by the author and from replies to a questionnaire on educational policies of non-governmental organizations in the UK and Europe (mainly German and Scandinavian).
10. US General Accounting Office (1989), Appendix 2, p.70.
11. CEAAL (1989), p.34 (translated from Spanish).
12. D. Kandiyoti (1988), p.9.

CHAPTER 20

Recommendations

The 1980s were indeed a 'lost decade' for development. This book shows the widespread reverses which have hit the education sector. Education may not be a panacea for under-development, but it is certainly a precondition for development. Just as the environmental crisis affects the natural resources on which life ultimately depends, so the education crisis threatens the human resources of knowledge, skills and self-confidence.

Despite the positive targets established by the 1990 World Conference on Education for All, the task of educational renewal is unlikely to succeed unless fundamental and radical changes can be brought about. The obstacles that stand in the way of education for all are illustrated in this book. They arise above all from the continuing inequalities between Northern industrialised countries and the states of the South and from the divisions and inequalities within societies. They include:

- the debt burden;
- inequitable international trading relations;
- war and civil conflict, often prolonged and promoted by external powers;
- widespread infringement of human, democratic and educational rights;
- the failure of the international community to give development issues the priority they deserve and require.

Many important recommendations arise from this book in relation to educational priorities, styles, techniques and curricula. The book has also highlighted the heroic efforts of individuals, communities and movements to establish their own educational initiatives in the face of poverty, discrimination, oppression and violence. These efforts need our support and solidarity.

Nevertheless, educational ideas are difficult to practise without resources, where children need to work to survive, or in the middle of a war. People's education initiatives will always have value in demonstrating innovative ideas and techniques, but tend usually to develop as a response to defective, discriminatory or inadequate state provision.

The state should provide a proper education for all its citizens, while allowing space and freedom for genuine and active community participation and initiative. Education should contribute to and reinforce democratic practices. In today's crisis, many states deliberately deny sections of their population educational rights and attempt to impose an education that runs counter to the interests of the recipients. Other nations are prevented from achieving their educational aspirations by poverty, recession, debt, unequal trade relationships, local, regional or global conflicts, and the impact of inadequate or inappropriate international development and adjustment policies.

Our recommendations, therefore, cannot be put into practice unless the economic and political causes of the education crisis and the obstacles to its resolution are addressed. The crisis cannot be resolved piecemeal through national level approaches alone. Nor should governments or agencies approve solutions gained at the expense of developments in other areas, such as health and the environment. Mere switches of aid priorities between sectors are not an appropriate response. Whilst countries in the South can exercise their sovereignty in many ways to improve educational opportunities for their citizens, only a global approach can seriously address the obstacles which litter their path.

The economic context

Our recommendations cannot be fully realized unless the following changes in the economic context are initiated and maintained:

A *major revision of global development policy*

Global policies for development are half-hearted, self-interested, non-existent or ignored. These policies are made and controlled in the industrialized countries of the North. They need to be changed, and the people and organizations of the North should play a major part in bringing about these changes, by raising awareness of the issues in the North and by lobbying their own governments to give international development a higher priority.

New initiatives to relieve the burden of debt

The burden of debt service on developing economies has led to negative North–South resource flows, disrupted economies and chronic foreign exchange shortages. This burden should be lifted if the education crisis is to be successfully resolved. Efforts to date have achieved only limited relief and dramatic new initiatives are essential.

Commercial banks
– should write off a large proportion of their debts: 50 per cent of commercial debt to middle-income countries and 100 per cent for the

poorest countries. Northern country governments should alter the tax regime to encourage their banks to write off Southern debt. Banks *can* afford whole or partial debt forgiveness.

Government to government debt
– should be reduced in a similar proportion, through write-offs, conversion to grants, conversion to concessional interest rates or by being exchanged for educational and other expenditures in local currencies.

Multilateral agency debt
– debts owed to multilateral agencies, such as the World Bank, should be refinanced under much easier terms. New loans should be made in the context of revised development-oriented objectives for the multilateral agencies and only at concessional rates of interest. Conditions attached to loans should be designed to encourage the protection of poor and marginal communities.

Repayment rules
– should be established to ensure that debt service and repayment can never again threaten the survival of citizens of debtor nations, or the loss of their capacity to develop. Such rules could, for instance, limit debt payment to a certain percentage of export earnings.

Aid

– the UN aid target of 0.7 per cent of GNP should be met by all OECD countries;
– the UN aid target of 1 per cent of GNP including private money should also be met. This means that negative private flows (money moving from South to North), should be reversed, by stemming capital flight and reducing debt service, in addition to increasing official aid;
– aid to the newly democratizing nations of Eastern Europe should be additional to these North–South flows;
– aid should not be tied to purchases from the donor country;
– aid should be designed to reach the poorest and most disadvantaged;
– the objectives, organization and working practices of the international financial institutions (the IMF, World Bank and regional development banks) should be revised to ensure that development aims have priority over immediate pressures to repay loans. These agencies should disclose information, decisions and the assumptions on which they work, so as to make them more publicly accountable;
– cutting the defence spending of industrialized countries by 10 per cent could pay for a doubling of aid by the year 2000. Changes in East–West relations offer an unprecedented opportunity for redirections in military expenditure in the North, and for the resolution of proxy conflicts in the South. The major part of such savings should be directed towards aid and development objectives.

Trade

– a renewed effort is required by the industrialized countries individually and in the context of UNCTAD, GATT and the Lomé Convention to redress the North–South imbalance in trade relationships. Policies and practices should be developed to ensure that developing economies are not vulnerable to massive fluctuations in commodity prices, and to end protectionist trade policies which undermine their development prospects.

Recommendations

1. A World Convention on Educational Rights

– should be internationally agreed. It should outlaw the denial of education on grounds of gender, race, ethnic origin, language or politics and guarantee access to full-time education for all children up to minimum age. It should protect the human rights of teachers, students and academic staff, particularly the rights to organize, and to pursue, develop and transmit knowledge. Existing international instruments, such as the Universal Declaration on Human Rights and the International Convention on the Rights of the Child, do not detail educational rights. A new instrument is needed to ensure that education, or its denial, cannot be used as a tool for political oppression. The WUS Lima Declaration on Academic Freedom and Autonomy of Institutions of Higher Education is a useful starting point.

2. The State

– should provide education for all children, youth and adults. This education should ensure genuine community participation in decision-making and should be conducive to social equity. Education should be seen as a lifelong process encompassing pre-school provision and adult literacy and training programmes as well as formal schooling. Governments should take active measures to remove educational disparities on grounds of gender, ethnicity or wealth. Privatization, 'cost-recovery' and fee-charging further disadvantage poor people and communities and should be avoided unless adequate compensatory measures are in place.

3. Non-formal and popular education

– should be protected from state repression. The convention on educational rights (see 1 above) should ensure the freedom of communities to develop popular and alternative educational initiatives. Grassroots education initiatives should be given greater recognition and priority in national plans for education and in educational aid provision. Governments should respond positively to innovations generated by non-formal and popular education initiatives.

4. Teachers

– are the key resource for basic education. Their rights and freedoms should be protected (see 1 above). Their salaries, conditions and career prospects should be at a level to minimize the loss of trained teachers and to avoid teachers taking on additional employment in order to survive. Significant investment in teacher training is essential, as is recruitment of numbers sufficient to ensure reasonable class sizes.

5. Curriculum development

– should be related to people's history and culture and should provide a basis for critical analysis and independent thinking. Curricula should be developed which aim both to empower communities economically by paying attention to the pattern of skills required for the development of their society and to enable a full participation in civic and political life.

6. Women and girls

– should be given equal access to educational opportunities at all levels and in all subject areas (not only in areas considered traditionally appropriate). Educational plans and programmes should take account of women's and girls' domestic, agricultural and other workloads. Curricula should be developed which eradicate gender stereotyping and empower women to define their own educational needs. Education should be used to raise awareness of women's rights, including reproductive rights and legal and employment rights. All educational research should provide gender-related information.

7. Refugees

– should be be given greater educational assistance, enabling them to use their skills in the education of their communities. Most governments have formally accepted responsibility under the UN Convention on Refugees for refugee education, but many are unable or unwilling to provide the necessary resources. The financial crisis facing the work of the UNHCR (the major agency assisting refugee education) should be urgently resolved through enhanced contributions by donor governments. Refugee education should pay attention to refugees' particular cultural and language needs, to the likelihood that their education has been disrupted by flight and exile, and to the need to address the psychological and physical traumas associated with the refugee experience. At the same time, refugee education should take into account the needs and aspirations of host communities.

8. Working children

– should not be excluded from education because of their financial deprivation. Child labour is, in principle, unacceptable. No household should depend for its livelihood on the income or labour of children, and the state is responsible for ensuring that children are not driven to work in order to survive. However, given that many children in today's world are forced to work, ways should be found to ensure that they have access to basic education. Possible methods are part-time (evening) study for working children, out-of-school catch-up programmes and appropriately designed extensions to adult education and literacy programmes.

9. Research

– is needed in order to inform the development of educational plans and priorities. The state of education globally is poorly documented. The capacity for research and the knowledge base within Southern countries needs to be strengthened, and the dependence on research conducted from the industrialized North and by Northerners correspondingly reduced. All research should recognize particularly the need for gender-related statistics.

10. International co-operation

– must be increased: in particular, Unesco, as the UN agency with a particular responsibility for education, should be supported. Governments which have withdrawn from Unesco should reconsider their position in the light of the education crisis.

11. Government aid

– education should be a priority, and should account for at least 20% of total aid. Such an objective should be adopted by the Development Assistance Committee (DAC) of the OECD, whose members' aid to education has fallen during the 1980s from 17 per cent to 10 per cent. This should be in the context of increasing totals so as to ensure that it is not achieved at the expense of other sectors;
– educational aid should be in the form of grants, not loans. If loans are provided for education, they should always be at concessional rates of interest;
– the quality, as well as the quantity, of educational aid needs to be

enhanced. A set of Guidelines for Educational Aid should be agreed by aid-giving governments, emphasizing teacher training, curriculum development, materials production and the need to increase educational opportunities for women, refugees, and the rural and urban poor.

12. Non-governmental organizations

– should review their policies with a view to giving education a higher priority;
– should increase their assistance in areas such as curriculum development, teacher upgrading and research, which support the formal sector without undercutting state responsibilities;
– should enhance the educational aspect of their programmes, ensuring that these are integrated into the planning stage, not merely added as an afterthought.

BIBLIOGRAPHY

References are arranged under thematic or country subheadings according to the section of the book in which they are used. Sources used more than once are cited in each of the relevant sections.

Part one: Education and international inequalities

Education, Debt and Structural Adjustment

'Adjusting education to economic crisis' (1989) *IDS Bulletin*, 20 (1), whole issue.

Bacchus, M.K. (1989) 'Curriculum development and education in the developing countries', *Development through Education*. Oxford.

Beraimah, K.L. (1988) 'Gender and textbooks: an African case study', in P.G. Altbach, and G.P. Kelly, (eds) *Textbooks in the Third World: Policy, Content and Context*. New York/London: Garland.

Berstecher, D. and Carr-Hill, R. (1990) *Primary Education and Economic Recession in the Developing World since 1980*. Paris: Unesco.

Bray, M., Clarke, P.B. and Stephens, D. (1986) *Education and Society in Africa*. London: Edward Arnold.

Bray, M. and Lillis, K. (1988) *Community Financing of Education: Issues and Policy Implications in Less Developed Countries*. Oxford: Pergamon Press.

Caillods, F. and Postlethwaite, N. (1988) 'Teaching and learning conditions in developing countries', Workshop on 'The future of strategic educational planning', Paris, Dec. 1988. Paris: International Institute for Educational Planning.

Clark, J. (1986) *For Richer, for Poorer: An Oxfam Report on Western Connections with World Hunger*. Oxford: Oxfam.

Colclough, C. and Green, R.H. (1988) 'Editorial: do stabilisation policies stabilise?', *IDS Bulletin*, 19 (1), 1ff.

Colclough, C. and Lewin, K. (1990) 'Educating all the children: the economic challenge for the 1990s'. Summary Paper for World Conference on Education for All, Jomtien, Thailand.

Coombs, P. (1985) *The World Crisis in Education: the View from the Eighties*. New York/Oxford: Oxford University Press.

Cornia, G.A. (1987) 'The adjustment stalemate: conventional approaches and new ideas'. Occasional Paper No. 3, Geneva: UN Non-Governmental Liaison Service, 5ff.

Cornia, G.A., Jolly, R. and Stewart, F. (1987–88) *Adjustment with a Human Face*. 2 vols. Oxford: Clarendon Press.

Dziedzic, M.J. (1989) 'Mexico: converging challenges'. Adelphi Papers No. 242. London: International Institute for Strategic Studies.

George, S. (1988) *A Fate Worse than Debt*. Harmondsworth: Penguin Books.

Ghai, D. and Hewitt de Alcántara, C. (1989) 'The crisis of the 1980s in Africa, Latin America and the Caribbean: economic impact, social change and political implications'. Discussion Paper No. 7. Geneva: United Nations Research Institute for Social Development.

Griffith-Jones, S. and Sunkel, O. (1989) *Debt and Debt Crises in Latin America: the End of an Illusion*. Oxford: Clarendon Press.

Hewitt, A. and Wells, B. (eds) (1989) *Growing Out of Debt*. London: Overseas Development Institute.

Heyneman, S. (1989) 'Economic crisis and the quality of education: tables and figures for presentation at the conference on Development through Education'. Oxford, Sept. 1989.

Hinchcliffe, K. (1989) 'Economic austerity, structural adjustment and education: the case of Nigeria', *IDS Bulletin*, 20 (1), 5ff.

Inter-American Development Bank (1988) *Economic and Social Progress in Latin America 1988*. New York.

ILO World Employment Programme (1985) 'The crisis in the North and the South: the impact of the world recession on employment and poverty in developing countries'. Working Paper No. 59, Geneva.

——— (1986) 'Stabilisation, adjustment and poverty'. A collection of papers presented at an informal ILO expert group meeting, International Employment Policies, Working Paper No. 1, Geneva.

International Monetary Fund (1989) *World Economic Outlook*. Washington, DC.

Jolly, R. and van der Hoeven, R. (1989) 'Protecting the poor and vulnerable during adjustment: the case of Ghana'. New York: Unicef.

King, K. (1988) *Aid and Educational Research in Developing Countries: The Role of the Donor Agencies in the Analysis of Education*. Edinburgh University: Centre for African Studies.

Lewin, K. (1988) 'The organisational response to parsimony', *Compare*, 18 (1), 11ff.

Lewin, K. and Berstecher, D. (1989) 'The costs of recovery: are user fees the answer?', *IDS Bulletin* 20 (1), 59ff.

Lockheed, M.E. and Verspoor, A. (1990) *Improving Primary Education in Developing Countries: a Review of Policy Options* (draft). Washington, DC: World Bank.

Lovell, C.H. and Fatema, K. (1989) *Assignment Children: the BRAC Non-formal Primary Education Programme in Bangladesh*. New York: Unicef.

Miller, R.M. (1987) 'The Fading Future', *Comparative Education Review*, 31, 218ff.

——— (1985) 'Human resource development: the role of education', in T. Rose (ed.) *Crisis and Recovery in Sub-Saharan Africa*. Paris: Development Centre, OECD, 124ff.

'Structural Adjustment' (1988) *The Courier: Africa–Caribbean Pacific–European Community*, 111, whole issue.

Tibi, C. (1988) 'The internal allocation of resources for education: an international perspective', in D. Monk (ed.) *Ninth Annual Yearbook of the American Education Finance Association: Microlevel School Finance*. Cambridge, Mass.: Ballinger.

————— (1989) 'The financing of education: impact of the crisis and adjustment process' in F. Caillods (ed) *The Prospects for Educational Planning: a workshop organised by IIEP on the occasion of its XXVth anniversary.* Paris: Unesco/International Institute of Education Planning.

Unesco *Statistical Yearbook 1989.* Paris.

————— (1990) *Basic Education and Literacy: World Statistical Indicators.* Paris: Unesco, Office of Statistics.

Unicef (1989a) *The State of the World's Children 1989.* Oxford/New York: Oxford University Press.

————— (1989b) 'The social consequences of adjustment and dependency on primary commodities in sub-Saharan Africa'. New York.

Unicef (The Americas and the Caribbean Regional Office, Regional Programme, Women in Development) (1989) *The Invisible Adjustment: Poor Women and the Economic Crisis.* Second, revised edition. Santiago, Chile.

UN–NGO Workshop on 'Debt, adjustment and the needs of the poor'. Final Report, Oxford 19–22 Sept. 1987. Non-Governmental Liaison Service, Geneva.

Van der Hoeven, R. (1989) 'Debt and adjustment: the need for a global social contract'. Notes for the Africa–Europe Encounter of the Council of Europe, Porto Novo, Benin, 30 Aug–3 Sept. 1989.

Weeks, J.F. (ed.) (1989) *Debt Disaster? Banks, Governments and Multilaterals Confront the Crisis.* New York/London: New York University Press.

World Bank (1988) *Education in Sub-Saharan Africa: policies for adjustment, revitalization and expansion.* Washington, D.C.

World Bank, *Annual Report, 1988, 1989 and 1990.* Washington, DC.

————— *World Development Report 1989 and 1990.* Washington, DC.

————— *World Debt Tables 1989–90: the External Debt of Developing Countries,* vol. I. Washington, DC.

Wright C. (1989) 'Precursors to adjustment, revitalisation and expansion: an under-the-carpet view of the education crisis in sub-Saharan Africa', *Zimbabwe Journal of Educational Research,* 1 (1), 81ff.

Zymelman, M. and DeStefano, J. (1989) 'Primary school teachers' salaries in sub-Saharan Africa' World Bank Discussion Paper No. 45, Washington, DC.

Class, Gender and Ethnicity

Allison, C. (1985) 'Health and education for development: African women's status and prospects', in T. Rose (ed.) *Crisis and Recovery in Sub-Saharan Africa.* Paris: Development Centre, OECD, 111ff.

Arizpe, L., Salinas, F. and Velasquez, M. (1989) 'Effects of the economic crisis on the living conditions of peasant women in Mexico' in Unicef, *The Invisible Adjustment: Poor Women and the Economic Crisis.* Santiago, Chile.

Carnoy, M. and Samoff, J. (eds) (1990) *Education and Social Transition in the Third World.* Princeton: Princeton University Press.

Commonwealth Secretariat (1989), *Engendering Adjustment for the 1990s: Report of a Commonwealth Expert Group on Women and Structural Adjustment.* London.

George, S. (1988) *A Fate Worse than Debt.* Harmondsworth: Penguin.

Hedman, B. (1989) 'Statistics on women and men in development in

Zimbabwe'. Report from mission to Harare, Zimbabwe. Jan.–Feb. 1989. Stockholm: Statistics Sweden.

Hyde, K.A.L. (1989) *Improving Women's Education in Sub-Saharan Africa: a Review of the Literature*. Washington, DC: World Bank, Education and Employment Division: Population and Human Resources Department.

Kelly, G.P. (1990) 'Education and equality: comparative perspectives on the expansion of education and women in the post-war period'. *International Journal of Educational Development* 10 (2/3) 131ff.

Moser, C. (1989) 'The impact of recession and adjustment policies at the micro-level: low income women and their households in Guayaquil, Ecuador' in Unicef, *The Invisible Adjustment: Poor Women and the Economic Crisis*. Santiago, Chile.

Vargas Vega, R., Tupac, F., Tupac, C., Gonzales, V. and Gonzales, D. (1989) 'Mujer y educación en tres áreas rurales del Peru'. Lima, Peru: CELAE/Ministerio de Educación Pública.

Vélez, B. (1988) 'La educación de la mujer rural en Colombia: tres estudios de caso'. Medellín, Colombia: Unesco.

Young, K. (ed.) (1988) *Women and Economic Development: a Critical Assessment of Local, Regional and National Planning*. Oxford: Berg.

Literacy and Development

Archer D. and Costello, P. (1990) *Literacy and Power: the Latin American Battleground*. London: Earthscan.

Bown, L. (1990) 'Preparing the Future: Women, Literacy and Development. The Impact of Female Literacy on Human Development and the Participation of Literate Women in Change'. Development Report No. 4. London: ActionAid.

Carron, G., Mwiria, K. and Righa, G. (1989) *The Functioning and Effects of the Kenya Literacy Programme*. Paris: International Institute for Educational Planning.

Consejo de Educación de Adultos de América Latina, Programma de Alfabetización Popular (1989) *Formación de Educadores Populares: cuatro experiencias latinoamericanas*. Santiago, Chile: CEAAL.

Freire, P. and Shor, I. (1987) *A Pedagogy for Liberation: Dialogues on Transforming Education*. Basingstoke: Macmillan.

Freire, P. and Macedo, D. (1987) *Literacy: Reading the Word and the World*. London: Routledge & Kegan Paul.

Ganter, E. and Edkins, D. (1988) *Marotholi: Theatre for Another Development*. Maseru, Lesotho: The Village Technology Information Service, Christian Council of Lesotho.

German Adult Education Association (1990) *Adult Education and Development*, 31 and 35 (whole issues).

Hinzen, H. (1989) 'Literacy policy and practice: issues for debate', in *Prospects* (Unesco) 19 (4) 505ff.

Lind, A. (1988) *Adult Literacy: Lessons and Promises: Mozambican Literacy Campaigns 1978–1982*. University of Stockholm: Institute of International Education.

Lind, A. and Johnston, A. (1986) *Adult Literacy in the Third World: a Review of Objectives and Strategies*. Stockholm: SIDA.

Oxenham, J. (1980) *Literacy: Writing, Reading and Social Organisation*. London: Routledge & Kegan Paul.

Rafferty, M. (1988) 'Women, development and adult education in Tanzania', in M. Hodd (ed.) *Tanzania after Nyerere*. London: Pinter.

Unesco/Unicef (1988) *Women's Education in Africa: a Survey of Field Projects in Five Countries*. Paris.

World University Service (UK) (1990) *Literacy and Liberation*: Report of the WUS Annual Conference. London.

Part two: The debt crisis, politics and educational policy

Profile of the case study regions

Inter-American Development Bank (1988) *Economic and Social Progress in Latin America 1988*. New York.

Johnson, P. and Martin, D. (1989) *Apartheid Terrorism: the Destabilisation Report*. London/ Bloomington, Ind.: Commonwealth Secretariat.

Unicef (1989) *Children on the Front Line: the Impact of Apartheid, Destabilisation and Warfare on Children*. New York/Geneva.

World Bank, *World Development Report 1989*. Washington, DC.

Zambia

Andersson, P-A. and Kayizzi-Mugerwa, S. (1989) 'Mineral dependence, goal attainment and equity: Zambia's experience with structural adjustment in the 1980s'. University of Göteborg.

Clark, J. and Keen, D. (1988) *Debt and Poverty: a Case Study of Zambia*. Oxford: Oxfam.

Colclough, C. (1988) 'Zambian adjustment strategy – with and without the IMF', *IDS Bulletin*, 19 (1), 51ff.

Coombe, T. (1988) 'Integral planning for the staffing function in education'. Workshop on 'The future of strategic educational planning', Dec. 1988. International Institute for Educational Planning, Paris.

Johnston, A., Kaluba, H., Karlsson, M. and Nyström, K. (1987) *Education and Economic Crisis: the cases of Mozambique and Zambia*. Education Division Documents, No. 38. Stockholm: SIDA.

Kaluba, L.H. (1986) 'Education in Zambia: the problem of access to schooling and the paradox of the private school solution', *Comparative Education*, 22 (2), 159ff.

Kelly, M.J. (1988) 'Financing Education in Zambia'. Study prepared for the International Institute of Educational Planning, Paris. University of Zambia: School of Education.

Kelly, M.J. (1987) 'Education in an economy under decline: the case of Zambia'. University of Zambia: School of Education.

Kelly, M.J., Nkwanga, E.B., Kaluba, L.H., Achola, P.P.W. and Nilsson, K. (1986) 'The provision of education for all: towards the implementation of Zambia's educational reforms under demographic and economic constraints 1986-2000'. University of Zambia: School of Education.

Lubasi, R., Nudenda, G. and Odin, B. (1989) 'An evaluation of Self-Help Action Plan for Education (SHAPE) in Zambia'. Lusaka: SIDA.

McNab, C., Chidumayo, S., Fägerlind, I., Idemalm, A. and Mweene, B. (1989) 'Supporting Zambian education in times of adversity: an evaluation of Swedish–Zambian cooperation in education 1984–89'. Education Division Documents, No. 44. Stockholm: SIDA.

Reinikka-Soininen, R. (1990) *Theory and Practice in Structural Adjustment: the Case of Zambia.* Helsinki: Kauppakorkeakoulin Julkaisuja.

Silanda, E. and Tuijnman, A. (1989) 'Regional variations in the financing of primary education in Zambia', *International Journal of Educational Development,* 9 (1), 5ff.

Zimbabwe

Chivore, B.R.S. (1986a) 'Form IV pupils' perception of and attitude towards the teaching profession in Zimbabwe', *Comparative Education,* 22 (3), 233ff.

――― (1986b) 'Teacher education in post-independent Zimbabwe: problems and possible solutions', *Journal of Education for Teaching* 12 (3), 205ff.

Chung, F. (1989) 'Government and community partnership in the financing of education in Zimbabwe'. Conference on 'Development through education' Oxford, Sept. 1989.

Davies, R. and Saunders, D. (1987) 'Stabilisation policies and the effects on child health in Zimbabwe', *Review of African Political Economy,* 38, 3ff.

Dorsey, B.J., Gaidzanwa, R.B. and Mupawaenda, A.C. (1989) *Factors affecting Academic Careers for Women at the University of Zimbabwe* (Harare). University of Zimbabwe, Human Resources Research Centre.

'Education in the new Zimbabwe' (1988) Proceedings of a conference held at Michigan State University in collaboration with the Faculty of Education, University of Zimbabwe, June 1986. Michigan State University, East Lansing, Mich., 1988.

Government of Zimbabwe (1988) *Quarterly Digest of Statistics.* Harare: Central Statistical Office.

――― (1986, 1987) *Annual Report of the Secretary for Education.* Harare: Ministry of Education and Culture.

Government of Zimbabwe (1990) 'Political mobilisation in enhancing education for all in a newly independent Zimbabwe'. World Conference on Education for All, Jomtiem, Thailand, 5–9 March 1990. Harare: Ministry of Education and Culture.

――― (1988) *Report on PHC/MCH/ARI Surveys.* Harare: Ministry of Health.

Mandazo, I. (ed.) (1986) *Zimbabwe: the Political Economy of Transition 1980–1986.* Dakar: CODESRIA.

Riddell, A.R. (1988) 'School effectiveness in secondary education in Zimbabwe: a multi-level analysis'. Ph.D., Institute of Education, London University.

Stoneman, C. and Cliffe, L. (1989) *Zimbabwe: Politics, Economics and Society.* London/New York: Pinter.

Zimbabwe Foundation for Education with Production (ZIMFEP) (1986) 'Education in Zimbabwe'. Papers from a seminar organised by the Ministry of Education/Dag Hammerskjold Foundation, Harare.

Zvobgo, R.J. (1986) *Transforming Education: the Zimbabwean Experience.* Harare: College Press.

Costa Rica

CSUCA Research Project, 1989, for WUS(UK) supervised by Dr Mario Lungo Uclés and researched by Ethel Romano, (hereafter, CSUCA Research Project).

Government of Costa Rica (1987) *Censo de Población 1984*. San José: Ministerio de Economía, Industria y Comercio.

―――― (1985) 'Las incidencias de la crisis socioeconómica en la deserción escolar del sistema educativo costarricense'. San José: Ministerio de Educación Pública/ Ministerio de Planificación Nacional/Organisación de Estados Americanos.

Quiros, T. (1987) *Plan nacional de alfabetización y educación basica de adultos*. San José: Projecto Regional de Educación de Adultos y Alfabetización (PREDAL)/Organización de los Estados Americanos/ Ministerio de Educación Publica.

Romero, S. (1987) 'Costa Rica: la educación en la mira de la crisis', *OCLAE*, 1-2.

Vargas, A.R. (1987) 'La deuda externa de Costa Rica 1970-85', *Estudios Sociales Centroamericanos*, no. 45, 121ff.

Villasuso, J.M. (1987) 'Costa Rica: crisis, adjustment policies and rural development', *CEPAL Review*, 33, 107ff.

Mozambique

Frelimo (1989) 'Report of the Central Committee to the Fifth Congress: For the normalisation of life'. Maputo.

Frieling, I.M. (1987) 'Population and employment in Mozambique, with a case study for two Maputo suburbs', Lusaka, Zambia: ILO World Employment Programme, Southern African Team for Employment Promotion. Working Paper.

Government of Mozambique (1988) *Relatório do Ministério da Educação*. Maputo: Council of Ministers.

Hermele, K. (1988) *Country Report, Mozambique: War and Stabilisation: a mid-term review of Mozambique's economic rehabilitation programme (PRE) with implications for Swedish Development Assistance*. Stockholm: SIDA, The Planning Secretariat.

Johnston, A. *et al* (1987) *Education and Economic Crisis: The Cases of Mozambique and Zambia*. Stockholm: SIDA.

Johnston, A. (1989) *Study, Produce and Combat! Education and the Mozambican State 1962–1984*. University of Stockholm: Institute of International Education.

Johnston, A. (1990) 'The Mozambican state and education', in M. Carnoy and J. Samoff (eds) *Education and Social Transition in the Third World*. Princeton: Princeton University Press.

Marshall, J. (1985) 'Making Education Revolutionary' in J.S. Saul (ed) *A Difficult Road: The Transition to Socialism in Mozambique*. New York: Monthly Review Press.

―――― (1988) 'Why shoot the teacher? War and education in Mozambique'. Paper prepared for presentation at the African Studies Association Meeting, Chicago, 27–30 Oct, 1988.

―――― (1990) 'Economic recovery for whom? The social costs of SAP in Mozambique', a paper presented to 'SAP, multilateral imperialism, and African strategies for development', a conference organized by the Institute of African Studies, Columbia University, New York, April 1990.

Unicef (1989) *Children on the Front Line: the Impact of Apartheid, Destabilisation and Warfare on Children*. New York/Geneva.

Nicaragua

Archer, D. and Costello, P. (1990) *Literacy and Power: the Latin American Battleground.* London: Earthscan.

Arrien, J.B. and Lazo, R.M. (eds) (1989) *Nicaragua: diez años de educación en la revolución.* Managua: Ministry of Education/Mexico, DF: Claves Latinoamericanas.

Arnove, R.F. (1986) *Education and Revolution in Nicaragua.* New York/London: Praeger.

Bevan, J. (1989) 'Slashed budgets but no closures', *Times Educational Supplement*, 6 Oct. 1989.

Black, G. and Bevan, J. (1980) *The Loss of Fear: Education in Nicaragua before and after the Revolution.* London: Nicaragua Solidarity Campaign/WUS.

Cabieses, H. (1986) *Economía Nicaraguense 1979-86.* Managua: UNAN/Free University of Amsterdam.

Carnoy, M. and Torres, C.A. (1990) 'Education and social transformation in Nicaragua, 1979–1989', in M. Carnoy and J. Samoff (eds) *Education and Social Transition in the Third World.* Princeton: Princeton University Press.

Close, D. (1988) *Nicaragua: Politics, Economics and Society.* London/New York: Pinter.

CSUCA Research Project 1989.

Freeland, Jane (1988) *A Special Place in History: the Atlantic Coast in the Nicaraguan Revolution.* London: War on Want/Nicaragua Solidarity Campaign.

Government of Nicaragua (1987) *El proyecto político–educativo de la revolución popular Sandinista.* Informe inaugural al IV Congreso Nacional de Anden del Dr Sergio Ramirez Mercado, Vice Presidente de la República. Managua: Presidency of the Republic.

────── Budgets 1983–86. Managua: Ministry of Education.

────── (1989) Enrolments/dropouts. Managua: Ministry of Education.

────── (1989) *Diez años en cifras.* Managua: INEC.

Melrose, D. (1985) *Nicaragua.* Oxford: Oxfam.

Molyneux, M. (1985) 'Mobilization without Emancipation? Women's Interests, the State and the Revolution in Nicaragua', *Feminist Studies* 11 (2), 227ff.

'Nicaragua: Development under Fire' (1988) *IDS Bulletin*, 19 (3), whole issue.

Sudan

Research project conducted for WUS(UK) by the Department of African and Asian Studies, University of Khartoum, supervised by Dr Medani M. Ahmed, in 1989 (hereafter University of Khartoum Research Project).

Barnett, T. and Abdul Karim, A. (eds) (1988) *Sudan: State, Capital and Transformation.* London: Croom Helm.

Fully, P.F. (1988) 'Education: total collapse', in *War Wounds: the development costs of conflict in Southern Sudan.* London: Panos Institute.

El Salvador, Guatemala and Honduras

Amnesty International (1989) *Guatemala: Human Rights Violations under the Civilian Government.* London.

────── (1989–90) Bulletins on Central America.

Antonio Orellana, V. (1985) 'La Desconcentración adminstrativa en el sector educativo [El Salvador] Logros y problemas', *Estudios Centroamericanos*, 435–36, 28ff.

Bueso, J.A. (1987) *El Subdesarrollo Hondureño*. Tegucigalpa: Universidad Nacional Autonomía de Honduras.

[Cabrera, E.] (1988) 'Importancia económica y implicaciones políticas de la ayuda norteamericana en El Salvador', *Estudios Centroamericanos*, 477, 661ff.

CSUCA Research Project 1989.

Edgar Jiménez, C., Raúl Benítez, M., Ricardo Córdova, M. and Alexander Segovia (1988) *El Salvador: Guerra, Política y Paz 1979–1988*. San Salvador: CINAS/CRIES.

Manz, B. (1988) *Refugees of a Hidden War: the Aftermath of Counter-insurgency in Guatemala*. New York: State University of New York.

National Union of Teachers/World University Service (UK) (1988) *Less Arms, More Education: Report of an NUT/WUS delegation to Honduras, Nicaragua and El Salvador, November 1987*. London: WUS(UK).

Painter, J. (1987) *Guatemala, False Hope, False Freedom*. London: Latin American Bureau.

Thomson, M. (1986) *Women of El Salvador: the Price of Freedom*. London: Zed Press/War on Want.

South Africa

Burman, S. and Reynolds, P. (1986) *Growing up in a Divided Society: the Contexts of Childhood in South Africa*. Johannesburg: Ravan Press.

Graaf, J.F. de V. (1989) 'Farm schools in the Western Cape: a different kind of bitterness'. RESA Conference, Essex University, 1989.

Gultig, J. and Hart, M. (forthcoming) 'Battleground Pedagogy: Schooling, Conflict and People's Education in Pietermaritzburg 1987–1990', in Research on Education in South Africa (RESA), volume on education in South Africa.

Indicator SA, issues from 1985 to 1989.

Kallaway, P. (ed.) (1983) *Education and Apartheid*. Johannesburg: Ravan Press.

National Education Crisis Committee (1989) Papers for the National Education Conference, Cape Town, Dec. 1989.

Republic of South Africa (1982, 1988) *Annual Report 1981* and *1987*. Pretoria: Department of Education and Training.

Nkomo, M. (1990) *Pedagogy of Domination* Trenton N.J.: Africa World Press Inc.

Research on Education in South Africa (RESA) (1988) 'Bantu education as a reformist strategy of the South African state'. Colchester, Essex. Paper No. 2.

Taylor, N. (1989) 'Falling at the first hurdle: initial encounters with the formal system of African education in South Africa'. Johannesburg: Education Policy Unit, University of the Witwatersrand, Research Report No. 1.

Namibia

Ellis, J. (1984) *Education, Repression, Liberation: Namibia*. London: WUS/CIIR.

WUS(UK) (1990) *Literacy and Liberation*. Report of the WUS Annual Conference. London.

Part three: Learning and teaching in marginal communities

Education and family income in Central America

CSUCA Research Project 1989.
Acker, A. (1986) *Children of the Volcano*. Toronto: Between the Lines.
Burgos-Debray, E. (1984) *I, Rigoberta Menchú: an Indian Woman in Guatemala*. London/New York: Women's Press.
Arzamendia Candia, C. (1985) 'Caracterización del analfabetismo en la zona urbana marginal de San José, "Ciudadela 15 de Setiembre"'. Master's thesis, University of Costa Rica.
Chant, S. (1985) 'Family formation and female roles in Querétaro, Mexico', *Bulletin of Latin American Research*, 4 (1), 17f.
D'Ciofalo, G. (1986) 'El trabajo infantil urbano en Managua'. Managua: Ministerio del Trabajo, Centro de Estudios del Trabajo.
'El Salvador: Conjunctura Económica' *Revista de la Universidad Nacional de el Salvador*, 11 (11).
Fundación Salvadoreña de Desarrollo y Vivienda Mínima (1987) 'Exploración preliminar sobre les condiciones de vide en los tugurios de San Salvador', *Estudios Sociales Centroamericanos*, 44, 79ff.
García, A.I. and Gomáriz, E. (1989) *Mujeres Centroamericanas*, vol. I: *Tendencias Estructurales*, vol. 2: *Effectos del Conflicto*. San José, Costa Rica: CSUCA/FLACSO/Universidad para la Paz.
González de la Rocha, M. (1988) 'Economic crisis, domestic reorganisation and women's work in Guadalajara, Mexico', *Bulletin of Latin American Research*, 7 (2), 207ff.
Montes, S. (1986) 'La familia en la sociedad salvadoreña', *Estudios Centroamericanos*, 450, 305ff.
———— (1988) 'Los derechos económicos, sociales y culturales en El Salvador', *Estudios Centroamericanos*, 476, 515ff.
Out of the Ashes: the Lives and Hopes of Refugees from El Salvador and Guatemala. London: El Salvador and Guatemala Committees for Human Rights/War on Want, 1985.
Painter, J. (1987) *Guatemala, False Hope, False Freedom*. London: Latin American Bureau.

Urban crisis: access to school education for poor communities in Khartoum

University of Khartoum Research Project

Education in Matabeleland South, Zimbabwe

Research project for WUS(UK) carried out by the Organisation of Rural Associations for Progress (ORAP) supervised by Sithembiso Nyoni and Sibangele Jamela in Kezi and Umzingwane districts, Province of Matabeland South, 1989.

Commonwealth Secretariat, (1989) *Engendering Adjustment for the 1990s.*

Fowles, A.R. (1985) 'Seasonal Aspects of Education in Eastern and Southern Africa', in P. Ndegwa, L.P. Mureithi and R.H. Green (eds) *Development Options for Africa in the 1980s and Beyond.* Nairobi/Oxford: Oxford University Press.

Government of Zimbabwe (1987) *Annual Report of the Secretary for Education.* Harare: Ministry of Education and Culture.

Muchena, O.N. (1980) 'Women in town: a socio-economic survey of African women in Highfield Township, Salisbury'. University of Zimbabwe: Centre for Applied Social Sciences.

Stoneman, C. and Cliffe, L. (1989) *Zimbabwe: Politics, Economics and Society.* London/New York: Pinter.

Education and marginalization in South Africa: Soweto, Natal and northern Transvaal

Research project for WUS(UK) carried out by researchers working with the National Education Crisis Committee (NECC), supervised by Yogesh Narsing, on Soweto and northern Transvaal, 1989.

Beall, J., Hassim, S. and Todes, A. (1989) '"A bit on the side?" Gender struggles in the politics of transformation in South Africa', *Feminist Review* 33, Autumn, 30ff.

Education Projects Unit and Career Information Centre (1988) 'Enrolment monitoring research'. Durban: University of Natal.

Gultig, J. and Hart, M. (forthcoming) 'Battleground Pedagogy: Schooling, Conflict and People's Education in Pietermaritzburg, 1987–1990'.

Muller, J. (1989) 'White school enrolments in Johannesburg'. Johannesburg: Education Policy Unit, University of Witwatersrand, Briefing Paper.

Narsing, Y.P. (1989) 'Learning in limbo, Part I: experiences of schooling in Soweto Jan.–June 1989'. Johannesburg: Education Policy Unit, University of Witwatersrand, Research Report No. 2.

Operation Hunger (1987) 'First report on estimating vulnerability in black rural communities in South Africa'. n.p.

Ritchken, E. (1990) 'Learning in limbo, Part II: experiences of secondary schooling in the Mapulaneng District, Lebowa'. Johannesburg: Education Policy Unit, University of Witwatersrand.

The Dilemmas of Refugee Education

Apeadu, N. and Karumuna, S. (1989) 'Mozambican refugees: Joint Consultancy Mission to Malawi'. New York/Addis Ababa: ILO/OAU.

Archer, D. and Costello, P. 'Maya Tecum, castellanisation and cultural genocide'. Unpublished manuscript.

COR Documentation Centre (1989) 'The refugee situation in the Sudan'. (Khartoum).

Ferris, E.G. (1987) *Central American Refugees.* New York/London: Praeger.

Gersony, R. (1988) 'Summary of Mozambican refugee accounts of principally conflict-related experience in Mozambique'. Washington, DC: State Department: Bureau for Refugee Programs.

Gorman, R.F. (1987) *Coping with Africa's Refugee Problem: a Time for Solutions.* Dordecht/Lancaster: Nijhoff and UNITAR.

Government of Nicaragua (1989) *Programma de Atención Integral a Deplazados, Repatriados y Refugiados.* Managua.

International Conference on Central American Refugees (CIREFCA), Guatemala City, 29-31 May 1989: 'Principles and criteria for the protection of and assistance to Central American refugees, returnees and displaced persons in Latin America'.

—— 'Document on the Republic of El Salvador: diagnosis, strategy and project proposals' (Feb. 1989).

—— 'Document on the Republic of Guatemala: diagnosis, strategy and project prosposals' (March 1989).

—— 'Document on the Republic of Costa Rica: diagnosis, strategy and project proposals' (Feb. 1989).

—— 'Document on the United Mexican States: diagnosis, strategy and project prosposals' (March 1989).

Loescher, G. and Monahan, L. (1989) *Refugees and International Relations.* Cambridge: Cambridge University Press.

Manz, B. (1988) *Refugees of a Hidden War: the Aftermath of Counterinsurgency in Guatemala.* New York: State University of New York.

Mkangaza, C.D. (1989) 'Education and Training in Ukwimi Refugee Agricultural Settlement'. Lusaka: UNHCR.

Montes, S. (1986) 'El problema de los displazados y refugiados salvadoreños', *Estudios Centroamericanos*, 447–48, 37ff.

—— (1988) 'Migration to the US as an index of the intensifying social and political crises in El Salvador', *Journal of Refugee Studies*, 1 (2), 107ff.

Out of the Ashes: the Lives and Hopes of Refugees from El Salvador and Guatemala. London: El Salvador and Guatemala Committees for Human Rights/War on Want, 1985.

Oviedo Mendiola, M.M. (1989) 'Refugiados Salvadoreños en el area metropolitana de la ciudad de México'. Tesis/Licenciado en Sociologia, Universidad Nacional Autónoma de México.

Refugee Education: the Case for International Action. London: International Extension College/WUS(UK), 1986.

Refugee Service of World Council of Churches (1989) 'International debt and refugees', *Refugees*, 100E.

—— (1989) 'Refugees in Central America', *Refugees*, 101E.

Romano, E. (1989) 'Reportaje sobre refugiados salvadoreños en Costa Rica', San José: CSUCA, unpublished report for WUS(UK).

Seminar on the Protection and Education of Mozambican Refugees: Papers on Zambia, Zimbabwe, Malawi. Harare, 1990.

—— J.K.D. Foli, 'Protection and education of the Mozambican refugees'.

—— 'Preliminary report by the Camp Administration of the Mazoe River Bridge Camp, Zimbabwe.

UNHCR (1989) Fact Sheets on Refugees.

—— (1989) *UNHCR activities financed by voluntary funds: Report for 1988/89; Part I: Africa; Part IV: Latin America and the Caribbean.* Geneva.

—— *Refugees* (1988–89).

Part four: Breaking the culture of silence: organizing for literacy

Archer D. and Costello, P. (1990) *Literacy and Power: the Latin American Battleground.* London: Earthscan.

Bown, L. (1990) 'Preparing the Future: Women, Literacy and Development'. London: ActionAid.

CEAAL (1989) *Formación de Educadores Populares: cuatro experiencias latinoamericanas*. Santiago, Chile.

Government of Nicaragua (1988) 'Memorias del proyecto educativo en el valle de Jalapa'. Jalapa: Ministry of Education, Region I.

Grainger, I.P. (1987) 'The literacy campaign in Zimbabwe', *Journal of Social Development in Africa*, 2 (2), 49ff.

Lind, A. (1988) *Adult Literacy: Lessons and Promises: Mozambican Literacy Campaigns 1978–1982*. University of Stockholm: Institute of International Education.

Lind, A., Gleditsch, M. and Henson, T. (1986) 'Literacy and income-generating activities in Zimbabwe'. Oslo: NORAD Consultancy Report.

Miller, V. (1985) *Between Struggle and Hope: the Nicaraguan Literacy Crusade*. Boulder/London: Westview.

Pearce, J. (1986) *Promised Land: Peasant Rebellion in Chalatenango, El Salvador*. London: Latin America Bureau.

Romano, E. (1989) 'Analisis de experiencias innovadoras en educación de adultos y alfabetización, en que han participado universidades del área centroamericana'. San José, Costa Rica: CSUCA.

Toledo Hermosillo, E. (1990) *Alfabetizar bajo la guerra: la educación popular en El Salvador*. Mexico City: Edimar/ANDES.

Urdang, S. (1989) *And Still They Dance: Women, War and the Struggle for Change in Mozambique*. London: Earthscan.

Wedepohl, L. (1984) 'A Survey of Adult Illiteracy in South Africa'. University of Cape Town, Centre for Extra-Mural Studies.

Part five: The future of education in the south

Ayres, R.L. (1983) *Banking on the Poor: the World Bank and World Poverty*. Cambridge, Mass.: MIT Press.

Campbell, B.K. and Loxley, J. (eds) (1989) *Structural Adjustment in Africa*. Basingstoke: Macmillan.

Colclough, C. and Lewin, K. (1990) 'Educating all the children: the economic challenge for the 1990s'. Summary Paper for World Conference on Education for All, Jomtien, Thailand.

Connable, B. (1990) Address by Barber B. Connable, President, The World Bank Group, to the World Conference on Education for All, Jomtien, Thailand, 6 March 1990.

Griffith-Jones, S. and Sunkel, O. (1989) *Debt and Debt Crises in Latin America: the End of an Illusion*. Oxford: Clarendon Press.

Hawes, H. and Coombe, T. (eds) (1986) *Educational Priorities and Aid Responses in Sub-Saharan Africa*. London: Overseas Development Administration/University of London, Institute of Education.

Hayter, T. and Watson, C. (1985) *Aid: Rhetoric and Reality*. London: Pluto.

Hewitt, A. and Wells, B. (eds) (1989) *Growing Out of Debt*. London: Overseas Development Institute.

Kandiyoti, D. (1988) 'Women and rural development policies: the changing agenda'. IDS Discussion Paper No. 244.

King, K. (1988) *Aid and Educational Research in Developing Countries: the*

Role of the Donor Agencies in the Analysis of Education. Edinburgh University: Centre for African Studies.

Mistry, P.S. (1988) *African Debt: the case for relief for Sub-Saharan Africa*. Oxford: Oxford International Associates.

OECD (1985) *Twenty-five Years of Development Cooperation: a Review. 1985 Report*. Development Assistance Committee, Paris.

OECD (1989) *Development Cooperation in the 1990s. 1989 Report*. Development Assistance Committee, Paris.

Overseas Development Administration (1989) *Into the Nineties: an Education Policy for British Aid*. London.

Parfitt, T.W. and Riley, S.P. (1989) *The African Debt Crisis*. London: Routledge.

Singer, H.W. and Sharma, S. (eds) (1989) *Economic Development and World Debt*. Basingstoke: Macmillan.

Swedish International Development Authority (SIDA) (1988) *Annual Report 1988: Education, Culture and Public Administration*. Stockholm.

―――― (1986) *Guidelines for Education Assistance*. Stockholm.

United Nations Economic Commission for Africa (1989) *African Alternative Framework to Structural Adjustment Programmes for Socio-economic Recovery and Transformation*. Addis Ababa.

United States Agency for International Development (1990) *USAID's Partnership for Basic Education*. Washington, DC.

US General Accounting Office (1989) *Central America: Impact of US Assistance in the 1980s*. Report to the Chairman, Committee on Foreign Relations, US Senate. Washington, DC.

Weeks, J.F. (ed.) (1989) *Debt Disaster? Banks, Governments and Multilaterals Confront the Crisis*. New York/London: New York University Press.

World Bank, *Annual Report 1988, 1989 and 1990*. Washington, DC.

World Bank (1990) *The Dividends of Learning: World Bank Support for Education*. Washington, DC.

World Bank, *World Development Report 1989 and 1990*. Washington, DC.

'World Declaration on Education for All: Meeting Basic Learning Needs', Jomtien, Thailand, 9 March 1990.

Young, K. (ed.) (1988) *Women and Economic Development: a Critical Assessment of Local, Regional and National Planning*. Oxford: Berg.

Subject Index

Countries/Regions Index